The Ultimate Solution Roadmap

D0360491

Microsoft Proxy Server 2 On Site

This book will take you on a journey through islands of valuable _____ designed to help you provide secure, high-performance Internet access for your organization. You can use the Ultimate Solution Roadmap to find the shortest route to the information you need to know, when you need to know it. There's a lot to know about planning, installing, and administering Microsoft Proxy Server, and the roadmap makes the trip more enjoyable.

The following seven major tasks form the departure points for the roadmaps:

- Understand the Proxy Server implementation plan.
- Conduct the Internet access needs assessment.
- Conduct the Internet security assessment.
- Plan the Proxy Server installation.
- Install Proxy Server.
- Administer Proxy Server.
- Administer Proxy Server clients.

Simply pick the appropriate journey and follow the roadmap to the destination of your choosing. Then turn to the indicated page numbers to find out more about what you need to know. Use the roadmaps often and enjoy your excursions into the depths of Proxy Server.

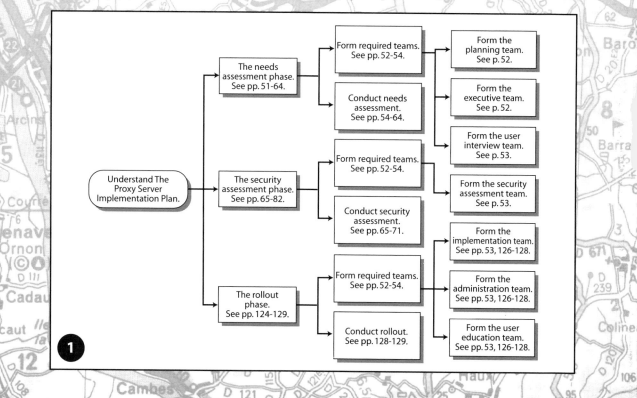

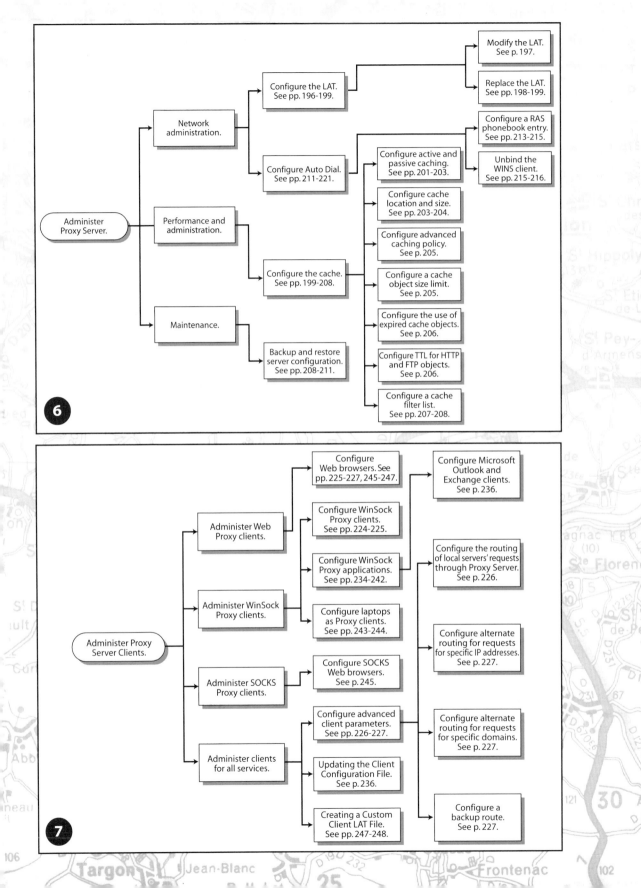

6

Administer Proxy Server.

- Network administration.
  - Configure the LAT. See pp. 196-199.
    - Modify the LAT. See p. 197.
    - Replace the LAT. See pp. 198-199.
  - Configure Auto Dial. See pp. 211-221.
    - Configure a RAS phonebook entry. See pp. 213-215.
    - Unbind the WINS client. See pp. 215-216.
- Performance and administration.
  - Configure the cache. See pp. 199-208.
    - Configure active and passive caching. See pp. 201-203.
    - Configure cache location and size. See pp. 203-204.
    - Configure advanced caching policy. See p. 205.
    - Configure a cache object size limit. See p. 205.
    - Configure the use of expired cache objects. See p. 206.
    - Configure TTL for HTTP and FTP objects. See p. 206.
    - Configure a cache filter list. See pp. 207-208.
- Maintenance.
  - Backup and restore server configuration. See pp. 208-211.

7

Administer Proxy Server Clients.

- Administer Web Proxy clients.
  - Configure Web browsers. See pp. 225-227, 245-247.
    - Configure Microsoft Outlook and Exchange clients. See p. 236.
- Administer WinSock Proxy clients.
  - Configure WinSock Proxy clients. See pp. 224-225.
  - Configure WinSock Proxy applications. See pp. 234-242.
    - Configure the routing of local servers' requests through Proxy Server. See p. 226.
  - Configure laptops as Proxy clients. See pp. 243-244.
    - Configure alternate routing for requests for specific IP addresses. See p. 227.
- Administer SOCKS Proxy clients.
  - Configure SOCKS Web browsers. See p. 245.
- Administer clients for all services.
  - Configure advanced client parameters. See pp. 226-227.
    - Configure alternate routing for requests for specific domains. See p. 227.
  - Updating the Client Configuration File. See p. 236.
  - Creating a Custom Client LAT File. See pp. 247-248.
    - Configure a backup route. See p. 227.

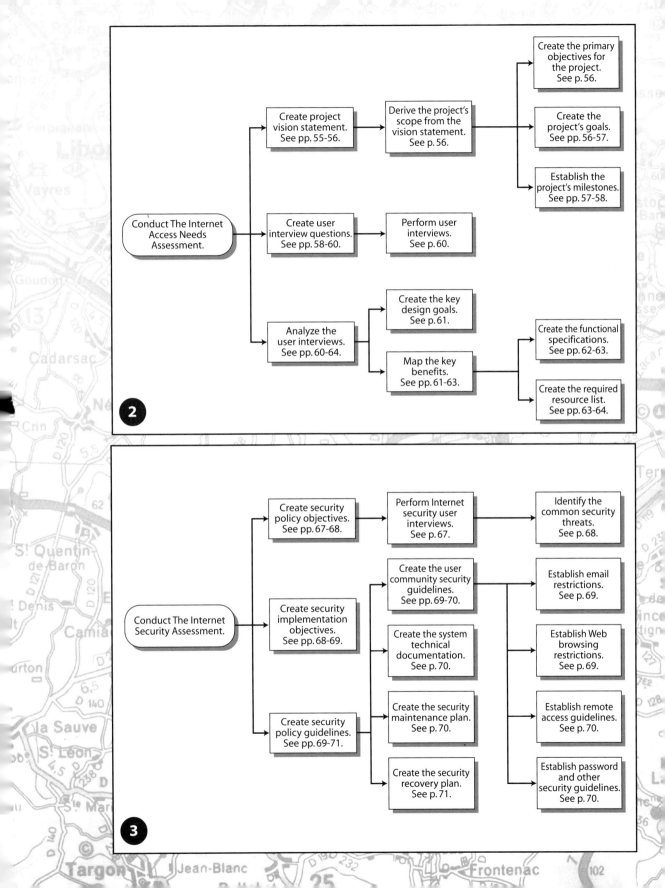

Panel 2

Conduct The Internet Access Needs Assessment.

→ Create project vision statement. See pp. 55-56.

→ Derive the project's scope from the vision statement. See p. 56.

→ Create the primary objectives for the project. See p. 56.

→ Create the project's goals. See pp. 56-57.

→ Establish the project's milestones. See pp. 57-58.

→ Create user interview questions. See pp. 58-60.

→ Perform user interviews. See p. 60.

→ Analyze the user interviews. See pp. 60-64.

→ Create the key design goals. See p. 61.

→ Map the key benefits. See pp. 61-63.

→ Create the functional specifications. See pp. 62-63.

→ Create the required resource list. See pp. 63-64.

Panel 3

Conduct The Internet Security Assessment.

→ Create security policy objectives. See pp. 67-68.

→ Perform Internet security user interviews. See p. 67.

→ Identify the common security threats. See p. 68.

→ Create security implementation objectives. See pp. 68-69.

→ Create the user community security guidelines. See pp. 69-70.

→ Establish email restrictions. See p. 69.

→ Create the system technical documentation. See p. 70.

→ Establish Web browsing restrictions. See p. 69.

→ Create security policy guidelines. See pp. 69-71.

→ Create the security maintenance plan. See p. 70.

→ Establish remote access guidelines. See p. 70.

→ Create the security recovery plan. See p. 71.

→ Establish password and other security guidelines. See p. 70.

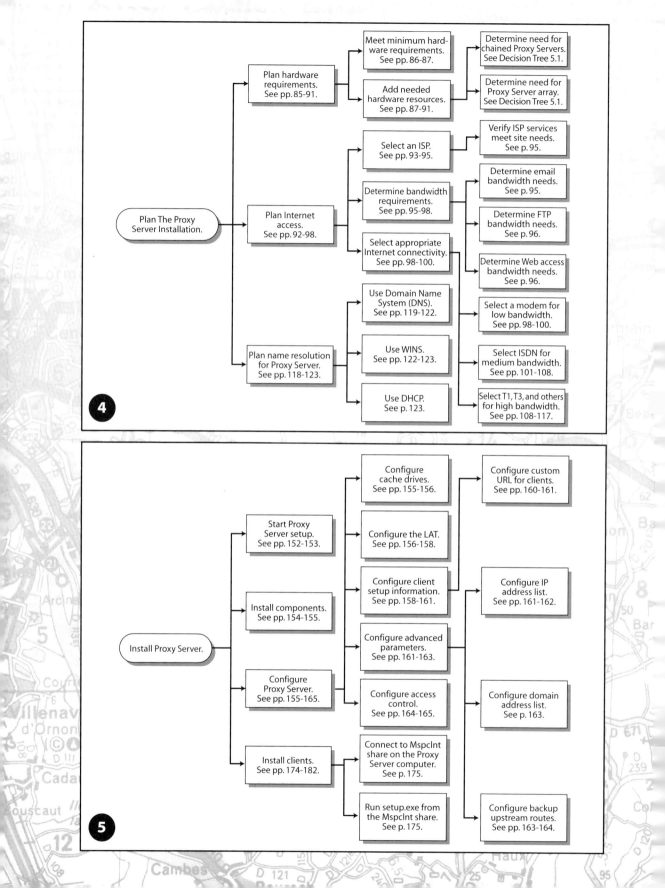

4

Plan The Proxy Server Installation.

- Plan hardware requirements. See pp. 85-91.
  - Meet minimum hardware requirements. See pp. 86-87.
    - Determine need for chained Proxy Servers. See Decision Tree 5.1.
  - Add needed hardware resources. See pp. 87-91.
    - Determine need for Proxy Server array. See Decision Tree 5.1.
- Plan Internet access. See pp. 92-98.
  - Select an ISP. See pp. 93-95.
    - Verify ISP services meet site needs. See p. 95.
  - Determine bandwidth requirements. See pp. 95-98.
    - Determine email bandwidth needs. See p. 95.
    - Determine FTP bandwidth needs. See p. 96.
  - Select appropriate Internet connectivity. See pp. 98-100.
    - Determine Web access bandwidth needs. See p. 96.
- Plan name resolution for Proxy Server. See pp. 118-123.
  - Use Domain Name System (DNS). See pp. 119-122.
    - Select a modem for low bandwidth. See pp. 98-100.
  - Use WINS. See pp. 122-123.
    - Select ISDN for medium bandwidth. See pp. 101-108.
  - Use DHCP. See p. 123.
    - Select T1, T3, and others for high bandwidth. See pp. 108-117.

5

Install Proxy Server.

- Start Proxy Server setup. See pp. 152-153.
  - Configure cache drives. See pp. 155-156.
    - Configure custom URL for clients. See pp. 160-161.
  - Configure the LAT. See pp. 156-158.
  - Configure client setup information. See pp. 158-161.
    - Configure IP address list. See pp. 161-162.
- Install components. See pp. 154-155.
  - Configure advanced parameters. See pp. 161-163.
- Configure Proxy Server. See pp. 155-165.
  - Configure access control. See pp. 164-165.
    - Configure domain address list. See p. 163.
- Install clients. See pp. 174-182.
  - Connect to Mspclnt share on the Proxy Server computer. See p. 175.
  - Run setup.exe from the Mspclnt share. See p. 175.
    - Configure backup upstream routes. See pp. 163-164.

Here's praise for Certification Insider Press's best-selling Exam Cram series. These comments come to us via craminfo@coriolis.com. We look forward to hearing from you, too.

First of all, I want to say how impressed I am with the *Exam Cram* series. I passed both the NT 4 Workstation and Server on the first try! Your books are concise and refer exactly to where to study further.

—Miriam Strysik, Associate Systems Programmer
   Kaiser Permanente

This book has been the best educational computer book that I have ever read.

—Mark Freeman
   XLConnect Solutions, Inc.

Thank you for offering the MCSE *Exam Cram* books. They are the best reference books for the MCSE tests indeed. I am glad to recommend them to my friends.

—Yu-Ting Swenson, MCP

Tomorrow I'll be taking the TCP/IP exam, and after spending a few weeks with your book and various Net sources, I feel quite confident about the results. This will be my fourth test. I relied on your *Exam Cram* series for Workstation, Server, and Enterprise, and scored 882, 909, and 921 on them respectively, all on my first try. Many thanks for saving me so much time!

—Thomas Mullen, MCP

I just took the Windows 95 test last Thursday and passed with an 899; nothing beats preparation. We have at least 15 people currently in various stages of MCSE testing and all of them are using *Exam Crams* to prepare.

—Greg Conroy

I really do think you guys have a great idea with the *Exam Cram* books. I think they are even better than those "For Dummies" guys because they target a market that has never been catered to before. The books out there right now are always boring and too technical for their own good. I must commend your ideas on creating a set of books designed just for exam purposes. I think that this is needed in the market.

—Lorne Boden
   Executive Education

The (*MCSE TCP/IP Exam Cram*) book was great. I read it along with 2 others. I passed my test and am now part of the 7% of MCSEs that are women.

—Alice Goodman, MCSE
   IT - Pioneer Human Services

Let Us Help You Jumpstart Your Career

I remember the first job I had right out of college. Armed with a computer science degree and too much confidence for my own good, I was ready to take on the world. Unfortunately, my lack of real-world experience and day-to-day problem-solving abilities got me into more trouble than I like to admit. But one thing I learned quickly was that teaming up with other people who knew how to quickly detect and solve tricky problems was a surefire way to greater success. (It also makes people think you're really smart!)

In developing our new *On Site* series, we started with one simple goal—to create books and software that could help you solve problems like a seasoned pro. Let's face it, implementing technologies like Proxy Server or Exchange Server across an enterprise network can turn into a complicated mess, especially if you haven't done it before. In each *On Site* guide, you'll find hundreds of pages of useful tips and techniques for planning, deploying, configuring, and troubleshooting network technology.

We've incorporated a number of unique features throughout each *On Site* book to help you become an "in-demand" expert. Inside the front cover we start with a tear-out visual problem-solving card to help you get your bearings. If you are having difficulty solving a problem, simply look up your problem and the card will direct you to solutions inside the book. Later, you'll find useful visual decision trees and checklists to help you solve complex problems, step-by-step. You'll also find numerous time-saving tips that are designed to keep you from wasting your valuable time. Last but not least, we've included a sample chapter from our *MCSE Proxy Server 2 Exam Cram* to help you get a "taste" of what's involved with MCSE certification.

I hope that you find each *On Site* book up to the standards of our best-selling *Exam Cram* and *Exam Prep* books. Whether you are certified, planning to get certified, or just implementing Microsoft network technology, we want you to be able to count on getting the expert advice you need from our *On Site* series.

To help us continue to provide the very best problem-solving and certification guides, we'd like to hear from you. Write or email us at **craminfo@coriolis.com** and let us know how our *On Site* books have helped you in your work, or tell us about new features you'd like us to add. If you send us a story about how an *On Site* book has helped you and we use it, we'll send you an official *Certification Insider Press* shirt for your efforts.

Keith Weiskamp
Publisher, Certification Insider Press

ON SITE™

Microsoft
PROXY
SERVER 2

PLANNING
DEPLOYMENT
CONFIGURATION
TROUBLESHOOTING

Microsoft Proxy Server 2 On Site

Copyright © The Coriolis Group, 1998

Limits of Liability and Disclaimer of Warranty

Trademarks

The Coriolis Group, Inc.
An International Thomson Publishing Company
14455 N. Hayden Road, Suite 220
Scottsdale, Arizona 85260

602/483-0192
FAX 602/483-0193
http://www.coriolis.com

Technical Illustrations by Kathy Schuler

Library of Congress Cataloging-in-Publication Data
Schuler, Kevin.
    Microsoft Proxy Server 2 on site / by Kevin Schuler.
        p.   cm.
    Includes index.
    ISBN 1-57610-259-9
    1. Web servers—Computer programs.   2. Microsoft Proxy server.
I. Title.
TK5105.888.S38   1998
005.7'1376—DC21   98-13406
                                                                CIP

Printed in the United States of America
10 9 8 7 6 5 4 3 2 1

an International Thomson Publishing company

Albany, NY • Belmont, CA • Bonn • Boston • Cincinnati • Detroit • Johannesburg • London • Madrid
Melbourne • Mexico City • New York • Paris • Singapore • Tokyo • Toronto • Washington

Publisher
Keith Weiskamp

Acquisitions
Shari Jo Hehr

Project Editor
Ann Waggoner Aken

Production Coordinator
Kim Eoff

Cover Design
Anthony Stock

Layout Design
April Nielsen

CD-ROM Development
Robert Clarfield

Marketing Specialist
Cynthia Caldwell

This book is dedicated to my grandmother, Clara Schuler, who at age 98 continues to inspire us with her wisdom and faith.

About The Author

Kevin Schuler is President of InDepth Technology, a technical consulting firm dedicated to delivering to its clients an in-depth understanding of Microsoft's emerging technologies. Additionally, Kevin serves as a Microsoft Regional Director. In that capacity, Kevin assists Microsoft by conducting Microsoft Developer Days in Columbus, Ohio, assisting in the establishment of user groups, and building technical communities. Kevin also is a member of the Microsoft TechEd advisory board, assisting with the creation of content for Microsoft's largest channel event. Kevin also serves as a consultant to Microsoft for its MCSD (Microsoft Certified Solutions Developer) program.

Before establishing InDepth Technology, Inc., Kevin worked from 1988 to 1997 as Executive Vice President and General Manager for Babbage-Simmel, a technology consulting and training firm. He began programming microcomputers in 1979. He established one of Microsoft's first Authorized Training Centers. Subsequently, he helped found the Ring Zero Group, a small circle of industry professionals working with Microsoft, to spearhead the adoption of Microsoft's SQL Server throughout corporate America. He has spoken about the impact of the digital communications revolution at several important venues including Ohio State University, the University of Georgia, and the University of Maryland. Kevin also coauthored *Microsoft Exchange Server 5.5 On Site*, published by The Coriolis Group.

Acknowledgments

Books are never written solely by the author. There are many people who come together, albeit often electronically, to create a work such as this. I owe a debt of gratitude to each and every one who helped make this book possible.

My first thanks go to all my friends at Microsoft Corporation in Redmond. For several years, numerous Microsoft employees urged me to write a book. My special thanks go to Michael Werner and Kostas Mallios for finally driving the point home. Their creative energy and enthusiasm were instrumental in this undertaking.

Writing a book takes a lot of time, some great advisors, and a sense of humor. I thank the Executive Board of COUNT (Central Ohio Users NT) for their combination of good technical advice and humor. Thank you Brian Keller, Jeff Schmidt, Mary Ann Schull, and Ed Zirkle. You made the job much more enjoyable and offered some great suggestions.

A big thanks goes to all the Microsoft Regional Directors. This is a great group of individuals from around the world. Regional Directors assist Microsoft in building technical communities and putting on Microsoft's largest conference, Developer Days, each year. I learned a lot from each of you. An extra big thanks goes to Ken Spencer for his sage advice about writing technical books.

I'm a big fan of planning. I also know that you can't plan everything. When preparing to write this book, I put extra disaster recovery mechanisms in place. I heard the horror stories about losing a good portion of a book to power outages, disk failures, and so on. So I beefed up our UPS systems, performed regular and redundant back up—in short, I prepared for the worst. Midway through the writing, we were hit by a terrible storm. Tornadoes danced within a stone's throw, and our electrical power and telecommunications systems were out cold for a couple of days. Everything survived but the ISDN line and adapter. The ISDN equipment at Ameritech's central office was fried along with the ISDN adapter at our premises. Thank you Ameritech for getting the ISDN line up and running so quickly—it could have been a horror story. Also, special thanks to 3COM for replacing our ISDN adapter so quickly.

Acknowledgments

My publisher offered great support throughout the project. There are some terrific people who worked hard behind the scenes to make this book possible. I thank the following Coriolis associates for their positive reinforcement and close attention to detail: Ann Waggoner Aken, Project Editor; Robert Clarfield, CD-ROM Developer; Kim Eoff, Production Coordinator; Cynthia Caldwell, Marketing Specialist; Anthony Stock, Cover Design; and, Paulette Kilheffer, Copy Editor. I also offer my thanks to Allen Wyatt who served as the Technical Editor of this book. Allen read the manuscript with a sharp eye and made countless insightful suggestions.

I also am grateful for the friendship and advice of my colleagues. In particular, my gratitude goes to David Mader for "keeping me in the loop." David's technical competency, spiritual well being, and musical musings were remembered often in the thick of this project. Another big thank you goes to Ty Wait for his friendship and assistance throughout the duration of this endeavor. Ty not only offered some great advice, but also helped organize and co-delivered content for several of my speaking engagements when my time was curbed by project deadlines.

Finally, and most importantly, I am most grateful for the patience, understanding, and hard work of my wife Kathy. She was not only supportive throughout the project, but she initiated the vendor relationships and secured the content for the companion CD-ROM. Additionally, her outstanding illustrations appear throughout the book, helping to make clear some rather complex technical concepts. Without her help, this book simply would not have been possible.

Table Of Contents

Part II   Understanding Your Internet And Security Needs

Introduction

Everyone from large corporations to small offices and home offices (SOHOs) are rushing to connect their users to the Internet. Microsoft Proxy Server 2.0 offers a secure, high-performance, reliable solution to this business and security challenge. The industry reviews are outstanding: Microsoft Proxy Server is the clear winner on the Windows NT platform.

Proxy Server does much more than its name implies. New with Proxy Server 2.0 are industrial strength firewall features to protect your organization's private network. When configured appropriately, Proxy Server is a flexible, high performance product with powerful tools for administration and management. In fact, Microsoft Corporation itself uses Proxy Server to connect its thousands of employees to the Internet.

This book will teach you how to properly implement Microsoft Proxy Server 2.0 for your organization. While you will have peace of mind because your private network is safe and secure, your user community will enjoy a high-performance and reliable connection to the Internet. This book's content is designed to help you realize Proxy Server's role as a secure, high-performance gateway between your private network and the public network of the Internet.

Who Should Read This Book

This book is for systems professionals, network administrators, and SOHO power users who want an in-depth understanding of Microsoft Proxy Server 2.0. Filled with procedures, decision trees, illustrations, and clear explanations of its background technology, this book will help you accelerate your understanding of Proxy Server's technical details.

Just learning how Proxy Server works is not enough; you'll also need to know how to assess Internet access needs and requirements of your user community. You will learn how to do this by bringing the persons who will be accessing the Internet into the planning process early on. Therefore, the Proxy Server is implemented more *effectively*, and the rollout is more likely to be viewed as a *success*. Try this process once, and you will appreciate how important it is and how well it works.

How This Book Is Organized

I organized this book into four major parts:

➤ The Product

➤ Understanding Your Internet And Security Needs

➤ Planning And Installing

➤ Administering The Server, Clients, And Security

The organization of the book guides you through a truly effective implementation of Proxy Server. First, by understanding the product's features and architecture you will be able to communicate the possibilities of the technology. Then, you learn how to map the Internet access and security needs of your organization to the capabilities of the product. Next, you learn how to plan and install Proxy Server 2.0. Finally, your Internet needs will change over time, so you'll learn about administering the server, clients, and security. Additionally, in the appendixes, you'll find great information about troubleshooting, TCP/IP, and additional resources to further your knowledge. The following is a brief tour of the book.

Part I: The Product

Part I explains the basics of Microsoft Proxy Server 2.0 and why this product is such a significant technology. Internet access is more than important for today's organizations—it is crucial. Proxy Server has numerous features and benefits that make Internet access secure, convenient, and fast. Chapter 1 furnishes the basic, high-level understanding of Proxy Server's features that is critical to its proper implementation.

It's also important to understand the architecture of the three major proxy services that comprise Microsoft Proxy Server: The Web Proxy service, WinSock Proxy service, and SOCKS Proxy service. Chapter 2 explains how each of these services plays a distinct and important role in Internet access for your organization. Understanding these lower-level details about Proxy Server's underpinnings will help you create the appropriate Proxy Server configuration for your organization.

Part II: Understanding Your Internet And Security Needs

Part II guides you through the initial parts of a successful Proxy Server Implementation Plan: needs assessment and security assessment. A well-functioning private network infrastructure has long been a critical factor in the attainment of business objectives. Now, Proxy Server allows you to expand the reach of your organization's private network to the worldwide public arena of the Internet. Chapter 3 illustrates how you use the needs of your business and user community to drive the implementation process.

Security is a huge issue when connecting your private network to the public Internet. What are the threats to your network? How do you determine the security objectives of your organization and create security policies? Chapter 4 furnishes the clear instructions you need to perform a security assessment that will help you plan the network security for your organization. Also, Microsoft Proxy Server combines with and enhances the native Windows NT security. This chapter explains the critical parts of the Windows NT Security model as it relates to Proxy Server and offers a checklist to guide your configuration of Proxy Server security.

Part III: Planning And Installing

Part III guides you through the planning and hands-on implementation of Proxy Server. First, you learn how to plan the implementation. In Chapter 5, you'll learn not only the hardware requirements for Proxy Server, but also the breadth of your Internet connectivity options. The strengths and weaknesses of modems, ISDN, T1 and T3 lines, and more are discussed. Additionally, in this chapter you'll learn how to organize an effective Proxy Server rollout plan for your organization using the information you garnered from your needs and security assessments.

Chapter 6 takes you systematically through a Proxy Server installation. As most of your planning was done up front, this process is swift and straightforward. Starting with configuring Windows NT through installing Proxy Server itself, you're taken completely through each option of the setup process. Configuring the cache, the Local Address Table (LAT), access control, and more are explained in this chapter.

Part IV: Administering The Server, Clients, And Security

Once set up, you'll enjoy learning about Proxy Server's administrative features. The remaining chapters feature an in-depth examination of the procedures and options available for administering the server, clients, and even administering Proxy Server in multi-server environments.

In Chapter 7, you'll learn how to administer Proxy Server 2.0 from the command line or from menu-based utilities. Both methods and their options are discussed in detail. You'll also learn how to create custom HTML error messages, configure Auto Dial, configure the cache, and more. However, just learning how to administer the server is not enough, so in Chapter 8 you'll learn how to administer Proxy Server clients. You'll master the details of the client configuration file, you'll learn what actions the command entries perform, and you'll learn when to make changes.

In Chapter 9, you'll also learn how to administer Proxy Server security. For example, using Proxy Server Access control allows you to be able to determine exactly which

Internet services are available to the entire organization, members of specific groups, or individual users. In addition, you'll learn how to use security enhancements normally found only in full-featured Internet firewall products. You'll be able to automatically filter packets, setup security alerts, and create logs.

Finally, in Chapter 10 you'll learn how to create Proxy Server Arrays, chains of Microsoft Proxy Servers, or a Microsoft Proxy Server chained with 3rd party CERN-based proxy servers or other firewall products. You'll even be able to configure Proxy Server to listen and respond on behalf of Web servers or other servers, such as Microsoft Exchange, that are located behind the Proxy Server.

Appendixes

The appendixes contain important, real-world information to make Proxy Server work for you. Appendix A contains valuable information about troubleshooting Proxy Server. Included with Proxy Server is a utility that helps you detect and diagnose common configuration problems. I explain troubleshooting by using this utility, along with the various logs that Proxy Server creates.

Appendix B is a basic guide to TCP/IP. This appendix gives you detailed information about TCP/IP that you need to know to implement and administer Proxy Server. If you've ever wondered about the intricacies of TCP/IP addressing, UDP and TCP ports, and "well-known ports," you'll find this appendix most helpful.

Appendix C is a detailed listing of the Windows Sockets API calls supported by Proxy Server. It's a useful guide if you need to implement custom WinSock applications.

Appendix D contains a wealth of information about Proxy Server third-party plug-ins, relevant URLs, and books to further your knowledge about Internet security.

Contacting The Author

I appreciate you buying this book. While writing it, I worked hard to make it useful and easy to read. What do you think? I really would like to hear from you. You can send your comments or suggestions to me at **kevins@indepth-tech.com**. Also, drop by **www.indepth-tech.com** for the latest information about Proxy Server and other projects of interest.

Now, let's start unraveling the mysteries of Proxy Server 2.0.

PART I

The Product

What Is Proxy Server?

What is Proxy Server? Answering this question will help ground your understanding of the features and capabilities of Microsoft Proxy Server 2.0. In this chapter, we'll examine a typical business case for deploying a proxy server and explore the three principal benefits of Microsoft Proxy Server. But first, let's pick apart the word "proxy."

"Proxy"—a rather legal sounding term, isn't it? A "proxy" usually designates a person authorized to act for another as an agent or a substitute. You might have heard of a "proxy vote," where a shareholder gives up his or her right to vote in person to another person or entity. So just what is a proxy server? It is simply a network server that is configured to act on behalf of the client computers connected to it.

Without the need for Internet access, there would be little use for a proxy server. Internet access, and the increased demands that access makes on network security, is the fundamental reason that your organization needs a proxy server. Let me give you a rather typical scenario.

> *A task, critical to the mission of your business, requires Internet access. Your organization does not have an enterprise-wide Internet connection because of economic, security, or management concerns. So the problem is quickly solved by attaching a modem to a PC and securing a dial-up connection to the Internet. Problem solved; but a concern lingers in your mind—"I just opened up my private network to Internet hackers." You rationalize that it's highly unlikely that someone would hack through that dial-up connection. Then another associate makes the case for a connection, then a third. Next thing you know, dial-up Internet connections are multiplying like January cold germs in the schoolyard. When something goes wrong, you have to fix it multiple times; administering all those dial-up connections is growing more impossible each day. It doesn't take long before you have a high-cost security and management nightmare on your hands. It's time for an intelligent solution.*

You've just realized that your business needs an intelligent technical solution for your Internet access that is economical, secure, and easy to manage. You need a proxy server. Your business also needs a security policy, but more on that a little later.

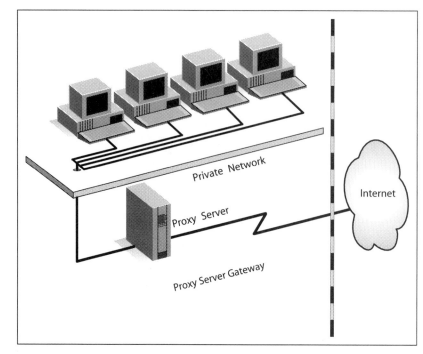

Figure 1.1 Proxy servers act as gateways between the private network and the Internet.

The need to access the Internet is critical for today's businesses. What a proxy server does is act as a secure gateway, or point of access, between the private network and the Internet. Figure 1.1 illustrates the basic role of a proxy server.

Let's take a look at exactly how an Internet proxy server works. Probably the most common Internet application in use today are Web browsers. In a few short years, the Web browser has grown to be the most popular *computer* application. Figure 1.2 illustrates the typical sequence for an Internet proxy service when browsing the Web.

Let's take a closer look at what happens when a user browses the Web with a proxy server in the chain:

1. A client application, such as a Web browser, makes a request for an object. In this example, the request is an HTML page on the Internet.

2. The client request is passed to the proxy server on the private network.

3. The proxy server translates the request and passes it to a host Web server on the Internet.

4. The host Web server on the Internet responds to the proxy server.

5. The proxy server passes that response back to the client application that made the original request.

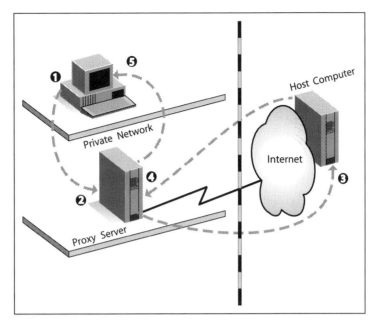

Figure 1.2   The proxy server routes requests and responses between the Internet and client computers.

Pretty straightforward isn't it? Actually, a lot more is going on behind the scenes; however, we'll get into those architectural details in Chapter 2. First, let's look at the principal reasons to place a proxy server between your private network and the Internet.

Principal Reasons For A Proxy Server

A proxy server simply routes requests and responses between the Internet and client computers. As illustrated in the previous example, the proxy server is continually acting as an agent between the client and the Internet. While at first that might seem like just a lot of extra work for the server, there are important reasons to add a proxy server to your system. I'll give you three compelling ones:

➤ Internet security

➤ Enhanced performance

➤ Simplified management

Microsoft Proxy Server 2.0 is an easy, secure way to bring the functionality of a proxy server to your organization. It runs on Microsoft Windows NT Server 4.0, it installs easily, and its friendly user interface makes it straightforward to administer. Users will enjoy the high performance Internet access that Proxy Server brings to the desktop. Internet security, enhanced performance, and easy management are the key benefits of Microsoft Proxy Server. Let's examine each of these benefits and their specific capabilities in depth.

Internet Security

Internet security is probably the most important reason to implement a proxy server. Remember those dial-up connections through modems attached to client computers on the private net that I mentioned previously? They're simply not secure. Your entire private network could become a hacker's dream. Proxy Server will solve that problem and more. For example, you might be considering hosting a Web site for your business, or allowing other forms of incoming access from the Internet. For that you need a firewall. That's okay, because Microsoft Proxy Server 2.0 expands the functionality of a typical proxy server to the realm of a true firewall. Your organization will benefit from both *outgoing* and *incoming* security with Microsoft Proxy Server 2.0. Proxy Server puts up a powerful barrier to intruders who attempt to gain illegitimate access from outside your internal network or, if specially configured, even between internal departments.

The security features in Proxy Server 2.0 are robust, providing a high level of protection for your private network from outside intruders. Proxy Server integrates with and expands the Microsoft Windows NT Server security model, allowing network administrators to have a high level of control over Internet access while protecting your intranet or Local Area Network (LAN). Proxy Server 1.0 provided outgoing service only, so in that respect, it was not a true firewall. Version 2.0 is a full-featured firewall, providing *outgoing* and *incoming* security features. This is a significant enhancement over Microsoft Proxy Server 1.0. Some of the new security features in Version 2.0 include:

➤ Dynamic packet filtering

➤ Multilayered security

➤ Packet event alerting and logging

➤ Shielding of internal network addresses

➤ Reverse proxy and virtual hosting

➤ Server proxying

➤ Shielding of Internet server applications

Dynamic Packet Filtering

A new feature in Microsoft Proxy Server 2.0 is support for packet layer security with dynamic packet filtering, both inbound and outbound. This eases the burden on a network manager, as Proxy Server intelligently and dynamically determines which TCP/IP packets are allowed to pass through to the secured network's circuit and application layer proxy services. Ports are opened automatically, only when needed, and ports are closed at the end of the communication. This means that it is unnecessary to manually pre-define and permanently open a set of ports for different applications. Inbound and outbound exposed ports are minimized, and security is enhanced.

A Short History Of Firewalls

Just a few years ago, the only firewall solutions that existed were built from scratch. It took an immense knowledge of TCP/IP and Unix for someone to custom craft a firewall. Not only were these firewalls quite costly, but as is the case with many custom solutions, they were difficult to manage.

In the early '90s, the firewall market initiated its first growth cycle and the first commercially available firewalls appeared. These products began to ease access problems, particularly for the larger organizations that could afford them. Most of these early firewall products were Unix-based, requiring fairly substantial technical skills to administer.

Today, several commercially available firewall solutions exist on various platforms, including Microsoft Windows NT. Typically, their cost ranges from $5,000 to $20,000. Microsoft positioned its Proxy Server 2.0 to be much less expensive than typical prices, and of equal or greater performance. Because Microsoft's Proxy Server is closely integrated with Windows NT, administering the proxy server is straightforward and economical. Now, Internet firewall protection is available and affordable for organizations ranging from the largest enterprises to the small office-home offices (SOHO).

Multilayered Security

I previously mentioned that Proxy Server 2.0 acts as a gateway to the Internet. Traditionally, gateways are implemented at one of three levels: *packet filtering, application,* or *circuit.* These gateway levels are sometimes referred to as security layers. To understand Microsoft's multilayer approach, it is important to know that Proxy Server 2.0 includes three types of proxy services. These services include:

➤ Web proxy

➤ WinSock proxy

➤ Socks proxy

The Web proxy service is implemented at the application level, working strictly with application protocols. The WinSock proxy and Socks proxy services are implemented at the circuit level. Dynamic packet filtering is always available, no matter which proxy service is in use. Figure 1.3 illustrates the multilayered security model implemented in Microsoft Proxy Server 2.0.

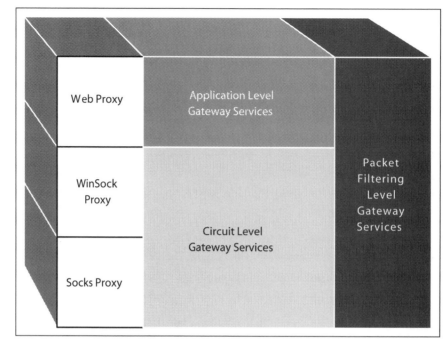

Figure 1.3   The multilayered security model implemented in Proxy Server 2.0.

Each of these proxy services works along with the dynamic packet filtering to provide a multilayered security model. We will go into the operational details of these three proxy services in Chapter 2, when I discuss Proxy Server's architecture. For now, let's separate out the application layer security and the circuit layer security and briefly discuss the available services.

Application Layer Security

The Web proxy is the only proxy service that supports application layer security. Because the Web proxy works at the application layer, content caching is available. The Web proxy service works by understanding commands within a protocol that an application, such as a browser, will issue.

For example, a browser uses HTTP as its application protocol. A user of the browser causes the client computer to issue various HTTP commands during the normal course of browsing. Microsoft Proxy Server 2.0 understands and interprets the HTTP command, then acts on behalf of the client PC and interacts with the Internet resource. Through this proxy process, the network's topology and IP or IPX addresses remain invisible to the outside network. Besides HTTP, the Web proxy also supports FTP and the Gopher protocol.

Circuit Layer Security

The Winsock proxy and the Socks proxy services use circuit layer security. These services provide non-cacheable, application-transparent circuit gateways. An inherent disadvantage with application level security is the small number of protocols actually supported. When circuit layer security is used, as with the WinSock proxy and Socks proxy services, multiplatform access to Telnet, RealAudio, NetShow, IRC, and many other Internet services is possible.

Packet Event Alerting And Logging

It would be nice if a network came under attack only when you were sitting at the system console. Of course, this is rarely the case. Proxy Server 2.0 has email and event-log alerts for protocol violations, dropped packets, and system events. You can configure Proxy Server to log dropped packets and stop proxy services if the hard disk is full. Also, Proxy Server will notify you via email or pager if an intruder is attempting to access your private network. There are several thresholds and variables that you can set to be sure that your proxy server remains safe and secure wherever you are.

Shielding Of Internal Network Addresses

It is much more difficult for an intruder to attack your private network if the private IP or IPX addresses remain hidden. Clients only need use a CERN-compatible Web browser, such as Microsoft Internet Explorer or Netscape Navigator, and the client's IP or IPX address is never known to the host computer. Browsing the Internet is popular; Proxy Server ensures that your organization's internal network addresses remain private.

Reverse Proxy And Virtual Hosting

Publishing to the Internet via a Web server is important for today's organizations. Yet your private network security can be compromised if the same Internet connection that you use to host your Web server is also used for your outward Internet access. Proxy Server 2.0 uses a method known as reverse proxying and reverse hosting to tighten up security when hosting Web services.

Here's how reverse proxying works. When an outside client makes a request for an HTML object across the Internet, the proxy server "impersonates" a Web server. The Web content is retrieved from the cache of the proxy server and fed back to the outside client. The real Web server is called on only if the proxy server cannot fulfill the client's request for Web content from its own cache. This Web publishing technique opens but a single "hole" in the firewall to fulfill HTTP requests, so your Web server remains secure and available for intranet services. Reverse proxy works at the application layer, so it only supports HTTP.

Virtual hosting is an extension of the reverse proxying concept. Virtual hosting, or reverse hosting as it is sometimes called, allows any server located behind the proxy server to publish to the Internet. Proxy Server 2.0 imitates virtual roots on the Web server and then redirects requests for a particular domain and root combination to a single Web server. This feature is great for a multisite intranet.

Server Proxying

Proxy Server 2.0 can proxy other servers that reside behind the proxy server firewall on the private network. Let's use a Microsoft Exchange Server as an example. The proxy server will "listen" for the incoming Internet packets that are intended for the Exchange Server. When packets intended for Exchange are detected, they are forwarded to the Exchange Server. Internet mail delivery is possible, and your Exchange Server is secure.

Server proxying is a circuit layer service, so a wide assortment of protocols are supported. Contrast this with Reverse Proxying, which is an application layer service and supports only HTTP.

Enhanced Performance

Performance is always an important issue, particularly to your organization's users. No one would be pleased if the addition of a proxy server caused noticeable speed degradation as your users browsed the Web. The good news is that in most cases, your users will see an apparent *increase* in Internet access speed.

Microsoft's Proxy Server actually enhances Web performance through the *active caching* of frequently visited Web sites. This means that Proxy Server is automatically updating its cached copies of your organization's most popular Web pages based on patterns of usage. Typically, members of a workgroup have a common set of Web sites that are critical to the fulfillment of their business mission. Workgroup members frequent these sites. Microsoft Proxy Server automatically maintains a central cache of these frequently visited sites. The benefits are reduced bandwidth requirements and faster loading of HTML files for your users.

Proxy Server 2.0 allows cached objects to be returned at LAN speeds, no matter what the speed of your Internet connection. Not only is client performance increased, but also bandwidth requirements are reduced by as much as 60%. Proxy Server 2.0 maintains both HTTP (Web) and FTP caches.

Proxy Server 2.0 implements caching in several ways. I'll explain each of them and briefly illustrate how they work.

Active And Passive Caching

Proxy Server 2.0 is able to cache Internet content both passively and actively. Passive caching is straightforward. When a client makes a request for an Internet object for the first time, the following sequence occurs:

1. The request is passed to the Proxy Server.

2. The Proxy Server passes the request to the host on the Internet.

3. The Internet host returns the object to the Proxy Server.

4. The Proxy Server passes the request to the client and stores, or caches, the Internet object for future requests for the same object.

Subsequent requests for the same Internet object, even by another client, will return the cached object until the object expires. Maintaining a centralized cache reduces Internet traffic. Simple enough, but you can see how passive caching can give impressive performance boosts and reduce Internet traffic.

Active caching is even more exciting. This type of caching is better described as active intelligent caching. What Proxy Server does is scrutinize the browsing habits of your users. It works continually in the background, keeping statistics of the most popular Web sites visited by your users. When the objects in the cache expire, Proxy Server automatically refreshes the content in the cache. Again, this reduces the Internet bandwidth requirements, and popular sites are typically returned at LAN speeds.

Distributed Caching

Distributed caching benefits larger organizations and even Internet Service Providers (ISPs) that require an enterprise-wide proxy solution. Basically, distributed caching brings the cached content closer to the users. For example, a large organization that has many departments might choose to implement a Proxy Server at each department, while a single Proxy Server acts as the Internet gateway and firewall. So, instead of a centralized cache, each departmental Proxy Server caches for its own department.

There is a growing trend toward technologies that "push" Internet content to the desktop. Indeed, Microsoft Internet Explorer 4.0 implements "push" technology in an important and exciting way. Now, important content arrives on a client's desktop without the user having to manually issue a request. While this technology is exciting, it has the potential to increase rather dramatically your Internet bandwidth requirements. Distributed caching will become increasingly important as organizations and ISPs support these "push" technologies. Proxy Server 2.0 works very efficiently at distributing the load of cached objects.

There are a few implementation choices you will have to make if your organization is of the size that will benefit from distributed caching. For example, distributed caching can be implemented using arrays, chaining, or a combination of both methods. Let's take a look at each method.

Proxy Arrays

A Proxy Array allows you to manage a group of Proxy Server computers as a single server. A Proxy Array works by synchronizing each Proxy Server's cache in the array with a single virtual cache. Figure 1.4 illustrates a Proxy Server Array. This method of distributed caching not only enhances performance, but also simplifies management because the array is administered as a single, logical entity. The main performance gain of the Proxy Server Array comes from the higher cache hit rates of the larger virtual cache size.

Chaining

Hierarchical caching, or chaining, involves the linking of multiple Proxy Servers in a prioritized chain. Figure 1.5 illustrates a hierarchical chain. With the hierarchical method of distributed caching, the cache is not synchronized; instead, the client requests follow a chain of priority that is based on the proximity of the cache. For example, the Proxy

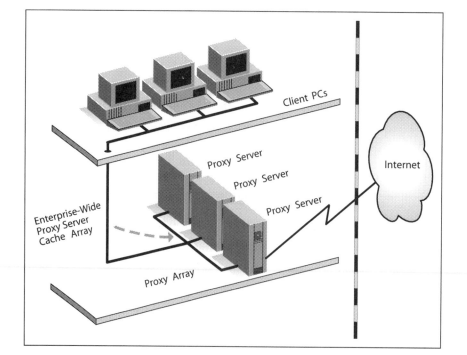

Figure 1.4   A Microsoft Proxy Server Array.

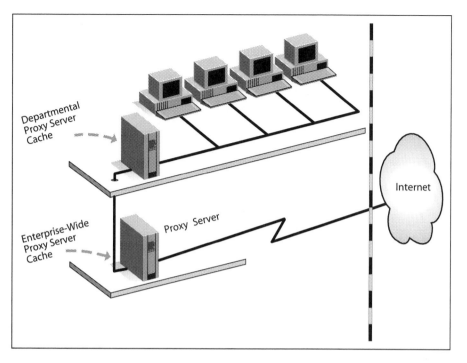

Figure 1.5   Hierarchical Caching of a Microsoft Proxy Server Chain.

Server cache closest to the client computer first attempts to service a request for an Internet object. If that request fails, it passes upstream to the next Proxy Server cache in the hierarchical chain. The object request moves through the chain until the object is found in a cache or, if the object is not cached, on an Internet host computer. Hierarchical caching effectively distributes the server load and fault tolerance across the entire proxy chain.

Combining Distributed Caching Methods

Proxy Server Arrays and Hierarchical Caches can be combined to create powerful distributed caching systems. Figure 1.6 illustrates a combination where an organization's departmental Proxy Servers are hierarchically linked to an enterprise-wide cached array of Proxy Servers. In this scenario, a client computer issues a request for an Internet object. If the object is found in the departmental Proxy Server, it is returned to the client. If the object is not found, the request routes the synchronized virtual cache in the Proxy Server array. The object is either returned to the client computer, or if the object is not in the cache, the request is routed to the Internet host and returned through the proxies to the client computer.

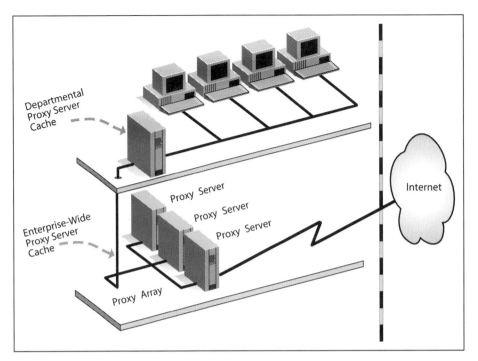

Figure 1.6   Departmental Proxy Servers are chained to an enterprise-wide Proxy Server Array.

Simplified Management

Managing technology can be costly, unless management tools are thoughtfully designed. Fortunately, the administration of Microsoft's Proxy Server 2.0 is easy and straightforward.

The management tools included with Proxy Server allow administrators to grant or deny inbound and outbound connections according to user, service, port, or IP domain. Access can be granted to only the sites you specify, or specific sites can be blocked. Microsoft Proxy Server is integrated closely with Windows NT Server. This is a big factor, particularly when it comes to cost of ownership. I remind you of my original scenario of dial-up connections that multiplied like cold germs in the schoolyard. The cost of ownership on all those connections is astronomical. On the other hand, with Microsoft Proxy Server 2.0, an administrator learns and uses a single set of tools to manage intranet and Internet access for the entire organization. A graphical interface, HTML-based administration, and support for command line scripting combine to make Microsoft Proxy Server exceedingly easy to manage.

In addition, the management tools integrate closely with Windows NT Server 4.0 services. This close integration with the operating system permits a single logon experience for the user, in addition to using the Windows NT *Server Performance Monitor* and *Event Log* for Proxy Server purposes. These management tools make Proxy Server affordable for organizations of all sizes. In Chapter 7, I'll go into the details of actually using the tools; what follows is an overview of the benefits provided by Microsoft's comprehensive approach to Proxy Server 2.0 management.

Central Administration

Microsoft Proxy Server 2.0 features a suite of centralized management tools. You have the choice of HTML-based administration, GUI-based administration, or Command Line-based administration. Let's briefly review the capabilities of each tool.

➤ The GUI-based administration is integrated with the *Microsoft Internet Information Service Manager*. This means that administrators learn one tool to manage both the Microsoft Internet Information Server (IIS) and Proxy Server. The tool is easy to use as both a local and remote administration tool.

➤ Command Line-based administration provides local and remote administration through MS-DOS prompts and batch files. Administrators can create a configuration script and send it to several Microsoft Proxy Servers for rapid configuration.

➤ HTML-based administration is flexible and easy to use. It provides both local and remote administration via a Web browser. The HTML-based administration even allows you to create customized HTML error pages.

The above management tools are integrated closely with the Windows NT Directory Service. So, while users benefit from a single logon experience for all network services and applications, the network administrator maintains complete control of access privileges. Administering arrays of Microsoft Proxy Servers is also easy, as administrative changes are automatically propagated to the other proxy servers in the array.

The Proxy Server 2.0 management tools give administrators the ability to control and monitor user access by setting user or group permissions by *protocol* in Web Proxy, WinSock Proxy, and Socks Proxy. Specific Internet services, or even access to certain Internet sites, can be granted or denied a particular user, group, or domain by the administrator.

Proxy Server 2.0 also includes tools for the backup and restoration of the Proxy Server configuration. A configuration can be backed up to a file or rolled back from a file to a previous configuration known to be good. All these management features make the rollout of Internet access via Proxy Server 2.0 uncommonly quick and efficient, while maintaining a great deal of control.

Let's say, for example, that one day the "Big Boss" asks you to restrict the members of the sales team to only the vendor Web sites required for their sales role. In addition, the "Big Boss" wants new employees still in training only to have access to the organization's human resources site. Also, the "Big Boss" wants unlimited Internet access for herself.

It's no problem. As the administrator you use the Proxy Server 2.0 management tools to restrict the Internet access of the *sales domain* to the specific vendor sites and restrict the *new employee domain* to only the HR intranet, with no Internet privileges. While you are at it, you give extra close attention to granting the user "Big Boss" unlimited access. All users do is simply log on to the Windows NT network or domain, and automatically they have the level of access that you granted them.

Site Management And Extensibility

What Web sites are important for members of your organization to visit? Proxy Server allows you to restrict access to remote Web sites. For example, you could deny access to all Web sites other than the specific ones you enable. Conversely, you could filter only those sites that your organization deems unacceptable. Some element of Web site scrutiny is required for most organizations.

Yet, managing long lists of inappropriate sites could soon grow to be a daunting task. The solution is to obtain any of several third-party software offerings that specialize in content filtering. As of this writing, such offerings include:

➤ SpyGlass' SurfWatch

➤ Secure Computing's SmartFilter

➤ CyberPatrol's Cyber Patrol Proxy

These software bundles help keep your organization's Internet access under control by using a professional service to monitor and rate Internet sites for content type and appropriateness.

Auto Dial

How much Internet access do you need? Microsoft Proxy Server reduces the bandwidth requirements through its caching model. With bandwidth of up to 128 kilobits per second (kbps) available through a dial-up ISDN, you might find that a dial-up connection is all you need. In fact, small workgroups that have limited access requirements have been pleasantly surprised at what a 28.8 modem can deliver with Proxy Server's caching features implemented.

Yet, dial-up connections, especially ISDN, can become costly if they remain live at all times. In addition, your ISP could become disturbed if you leave your line connected and inactive for too long a period. Read your agreement; they might even choose to cut your service! Microsoft Proxy Server 2.0 includes a cost saving auto dial feature. When a user issues a request for an Internet object, Microsoft Proxy Server automatically dials your ISP.

An administrator can specify which hours Internet access is enabled or disabled. Also, through Proxy Servers close integration with Windows NT Dial-Up Networking (DUN) and Remote Access Service (RAS), you can specify how long a connection remains live after Internet traffic has ceased. Administrators have complete control of dial-up Internet access.

Moving On

Microsoft Proxy Server 2.0 is a robust solution for your organization's Internet access. Its active caching can improve Internet performance from the largest organizations to SOHOs. Large organizations and even ISPs can benefit from Proxy Server's distributed caching model. Your organization's Internet users will delight in the enhanced speed delivered to the desktop when browsing the Web.

But Microsoft Proxy Server 2.0 is more than just a typical proxy server—it is a true firewall. The security features are multilayered, encompassing the protocol, circuit, and application layers. Your internal network addresses, whether TCP/IP or IPX, are shielded completely from the outside; Proxy Server will alert you if an intruder attempts to gain access to your private network. Your Microsoft Exchange server is secure behind the Proxy Server 2.0 firewall, and you can securely publish to the Web.

Yet all these robust features come in a package that is easy to manage. The management tools are integrated closely with Microsoft Windows NT, so administrators only have to learn a single set of tools to effectively manage Microsoft Windows NT, Internet Information Service (IIS), and Proxy Server 2.0. The administration of Microsoft Proxy Server 2.0 is centralized, allowing even large arrays of Proxy Servers to be managed at a single location.

In the next chapter, I'll peel apart the architecture of Proxy Server 2.0. We will take a closer look at how the Web Proxy, WinSock Proxy, and Socks Proxy work, and what capabilities are unique to each service. We will also take a look at the Cache Array Routing Protocol (CARP), the protocol that provides scalability and extreme efficiency when Proxy Servers are configured in an array.

Architecture

There are three major proxy services that comprise Microsoft Proxy Server: The *Web Proxy service*, *WinSock Proxy service*, and *SOCKS Proxy service*. While each of these services is secure and robust, individually they enjoy strengths and weaknesses based on their architectural underpinnings. In this chapter, I'll peel back the technology that makes these services work, exposing the architectural details that will help you make informed implementation decisions.

The word architecture can be somewhat intimidating. After all, there is a lot of complex coding that goes into a product such as Microsoft Proxy Server. Writing an application that specifically addresses the architecture of Proxy Server is a highly detailed and painstaking process. But this chapter is not intended to be a programming guide. Unless absolutely necessary, I avoid detailing specific programming calls, working instead with the underlying concepts that are important for a systems administrator or network manager to understand. Nevertheless, you should be fairly well versed in TCP/IP concepts before reading this chapter. If you feel you need a quick review, Appendix B, "TCP/IP Basics," will furnish the information you need.

One final note before you read on: Your mind might already be made up about what proxy service or services you wish to use. Still, I would strongly urge you to study this chapter and Decision Tree 2.1. You will better understand why you wish to take the course you chose in the first place, or this chapter might provide additional information that will cause you to alter your thinking somewhat. Either way, you come out way ahead. Now let's examine the Web Proxy service first.

Understanding The Web Proxy Service

The Web Proxy service is the cornerstone of Microsoft Proxy Server 2.0. The performance gains realized by your users will be the direct result of caching benefits provided by the Web Proxy Service. In fact, although using the Web Proxy service is not mandatory, I can't imagine implementing a Microsoft Proxy Server 2.0 for outgoing Internet access without it and, at minimum, implementing one of the several caching models. If you want caching, you must use the Web Proxy service.

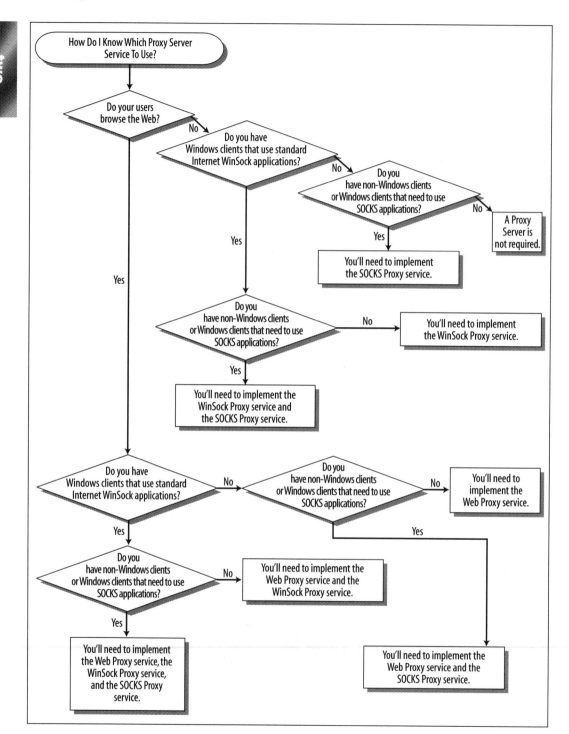

Decision Tree 2.1 How do I know which proxy server to use?

The Web Proxy service is the only one of the three proxy services in Microsoft Proxy Server 2.0 that works at the application level. More specifically, the Web Proxy service is an IIS server application, which acts on behalf of a user requesting an Internet object that can be retrieved using one of the protocols supported by the Web Proxy service. Buried in that definition is a significant downside of any application-level proxy service, including the Web Proxy service in Proxy Server 2.0. Application-level proxies have rather sparse protocol support. So, while most experts agree that an application-level gateway is the most secure, as a rule they are considered too restrictive and are often passed over in favor of proxy services implemented at the circuit or packet filtering level. Implementing an application-level gateway requires building special code for each Internet protocol. This is a daunting task; however, the universal popularity of the Web browser changed everything. Today an application-level proxy service makes sense because a single application, the Web browser, constitutes the vast majority of Internet access for many users.

It seems that everyone browses the Web. Throughout the globe, businesses have found that the World Wide Web (WWW) is a quick, low cost, highly effective way to communicate with their customers. So today, an application-level proxy service that works with popular Web browsers makes good sense. The Web Proxy service operates in conjunction with a Web Proxy client. The Web Proxy client is simply a client computer that uses a CERN compliant application, such as a popular Web browser, that is configured to use the Web Proxy service of Proxy Server. The client is configured through the setup program during the Proxy Server installation. I'll cover the installation process later, but from an architectural viewpoint, it is important to know that Web Proxy clients access the Internet through the Web Proxy service.

What Is CERN?

CERN is an acronym for the Conseil Europeén pour la Recherche Nucléaire (European Laboratory for Particle Physics). Located in Switzerland, CERN is the birthplace of the World Wide Web (WWW). In 1990, Tim Berners-Lee wrote the first WWW browser, which also functioned as an editor and ran under NeXTStep. In addition, he created the first WWW server, and defined URLs and the protocols HTTP and HTML. Tim is now the overall Director of the W3C. Founded in 1994, the W3C is an international industry consortium that develops common protocols for the evolution of the World Wide Web.

You will read terms such as "CERN capable browsers" throughout this book. These are simply browsers that adhere to the industry standards for application-aware proxy services over HTTP-based Client/Server communications. Most popular browsers, including those from Microsoft and Netscape, fit this description nicely.

The Quick Rise Of Web Browser Popularity

The Web browser is enormously popular, and it took a short period of time for its popularity to transpire. I recall a circumstance that drove this point home for me.

Not too long ago, I was a member of a volunteer committee comprised of several persons from all walks of life. The members' ages spanned from early 30s to late 60s. In September 1995, the committee was struggling to determine a means to inform an international audience about the committee's mission. With enthusiasm, I said, "A Web site would be an effective, low cost way to inform a large and growing audience about our mission." My proposal was brief and to the point. I finished and glanced around the room. Everyone sat in silent disbelief; then a voice cracked through the deafening silence saying, "That's awfully esoteric, we need a practical way to get the word out, like an advertisement in the newspaper."

No one had even heard of the Web, and the rest of the committee agreed with the newspaper idea. Yet we never did advertise in the newspaper; it was just too costly. But that's not the end of the story. In March 1996, just six months later, one of the more elderly committee members proposed we put up a Web site for the same purpose. Everyone talked about how the Web was the best and most exciting way to get the word out. Then a discussion broke out about which browser was best. This time it was I who sat in utter disbelief.

A single proxy application can fulfill a large percentage of an organization's Internet requests, and alleviate substantial security concerns at the same time. All that is required is a browser that is compatible with the standard CERN proxy protocol, such as Microsoft Internet Explorer or Netscape Navigator.

Proxy Server's Web Proxy service does support more than just the HyperText Transfer Protocol (HTTP) that browsers require. Besides HTTP, the Web Proxy service supports the File Transfer Protocol (FTP), Gopher protocol, and HTTP-S. HTTP-S is the protocol required for secure sessions using Secure Socket Layer (SSL) connections. But all communication with the Web Proxy client is through HTTP. IP packets are not passed between the Web Proxy service and the Web Proxy client.

Now, let's examine how the Web Proxy service works. My intent is to give you the details required to understand the process, but I'll stay away from specific program calls.

Inside The Web Proxy Service

The Web Proxy service uses HTTP for all communications with a Web Proxy client, yet FTP, HTTP-S, and the Gopher protocol are also available. I'll explain how that rather interesting feat works. First, take a look at how a normal browser works. For more information on whether to use Web Proxy or WinSock Proxy to FTP, see Decision Tree 2.2.

Directly Connected Browser

With a normal browser that is not configured to work with Proxy Server, HTTP requests are sent directly to the host computer. Prior to sending them, the browser parses them into an HTTP command form that the host computer can understand. Figure 2.1 illustrates this process.

Proxy Server And CERN Browser

When a CERN capable browser is configured for and using Proxy Server 2.0, the process works in a much different way. Let's break it apart by first looking at a browser request for a Web resource:

1. The browser sends the complete URL through the private network to a server running IIS.

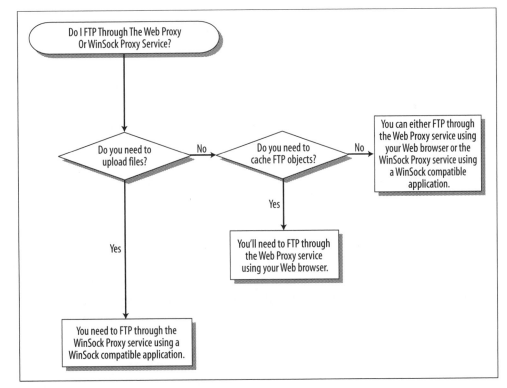

Decision Tree 2.2 Do I FTP through the Web Proxy or WinSock Proxy service?

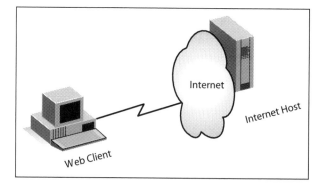

Figure 2.1   How a normal browser communicates with an HTTP host.

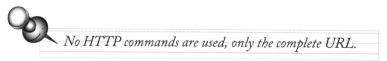

No HTTP commands are used, only the complete URL.

2. The IIS server receives the request and immediately calls the *Proxy ISAPI filter*, which filters the request for notification points such as monitor, log, modify, redirect, or authenticate requests.

3. The request is then forwarded back to the WWW service for a response action.

4. A response is issued by the WWW service, then the *Proxy ISAPI filter* is called again and the response is filtered again for notification points.

5. The response is then returned to the browser.

The above sequence shows how the Web Proxy service can handle multiple protocols. Because an ISAPI filter is called prior to the WWW service's attempt to process the HTTP request, the Proxy ISAPI filter can modify the request, adding the name of the Proxy application to the request. Look again at step 2 above. If the browser request is to be redirected to a proxy application such as FTP or Gopher, the *proxy application* is called in step 3 instead of the Web service, effectively bypassing further processing through IIS. Figure 2.2 illustrates the Web Proxy service architecture.

A little aside, if you're curious. The Web Proxy service is tightly integrated with Windows NT 4.0 as an IIS application. The Proxy ISAPI application and the Proxy ISAPI filter are in a single file: W3proxy.dll. The architecture of IIS allows this DLL to load once, when the Web server is started. After it loads, the Web server can call the DLL at any time. All necessary initialization is done once, making the requests much more efficient to process. The Web Proxy service's high performance and scalability are the result of close integration with Windows NT 4.0 and IIS.

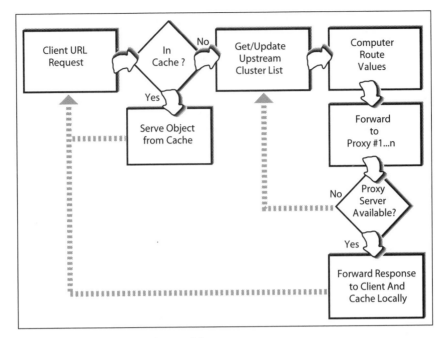

Figure 2.2   The Web Proxy service architecture.

Integration With IIS

Let me give you an example of how the Web Proxy service enhances performance by using HTTP connections to the Internet Information Service (IIS). There is a feature of HTTP called Keep-Alives. For it to work, both the browser and the Internet host must support this feature. It functions in a rather straightforward way: *by permitting TCP connections to remain intact even after a request and response are completed.* This prolonged connection improves performance substantially, because another connection does not have to be made if another request is made from the same client, to the same Internet host, within the specified time limit for connections.

Keep-Alives can enhance performance even if no further requests are made for a Web page. Here's how: A typical Web page has several links to separate graphic image files on a Web server. By keeping a connection to the Web server open, these objects can continue to load without again going through the connection process. Now recall I am writing about straight HTTP Keep-Alives; no proxy server has to be involved. So generally, the HTTP Keep-Alives feature increases performance even for regular, non-proxy browser communication. But for HTTP communication through Proxy Server, Keep-Alives are even more important.

Within your private network, every attempt to access HTTP, Gopher, and FTP Internet sites requires a connection from a browser to Proxy Server through IIS. In this scenario, IIS is functioning in the same way as an Internet host. Because IIS, the Web Proxy service, and Internet Explorer 3.0 (and higher) support HTTP Keep-Alives, there is a significant likelihood of reusing a connection between the same client and the same Proxy Server. These applications work together efficiently to provide high performance.

Tip

You might wish to verify that HTTP Keep-Alives are enabled. HTTP Keep-Alives are enabled by default, but can be disabled by adding the AllowKeepAlives value entry to the Registry and setting its value to 0. This is sometimes done for debugging purposes. Follow the instructions below to determine if Keep-Alives are enabled and to ensure optimal performance.

Check the Registry in the Windows NT 4.0 Server that is running Proxy Server for this entry:

```
HKEY_LOCAL_MACHINE\System\CurrentControlSet\Services\Inetinfo\Parameters
```

If the AllowKeepAlives entry does not appear, or if it appears and is set to 1, then Keep-Alives are enabled. If it is set to 0, change the value to 1.

Caching

Caching is simply maintaining a local copy of an object, in this case an HTTP object. Browsers cache all on their own, so why should we be concerned that the Web Proxy service caches? The main reason is that the Web Proxy service maintains a centralized cache. All of your users of the Proxy Server have access to this shared cache. Workgroups typically share common Internet access needs, so Internet object requests are returned by the shared cache a high percentage of the time.

A valid concern that arises with any proxy server's caching is security. While everyone benefits from the enhanced performance of a cached proxy server, security would be jeopardized if objects intended to be private were cached. It would be possible for some unscrupulous person to examine the cache and extract private information. With this concern in mind, let's take a look at exactly what is cached and, more importantly, what is not.

➤ **Passwords & Authentication**   Many services require a user to log in. Many of these Internet services use clear text as a means to exchange passwords. If these passwords were cached, rather obvious security problems could result. Proxy Server does not cache user logins or any form of user authentication.

➤ **Cookies**   Cookies are used by server applications to cause a client to return information to the server with each HTTP request. Cookies are used to personalize a page or to gather user information. Proxy Server will not cache cookies. Cookies are passed to the browser application to allow personalization to occur. Some users prefer to be warned before accepting cookies; however, this security feature must be turned on in the browser.

● ● *Tip* ● ● ●

Do you want to be warned before you accept a cookie while browsing with Microsoft Internet Explorer 3? Here's how to do it:

1. On the menu bar choose View|Options.
2. Click on the Advanced tab on the Options menu.
3. Mark "Warn before accepting cookies" checkbox.
4. Click on OK.

As you browse, a message box warning that "You have received a 'cookie' …" will pop up when you enter a site that delivers cookies. If you press "Yes", you will receive the cookie. Pressing "No" allows you to continue receiving the Web page, and the cookie is deleted from your hard drive.

➤ **Expiration Dates**   Internet objects pass the date and expiration date in the fields contained in the HTTP header. The date field contains the current date, and the expiration field contains the date that the object expires and should no longer be cached. For the Web Proxy service to cache the object, the expiration date must be later than the date contained in the date field.

➤ **Encryption**   This one is simple and rather obvious: Encrypted objects and objects protected by Secure Sockets Layer (SSL) are not cached.

➤ **Failed Requests**   HTTP defines a number of status codes that are returned to the server in response to a request. The status code 200 means "the action was successfully received, understood, and accepted." An object that returns a result code other than 200 is not cached. Therefore, only successfully returned objects can be cached.

➤ **Keywords**   The Web Proxy service looks for keywords in the HTTP response and request header. Objects that contain the keywords shown in Table 2.1 are not cached.

CARP (Cached Array Routing Protocol) Caching is a fundamental reason for deploying a proxy server. By holding frequently requested Internet objects in a central cache, users experience substantial performance gains. Yet these gains can be mitigated through inefficiencies in the caching process. These caching inefficiencies become even more apparent when using an array of proxy servers. As of this writing, a couple of competitive proxy servers use the Internet Caching Protocol (ICP). Microsoft examined ICP and found significant shortcomings, including:

➤ **Queries**   ICP arrays generate extraneous network traffic, as queries must be used to determine the location of cached objects.

Table 2.1   "Do not cache" keywords.

Keyword	Request/Response Header
Authorization	request
Vary	response
WWW-Authenticate	response
Pragma: no-cache	response
Cache-control: Private	response
Cache-control: no-cache	response
Set-Cookie	response

➤ **Scalability**   Adding proxy servers to an ICP array creates "negative scalability," as the proxy servers must conduct further querying between themselves to determine the location of cached objects in the array.

➤ **Redundancy**   Each server in an ICP array contains largely the same information, an inefficient use of resources.

These problems are significant. Ideally, the browser or downstream proxy server knows whether the Internet object is cached or not and exactly where in a proxy array the object is stored. ICP is too query-intensive to be viable. The problems with ICP led Microsoft to create a new method of caching Internet objects: the Cached Array Routing Protocol (CARP). CARP is much more powerful because it permits "queryless" distributed caching. Take a look at the ways CARP improves on ICP:

➤ **Queryless**   CARP uses a method of *hash-based routing* instead of queries, to resolve requests for cached Internet objects in a single hop.

➤ **No Redundancy**   Internet objects are kept in only one proxy server in an array, so the array acts as a single logical cache.

➤ **High Scalability**   CARP actually allows proxy servers to become faster and more efficient as proxy servers are added to the array.

CARP solves the problems of ICP and also provides some additional benefits. For example, it uses standard HTTP to maintain compatibility with other firewalls and proxy servers. In addition, clients use the industry standard client Proxy Auto-Config (PAC) file, so the benefit of single-hop resolution is extended to clients, not just proxy servers.

What Is Hashing?

Much of my life is spent finding things. Do I hear a chuckle? No, I'm not a bit surprised that much of your precious time is spent the same way. Actually this is an age-old problem that has found its way to computer technology. Hashing is a method to find things faster, that is, for computers to find things faster.

Human beings like to sort things that they want to find fast into some kind of order, such as alphabetic order. Computers, on the other hand, prefer random order. Hashing systems are based on the antithesis of sorting. Proxy Server's hashing algorithm is a pseudorandom function that is applied to the URL's key value in order to scatter URLs randomly throughout the cache. When an Internet object is added to the cache, the object's URL is fed to the hash function, which calculates a location in the cluster list where the data can be placed. At that location, a *bucket* can hold a fixed number of URLs. A bucket is simply the amount of space reserved in each position in the cluster list. When the bucket is filled with URLs and Proxy Server attempts to place another URL in the bucket, it overflows and another bucket is created. Searching the cluster list for a particular URL is performed by feeding the URL into the hash function. The output of the function is the bucket location where the URL is stored. The URL can then be retrieved using the cluster list.

While such a technique would drive humans crazy, this method allows computers to find the data, typically with a single memory access. Hashing provides fast access, low maintenance, and efficient use of space compared with other data access methods.

Understanding CARP

Let's pick apart how CARP works. Figure 2.3 illustrates the CARP's distributed caching model. Here's how the process works:

1. The client makes a request for a URL.

2. Proxy Server determines if the URL is in the cache. If it is, the cache serves the requested URL. If it is not in cache, proceed to step 3.

3. The item was not in the cache, so get the *Upstream Cluster List* (also called the *Membership List*).

4. Compute route values.

5. Forward to Proxy #1…*n*.

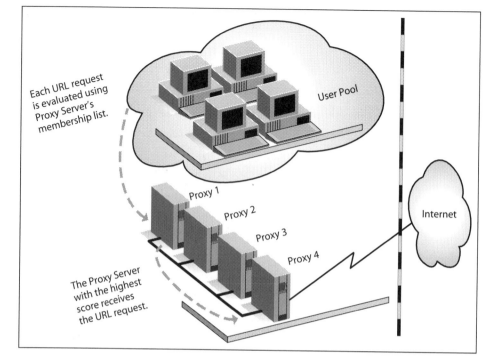

Figure 2.3   CARP's distributed caching model.

6. Determine if the Proxy (*n*) is available. If it is, proceed to step 7. If not, go back to step 3.

7. Forward Response to Client & Cache Locally.

CARP uses a routing algorithm that is "deterministic." In other words, the Web browser or downstream proxy server knows exactly in which cache a requested URL resides, or where it will reside when cached. CARP computes a hash that results in identical scores for identical sets of inputs. Here's the basic four-step process:

1. **Result A:** Proxy Server 2.0 computes a hash of each (*n*) proxy server.

2. **Result B:** Proxy Server 2.0 computes a hash of the requested URL.

3. **Result C:** Each Result A is combined with Result B, to create a total of *n* scores.

4. **Action:** The proxy server with the highest score is the first proxy to receive a URL request. If that request fails, the URL routes to the next highest score and so on.

Let's take a look at how CARP works. Don't worry if you have a math phobia, the numbers used in Tables 2.2–2.4 are for illustrative purposes only. You don't have to do math on these numbers. In these examples, we are only concerned about the highest

Table 2.2 Proxy Server 2.0 computes a hash of each (*n*) proxy server.

Proxy(*n*)	Hash Result A
Proxy1	6
Proxy2	9
Proxy3	22
Proxy4	14

Table 2.3 Proxy Server 2.0 computes a hash of the requested URL.

URL	Hash Result B
www.microsoft.com	6

Table 2.4 Each Result A is combined with Result B to create a total of *n* scores.

Proxy(*n*)	Proxy Hash Result A	URL Hash Result B	Score Result C
Proxy1	6	6	4
Proxy2	9	6	6
Proxy3	22	6	8 ← Action
Proxy4	14	6	2

value. Also, the actual values computed by the hashing algorithm are 2^{32} (10 digits)—much too unwieldy to work with as examples.

In Tables 2.2 to 2.4, Proxy3 would hold the URL for microsoft.com. So Proxy Server 2.0 would perform the action of retrieving the URL from Proxy3. Remember I said that Proxy Server 2.0 works with 2^{32} hash. This is a huge number, allowing every URL to have a unique hash.

Load Balancing

Proxy Server load balances the cache through *distributed caching*. Cached arrays, chains, or a combination of each are means of implementing distributed caching. The process of distributed caching enhances active and passive caching by distributing evenly the load of cached objects. Also, if one Proxy Server computer suddenly becomes unavailable, fault tolerance is provided by distributed caching. The uniqueness of every URL's hash provides an effective way for Proxy Server 2.0 to manage this balancing act among the proxy servers. For example, only the Result Cs (scores) are shown for each URL in Table 2.5.

URL	Proxy1 Score	Proxy2 Score	Proxy3 Score	Proxy4 Score
www.microsoft.com	4	6	8	2
www.xyz.com	9	3	1	7
www.abc.com	3	6	2	7
www.yourcompany.com	1	7	3	5

Table 2.5   Distributed caching balances the load.

As shown in Table 2.5, the high scores are distributed equally across each server. Statistically, the hashing algorithm would naturally balance the cache load equally across all the proxy servers.

Adding And Deleting Proxy Servers

An additional benefit to the CARP algorithm is that adding or deleting proxy servers causes only a fractional change in the cached URLs. The change would be 1/n, where n is the number of proxy servers in the array.

Here's how it works: Recall that a URL's hash is combined with the hash of all available proxy servers, and the highest score is the proxy server that holds the URL. So when a proxy server is added to an array of, let's say, four proxy servers, approximately $1/5^{th}$ of the cache would be reassigned. Statistically, the chances are one out of five that the new proxy server would have the highest score. A similar outcome occurs when a server is deleted from the array. Only a fraction of the total cached URLs is lost.

Adding or deleting proxy servers from an array only affects a fractional portion of the total cache. Therefore, making changes only to array membership is of minimal consequence. This resiliency to change is in marked contrast to ICP, which must rebuild the entire cache with any change in array membership. CARP provides a better and easier way to manage a cache.

CARP Routing

CARP provides the routing features of Proxy Server 2.0. There are two types of routing that CARP supports: distributed and hierarchical. In the previous section on load balancing, we examined how CARP works with a distributed cache of proxy servers in an array. Let's now take a look at how CARP works with hierarchical routing.

CARP's hierarchical routing operates similarly to its distributed routing. The basic difference, as shown in Figure 2.4, is that hierarchical routing involves a downstream proxy that can route requests to n upstream proxies. The downstream proxy routes to an upstream proxy in the same way as a proxy array routes requests to a distributed cache: by

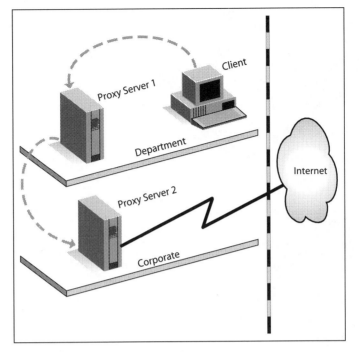

Figure 2.4   CARP's hierarchical caching model.

using the proxy membership list and hash based routing. Using the same methodology for both distributed and hierarchical caching not only is very efficient, but also provides the flexibility of mixing caching models.

Another benefit is that distributed and hierarchical caches can be combined to create, effectively, a single large cache. A large corporation that has sizable departments whose employees make heavy use of the Internet might use this approach. Figure 2.5 illustrates a combination proxy model in use at a large corporation. In this scenario, the department has its own proxy server array, which in turn feeds into a corporate-wide proxy server array. Let's look at how the routing process works with two arrays, organized in a hierarchy:

1. The client forwards a request for a URL to Departmental Proxy 1. Departmental Proxy 1 applies the routing algorithm against its own copy of the array membership list and determines that its Departmental Proxy 2 has the high score. The request is then forwarded to Proxy 2.

2. Departmental Proxy 2 applies the routing algorithm against its own copy of the array membership list and determines that it should handle the request.

3. Departmental Proxy 2's cache does not contain the URL. Departmental Proxy 2 applies the routing algorithm against the membership list of the corporate-wide proxy array and forwards it to Corporate Proxy 3.

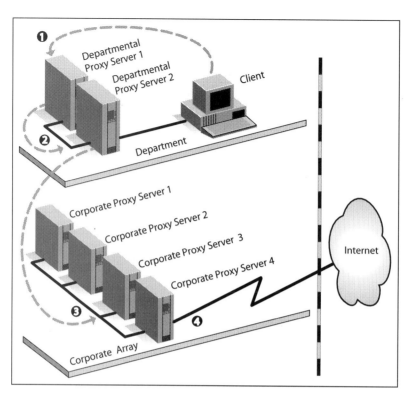

Figure 2.5   CARP's combination distributed and hierarchical caching model.

4. Corporate Proxy 3 applies the routing algorithm against its copy of the corporate-wide array's membership list and determines that it should handle the request. The URL is not in its cache, so it forwards the request to the Internet.

It is clear by the above example that the array membership list is an important piece in the CARP model. You might ask, "Just which proxy server in an array is responsible for managing the membership list?" The answer is that all proxy servers are responsible for maintaining their own list. Proxy Server 2.0 uses an "array manager" to maintain the current list of array members in a specific proxy array. The array managers communicate through HTTP and remote procedure calls (RPCs) to keep the membership list up-to-date.

A real advantage is that the array manager can "publish" the membership list via HTTP to any application that can understand HTTP. Even browsers could route CARP requests, making locating a URL in the cache of a Proxy Server 2.0 array very efficient. Yet even if the browser does not support CARP, a single request to a randomly selected array member is all that is required to produce the correct routing for a URL request. All array members always have up-to-date membership lists.

CARP is a significant advance for cached proxy servers. This is particularly true when using hierarchical or distributed routing. Technically, CARP represents a dramatic improvement over ICP. Using the hashing method for identifying proxy servers and URLs means Proxy Server 2.0 never needs to use the slower query method to find a URL or an array member. Content is never duplicated in an array, so Proxy Server 2.0 is very efficient with hard disk space. In addition, the architecture of CARP allows Proxy Server 2.0 to be highly scalable, providing an effective solution for the largest organization or ISP to small SOHOs.

The WinSock Proxy Service

The Web Proxy Services are secure and high performance solutions for Internet access, through Web browsers and other applications that support HTTP. So why do we need the WinSock Proxy Service? First, to access all the Internet applications that use protocols other than HTTP, FTP, and Gopher. That includes: NetShow, RealAudio, IRC, and other Internet applications that are written to use Windows Sockets over TCP/IP.

Yet there are other equally important reasons to use the WinSock Proxy Service. For example, many believe the IPX/SPX protocols to be ideal, routable protocols for private networks. The WinSock Proxy Service acts as an IPX gateway if TCP/IP is not installed on the private network, allowing access to the Internet while still running IPX/SPX internally. Also, the WinSock Proxy Service is a stand-alone Windows NT 4.0 application, which means that the service provides Windows NT challenge/response authentication between the client and the server.

Before we examine the WinSock Proxy service in detail, let's review how Windows Sockets, or WinSock, came about and why it is used. This understanding will help clarify some of the details of the WinSock Proxy service process.

Understanding Windows Sockets

It wasn't long ago that each programmer would develop his or her own communications interface between a client application and an Internet host. As the Microsoft Windows platform grew increasingly popular, it became clear that a more efficient programming interface was required to keep up with the increasing demand for new Internet applications. Internet developers, along with Microsoft itself, knew that a standard Internet programming interface for Windows would benefit programmers and consumers alike.

A common Internet programming interface already existed for the Berkeley (BSD) Unix operating system, called "sockets." Programmers have an aversion to reinventing the wheel; they would much rather be innovating than re-coding. So they took the basic programming conventions of Berkeley Sockets and converted it to work with the Windows family of operating systems. The new Internet programming interface was dutifully called "WinSock," in honor of its heritage.

two

WinSock Versions

Often, great ideas are born when diverse people of like interests gather to brainstorm and consult. The original WinSock was conceived in the fall of 1991 during a "Birds of a Feather" session at an Interop conference. Interop is a large annual conference comprised of networking, Internet, and intranet experts. The combination of great programming minds and strong vendor support produced the initial version of WinSock.

The current version of WinSock is 1.1. The vast majority of Internet applications in use today support WinSock 1.1. There is a new WinSock specification on the horizon: *WinSock 2*. WinSock 2 provides multiprotocol support, quality of service, a layered provider architecture, and numerous other performance enhancements over WinSock version 1.1. As of this writing, WinSock 2 is available in Microsoft Windows NT 4.0 and soon will be incorporated in the upcoming release of Windows 98. You might wish to check out http://www.intel.com/ial/winsock2/ for up-to-date information on WinSock 2.0.

The beauty of WinSock for the programmer is that low-level network programming is not required. Instead, a single standard Application Programming Interface (API) exists for programmers to write to. As Figure 2.6 shows, WINSOCK.DLL simply acts as a

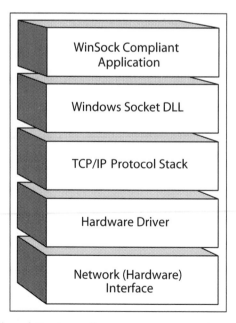

Figure 2.6   The WinSock architecture allows programmers to concentrate on the high-level application programming.

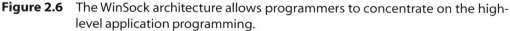

layer between the WinSock applications and the TCP/IP stack. Understanding Windows Sockets and the WinSock Proxy service requires a basic knowledge of TCP/IP and Internet protocols. If you're a little fuzzy on TCP/IP, now would be a good time to turn to Appendix B, "TCP/IP Basics," for a review.

WinSock applications communicate with the WINSOCK.DLL; which, in turn, translates these commands to the TCP/IP stack; and the TCP/IP stack passes them on to the Internet host computer. The WinSock model leaves the details of TCP/IP, hardware drivers, and network interfaces to the WINSOCK.DLL. Programmers write to Windows Socket APIs to perform these six basic communication commands for a WinSock application:

➤ **Open**   Establish a socket.

➤ **Send**   Send data to a socket.

➤ **Receive**   Receive data from a socket.

➤ **Status**   Obtain status information about a socket.

➤ **Close**   Terminate a connection.

➤ **Abort**   Cancel an operation and terminate the connection.

The first four basic commands deal with opening, sending data to, receiving data from, or obtaining information about a "socket." A *socket* is a data structure that represents a communication channel. It consists of an IP address and port number. The last two commands in the above list simply end or nullify the communication channel.

Rather than get into the details of the actual coding of Windows Sockets, I'll give an overview of the Windows Sockets' communication process. This overview will assist your understanding of the WinSock Proxy service in Microsoft Proxy Server.

TCP sockets have two transport mechanisms: *TCP* (Transmission Control Protocol) and *UDP* (User Datagram Protocol). TCP is used for stream-oriented, point-to-point communications. The TCP data stream mechanism is reliable: If data errors occur, the data is retransmitted. On the other hand, UDP is used for datagram-oriented, connectionless communications. UDP does not retransmit on error. Programmers will choose TCP or UDP based on the type of connection required for an application.

TCP Sockets

Connection-oriented TCP sockets are far more common than UDP. For example, FTP, HTTP, and the Gopher protocol use TCP sockets because of their inherent reliability. Application protocols such as FTP (File Transfer Protocol) require high reliability because the data received must be the same as that which was transferred. Lost bits just wouldn't be acceptable. So a virtual connection is set up between the client and the Internet host. Here is how this connection-oriented process typically works:

1. The client initiates the connection to a server, sending a request for an explicit application through TCP to an Internet host. A local IP address and port combination is associated with the socket.

2. The Internet host acknowledges the client's request by establishing a connection. The host sends or receives the data and queries the client for the local and remote address and port pairs.

Less commonly, the server could initiate the connection request. The above communication is in a *connected state* because both the client and the Internet host confirm the communication. Because of the connected state, TCP sockets are considered relatively secure. Also, the data transfer is *stream oriented*. In other words, streams of data can be passed between the client and Internet host. In the case of an FTP application, an entire file can be passed from the client to the Internet host, or vice versa. A *checksum* is used to ensure that the data received is identical to that sent. Of course, the downside to all this housekeeping is a reduction in transfer speed.

UDP Sockets

UDP sockets are *connectionless*. In other words, UDP sockets simply deliver the data, there is no checking to determine if the data was sent to, or is coming from, the correct address. UDP does not check if the correct data was received or sent. UDP sets up *datagram-oriented communications*. This simply means that small, uniform lengths of data are sent unacknowledged by the Internet host. Here's how the connectionless process works:

1. The client initiates the connection to a server, sending a request for an explicit application through UDP to an Internet host. A local IP address and port combination is associated with the socket.

2. The Internet host immediately sends or receives the data to the IP address and port specified by the client.

Contrast the UDP connectionless process above with TCP. It is much simpler and, as you might guess, it is more prone to error and security breaches than TCP. So why would anyone want to use UDP? Primarily, speed. UDP does not have the housekeeping overhead of TCP, so it can transmit at much faster rates than TCP. Real-time applications such as RealAudio and VDOLive use UDP. A second benefit of UDP is that it supports the sending of the same data to multiple clients simultaneously. This is called a *multipoint connectionless service*.

Standards Prevail

WinSock vendors, including Microsoft, agree to adhere to the Windows Sockets standard set of APIs. All Windows-based TCP/IP protocol stacks and WinSock applications support these standard APIs. Besides TCP/IP, some WinSock implementations support the IPX/SPX and NetBEUI protocols.

So programmers don't have to concern themselves if they are using the WINSOCK.DLL that came with Windows 95, Trumpet WinSock, or the WinSock Proxy service that is part of Microsoft Proxy Server 2.0. It all just works. Customers can choose the WinSock compliant application that suits their needs. Terminal emulators, e-mail systems, IRC (Internet Relay Chat), Web browsers, file transfer utilities, search engines, virus scanners, paint programs, and newsreaders are among the hundreds of applications written for WinSock.

Understanding WinSock Proxy

Let's begin by thinking of the WinSock Proxy service as a shared WinSock. Like any WinSock, the WinSock Proxy service permits client applications to send Windows Sockets APIs to server applications running on an Internet host computer. Just like a normal WinSock, the client application appears to the Internet host to be directly connected. The WinSock Proxy service is transparent to WinSock applications and the user.

Yet there is a significant difference: The WinSock Proxy service on the Proxy Server captures the WinSock API calls and redirects them to the Internet host computer. Although it appears to both the client and host that a single connection exists between them, this is not the case. There are two connections: one on the private network from the client to the proxy server and one over the Internet from the Internet host to the proxy server. The WinSock Proxy service allows the client application to function as if it were connected directly to the Internet host, even though it is not. In other words, the proxy server acts as a WinSock gateway.

There are other technical differences as well. For example, a typical WinSock consists of a single DLL (Dynamic Link Library), named WINSOCK.DLL, installed on the client computer. On the other hand, the WinSock Proxy service consists of two parts: a DLL running on each client and a service running on the proxy server. I'll show you how the WinSock server service works, then the WinSock client.

Understanding The WinSock Server Service

Let's examine the WinSock Proxy service running on the proxy server. The WinSock Proxy service runs as a stand-alone service on Windows NT 4.0. Its primary responsibility is establishing gateway connections between the WinSock applications on the client and the Internet host. These communications remain secure as they are all channeled through the proxy server. Also, you are not limited to using TCP/IP on your private network; if you wish, you could use the IPX/SPX protocols. The proxy server acts as an IPX/SPX to TCP/IP gateway between the private network and the Internet, while the WinSock Proxy service performs the data pumping between the two communication channels.

Another benefit of the application-level communications being channeled through the proxy server is that the WinSock Proxy service can provide application-level event monitoring for redirected Windows Sockets applications on the internal network. This provides the proxy server administrator with a wealth of performance, security, and management options.

The WinSock Proxy service can redirect most Internet applications that communicate by using Windows Sockets 1.1. Although Windows NT 4.0 and Windows 98 support Windows Sockets 2.0, these APIs are not supported by Microsoft Proxy Server 2.0 at this time. A couple of other issues are important to note. First, Internet hosts will see only the address of the proxy server, no matter which client is accessing the Internet host. Also, client applications that bind to a specific port can present problems if that port is in use by another client. WinSock applications that are able to bind to any port will not exhibit this problem. However, most WinSock applications should work well with the WinSock Proxy service.

Understanding The WinSock Client

When the Microsoft Proxy Server is installed on a client computer, the original Windows Sockets DLL is renamed and a special Proxy Server version of the Windows Sockets DLL is installed. This new DLL is responsible for redirecting Windows Sockets API calls from the client to the Internet host. The Proxy Server version of the Windows Sockets DLL adopts the name of the original DLL. Windows Sockets DLLs are named according to the following conventions:

➤ WINSOCK.DLL—for 16-bit Windows clients: Windows 3.1, Windows for Workgroups 3.11, and Windows 95.

➤ WSOCK32.DLL—for 32-bit Windows clients: Windows 95 and Windows NT.

As you can see from the above list, Windows 95 gets both the 16-bit and 32-bit versions of the Windows Sockets DLL. This allows 16-bit and 32-bit Windows Socket applications to coexist on the same Windows 95 client computer.

Recall that the original Windows Socket DLL is not discarded, only renamed. This allows the original DLL to still be used for passing Windows Socket API calls to WinSock applications on the private network. So WinSock applications on the private network can continue to operate normally. If a third party WINSOCK.DLL was installed prior to installing the Proxy Server client, it is that Windows Sockets DLL that is renamed and used for private network communications.

Windows clients communicate with the WinSock Proxy service through the newly installed Proxy Server version of the Windows Sockets DLL. Windows Sockets API calls now are redirected to a special *control channel* that uses UDP for communication. UDP is used for two reasons: It's fast, and it allows multi-point connections. This is a very efficient method of connecting clients, as only a single socket is required for communication with all clients. Typically, the problem to this approach is that UDP communication is unreliable. Microsoft overcame that problem by designing a unique acknowledgment protocol. This acknowledgment protocol, utilized between the client and the proxy server, ensures that control channel communication is reliable—a very innovative solution.

The control channel uses UDP port number 1745. However, the actual TCP connections and UDP data use arbitrary ports. Ports in the range of 1024-5000 are used by WinSock applications, unless the applications binds with port 0, in which case Windows NT will choose a port on its own.

The WinSock Proxy service uses three different procedures for using the control channel.

➤ **The control channel is used to set up TCP connections for WinSock Proxy clients to Internet hosts.** The control channel is used to establish a virtual connection with the Internet host; however, the control channel is no longer required once the connection is established.

➤ **The control channel is used to maintain UDP communications between the WinSock Proxy client and the proxy server's WinSock service.** When binding to a UDP socket, WinSock Proxy clients contact the proxy server's WinSock service through the control channel. Multiple remote applications communicating with an internal application also require the control channel. Each time an Internet host sends data, port-mapping information is sent to the client DLL. The control channel is not needed for sending and receiving data between known peers.

➤ **The control channel is used to manage database requests between WinSock Proxy clients and WinSock Proxy servers.** Requests for DNS (Domain Name System) name resolution are handled through the control channel. The control channel is used when passing the client request to the WinSock Proxy service and when forwarding the response to the client WinSock DLL.

Here is how Windows Sockets uses the control channel:

1. A client attempts to make its initial Windows Sockets connection.

2. The WinSock Proxy DLL loads and initializes.

3. The WinSock Proxy DLL establishes its own WinSock Proxy control channel with the WinSock Proxy service.

4. Using the control channel, the WinSock Proxy DLL notifies the WinSock Proxy service that it is active.

5. The WinSock Proxy service downloads the Local Address Table (LAT) to the client.

> *The client uses the LAT to determine which requests are routed to the Internet and which requests remain within the private network.*

6. The WinSock Proxy service is now initialized. From this point on, the WinSock Proxy DLL will determine if WinSock applications are requesting connections with a computer on the private network or an Internet host. Windows Sockets API calls intended for private network computers are simply forwarded to the renamed original WinSock DLL for normal processing. Windows Sockets API calls intended for Internet hosts work with the WinSock Proxy DLL and WinSock Proxy service according to the three procedures stated earlier.

The client requires special processing through the control channel only when first establishing a connection with an Internet host. Beyond that point, standard Windows Sockets and Win32 APIs are used by the WinSock application. The application believes it is communicating directly with the Internet host, when in fact it is communicating with the WinSock Proxy service, which forwards the request on to the Internet host.

Redirecting TCP

Recall that the control channel is used to set up TCP connections for WinSock Proxy clients to Internet hosts. Two connections are established by the WinSock Proxy service each time a private network application requests a TCP connection: one between the client application and the WinSock Proxy service, and the other between the WinSock Proxy service and the Internet host. Yet the application and the Internet host function as if they were directly connected.

The following list represents the TCP redirection process:

1. A TCP redirected connection with the Internet host is established, using the control channel. The control channel is no longer used once the connection is established.

2. The private network application then initiates an outbound TCP connection to an Internet host.

3. Data is sent and received using standard Windows Sockets APIs. When sending and receiving data, the WinSock Proxy DLL forwards the request to the original, renamed Windows Sockets DLL.

The Internet host application believes it is communicating directly with the private network application, but it "sees" only the IP address of the Proxy Server. TCP redirection works even for applications like FTP that need to "see" the Internet application's IP address. The Internet host believes it is communicating directly with the proxy server, and the WinSock Proxy service redirects the requests and data back to the client.

Windows Socket applications also can listen for a TCP connection from an Internet host or a computer on the private network. In this case, a slightly different scenario exists. In order to determine whether the communication should be redirected, WinSock Proxy examines the local IP address to which the application socket is bound. Upon examining the IP address, WinSock Proxy does one of the following:

1. If WinSock Proxy determines the address to be part of its own private network, the listen request is passed to the Windows Sockets DLL.

2. If WinSock Proxy determines the address to be that of Proxy Server's, the listen request is redirected to the Internet host.

The following process takes place if the listen request is redirected:

1. WinSock Proxy listens on behalf of the private network application for a socket connection. The WinSock Proxy service will listen on the proxy server's Internet IP address and the port that was specified as the local port in the private network application's socket bind.

2. Meanwhile, the private network application continues to listen for a connection. When an Internet host connects to the proxy server, the WinSock Proxy service creates a socket connection between the private network application and the WinSock Proxy service, using the local port specified by the application. The WinSock Proxy service uses the proxy server's Internet address and an arbitrary port for its connection with the Internet host.

Redirecting UDP

Windows Sockets applications that use UDP have different redirection requirements from those that use TCP. Because UDP is connectionless and supports multiple applications that communicate with another application on the same UDP socket, some unique problems arise when implementing a proxy server. For example, there could be multiple sources of data sent to a single destination socket.

To illustrate the problem, let's examine the following scenario, showing what happens when a client on the private network receives a packet over UDP from the Internet.

1. The WinSock Proxy service forwards a packet from an Internet source to a private network client.

2. The packet header just forwarded contains the source IP address of the Proxy Server, not the Internet source.

3. Consequently, before the internal application can receive the data, the WinSock Proxy client DLL must change the source port and IP address to that of the actual Internet source.

That might be okay, except for one important detail. UDP allows for multiple sources of data sent to one destination socket. So the client application would never know from which Internet source the packet came.

A solution offered by other proxy server implementations is to have the proxy server add a header to the data prior to forwarding it to the computer on the private network. The new header, of course, would contain the original source port and IP address. The client DLL then removes the header, modifies the source IP address and port, and passes the data to the application. This is a lot of overhead for the application, as every packet would have to be processed. This is a particularly thorny issue and a common reason to use UDP in the first place, if only for its inherent speed. Such an awkward solution slows down the transmissions dramatically.

Microsoft Proxy Server offers a more sensible approach. It simply creates a new UDP socket for each Internet source, while the WinSock Proxy service maintains a port mapping table. Let's examine the process in detail:

1. An initial data packet is received from a new Internet port and IP address.

2. The WinSock Proxy service creates a new UDP socket on an arbitrary local port in Proxy Server.

3. An entry is made in a table that maps Internet ports and IP addresses to the port number of the WinSock Proxy service.

4. The mapping table is forwarded to the WinSock Proxy client DLL through the control channel.

This process is very efficient. Only a single control channel is required, and the data is not modified. The trade-off is that the proxy server computer requires extra resources when a private network application needs to communicate with many Internet peers. This factor should be understood when implementing a proxy server system for your organization. But taken as a whole, this is a reasonable trade-off. Typically, your users will require two types of UDP applications:

➤ Applications that use a single Internet host that communicates with many users on your private network, for example, RealAudio or VDOLive.

➤ Applications where the number of Internet peers communicating with the client is small.

Applications where many Internet sources communicate with a private network client are quite rare.

TCP/IP Private Networks

TCP/IP is an increasingly popular protocol for private networks. The popularity of intranets is a major reason to deploy TCP/IP on the private network. Private network clients can use a TCP/IP application on the Internet or on a private network. Proxy Server coexists nicely with TCP/IP running on a private network.

The key to WinSock Proxy's ability to distinguish a private network request from an Internet request is the Local Address Table (LAT). The LAT contains a list of all the IP addresses and subnets that comprise the private network. The LAT is forwarded to the private network client through the control channel when the WinSock Proxy client initializes. The WinSock Proxy DLL assumes the responsibility of the client's WinSock Proxy DLL to route IP addresses to the private network via the normal Windows Sockets DLL or to the Proxy Server to be redirected to the Internet.

There are some potential dangers to be aware of when using WinSock Proxy with TCP/IP. For example, if the WinSock Proxy is unable to determine if an IP address is for the Internet or a private network, it will assume the address is for the more secure of the two: *the private network*. Also, an environment where multiple servers connect to the Internet through a proxy server could prove to be problematic. For example, suppose that two servers are connected to the Internet using the same IP address and each server is configured to do a redirected listen on port 25 for a Simple Mail Transfer Protocol (SMTP) application. In this case, mail services would fail because both internal servers are listening on the same port and are redirected to the same port on the proxy server computer. The WinSock Proxy service has no way to know which mail server a data packet is for. If different IP addresses are used, the data packets are redirected appropriately.

IPX Private Networks

Running IPX/SPX on the private network is a popular alternative to TCP/IP. The packets are compact and routable. The WinSock Proxy service acts as a protocol gateway for an IPX/SPX network. The Windows Sockets redirection method on an IPX/SPX network parallels that of a TCP/IP network, with one exception: IPX is used on the control channel instead of UDP. The WinSock Proxy DLL simply changes the Windows Sockets API parameters to match what the IPX/SPX network requires. In other words, when a local IP address is specified, WinSock Proxy converts it to a local IPX/SPX address. From that point, the WinSock Proxy service communicates with the client over IPX/SPX.

When the private network is running IPX/SPX exclusively, the WinSock Proxy service will redirect to the Internet any attempt by a Windows Sockets application to communicate over TCP/IP. In this case the WinSock Proxy service is acting as a protocol gateway to the Internet.

two

The SOCKS Proxy Service

The SOCKS Proxy service is a nontransparent proxy service. The Web Proxy and the WinSock Proxy services by contrast are transparent. In other words, the SOCKS Proxy service requires applications that are specifically designed to run with a SOCKS proxy in place; the Web Proxy and WinSock Proxy services do not require any modifications to standard Internet applications.

The WinSock Proxy client application and SOCKS client application provided by Microsoft Proxy Server 2.0 are incompatible; therefore, you must disable the WinSock Proxy client application if you are running the SOCKS client application through the SOCKS Proxy service. However, the WinSock Proxy service can still run on the server for other WinSock Proxy clients that might exist on the private network.

The SOCKS Proxy service supports the SOCKS version 4.3a standard. SOCKS is a circuit level firewall designed to support the lowest-common-denominator UNIX sockets. SOCKS does not support UDP-based applications, such as VDOLive and NetShow. There are many SOCKS applications available, including Telnet, FTP, Whois, and Gopher. One advantage to SOCKS is that it never needs to know about the application protocol. This makes it easy to adapt to a variety of applications including those using Windows NT challenge/response authentication.

Perhaps the clearest way to understand the SOCKS Proxy service is to compare and contrast it with the WinSock Proxy service. The SOCKS Proxy service functions similarly to the WinSock Proxy service in that access control is applied at the beginning of each TCP session. Beyond that point, the SOCKS Proxy service simply redirects the data between the client on the private network and the Internet host. In addition, while the WinSock Proxy service uses global domain filters that support DNS names as well as IP addresses, the Socks Proxy service defines filters only by the destination IP addresses.

Proxy Server supports the SOCKS standard configuration file. The SOCKS Proxy service uses standard IP addresses and the Identification (*Ident*) protocol to identify and authenticate a SOCKS Proxy client. All security is based on TCP header information, such as addresses, port numbers, and Internet hosts. Here is the way the process works:

1. The client on the private network connects to the SOCKS service running on the proxy server and sends a request to establish a connection to an application server on the Internet.

2. The client includes in the request packet the IP address and the port number of the destination host, and the userid.

3. The SOCKS server checks to see whether such a request should be granted, using the Ident protocol (RFC 1413). Granting permission can be based on any combi-

nation of source IP address, destination IP address, destination port number, the userid, and other information.

4. If the request is granted, the SOCKS service makes a connection to the specified port of the destination Internet host.

5. The SOCKS service sends a reply packet to the client on the private network when either the connection is established, the request is rejected, or the operation fails.

For the SOCKS Proxy service to operate successfully, the Web Proxy service must be running. So, stopping the Web Proxy service also stops the SOCKS Proxy service from functioning. SOCKS is very flexible when it comes to client platforms. Cross-platform support for SOCKS is extensive. The Microsoft Proxy Server's SOCKS Proxy service is compatible with all popular client operating systems and client hardware platforms, including Windows, Macintosh, and UNIX.

Moving On

The Web Proxy service, WinSock Proxy service, and SOCKS Proxy service comprise a total proxy and firewall solution for your organization. The architectural details provided in this chapter not only ground your understanding of the technology, but also help guide your thinking as you design the Microsoft Proxy Server solution for your organization.

Now you can start asking yourself some questions. For example, is your design driven by users who need to access Web services? If so, you probably need to implement the Web Proxy service. But what kind of caching is required: distributed, hierarchical, or perhaps a combination model? Is your organization large, divided into several departments? Do departments need to access a common set of Web sites? Do your users need access to VDOLive or RealAudio? You know the WinSock Proxy service fits the need for these UDP applications. And of course there's the SOCKS Proxy service. Does your organization use SOCKS applications?

You know the technical architecture of Proxy Server, but do you know the archetype of a successful deployment plan for your organization's Proxy Server services? A model for a truly effective technical deployment plan begins by bringing your user's needs and concerns into the picture. Then we can match those needs with the technical capabilities of the product. That's where needs assessment comes to the rescue, and guess what?—that's the topic of our next chapter.

PART II

Understanding Your Internet And Security Needs

Needs Assessment

The Internet is full of resources of potential benefit to your organization. Your Proxy Server is your organization's gateway to all the benefits, as well as the pitfalls, of the Internet. By carefully planning your Proxy Server installation, you will enable your organization to enjoy all of Proxy Server's advantages, while steering clear of Internet risks. The Proxy Server implementation plan begins with needs assessment. No matter what the size of your organization, a good Proxy Server system must meet the Internet access needs of your user community. In this chapter, you will learn how to best assess those needs and create an effective implementation plan.

Proxy Server's Role In The Network Infrastructure

For most organizations, a well-functioning private network infrastructure is a critical factor in the attainment of business objectives. With Proxy Server, you can expand the reach of your organization's private network to the worldwide public arena of the Internet. But to do so without taking into account the business needs, user needs, and security risks of such an endeavor would be foolhardy.

Your private network exists for several important reasons. For example, networks facilitate communication, allow for the exchange of information, and assist with the organization of your company's knowledge capital. In other words, your private network helps your organization attain its mission-critical business objectives. As an administrator of your company's network, you are a crucial player in the successful implementation of technology for your organization. However, just understanding technology is not enough. You also must have the keen understanding of your organization's business processes, and the people that make it all work.

The Proxy Server Implementation Plan

The Proxy Server implementation plan provides the basic model for successful implementation of Proxy Server into your organization's network. The Proxy Server implementation plan is made up of three major phases, which are covered in this chapter and the next two chapters of this book. The following list shows the three phases and their corresponding chapters:

➤ **Needs Assessment**   Chapter 3 (This chapter)

➤ **Security Assessment**   Chapter 4

➤ **The Rollout Plan**   Chapter 5

A quick note on the implementation plan's scalability: As you read the details of the implementation plan, you might think that your organization is either too large or too small to use the model. However, the plan scales easily to any size organization. If your organization is small you wear many "hats," and you might assume several roles in the implementation plan. Conversely, if your organization is large you might have several persons performing the same role, with responsibilities divided by departmental or geographical boundaries. As the teams and the roles are described in the following sections, think about how the Proxy Server implementation plan might scale to your organization.

You might find that some of the teams or roles are already in place in your organization with slightly different responsibilities. If so, this is great news. Use this plan as a guide for organizing your implementation. Strict adherence is not required.

Team Formation

A good implementation plan is supported by project teams that are clearly focused on their mission. Quality and efficiency are the hallmarks of a well-working team. The teams are interdependent with each other, so cross-staffing is not only acceptable, it's desirable; of course, with smaller organizations cross-staffing is a necessity.

➤ **The Planning Team**   The mission of this team is to oversee the progression of the project through the implementation phase. This team has the responsibility of *approving* the *Function Specification Document* and the overall corporate standards for Internet connectivity. This team is active during all project phases. This team consists of the team leaders from each of the following teams and the *Logistics Manager*. The leader of the Planning Team is the *Implementation Project Manager*.

➤ **The Executive Team**   The mission of this team is to make top-level decisions about the appropriate level of Internet access and security. This team is active during all project phases. The team consists of the organization's top-level executives, the *Implementation Project Manager* and the *Logistics Manager*. The *Implementation Project Manager* is the leader of this team and acts as a technical liaison.

➤ **The User Interview Team**   The mission of this team is to determine Internet access needs as they relate to the business requirements of the organization. This team is active during the needs assessment phase. The team consists of representative members of the user community. The leader of this team is the *Proxy Server Technology Manager.*

➤ **The Security Assessment Team**   The mission of this team is to align the needs assessment and the security assessment needs to Proxy Server's security features. This team is active during the security assessment phase. The team consists of *Windows NT/Proxy Server Engineers.* The leader of this team is the *Proxy Server Technology Manager.*

➤ **The Implementation Team**   The mission of this team is to complete all aspects of the installation of the Proxy Server system. This team is active during the rollout phase and is responsible for assuring that the project's objectives are met. This team consists of *Windows NT/Proxy Server Engineers,* the *Testing Engineer,* and the *Logistics Manager.* It is led by the *Implementation Project Manager.*

➤ **The Administration Team**   The mission of this team is to administer and support the Proxy Server system, including the server and its clients, during the rollout phase and beyond. Members of the Security Assessment Team are absorbed into this team during the rollout phase and remain assigned for long-term security support. This team is active during the rollout phase and remains active after the implementation of the project. The leader of this team is the *Proxy Server Technology Manager.*

➤ **The User Education Team**   The mission of this team is to provide training to the user community for the Proxy Server system, including Security Policies. This team is active during the rollout phase and remains active after the implementation of the project. This team consists of those persons in the organization who are responsible for the technical training of the user community. The leader of this team is the *User Education Manager.*

Team Roles

The team roles identified in the Proxy Server implementation plan include:

➤ **Proxy Server Technology Manager**   This is the *overarching management* role for the implementation project and the administration of the Proxy Server system once it is in place. Initially, this person is charged with building the business case for the project, including identifying and setting priorities. This role has the ongoing duty of continuing to deliver a system that meets the business needs.

➤ **Implementation Project Manager**   This is the *technology management* role for the Proxy Server implementation project. The responsibilities of this role include developing the Functional Specification Document and facilitating the day-to-day coordination of the implementation project. The Functional Specification Document describes the technical and business requirements for the Proxy Server system. This role has the responsibility of developing the corporate standards and serves as the technical liaison between the technical and non-technical team members.

➤ **Windows NT/Proxy Server Engineer**   This *technical* role has the hands-on responsibility of implementing the Windows NT and Proxy Server technologies required and offering technical suggestions and advice throughout the implementation project. After implementation, persons fulfilling this role provide administrative support for the clients and servers that comprise the Proxy Server system. Additionally, this role maintains the Windows NT and Proxy Server security systems.

➤ **Testing Engineer**   This *technical testing* role has the responsibility of uncovering potential problems or issues before the final rollout of the Proxy Server system.

➤ **User Education Manager**   This role has the responsibility of *designing, developing, and publishing instructional materials* for the user community. This role ensures that the users of your organization's Proxy Server system understand the proper operation of the Internet-based tools. Also, this role informs and instructs the user community about their maintenance and security responsibilities.

➤ **Logistics Manager**   Throughout the Proxy Server implementation process, the person in this role works with all teams *to ensure a smooth and timely project progression*. In addition, this role is responsible for the timely arrival of all equipment and services for the project.

Team Membership

Table 3.1 describes the team membership, its leader, and the phase or phases in which the team is active. For reference, the table also lists the chapter in this book where you can find more information.

The Needs Assessment Phase

Every Proxy Server implementation project needs clearly defined vision and goals to have a successful outcome. But how is this accomplished? Seldom are needs determined by a single person. Rather, the people that comprise your organization must reach a shared vision of a successful project outcome. Tremendous benefits can result from the secure Internet access that Proxy Server provides. Your organization's executives, technical professionals, and user community all have their own unique understanding of the organization's business processes and how Internet access through Proxy Server might benefit the enterprise. In the needs assessment phase, these individuals reach consensus about the vision and goals of Internet access through a Proxy Server system.

Table 3.1			Proxy Server team membership information.	
Team	**Phase**	**Chapter**	**Membership**	**Leader**
Planning	All	5	Team leaders from each of the teams and the Logistics Manager	Implementation Project Manager
Executive	All	5	Top-level executives in the organization, the Implementation Project Manager, and the Logistics Manager	Implementation Project Manager
Needs Assessment User Interview	Needs Assessment	3	Representatives from the user community	Proxy Server Technology Manager
Security Assessment	Security Assessment	4	Windows NT/Proxy Server engineers	Proxy Server Technology Manager
Implementation	Rollout	5	Windows NT/Proxy Server engineers, the Testing engineer, and the Logistics Manager	Implementation Project Manager
Administration	Rollout (after project's end)	5	Security Assessment Team members, Implementation Team members	Proxy Server Technology Manager
User Education	Rollout (continues after project's end)	5	Persons in the organization who are responsible for the technical training of the user community.	User Education Manager

The needs assessment process is iterative. While the Executive Team shapes the initial vision of the project, the Planning, Needs Assessment, and Security Assessment Teams offer detailed feedback that helps you obtain results that serve clearly defined business objectives that are outlined later in the process.

Vision

The first tangible outcome of the needs assessment phase is a *Project Vision Statement*. The Planning Team is responsible for creating the Project Vision Statement, and the Executive Team approves it. The Project Vision Statement supplies the overall objective of the project. Here's a sample Project Vision Statement:

Our vision for the Proxy Server implementation project is to provide secure, high-performance Internet access for our organization. The Internet will be used to provide swift communication with our customers, our vendors, and our field employees. Our Internet solution will be designed in a way that is simple for our IT department to manage and is cost-effective for our organization.

The Project Vision Statement becomes the fundamental reason for your Proxy Server implementation project, stating in a clear way the benefits to your organization. It focuses on the business value of the Proxy Server solution rather than on the technical feasibility. Also, because the project was developed with representatives from your organization's executives and user community, it is likely that it will receive broad support from your entire organization.

Project Scope

The next step is to map your Project Vision Statement against the reality of what is required to achieve the vision. This is called the project scope. The Project Vision Statement is used to derive the project scope. The project scope consists of three key elements:

➤ **Project Objective** The broad factors that describe a successful implementation of Internet access capabilities for the organization through Proxy Server.

➤ **Project Goals** The items that can be measured as indicators of meeting the above objectives successfully.

➤ **Deliverables** The tangible items that, when completed, comprise the successful implementation of Proxy Server.

Primary Project Objectives

Creating project objectives is a little like detective work. The objectives are buried in the vision statement and the user interviews. You discover the project objectives in the information you now have. Now let's turn our sample Project Vision Statement into a set of high-level objectives. This project's primary objectives are to design and implement a Proxy Server solution that:

➤ Provides secure Internet access for the organization.

➤ Provides high-performance Internet access for the organization.

➤ Is simple to manage for the IT department.

➤ Is cost-effective for the organization.

Project Goals

Next, you also must provide a means to measure the Proxy Server implementation project's success. Goals are things that you can measure. Some of the measurements will be specific to your organization, while others will be technical. Because we understand the technical capabilities of Proxy Server, we can map some of Proxy Server's technical features to the project objectives to derive our goals. So, to accomplish the project objectives, Internet access through Proxy Server should:

➤ Implement Proxy Server's application and circuit layer security.

➤ Provide alerts through private network mail if a security breach should occur.

➤ Provide Internet access to the desktop of all private network users through a secure Proxy Server connection.

➤ Increase Web performance by providing organizational and departmental caching for Web access.

➤ Allow administration through easy-to-use, menu-based tools.

➤ Centralize enterprise-wide Internet access to simplify troubleshooting and minimize support costs.

Of course, the above is simply an example. Your project objectives will include the objectives and features that fit the specific needs of your organization.

Project Milestones

Milestones mark the progression of the Proxy Server implementation project through receipt of project *deliverables*. A deliverable is a tangible outcome of a team's work. Table 3.2 shows some of the milestones and the teams responsible for the Proxy Server Implementation Plan deliverables.

Table 3.2   Project milestones.

Milestones	Team Responsible	Completion Target Date	Actual Completion Date
Team formations approved	Planning		
Vision statement approved	Executive		
Scope approved	Planning		
Vision scope document	Planning		
Security requirements document	Security		
Produce user survey questions	User Interview		
Conduct user interviews	User Interview		
Produce an analysis of the user interviews for the planning team	User Interview		
Functional requirements document	Planning		
Required resources list	Planning		
Security policy objectives	Security		

Continued

three

Table 3.2   Project milestones (Continued).

Milestones	Team Responsible	Completion Target Date	Actual Completion Date
Security implementation objectives	Security		
Security policy guidelines	Security		
Complete lab tests of the Proxy Server client configuration	Implementation		
Conduct the pilot rollout (adjust procedures as required)	Implementation		
Conduct the final rollout	Implementation		
Set and verify all Proxy Server configuration parameters	Administration		
Set and verify all Proxy Server client configuration parameters	Administration		
Complete user training for the Proxy Server system and the security policies	User Education		
Construct ongoing training schedule	User Education		
Design and implement help desk procedures	User Education		

User Interviewing

To fully understand the Internet access needs of an organization, you must include the user community in the process. While the Internet is changing the way business works, it is still people who make your organization successful. Your user community understands the organization's business processes and, when given the opportunity, will come up with innovative uses of the Internet.

In the user interview phase of the Proxy Server implementation project, your organization's people should be encouraged to use both their expertise and their imaginations to come up with ideas about the importance of connecting to the Internet. A key assumption you can make is that everyone in your organization can benefit from Internet access. Therefore, it's important to include representation from all departments—sales, accounting, executive, technical, and so forth; everyone needs Internet access. But, rather than focusing first on the technology, begin by focusing on the business issues. You need to ask your users how Internet access can make their job responsibilities easier, better, more efficient, and less costly.

Your approach to user interviews will vary based on the size of your organization. There are many ways to conduct user interviews. For larger organizations, a more formal survey approach makes sense; a survey is more efficient, and the results can be tabulated in a more scientifically verifiable way. Smaller organizations will benefit from a more open-ended approach, where everyone has an opportunity to "brainstorm" together. You might find that a combination of a survey and an open-ended approach to user interviews works well.

Interview Questions

Each organization will create interview questions that are specific to its business needs. But, before you get specific, it's a good idea to ask more general questions. The following are examples of some general questions in an open-ended format that you might ask your users:

➤ Why do you believe Internet access is important?

➤ How many computers are in your department or work group?

➤ How important is the internal email system to your job function?

Next, move to more specific, business-related questions:

➤ What are the most important business processes in which you regularly engage (please list all that apply)?

➤ Of the above business processes, how many involve individuals or organizations outside of our own (please list all that apply)?

➤ Of the above, name the outside individuals or organizations. If individuals, please state the organization they are affiliated with (please list all that apply).

Next, the questions become more specific and technical:

➤ Which individuals or organizations important to your job function use Internet email?

➤ How would our organization benefit by using Internet email?

➤ Which individuals or organizations important to your job function have Internet Web sites?

➤ Which individuals or organizations important to your job function offer ways to interact with their business, such as providing electronic commerce through their Internet Web sites?

➤ Do the individuals or organizations that have electronic commerce Web sites listed above offer discounts for their services when purchased using the Web site?

➤ Of the above, which Web sites would most benefit you in your job function (please list all that apply)?

➤ Which individuals or organizations important to your job function offer ways to interact with their business, such as providing valuable information by downloading files from their Web sites?

The above questions are stated from the viewpoint of a *user of Internet information*. You also might ask questions from the viewpoint of your organization's being a *provider of information*, as listed below:

➤ Which individuals or organizations important to your job function would benefit from interacting with our business by acquiring valuable information or electronic commerce through our own Internet Web site? Please describe.

➤ Of the above, which individuals or organizations would most benefit from our Web site (please list all that apply)?

➤ What specific information could our organization publish on a Web site that would prove valuable to the above individuals or organizations?

Again, these are only sample questions. However, they should prove valuable as a starting point for developing your own.

You shouldn't be too concerned about technical limitations at this stage. Later in the plan you'll be able to sort out the inspired ideas from the impractical ones. In fact, these questions will help identify the Proxy Server services, protocols, and ports required for the associated WinSock applications. For now, the team's leadership should provide clear direction without introducing preconceived limitations. The basic concept at this stage is to encourage the ideas to come out. I promise you, you'll discover some great ones.

Analyzing The User Interviews

As you sift through the information, your goal is to uncover the user needs. These needs will form the basis of the key design goals and key design benefits for the project, which are contained in the *Functional Specifications Document*. The Planning Team, led by the Implementation Project Manager, is responsible for the creation of the document.

For example, here is a sampling of statements that your users might come up with in response to the User Interviews:

➤ **Purchasing**   One of our primary vendors has a Web site that allows our organization to check inventory availability in real time. They say it's secure—something about 128-bit security. In addition, a two percent discount is offered for orders placed on the Web. We could make most, if not all, of our purchases using their Web site. This would save the organization both time and money.

➤ **Customer Support**   Our customers often ask if we can provide our internal support database directly to them via a Web site. So, often when someone calls for assistance, I just read the answer in our support database. We have so many calls now, it's hard to keep up. I believe we could reduce our support calls by 40 percent by providing our database through the Internet.

➤ **Marketing**   Up-to-date company profiles are offered on an FTP site on the Internet. We use profiles to help us target new customers for our products. While we currently have traditional books that contain this information, they go out of date quickly, and it takes a lot of time to research. Sometimes I have to wait until someone else returns the book to the shelf before I can even start the research. If I had FTP access, my research time would be reduced by 60 percent. Also, we currently fax the company profiles to our field offices. If we could use FTP to upload those files, it would save us even more time and money.

➤ **Sales**   When I am out of town, it's difficult to contact my sales manager using the phone. Voice mail is an option, but I often need to give detailed messages that require detailed answers. Voice mail doesn't work well in that case. If we had Internet email I could stay in touch with the office and get the detailed answers I need to close the big sales. I estimate our sales would increase by 20 percent.

Key Design Goals

The above statements are then turned into key design goals. For example:

➤ Our Proxy Server system will bring secure 128-bit Web access to every desktop.

➤ Our Proxy Server system will use reverse hosting to publish our customer support database to the Web.

➤ Our Proxy Server system will use the WinSock Proxy service to provide our sales managers the ability to upload and download files using FTP.

➤ Our Proxy Server system will use reverse hosting to allow secure POP3 access to our Microsoft Exchange Server for our field associates.

Key Benefits

You also use the original user interview responses to map the key benefits. Below are a few examples:

➤ Lower our purchasing costs by two percent using electronic commerce on vendor Web sites.

➤ Improve our customer support by publishing our internal support database on the Web.

three

> ➤ Reduce the research time of our marketing associates by 60 percent by providing Internet Web access.

> ➤ Increase sales by 20 percent by implementing Internet email system for our field sales associates.

Functional Specifications Document

The Planning Team uses the responses from the user interviews as the basis for the Functional Specifications Document. The key design goals and benefits of the Proxy Server implementation project are combined with the technical specifications to make up the Functional Specifications Document. The following is an abbreviated example of some of the information contained in a Functional Specifications Document for a fictitious organization.

Example Functional Specifications Document

Our fictitious organization's Proxy Server specifications can be divided into two basic categories: *user of information* and *provider of information*. Activities included under the user of information category call for *outbound* Internet access. This is the traditional role for a Proxy Server system. Activities included under the provider of information category call for *inbound* Internet access. Applications that use Proxy Server reverse proxy and reverse hosting features are organized under the provider of information category.

User Of Information

During our user interviewing, we discovered that our users need outbound Web Proxy and WinSock Proxy services. We identified the following requirements:

> ➤ Web browsing using a browser capable of 128-bit security.

> ➤ FTP services using an FTP application capable of downloading and uploading files.

Provider Of Information

During our user interviewing, we discovered that our users and customers need inbound Internet services. We identified the following requirements:

> ➤ Web hosting through Proxy Server's reverse hosting feature.

> ➤ FTP hosting through Proxy Server's reverse hosting feature.

> ➤ POP3/SMTP hosting (Microsoft Exchange Server) through Proxy Server's reverse hosting feature.

User Community Size And Structure

We have 2,100 associates who have computers on their desktops, which comprise six departments. All departments, except Administration, responded that they would be moderate to heavy users of Web sites. Moreover, when asked what individuals or organizations had Web sites, the respondents reported a great deal of similarity within the departments. The use of departmental Proxy Servers chained to a Proxy Server array that is directly connected to the Internet will provide the high-performance Internet access called for in our mission. Table 3.3 details the user community size and structure.

Internet Access Requirements

A dial-up connection was ruled out. Because of the size of the organization, the anticipated usage of the Internet alone is enough to rule out this option. However, we also need to use the reverse hosting features of Proxy Server to provide access to a customer support Web site, FTP services, and POP3/SMTP mail. Therefore, a persistent connection through a T-1 line is recommended.

Applications

The Internet applications required by the user community are detailed in Table 3.4.

The Required Resource List

After completing the Functional Specification Document, the Planning Team begins work on the next deliverable, the *Required Resource List*. The Logistics Manager creates the Required Resource List for the Proxy Server implementation plan in consultation with the other members of the Planning Team, departmental managers, vendors, and other outside services. The goal is to create a list that will ensure that resources are available as the project requires. What are resources? Anyone or anything that is required to complete the project: hardware, software, communications connections, and the people to put it all together.

Table 3.3 User community size and structure.

Department	Associates	Departmental Proxy Server
Accounting/Finance	90	No
Administration	750	No
Customer Support	400	Yes
Executive	60	No
Marketing	300	Yes
Sales	500	Yes

Table 3.4   Required Internet applications.

Application	Downstream	Upstream	Notes
Normal Web browsing	Yes	No	
Secure Web browsing (HTTP-S)	Yes	No	128-bit
Web hosting	No	Yes	
Email	Yes	Yes	Avg. 18 messages per day per user
FTP upload/download	Yes	Yes	Biased towards download
Newsgroup reading	Yes	No	

Moving On

The needs assessment phase is an important part of the Proxy Server implementation plan, but don't be too apprehensive about its magnitude. For example, roles don't necessarily mean people. In other words, smaller organizations will have one person filling several roles. But the roles still need to be filled. In a company of one, your role is accountant, salesperson, receptionist, and maybe even janitor. As your company grows, you can begin to spread out the roles and the work involved with each. The same is true with a Proxy Server implementation. No matter what the size of the organization, you need to determine your Internet access needs and your security needs.

In the next chapter, you'll learn how to assess your security needs. The process is similar to needs assessment in that your user community needs to be actively involved. In that way, you can achieve truly transparent access to the Internet while maintaining tight security.

Security Assessment

Internet security is the reason most organizations turn to a technology like Proxy Server in the first place. Proxy Server's security is very flexible and full featured. While it's great to have all the security options of Proxy Server, those same options increase the need for effective security plans. In this chapter, you will learn how to conduct a Proxy Server security assessment. The security assessment helps you identify the proper configuration for your Proxy Server computer. You will also learn some of the basic technical issues involved in configuring Proxy Server security.

Security Assessment Milestones

The deliverables, or milestones, in the Proxy Server security assessment phase are the *Security Policy Objectives*, the *Security Implementation Objectives*, and the *Security Policy Guidelines*. These documents must meet the Proxy Server security requirements, as set forth in the project's scope described in Chapter 3. The plan also affords the opportunity to devote focused time and resources to mitigating the security risks inherent in any Internet connectivity project. As in the needs assessment phase, the Security Team involves the user community in the development of the Security Policy Guidelines. Proxy Server security assessment is an extremely important phase. A security mishap could destroy the confidence of management and the user community in the Proxy Server system.

Yet your user community, if typical, will put access above security. This creates a natural tension between users, who simply want access, and the security professional, whose mission is to protect and restrict. In the best of worlds, Internet users are unaware of the underlying technology of the security system that protects the organization. Other than password authentication, security measures can be transparent to the user. In fact, security measures that are too strict jeopardize the success of the project.

Top-Level Security Objectives

It is important to involve the user community in Proxy Server security planning. The people who work with the organization's valuable information each day have the best understanding of exactly what needs to be protected. Once security needs are identified, the security professional can determine the technical solutions that will best protect the data and are most feasible. Keep these high-level objectives in mind when developing a reasonable security plan:

➤ By involving the user community in the planning phase, you will uncover the most significant security risks, but you will not find all risks.

➤ Even with the risks you find, you can't predict everything—so create contingency plans.

➤ Decide the amount of loss that is acceptable—you can't prevent all loss.

➤ Put strong procedures in place and document them well. If a loss does occur, your adherence to reasonable and prudent security efforts might diminish your legal liability.

Common Security Threats

You also need to guide the user community in the identification of specific types of Internet security threats. A few broad-stroke examples will help users identify the organizational security threats that could be the most damaging. The three most common categories of Internet security threats are: *unauthorized access, data loss,* and *denial of access.* The following list describes these threats:

➤ **Unauthorized Access** An intruder intentionally gaining access to a private network is the typical form of unauthorized access. However, unauthorized access many times is accidental, resulting from careless or improper security procedures. This type of threat could result in the improper exposure of confidential information.

➤ **Data Loss** Sometimes data loss is linked with unauthorized access. If data is deleted or written over, it could be lost forever. The best forms of protection are good security procedures and a reliable backup system. The backup system must include procedures that are simple, used and checked frequently, and modified when required.

➤ **Denial of Access** This is a growing threat to networks that are connected to the Internet, as executing a denial of access attack is relatively easy. Even large organizations, including Microsoft Corporation, recently have experienced denial of access attacks. Denial of access prevents an authorized user from obtaining a needed resource. This type of threat is serious and can shut down a business for the period that access to the network is blocked.

The Proxy Server Security Assessment Plan Process

Your security assessment plan is a process whereby documents are developed that describe security objectives on three different levels. The Security Policy Objectives consist of *high-level* objectives presented from the perspective of a user, focusing on *what* needs to be protected. Subsequently, these objectives are used in the development of the Security Implementation Objectives. The Security Implementation Objectives consist of *mid-level* technical objectives that focus on *how* the security system will be put in place.

Finally, technology alone cannot protect your private network. Security procedures, documentation, and user cooperation are important factors in any security system. The Security Policy Guidelines are the *low-level* details that describe the *procedures* and *user responsibilities* required to maintain the system. Figure 4.1 describes the security assessment plan process.

Security Policy Objectives

As in the user assessment phase, the user community plays a role in the development of these objectives. Your users have the best understanding of the specific information that is at risk, along with who should be afforded access rights. Therefore, security interviews must be conducted with the user community. Later, the Security Team will analyze the user responses and create the Security Implementation Objectives document.

It is difficult for the security professional to create Security Policy Objectives without help from the user community. Computer professionals prefer discussing protocols, ports, authentication, and other implementation details. The user community, on the other hand, often finds implementation details boring. The common ground between the computer professional and the user community is the information that must be protected. The user community understands the sensitivity of information relevant to their work and will be more than willing to help formulate the Security Policy Objectives. Additionally, the user community will be much more supportive of the organization's security policies when they participate in their creation.

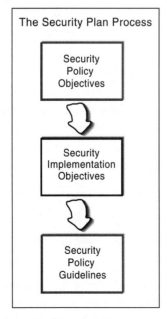

Figure 4.1   The security assessment plan process.

You can use the following questions as a starting point for querying your user community about Security Policy Objectives:

➤ What information is specific to your department that needs to be protected?

➤ What information should be available for viewing, but shouldn't be deleted or modified?

➤ Does documentation exist for the files or data you wish to protect?

➤ Does your department have a policy on the use of floppy disks or other removable media?

➤ Have you isolated the information that is public from the information that needs to be kept private?

➤ Do restrictions exist on remote access of private information?

➤ How does your department ensure the confidentiality of passwords?

Security Implementation Objectives

You develop the Security Implementation Objectives by using the Security Policy Objectives as the known high-level requirements and then interpolating the mid-level technical requirements. In other words, you take into account the technology required to implement the objectives, but leave the precise technical details, procedures, and user responsibilities for the Security Policy Guidelines document.

For example, consider the following statement, made during an interview with the Customer Service Department about the Security Policy Objectives:

We need to protect our Customer Service reports, as these reports contain confidential information about our customers and products. On the other hand, our Customer Service database contains valuable troubleshooting information for our customers. We really want them to have access to this information—it could be a real time saver for our department. But we sure wouldn't want anyone to delete that information. Can we give our customers Internet access to this information, but keep the files secure?

From the above, the following security objectives are established:

➤ Our Proxy Server system will implement the security systems and procedures required to permit the publishing of our customer support database to the Web using Proxy Server's reverse hosting feature.

➤ The Customer Database support system will remain in the Microsoft SQL Server Database. We will keep active the current security system for the database. The IP address for this computer system will be contained in the Proxy Server Local Address Table (LAT) along with all other private network IP addresses.

➤ A partial mirror of the Customer Service database, containing only the trouble-shooting tables, will reside on a Microsoft Windows NT Internet information server. Customers will have read access to this server. Only the Customer Service database administrator will be able to modify or delete information. Periodically, a script will automatically update the database from the Microsoft SQL Server system.

In this way, Security Implementation Objectives meet the needs of the user community and serve as a technical blueprint for the more detailed Security Policy Guidelines.

Security Policy Guidelines

The Proxy Server Security Policy Guidelines define, in detail, how the security system will be built and maintained. There are four basic parts to the Security Policy Guidelines:

➤ The User Community Security Guidelines

➤ The Security System Technical Documentation

➤ The Security Maintenance Plan

➤ The Security Recovery Plan

The User Community Security Guidelines

These are the high-level guidelines that detail the user's responsibility for a secure system. Common topics for these guidelines include Internet email restrictions, Web browsing restrictions, and remote access guidelines. Also, it's a good idea to go into detail about the user's responsibility for maintaining password security. The user guidelines must be written from the perspective of a user, free from technical jargon that would confuse a user's understanding.

Why Internet email restrictions? Unfortunately, email can contain attached documents infected with macro viruses that, once the attachment is opened, wreak havoc on any document you open with your word processor. Because of the insidious nature of these macro viruses, it could take months to eradicate them. Also, bandwidth attacks are possible. A bandwidth attack occurs when a user's mailbox is flooded with hundreds, or even thousands, of unwanted email messages. Typically, this is because a user joins a list server and, subsequently, the list is hacked.

You also should explain to your user community what content is prohibited when browsing the Web. While Proxy Server allows you to filter particular URLs or use third-party filters, the list will never be complete. Even third-party content filter vendors can't guarantee 100 percent accuracy. So your users should know what content is acceptable and unacceptable to your organization. An alternative is to only grant access to sites "approved" by the organization. However, such an option is far too restrictive for most organizations. Additionally, it could create a significant amount of administrative overhead.

The user guidelines for remote access are also important. Yes, your security systems should prevent unauthorized entry, but if a user knows in advance exactly what can be accessed, support calls and user frustration will be minimized. Also, it might be desirable to limit remote access to certain times of the day that can be monitored by security professionals. Let the user know when remote access services are available and unavailable, and that their actions are monitored. If remote access is not specifically required, by all means do not implement it—but let the user community know why remote access is not an option.

You probably already know that a stolen password is the most common security breach. But do your users know? Make sure that your users, especially those who have administrative rights, know how to construct a difficult-to-guess password. Good passwords are long, but not so long that they cannot be memorized. Also, using mixed-case and mixed numbers and letters helps. You might have other suggestions. Be sure to put this information in the User Community Security Guidelines.

Of course, there will be many other high-level user guidelines to include, based on your organizational requirements: the storage of passwords, the use of floppy disks, the attaching of files to email, and more. You should determine which guidelines are the most important for your organization. Again, be sure to write this document in a high-level, user-directed manner. Your users want to understand the security issues, but they probably don't care about the bits and bytes.

The Security System Technical Documentation

This document serves two purposes. Initially, it documents, in detail, how Proxy Server security, Windows NT security, and the other related security systems were implemented. But it also helps if something goes wrong. During a system problem, well-documented procedures often make the difference between an orderly resolution and an embarrassing disaster. Several of the procedures outlined in this chapter and throughout the book can be used as a starting point for the Security System Technical Documentation.

The Security Maintenance Plan

Procedures will need to be created for the maintenance of the Security Policy Guidelines. Security needs change over time, along with the information that needs to be protected. It is necessary to perform periodic review of the Security Policy Guidelines. This usually takes the form of periodic meetings between the security professional and the user community to uncover changes in the information-protection needs. Alternatively, a user from each department can be appointed as a security liaison. Their responsibility would include meeting periodically with both the department's employees and those responsible for the Proxy Server security. Either way, the goal is to keep the security information up-to-date.

The Security Recovery Plan

You will also need to create procedures to be used if a security breach occurs. If security fails, your users might be left with no access to the Internet and your customers without a way to reach your organization through Internet mail, FTP, or Web services. With increasing reliance on the Internet, the loss of business could be substantial. You need to create procedures that isolate the steps required to re-establish the security system and Internet access. It is far better to create levelheaded procedures prior to a security breach that clearly indicate responsibilities, rather than to have to confront this task in the midst of a problem. You need to plan for issues such as a backup route to the Internet, server restoration, the location and maintenance of hot spares, and third-party technical support.

Windows NT Security

Proxy Server's close integration with Windows NT means that the Security Team members need a solid understanding of the Windows NT Security Model, along with the particulars of Internet security. The following sections highlight some of the important Windows NT security considerations when managing a Proxy Server computer.

Windows NT Domains

You should configure Proxy Server as a standalone server in your current domain, if at all possible. This avoids any security problems that might arise from the improper configuration of Windows NT domains. Proxy Server configured as a standalone server is considered the most secure.

However, if you're working with a larger private network and you understand the Windows NT Domain model, you can set up Proxy Server as a primary domain controller (PDC) within its own domain. You do this by setting a single one-way trust relationship to another domain on your private network. In this relationship, the domain used for Proxy Server is the trusting domain and another internal domain is specified as the trusted domain (see Figure 4.2).

In the above example of a one-way trust relationship, the resources that become available are in the trusting domain, or specifically in this case, the Proxy Server computer. So

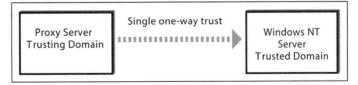

Figure 4.2   A single one-way trust relationship from Proxy Server to another domain.

the Proxy Server domain trusts the domain controllers in the other domain on the private network to validate user accounts to use its resources.

A one-way trust relationship limits access to the Proxy Server computer and, therefore, reduces the private network's exposure to an Internet attack. For example, because no Windows NT-based servers on the private network trust the domain used for Proxy Server, those private network domains remain secure from an Internet intrusion. If you need to add other Proxy Server computers, they would become members of the domain created for the original Proxy Server computer.

Windows NT User Management

The User Manager for Domains is the tool used to manage security for domains, member servers, and workstations. Using User Manager for Domains, you can administer computers or domains, create and manage user accounts, create and manage groups, and manage the security policies. You can use the Account Policy dialog box under Policies on the User Manager for Domains menu to configure strict account policies for user passwords. The objective is to protect the server against exhaustive or random password attacks. The following describes account policies you can enforce that will help protect the server:

➤ **Administrator Group Membership**   You should limit the members of the administrator group to only those who have administrative responsibilities on the Proxy Server computer.

➤ **User Rights**   Restrict user rights to precisely the permissions that are required.

➤ **Password Expiration**   Use the Account Policy dialog box to force users to regularly change passwords.

➤ **Unsuccessful Logon Attempts**   Use the Account Policy dialog box to lock out the user after three to five unsuccessful logon attempts.

➤ **Guest Account**   Disable the Windows NT guest account.

Client Logon, Authentication, And Access Control

Proxy Server uses three different mechanisms to provide secure Internet access: *client logon, authentication,* and *access control.* To adequately configure Proxy Server security, you need to understand the purpose of each security mechanism used in the Proxy Server system. These security mechanisms are defined as follows:

➤ **Client Logon**   A client logon request occurs whenever a client requests an object from IIS. Because the Web Proxy service uses the WWW service of IIS, a client logon request occurs whenever a Web browser configured to use Proxy Server requests an Internet object. The logon process simply determines if the client is allowed or denied access to a resource on the server.

➤ **Authentication**   Authentication, on the other hand, is a server mechanism used to validate users during the logon process. Authentication can take many forms, ranging from the simple assignment and verification of passwords to more complex encryption methods used to create a secure communication channel between the client and the server.

➤ **Access Control**   Proxy Server has an additional security mechanism, called access control. In order to provide distinct security permissions for individual users or groups, access control must be enabled. Access control is available to both the Web Proxy service and WinSock Proxy service. When access control is enabled for the Web Proxy service, Proxy Server uses a combination of the Web Proxy service's permissions and the password authentication settings configured for the various IIS services.

Password Authentication Methods

There are three types of password authentication: anonymous logon, basic (clear-text) authentication, and challenge/response. All three authentication methods are available to the Web Proxy service. The Web Proxy service uses the password authentication method(s) configured for use on the Internet Information Server's WWW service on the Proxy Server computer.

While all three authentication methods are available to the Web Proxy service, the WinSock Proxy service uses the Windows NT challenge/response authentication. This provides a secure communications path for all Windows Sockets applications. For either service, authentication is only used when access control is enabled in the respective service. The following sections describe anonymous logon, basic (clear-text) authentication, and challenge/response.

Anonymous Logon

The anonymous logon method is available to the Web Proxy service. It is the default logon method for this service. Anonymous logon uses a standard logon account to provide guest access to Internet resources. The username *anonymous* is used in TCP/IP to refer to a guest account that has read-only access to public files and directories.

As previously mentioned, the Web Proxy service relies on IIS for much of its functionality. During installation, IIS creates a default anonymous user account named IUSR_*computername*, where *computername* is the server computer. For example, if IIS is installed on a computer with the name *Proxy1*, the default anonymous user account is named IUSR_*Proxy1*. When Proxy Server is installed, this account is granted permissions to the Web Proxy service by default.

four

A variety of problems arise when using the anonymous IUSR_*computername* account. For example, the IUSR_*computername* account does not work well in these multi-server situations:

➤ If you have multiple Proxy servers configured as an array.

➤ If you want to allow "anonymous" access to Web publishing from the local IIS computer.

➤ If you want to authenticate users for client requests that pass through the Web Proxy servers.

Therefore, using the IUSR_*computername* with arrays, reverse proxying, or reverse hosting is not advisable. In addition, when only anonymous logon (and no other authentication method) is allowed, access control and all other items on the Web Proxy Permissions tab are disabled. This removes the ability to configure individual or group permissions for the WWW (HTTP and HTTP-S), FTP, Gopher, or Secure Socket Layer (SSL) connections.

I discourage the use of anonymous logon with Proxy Server. Weak security and the inability to use access control alone are reasons enough. If you are compelled to use the IUSR_*computername* account, use the following procedure to enable anonymous logon:

1. Double-click the computer name beneath the WWW service in the Internet Service Manager.

2. Select the Allow Anonymous checkbox in the WWW Service Properties dialog box.

3. Click Apply, and then click on OK.

Basic Authentication

The standard HTTP mechanism for authentication is basic authentication. A logon with basic authentication sends and receives user information as clearly readable text characters. While passwords and user names are encoded, no encryption is used with basic authentication. The following describes the authentication procedure for basic authentication:

1. The client prompts the user for username and password credentials.

2. The credentials are then encoded by the client and sent to the server.

3. The username is verified as being an account on the Proxy Server computer or in a trusted domain of that computer.

● ● ● *Tip* ● ● ● ●

Users having accounts in a trusted domain must include the domain's name in the username credential. For example:

```
username=domain\account
```

Although basic authentication is one step above anonymous logon and you can enable access control, the security it offers is still fairly weak. For example, anyone can use a freely available utility named Uudecode to decode passwords and usernames. Basic authentication also restricts your use of Web browsers (see the sidebar *Web Browsers & Challenge/ Response Authentication*). Unfortunately, basic authentication is the only authentication available for some Web clients, such as those that use UNIX. Supplementing basic authentication with another encryption method is a good idea for those clients. I advise using Windows NT challenge/response authentication for Microsoft Windows-based clients. Windows NT challenge/response authentication is described in the next section.

You can use the following procedure to set basic authentication for *all* users:

1. Double-click the computer name next to the WWW service in Internet Service Manager.

2. Under Password Authentication, select the Basic (Clear Text) checkbox, and click to clear the Windows NT Challenge/Response checkbox.

3. Click to clear the Allow Anonymous checkbox.

4. Click Apply, and then click on OK.

5. Double-click the computer name next to the Web Proxy service.

6. Click the Permissions tab, and then click to clear the Enable Access Control checkbox.

7. Click Apply, and then click on OK.

You can use the following procedure to set anonymous logon for specific users and to set basic authentication for all other users.

1. Double-click the computer name next to the WWW service in Internet Service Manager.

2. Under Password Authentication, select the Basic (Clear Text) checkbox, and click to clear the Windows NT Challenge/Response checkbox.

3. Next, select the Allow Anonymous checkbox, click Apply, and then click on OK. At this point, IIS will use anonymous logon and basic authentication, but not Windows NT Challenge/Response authentication.

4. Double-click the computer name next to the Web Proxy service.

5. Click the Permissions tab, select the Enable Access Control checkbox, and then click Add.

6. In the Add Users and Groups dialog box, in Names, select the appropriate users from the list, verify that they appear under Add Names, and then click on OK.

7. Click Apply, and then click on OK.

The users and groups you add under Add Names will use basic authentication, and all other users will use anonymous logon. Also, when you enable access control, you need to assign user permissions for access rights to each service. See Chapter 9 for more information about configuring and administering access control.

Challenge/Response Authentication

Windows NT challenge/response authentication offers the highest level of security to Proxy Server clients. As an integral part of the Windows NT Security model, it encrypts usernames and passwords to set up a secure channel. It also offers a single logon to the client computer, so Proxy Server services are available as soon as someone logs on to the private network.

Windows NT challenge/response authentication does have limitations. For example:

➤ The client and server computers must be located in the same or trusted domains.

➤ The Web browser must support Windows NT challenge/response authentication. (See the sidebar *Web Browsers And Challenge/Response Authentication*.)

But if you can live with its limitations, it is the recommended choice. You use the following procedure to set challenge/response authentication for all users:

1. Double-click the computer name next to the WWW service in Internet Service Manager.

2. Under Password Authentication, select the Windows NT Challenge/Response checkbox, click to clear the Basic (Clear Text) and Allow Anonymous checkboxes.

3. Click Apply, and then click on OK.

4. Double-click the computer name next to the Web Proxy service.

5. Click the Permissions tab.

6. Click to clear the Enable Access Control checkbox.

7. Click Apply, and then click on OK.

Web Browsers And Challenge/Response Authentication

Challenge/response authentication with the Web Proxy service adds an extra measure of security. However, currently only Microsoft Internet Explorer version 4.0 fully supports challenge/response authentication used by Proxy Server through IIS. Other browsers exhibit problems with rejecting client configuration scripts (JScripts). Also, HTTPS pages that use the Secure Sockets Layer (SSL) are improperly displayed. If you need to use a Web browser other than Microsoft Internet Explorer version 4.0, use basic authentication.

You also can set anonymous logon for specific users and set challenge/response authentication for all other users by using the following procedure:

1. Double-click the computer name next to the WWW service in Internet Service Manager.

2. Under Password Authentication, select the Windows NT Challenge/Response checkbox, and click to clear the Basic (Clear Text) checkbox.

3. Select the Allow Anonymous checkbox.

4. Click Apply, and then click on OK.

5. Double-click the Proxy Server Service for which you wish to add access control (either the WinSock or Web Proxy service). Then, click the Permissions tab.

6. Select the Enable Access Control checkbox, and then click Add.

7. In the Add Users and Groups dialog box, in Names, select the appropriate users from the list, verify that they appear under Add Names, and then click on OK.

8. Click Apply, and then click on OK.

The users and groups you add under Add Names will use Windows NT challenge/ response authentication, and all other users will use anonymous logon. Also, when you enable access control, you need to assign user permissions for access rights to each service. See Chapter 9 for more information about configuring and administering access control.

Proxy Server Security

Proxy Server's maximum security is dependent on having numerous security parameters properly set. Because Proxy Server's role is a gateway between your private network and the public network of the Internet, attention to these security settings is critical. Fortunately, Proxy Server self-configures itself during setup to provide a reasonable level of security. Although this makes Proxy Server setup relatively straightforward, it might not provide the security level required by your organization. Careful study of the specific Proxy Server configuration details and procedures contained in this book's remaining chapters will provide the understanding you need to create a Proxy Server system that meets the security requirements of your organization.

Access Control

Proxy Server's access control features allow you to set access to specific protocols by individuals, groups, domains, or the entire organization. Access control eliminates any security holes that might exist if all ports and protocols were always open. Also, password authentication settings are available when access control is turned on. Therefore, enabling access control is highly recommended. Table 4.1 is useful for determining how best to implement Proxy Server's access control for your organization. See Chapter 9 for more information.

Table 4.1   Access control planning worksheet.

User's Application	Protocol	Access Required by Everyone	Access Required by Group or Domain	Access Required by Individual
	AlphaWorld			
	AOL			
	Archie			
	DNS			
	Echo (TCP)			
	Echo (UDP)			
	Enliven			
	Finger			
	FTP			
	Gopher			
	HTTP			
	HTTP-S			
	ICQ			
	IMAP4			
	IRC			
	LDAP			
	MS NetShow			
	MSN			

Continued

User's Application	Protocol	Access Required by Everyone	Access Required by Group or Domain	Access Required by Individual
	Net2Phone			
	Net2Phone registration			
	NNTP			
	POP3			
	Real Audio (7070)			
	Real Audio (7075)			
	SMTP (client)			
	SuperUserPseudoTelnet			
	Time (TCP)			
	VDOLive			
	Vxtreme			
	WhoIs			
	Other			

Table 4.1   Access control planning worksheet (Continued).

Disable RPC Listening On The Internet Adapter

It's a good idea to disable ports used for remote procedure call (RPC) listening on the Internet adapter. Windows NT TCP/IP services use ports 1024 through 1029 for RPC listening. It is a security risk to have RPC listening enabled on the Internet adapter. Use the following procedure to disable external ports used for RPC listening.

1. Create a backup of Registry.

2. Click Start, click Run, type **regedit** in the Open box, then click on OK.

3. Open the following key:

    HKEY_LOCAL_MACHINE\SYSTEM\CurrentControlSet\Services

4. Click the entry underneath the above key that represents your internal network adapter. Write down the name of the entry selected.

5. Click Services, then click Edit, point to New, and click Key.

6. In the name field New Key #1, type **RPC**.

7. Click RPC, then click Edit, point to New, and click Key.

8. In the name field New Key #1, type **Linkage**.

9. Click Linkage, then click Edit, point to New, and click Key.

10. In the name field New Key #1, type **Bind**.

11. Click Bind, then click Edit, point to New, and click String Value.

12. In the name field New Value #1, enter the entry name that you wrote down in step 3. You do not need to enter a value under Data.

13. Click Registry.

14. Click Exit.

Basic Security Considerations

The following are a few basic considerations for maintaining Proxy Server security:

➤ **Disable IP Forwarding**   The Proxy Server setup program *disables IP forwarding* on the server. This allows Proxy Server to monitor and control the delivery of IP packets, thereby preventing unauthorized IP packets from penetrating Proxy Server's security. However, IP forwarding could become enabled inadvertently. For example, installing Windows NT's Remote Access Service (RAS) after Proxy Server is installed will enable IP forwarding.

➤ **Enable Access Control**   You cannot set any password authentication settings unless access control is enabled. See Chapter 9.

➤ **No External IP Addresses in the LAT**   Your Local Address Table (LAT) should not contain any external IP addresses. To do so would expose your private network to Internet servers and clients. See Chapters 6 and 7.

➤ **No Network Drive Mappings**   Do not use network drive mappings to other remote servers on your internal network.

➤ **Use Only NTFS Volumes**   The Windows NT file system NTFS includes the security features Proxy Server requires. It also supports data access control and ownership privileges, so you can limit access to portions of your file system for specific users and services.

➤ **Keep the Server Simple and Secure**   Run only the services and applications that you need. Use the Services tool in Control Panel to disable any services not absolutely required on the Proxy Server computer.

➤ **Turn Off Unneeded IIS Services**   Use the Internet Service Manager to turn off FTP or Gopher services if they are not used.

> *Your Proxy Server clients will still be able to use FTP and Gopher applications if these services are stopped.*

➤ **Unbind Unnecessary Services From Your Internet Adapters**   Unbind any unnecessary services from any network adapters connected to the Internet. For example: the WINS client and the Server Message Block (SMB) protocol.

➤ **On Proxy Server Clients, Remove DNS and Gateway References**   Don't let clients bypass Proxy Server to access the Internet while connected to the private network. This could jeopardize the security of the entire private network.

➤ **Configure Alerts**   Alerts are an important security feature. Alerts will inform you of suspicious network events, such as frequent protocol violations, SYN or FRAG attacks, or dropped packets, which can signal an attack.

➤ **Configure Logging**   Logging is another important security feature. Enable Proxy Server logging and review the log data frequently.

Security Checklist

Table 4.2 is a checklist that you will find handy when configuring the security parameters for a Proxy Server computer. If you use an array, or chain, of Proxy Server computers, you should use the checklist for each Proxy Server computer you implement.

Table 4.2	**Security checklist questions.**
Yes/No	**Questions**
	Has a secure password policy been implemented? Is it enforced?
	Is membership to the Administrator group limited to only the administrators who require such access?
	Are user rights limited?
	Are strict Windows NT account policies enforced?
	Have you disabled the ports used for Remote Procedure Call (RPC) listening on the Internet interface?
	Is IP forwarding disabled?
	Is access control enabled?
	Does the LAT consist only of internal IP addresses?
	Have all network drive mappings to other remote computers been removed from the Proxy Server computer?
	Continued

four

Table 4.2	Security checklist questions (Continued).		
Yes/No	**Questions**		
	Have you double-checked the permissions set on any shares created on the system if you are running the Server service on your Internet adapters.		
	Have you stripped the Proxy Server computer to only the services and applications required?		
	Are FAT volumes used on the Proxy Server computer? If so, convert them to NTFS volumes.		
	Have you disabled unneeded IIS services, such as Gopher and FTP?		
	Are all unused services unbound from your Internet adapters?		
	Have you removed the Domain Name System (DNS) and gateway references on your client configurations?		
	Have you configured alerts?		
	Have you configured logging?		

Moving On

Internet security is a huge topic. Proxy Server is the core of your organization's Internet security plan. You need to commit to an approach to Proxy Server administration based on both the needs of the organization and the availability of resources. The default configuration of Proxy Server, once set up, requires little administration. However, the tightest Proxy Server security—where you grant or deny access to users, services, ports, or domains that you specify—requires more frequent and detailed administrative attention. Selecting the right administrative/security mix is a balancing act. You don't want to build a Proxy Server system that requires more attention than you can possibly give; this will disappoint both your user community and yourself. Yet, you do need to provide adequate security. So choose your administrative approach carefully.

The security assessment plan outlined in this chapter will help you implement the Internet security your organization requires, while receiving the support of your user community. From a technical viewpoint, you also need to determine your server hardware and software requirements and the bandwidth requirements, and then select the appropriate Internet connection. In the next chapter, you learn how to do all this. Then you will learn the details of the rollout plan, the last phase of the Proxy Server implementation plan.

PART III

Planning And Installing

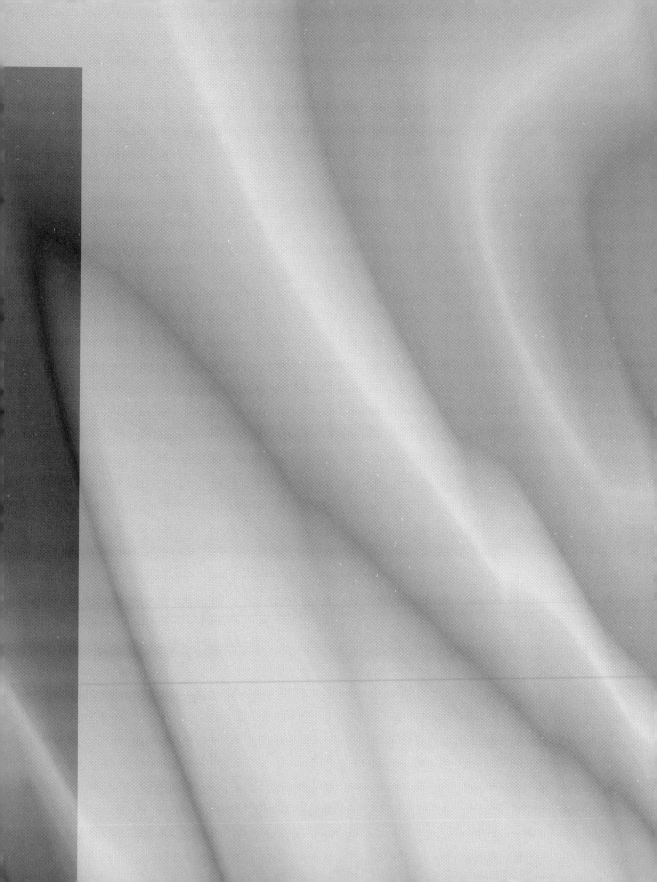

5

Installation Planning

Planning a Microsoft Proxy Server installation is an exercise in understanding the needs of your organization, the available technology, and the resources required to roll out the service. In Chapter 3, you learned how to assess the needs that are driven by your users. Then, in Chapter 4, you acquired the knowledge you needed to understand how to assess the security needs for your organization. Now you create the installation plan using that knowledge.

Your first step in planning the Proxy Server installation is to collect the information obtained from the needs assessment of your users and then blend it with your organization's security objectives. The result is a *needs-driven planning document* for your organization. This document serves as your Proxy Server installation road map as you survey the installation options provided in this chapter.

There are many decisions to make. You know that Microsoft Windows NT is Proxy Server's software platform, but there are some hardware choices to make based on the size of your organization and its needs. One of the most critical Proxy Server installation planning decisions is how to connect to the Internet. Of course, you want to make a choice that is appropriate for the size and needs of the organization, but your choice must also be cost-effective, scalable for future growth, and reliable and must provide the quality of service that your organization requires.

No two organizations are exactly the same; likewise, a single plan will not work for all organizations. This chapter will help you create a plan that is customized for your organization.

Hardware Requirements

Manufacturers of software are compelled to give out minimum requirements for their products. I'm always amazed at the gap between the manufacturer's stated minimum requirements and what I believe are the minimum requirements. Microsoft Proxy Server 2.0 minimum requirements are no different. The following are Microsoft's recommendations for minimum Proxy Server configurations:

Microsoft's Minimum Requirements For Proxy Server 2.0

➤ **Processor** Intel 486 or faster (Proxy Server also supports Alpha AXP).

➤ **Disk Space** At least 10 MB of available disk space for Microsoft Proxy Server after Windows NT Server has been installed. For caching, adequate free disk space for the Web Proxy cache (100 MB + 0.5 MB for each Web Proxy service client).

➤ **RAM** At least 24 MB (32 MB for RISC-based systems).

I would never configure a Proxy Server using the above minimum as a guide. Microsoft Proxy Server serves as your organization's gateway to the Internet. Scrimping on the performance capabilities of your Proxy Server will affect your entire organization. In my opinion, an Intel Pentium 100 is the minimum processor and the computer must have a PCI bus. These systems so far outperform an Intel 486-based machine that it makes little sense to waste your time on such a poorly performing configuration. You won't be happy, and your users won't be happy with you. For help in determining your hardware requirements for Proxy Server, see Decision Tree 5.1.

Besides the Pentium 100 processor minimum, your disk should be as fast as possible and perform well in multi-user environments. Put simply, a SCSI II disk drive should be considered the minimum requirement in all but the smallest Proxy Server installations. Yes, EIDI drives will work, but these drives do not multi-task well. Moreover, I use +1MB for each Web Proxy service client instead of .5 MB. The additional space for caching is an inexpensive safety net. As for RAM, I would begin with 32 MB for Intel-based systems and 48 MB for RISC-based systems. Given a choice and a higher budget, I would increase the RAM before I would increase the processor speed. My revised minimum requirement list follows.

Author's Minimum Requirements For Proxy Server 2.0

➤ **Processor** Intel Pentium 100 or faster.

➤ **Disk Space** At least 100 MB of available disk space for Microsoft Proxy Server after Windows NT Server has been installed. For caching, begin with adequate free disk space for the Web Proxy cache (100 MB + 1 MB for each Web Proxy service client). SCSI II drives are recommended as a minimum.

➤ **RAM** At least 32 MB (48 MB for RISC-based systems).

Configuring a Proxy Server has more to do with the load placed on that server than anything else. Hundreds of users will obviously require a more powerful server, or Proxy Server array, than a workgroup made up of eight members. Later, we will examine Proxy Server configuration recommendations that are scaled to small, medium, and large organizations. Now, let's look at how to pick a computer for a Proxy Server.

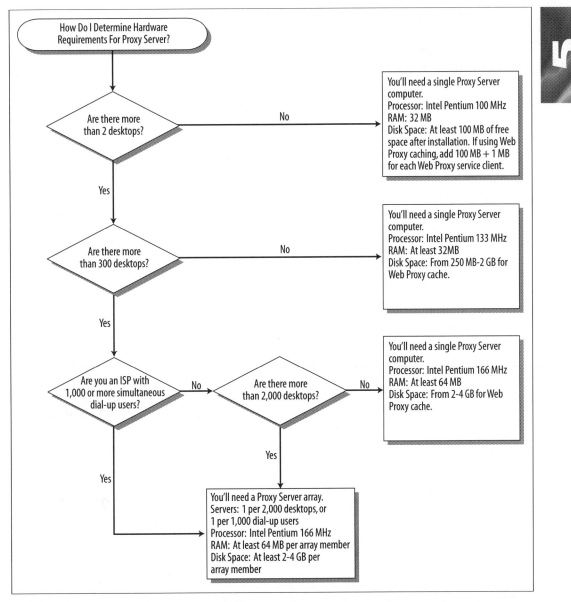

Decision Tree 5.1   How do I determine hardware requirements for Proxy Server?

Computer System Compatibility

Microsoft Proxy Server is integrated tightly with Microsoft Windows NT 4.0. So, it makes sense to start your hardware planning by making sure you have a machine that is stable while running Windows NT 4.0. Microsoft makes available a Hardware Compatibility List (HCL), which is found in the Support folder on the Windows NT 4.0 CD-ROM. The file is named Hcl.hlp. This is a list of computers and peripherals that have passed Microsoft's Windows NT 4.0 compatibility testing.

It's important to exercise a bit of caution with the HCL. For example, the system configuration is not listed in the HCL. Important items, such as BIOS (Basic Input Output Software) chips or controller cards, are changed over time by manufacturers. It is always a good idea to purchase a new machine with the vendor's understanding that Windows NT 4.0 compatibility is a requirement. You should also itemize the additional software, such as Microsoft Proxy Server 2.0, that must run on your new server. Reputable vendors will refund money or credit your account if the computer fails to perform the desired function. Another consideration about the HCL is that even though a computer is not on the HCL it still might run Microsoft Windows NT 4.0. In fact, many of the computers that I use every day are not on the HCL. I'm around computers as a profession, and consequently, I've accumulated a lot of non-mainstream computers and spare parts. By mixing and matching these parts, filling in with new technology where required, I've designed some great Windows NT servers at an economical price. Indeed, many of these computers perform more reliably than others that are on the HCL. But the practice of building from scratch takes time, patience, and experience. It is often less costly to buy a new machine that is guaranteed to work.

To summarize, in determining the base computer for a Microsoft Proxy Server:

1. Use the Microsoft Windows NT 4.0 HCL as a starting point for purchasing new computers, or for your own testing.

2. When purchasing a new computer, secure a money-back guarantee from the vendor. Make the purchase contingent on the successful running of Microsoft Windows NT 4.0 and Microsoft Proxy Server 2.0.

3. If you have time, experiment with hardware that is not on the HCL; you might be pleasantly surprised.

Also, I would use the above list for acquiring the other components required for your Proxy Server. Components such as network LAN (local area network) adapter cards, network ATM (Asynchronous Transfer Mode) adapter cards, network WAN (Wide Area Network) adapter cards, ISDN adapters, modems, and multi-port Serial Adapters all can be found on the HCL.

Network adapters are a crucial part of any server. For a single Proxy Server, you will need a minimum of a network adapter card for your private network and an external network adapter, ISDN adapter, or modem. There are a couple of exceptions. First, some installations might be connecting Proxy Server to another firewall. In this case, private network Proxy Servers require two private network adapter cards, one for your private network and one to connect to the other firewall. It is also possible to use Proxy Server only for Web caching or as an IP application-level gateway to support private network IPX clients—not for Internet access. In such a case, only a single internal network card is required.

Serial Ports

External modems and ISDN adapters might be part of your Proxy Server system, particularly if you have a small- to medium-sized organization. These external modems and ISDN adapters require a serial port. If you use one of these communication devices, all the data that is transmitted between your private network and the Internet will pass through the serial port. You want to make sure that the serial port is up to the task.

The serial port on your server should use an advanced UART (Universal Asynchronous Receiver Transmitter) chip to control the flow and reliability of the data between your serial port and your CPU. If you are going to use the serial port on your server, don't assume that your computer has an advanced UART; you have to determine this for yourself. A 16550 UART chip is the minimum required in order to get the maximum performance out of the modem's throughput. The 16550 allows data transfer rates between the modem and the serial port of up to 115.2 kbps. The speed that the serial port supports is called the *port speed*.

The older 8250 and 16540 UART chips' throughput is too slow or unstable to work adequately. These chips contain a single-byte FIFO (First In, First Out) buffer. Technically, these chips cannot keep up with the high interrupt rates of a multi-tasking operating system such as Microsoft Windows NT. Figure 5.1 illustrates that the operating system's communications driver must read and flush each incoming serial communications character, so while the operating system is busy processing another task, the buffer is overwritten and characters are lost. Here is how it works:

1. *Character 1* is received at the serial communications port.

2. The operating system's communications driver reads and flushes the *character 1* from the FIFO buffer.

3. Simultaneously, the operating system performs interrupts at a high rate for multi-tasking purposes, and the next incoming character, *character 2*, arrives to the serial communications port and is placed in the FIFO buffer.

4. Then, *character 3* arrives, overwriting the single-character FIFO buffer that was holding *character 2*.

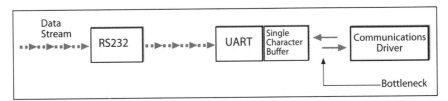

Figure 5.1   The operating system's communications driver must read and flush each incoming serial communications character.

5. Next, the operating system's communication driver turns its attention to the FIFO buffer and is unable to read *character 2* because the buffer contains *character 3*.

You get the picture, I'm sure: The whole process is fouled up at this point. The result is either that data is lost and must be retransmitted and reassembled or that the communications port locks up. Either way, this is not the communications speed and reliability you need for a server.

It is crucial that your motherboard or serial I/O card contain a compatible UART, such as the 16550. If the UART is an 8250 or 16450, it is incompatible with Windows NT and high-speed communications devices. You should be able to locate a socketed chip with the numbers *8250, 16450*, or *16550* on your motherboard or serial card. This is your UART. It might be inconvenient to tear apart your server to determine your server's UART. If this is the case, please read the sidebar "Is My Server's UART Compatible?" for a straightforward way to determine compatibility without tearing your server apart or using diagnostic utilities that often give erroneous results. Most of today's high-speed modems have a DCE-DTE (modem-computer) rate of 57,600. The 16550's port speed of 115,000 is adequate for these modems. A few External modems, such as the Hayes Optima and the latest external models from Diamond Supra, have DCE-DTE rates of 115,000. With these modems you might have better results following my recommendations for ISDN adapters, which follow.

Is My Server's UART Compatible?

Are you confused by all these numbers, need to test multiple computers, or just reluctant to hunt for a UART chip? Here is a surefire, easy way to test for an incompatible UART. It requires the use of a null modem cable, that is, a cable designed to directly connect two PCs through serial ports. Use your null modem cable to connect your NT Server's serial port to the known working serial port of another computer. Select identical baud rates, parity settings, and word lengths on both computers. Using a terminal program, such as HyperTerminal on the Windows NT server, type a few words. If a character or two appears on the other screen and the port hangs up or refuses to answer, you have an incompatible UART.

If you have an incompatible UART chip, your serial port is not functioning optimally. I don't recommend removing the chips from the motherboard. The chips are often soldered in, making them difficult to remove. In any case, it is usually far easier to add new components than to replace chips. I believe the best option is to disable the COM ports on the motherboard, or simply to replace the serial I/O card.

Third-party communications boards are relatively inexpensive and easy to install, and they provide dramatic improvements. Look for a communications board that will support at least 230.4 kbps. With faster modems and ISDN adapters becoming commonplace, the faster port speed will be beneficial.

I've had good experience with the Digi AccelePort C1 and C2, which use the 16C650 UART and special drivers to boost data transfer rates up to 460.8 kbps. The 16C650 UART has a FIFO buffer increased to 32 bytes. There are other manufacturers that market similar cards. In addition, Digi and others offer multi-port serial cards that enable a single server to have up to thousands of serial ports. All accelerated serial communications add-on cards require special drivers to function optimally. When choosing a serial communications card, be sure that the manufacturer offers drivers that are compatible with Microsoft Windows NT 4.0.

An ISDN adapter is often an excellent way to connect a small to medium size organization through a proxy server to the Internet. If you are using an external ISDN adapter (recommended), an accelerated serial communications add-on card offering at least 230.4 kilobits per second is a necessity. Why do you need such high port speed? With ISDN adapters that can support 2 B channels at 64 kbps each, or a total of 128 kbps, it is clear that even 115.2 kbps of the standard 16550 UART-based serial port is not enough. In addition, only 80 percent of the port speed is available to the communications device. So, the maximum throughput of a 115.2 kbps serial port is actually 92.2 kbps. As a general rule, I believe that the port speed should be one magnitude greater than the speed of the modem's or the ISDN adapter's highest communication speed. This accelerated speed reduces bottlenecks and improves overall performance.

DSU/CSU

Once you go beyond a dial-up connection using either a modem or ISDN adapter, you require a DSU/CSU (data service unit/channel service unit). This is a special piece of equipment that connects your computer network to the data network of your telephone company. Typically, the output of the DSU/CSU is connected to an Ethernet router. Your Proxy Server is then connected to the router through a LAN adapter card on a segment that is not connected to the private network. Figure 5.2 illustrates this configuration.

DSU/CSU and routers operate at different bandwidths. So make sure that your DSU/CSU and router work with the telephone service and ISP you will use for your Internet connection. In many cases, your ISP will furnish you with the appropriate DSU/CSU and router combination. It is often a wise choice to let your ISP handle the procurement and deployment of this equipment.

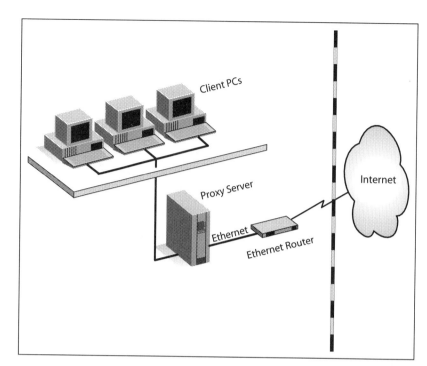

Figure 5.2 Proxy Server connected to the Internet through an Ethernet router.

Internet Connectivity Planning Concepts

Planning your Internet connectivity requirements is a difficult task. The Internet is as much a phenomenon as it is a reality. Businesses are constantly finding new and more innovative ways to use the Internet, while Internet services and content continue to grow at an astonishing rate. Whatever you believe your Internet connectivity requirements are today, they will change tomorrow.

Still, the best way to begin your planning process is to look at the expected use. Is your organization an Internet consumer, provider, or both? If your organization is an Internet provider, will the Proxy Server's Internet connection be shared? Also, what about Internet email: Will your Web browsing Internet connection be shared with the Internet email system? By now you know that Proxy Server's caching can reduce bandwidth requirements for Web browsing, but how much browsing is going on now? Using the material provided in Chapter 3, we have some of the answers.

Internet connectivity is highly scalable, based on your needs and budget. At the most basic level is modem connectivity. Simply using a telephone line, a modem, and a dial-up connection to an ISP will get you on the Internet with minimal bandwidth. At the other end are T1/T3 connections that can serve thousands of users. There is a good chance that your needs fall somewhere between these two extremes. In our search for the right answer for your organization, I will detail the full spectrum of your choices. I'll start with the ISP. The ISP is your organization's connection point to the Internet; every Internet packet goes through your ISP.

Selecting An ISP

Connecting businesses to the Internet is a growing and highly competitive business. It is best to shop for an ISP carefully. Price is always an issue, but it is seldom the only issue. ISPs can oversell their bandwidth and ports. Watch the ISP reviews carefully, the top ISP of last year might be on the bottom of the list this year. Of course, switching ISPs is an option. While it's not as easy as switching long-distance carriers, it is not as difficult as some have made it out to be. Still, it's best to choose your ISP wisely with the goal of developing a mutually beneficial relationship.

ISP Service And Services

Not all ISPs offer the same services. There are two broad markets that ISPs address: home and business. Some try to address both, but this is becoming increasingly difficult as the Internet community grows. Businesses, even if in the home, need to be assured of the quality of their access. ISPs addressing the business market need to provide uninterrupted, high-quality, low to high bandwidth to relatively few businesses; that is, few in contrast with the home market. Compare this with ISPs that address the home market. These ISPs need to provide occasional, low bandwidth access to large masses of users at a very low cost. One ISP that was attempting to address both markets reported some time ago that 80% of its revenue came from 20% of its customers—the business customers. That ISP later sold off its home users to an ISP whose main market was home users.

ISPs that address the business market need to offer the dial-up or leased-line service that you need today, in addition to the services that you might need in the future. Look for an ISP that provides dial-up analog, ISDN, 56 kbps, and T1. The location of the ISP's network operating center (NOC) is an important consideration. By all means, make sure it's close to your business operation. Also, make sure the ISP offers both DNS (Domain Name System) services and Network News services over NNTP (Network News Transfer Protocol).

Additionally, some ISPs offer Web hosting services. This is an excellent service to consider. Organizations often underestimate the time and cost involved in hosting their own Web site. The costs from an ISP are so minimal for this service, it's becoming increasing difficult to make a case for hosting your own site. For a small charge, your ISP can host your Web site on a powerful Web server, housed in a climate-controlled environment, connected to the Internet via T3, where frequent backups are the norm. In fact, many ISPs offer disaster recovery plans for your Web site—this is an important consideration for a commerce-based Web site.

Another consideration for allowing your ISP to host your Web site is that the Web site is then completely isolated from your organization's Internet connection. This means that having a large number of customers hitting your Web site does not reduce the bandwidth available to the Proxy Server. While you could purchase the needed bandwidth for your Proxy Server installation, it might be more costly. If all this sounds good, make sure that the ISP will use your organization's domain name. Workarounds that include the ISP's domain name with your address are unacceptable. Also, if Internet commerce is part of your requirements, be sure your ISP's Web provisions include these services. Today, many do.

You might wish to use one ISP to host your Web site and yet another to provide Internet connectivity to your Proxy Server. Because certain ISP's specialize in either Web site hosting or providing Internet connectivity, this division often works well. Splitting up ISP services beyond this point is generally not a good idea. Having a single bill and a single point of responsibility is an attractive feature. It is even more attractive when the ISP's service extends to leasing equipment. Most ISPs will sell or lease the equipment required to connect you to their NOC. Typically, the lease includes a compatible router and DSU/CSU, or the equivalent ISDN equipment, such as Terminal Adapters, NT1s, and ISDN-capable routers.

Backbone

Not all ISPs are alike when it comes to their Internet backbones. ATM and OC-3 optical fiber backbones are often used as high-speed Internet backbones by ISPs. Switched backbones offer quality of service, flexibility, and the ability to carry more access. These are today's premium backbones, fast and expensive. Their high expense leads to a good deal of sharing between ISPs. The closer you can get to the backbone, the better your Internet performance. ISPs freely give out information about their backbones. Backbone performance is important market differentiation for an ISP. If an ISP refuses to give out this information, I would look elsewhere.

One ISP truism: Your proximity to the Internet backbone is determined by the bandwidth you buy. That means not only that lower-speed connections will have lower bandwidth, but also that each Internet request must pass through more routers, or hops, before the packets make it to their destination. The fewer the hops, the higher the performance of your Internet connection. Performing a TRACERT through an ISP to a frequently visited URL will provide the number of hops it takes to reach a destination. However, please be aware that, because of the architecture of the Internet, these results might change.

Cost

Your ISP cost will be directly related to the amount of bandwidth your organization requires. Be sure you have a bandwidth upgrade path. Some ISPs will charge less for a lower speed connection and then penalize you for upgrading, while others make upgrading attractive, but charge a higher price up front. If your business is in growth mode, the latter probably would be the better choice. Additionally, Proxy Server caching model reduces the bandwidth requirements for Web browsing. Be sure to consider this factor when determining the bandwidth required for your organization.

It is likely that you will find more than one ISP that meets your requirements. So how do you choose? Of course price is one way; but beware, cheaper isn't always the best choice. Some ISPs market price over service; this is called "buying the market." These ISPs know that you will be attracted by the lower number on the bottom line. Just be sure that you have some assurance that the quality of service will remain up to your standards. An ISP just taking on a "buy the market" strategy might be undercapitalized and, therefore, unable to service the increased business. Now just to make things difficult, more expensive isn't always better either. Get to know your ISP candidates, get references, and talk to your peers and industry leaders about their experience. When you choose an ISP, you are choosing an Internet partner.

Bandwidth Requirements

The expected use of the Internet is what drives the need for bandwidth. Is your organization a user of Internet content, a provider, or both? You learned how to determine this in Chapter 3. If you went through the needs assessment process with the users in your organization, you now have an understanding of the applications and services anticipated for our Internet connection. All this information helps give us an idea how much Internet bandwidth your organization will need. Now let's take a look at the three most common Internet applications and the bandwidth guidelines for each.

Email Bandwidth Guidelines

Internet email typically does not require very much bandwidth. Email on the Internet is a store-and-forward operation. Even if you have huge amounts of bandwidth, your Internet email would not arrive instantaneously; it travels a rambling path through Internet routers and servers. For small organizations, a 28.8 kbps or higher analog modem might be enough bandwidth to start with. If your organization is larger, your users attach files often, or they simply send and receive large volumes of email, then a BRI ISDN connection (two, 64 kbps B-channels) is a good starting point.

Use these numbers as email bandwidth guidelines for each user of Internet email in your organization:

Email (ASCII text only)   *2 kbps/user*

Email (with attachments)   *5 kbps/user*

FTP Bandwidth Guidelines

Organizations whose users often transfer files over the Internet via FTP (File Transfer Protocol) need considerable bandwidth. Start with at least a BRI ISDN connection (two, 64 kbps B-channels); larger organizations need to start higher, based on the FTP activity. FTP simply chews up a lot of bandwidth. Start thinking about a fractional T1, or equivalent, to begin with and in any case invest in one of the scalable access solutions I mention later in this chapter.

Use the recommendations in Table 5.1 as *absolute minimum* FTP bandwidth guidelines for FTP users.

Web Access Bandwidth Guidelines

Web access benefits considerably from Proxy Server's caching capabilities. Very small workgroups that have limited Web browsing needs could get by with a modem if they often viewed the same Web sites and no more than one or two persons browsed at the same time. This is quite a limitation. I would advise even small workgroups to start with ISDN because of its scalability. Larger organizations would probably start with a fractional T1, or equivalent.

Use the recommendations in Table 5.2 as Web access bandwidth guidelines for each user who browses the Web.

Of course there are many other Internet applications. *Use these recommendations as a starting point only.* You also might need to combine user types. For example, one five-person workgroup might have three persons who browse the same site, two who browse randomly, one who FTPs files that typically are less than 1 MB, and all of whom use email. Table 5.3 illustrates how you would rough out the bandwidth requirements.

Table 5.1   Recommended minimum FTP bandwidths for FTP users.

Typical FTP File Size	Recommended Minimum Bandwidth
Under 1 MB	25 kbps/user
Above 1 MB, but less than 4 MB	50 kbps/user
Above 4 MB	100 kbps/user

Table 5.2   Web access bandwidth recommendations for users who browse the Web.

Web Access Requirements	Recommended Minimum Bandwidth
Low access (minimal graphics, workgroup visits same sites often)	15 kbps/user
High access (more graphics, workgroup does not visit the same sites often, or both)	25 kbps/user

Table 5.3   Estimating bandwidth requirements for a workgroup.

Users	Type	kbps/User	kbps Required
3	Web (low access)	15	45
2	Web (high access)	25	50
1	FTP	25	25
5	email (text)	2	10
Total Bandwidth Required in kbps			**130**

When Increasing Bandwidth Doesn't Help

Before you invest in increasing bandwidth for your Internet connectivity, examine the speed of the sites that your users find slow. All it takes is a quick PING to your slow site. PING (Packet Internet Grouper) is a DOS-based utility program that is included with Windows NT 4.0. PING works by sending an ICMP (Internet Control Message Protocol) echo request and then waiting for a response. For example, typing **PING ds.internic.net** at the Command Prompt of the Proxy Server computer would return the following:

```
ping ds.internic.net
Pinging ds.internic.net [204.179.186.65] with 32 bytes of data:
Reply from 204.179.186.65: bytes=32 time=80ms TTL=249
Reply from 204.179.186.65: bytes=32 time=90ms TTL=249
Reply from 204.179.186.65: bytes=32 time=80ms TTL=249
Reply from 204.179.186.65: bytes=32 time=80ms TTL=249
```

The above results are quite good for ds.internic.net. But what if the site you ping is over 400 milliseconds? That site can be declared sluggish. The good news is that the problem is not your bandwidth. Increasing your bandwidth to your ISP will not provide any increase in speed to this site. What's the bad news? Sorry, other than complaining to the owners of the site, there is not anything that you can do.

While you're at it, you might want to check the specific path your request takes through the maze of Internet routers. The total response time of every router through which your request passes determines your connection speed. If certain routers are consistently slow, complaining to your ISP might help. Please note, however, that some routers will silently drop packets with expired TTLs (Time To Live). Unfortunately, these routers are invisible to TRACERT.

five

In this case, ISDN (2 B-channels, 64 kbps/channel) would work well. However, I wouldn't take these numbers too literally. For example, your FTP user might only need files occasionally, and Web browsing might be sporadic. Use the guidelines as a starting point only. It is often a good idea to plan for growth in both access needs and your organization size. Nearly always, an access method that scales well is an important consideration.

Scaling Internet Connectivity

The biggest bottleneck for Internet connectivity is what telecommunications experts call "the last mile." They're referring to the connection from your site to your telephone company's CO (Central Office) and from the CO to your ISP, or both. "The last mile" is the most expensive upgrade for the RBOCs (Regional Bell Operating Companies) and for the growing list of carriers that compete with the RBOCs. Because of lagging upgrades in the last mile, we have many compromises to consider. There is no one right answer. In addition, the growing need for higher bandwidth generates new connectivity solutions at extraordinary rates. I'll start with the ubiquitous modem.

Modems

Modems are the most basic, lowest bandwidth means to connect to the Internet. Modems MODulate and DEModulate signals so that digital data can travel over analog wires. Basically, a modem puts a computer signal into a form that can be used with Plain Old Telephone Service (POTS). POTS, or analog dial-up service, is the only communications network service that truly is worldwide. Because of the universal diffusion of POTS and the high cost of upgrading "the last mile," modems will still be used for some time as the lowest common denominator connector.

Microsoft Proxy Server can use Windows NT's RAS (Remote Access Service) to connect to an ISP through a modem. Figure 5.3 illustrates a Proxy Server connected to the Internet via modem. The modem can be either internal or external. A little advice: Don't let an internal modem's lower cost attract you, this is not a good choice for a server. When problems arise, the superiority of an external modem is apparent. For example, if an internal modem needs to be reset, you must reboot the server, while an external modem would only need to be turned off and then back on—the server remains up. An additional benefit is that external modems give you status lights that keep you informed of the connections' condition. The status lights are valuable as a simple, reliable means of troubleshooting. There are software status lights available in the Preference Tab of Windows NT 4.0's Dial Up Networking Monitor. These status lights emulate those of an external modem. But software status lights are only moderately effective; when things go wrong, it is not uncommon for the software versions of modem status lights to display erroneous information.

Modems are of use with a proxy server only for very small installations. Of course, a dial-up modem connection to an ISP is the least expensive of all the connection options.

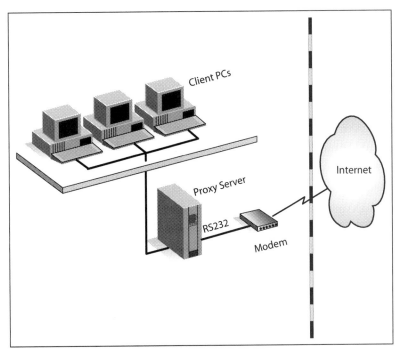

Figure 5.3   A Proxy Server connected to the Internet via a modem.

ISPs typically charge a low flat rate for an unlimited connection to the Internet. That is, when you can connect to the ISP. Modem connections aren't effective for most organizations unless there are only modest Internet connectivity needs. Web browsing, even with caching implemented, probably would be too slow if more than two users were browsing simultaneously.

Modem manufacturers would have you believe that the new crop of 56k modems will give you the equivalent speed of an ISDN link. Unfortunately, there are two problems with this assertion: lack of standards and the quality of the telephone lines.

Today, there are two competing standards for 56k modem technology: K56Flex from Lucent and x2 from 3Com (formerly U.S. Robotics). An official standard for 56k modem technology is unlikely to emerge until some time later in 1998. Because of the standards issue, ISPs have been slow to implement 56k technology. So if you are brave and buy one of these new modems, be sure that your ISP supports the 56k technology you buy. It also would be a good idea to make sure the modem has a flash ROM. Although this is typically a more expensive option, it might save a more costly upgrade when the 56k standard is finally set.

The second problem with modem transmission is the telephone lines themselves. If you have a 33.3 kbps modem today and it communicates at 24 kbps with your ISP, your shiny new 56k modem most probably will also communicate at 24 kbps. The problem is that phone lines were installed with voice capabilities in mind. While these phone lines work fine for voice, they fall short of delivering the required bandwidth demanded by high-speed modems. If you want to test your line for x2 capability, go to U.S. Robotics' Web page (**http://x2.usr.com/connectnow/linetest.html**) for instructions on testing your line. You do not require an x2 modem for the test. The only two requirements are:

➤ Any manufacturer's V.34 modem, installed and connected to a phone line.

➤ Any terminal application (such as Win95's HyperTerminal, RapidComm, QuickLink II, or MacComCenter).

There are some other reasons why 56k modems aren't quite up to ISDN. For example, right now FCC regulations limit the speed to 53k. Modem manufacturers plan on petitioning the FCC to increase this limit to the full 56 kbps, but right now 53 kbps is all you will get—and that's inbound only. Outbound bandwidth is reduced to 33.6 kbps with the Lucent 56kflex technology and 28.8 kbps with the U.S. Robotics x2 technology. Also, modems can take up to 30 seconds to negotiate a connection; ISDN typically connects in about 3 seconds.

Windows NT has the ability to bind together a pool of modems and aggregate the bandwidth. Modem pools normally combine a multiport serial card with a bank of modems. In addition, some modem manufacturers are making 67.2 modems that basically bond together two 33.6 modems using two phone lines. Some modem manufacturers are bonding two 56k modems for 112 kbps. There is even a hybrid modem/router technology available that is comprised of a four-port Ethernet router with three analog connections that can be combined to produce an Internet connection of up to 168 kbps downstream. On the surface these solutions look like a great way to wring some more life out of analog modem connections, and they might be appropriate for some installations. In particular, bonded modems might be appropriate in areas where ISDN installation and line costs remain high. But each modem connection requires a dedicated telephone line. Before you know it, the cost might be exceeding that of a digital connection to an ISP. As a rule, modem pools are better suited for incoming connections to a server by external client computers that connect private telephone lines with modems of equal or less speed capability.

A final note about modems. Modems can work reasonably well for Internet mail services for small workgroups. But even a small workgroup could bring a modem to its knees if its members are in the habit of sending large files attached to an email message. In that case, a modem would not have enough bandwidth. So, consider the bandwidth limitations of modem connectivity carefully before recommending that your organization connect to the Internet via a dial-up modem link to an ISP.

ISDN (Integrated Services Digital Network)

The next step up from analog modems is ISDN (Integrated Services Digital Network). ISDN began in 1968 as a concept by a CCITT (Consultative Committee for International Telephone and Telegraph) study group. The first set of standards recommendations was published in 1984 as a CCITT Red Book. No, ISDN isn't new. In fact, it is incredible that ISDN has been studied, standardized, and engineered over such a long period of time with such small adoption rates. The slow growth might lead you to conclude that ISDN is a poor choice for an Internet connection.

But don't give up on ISDN; in many ways ISDN is a solid solution for small bandwidth applications. Data communications over ISDN is a perfect match because ISDN's basic nature is digital, and ISDN is also scalable. There are currently two interfaces available: BRI (Basic Rate Interface), for lower speed applications; and PRI (Primary Rate Interface), for higher speed applications. I'll break apart the composition of ISDN in order to better explain the differences between the two interfaces. In the ISDN specifications, three channel types are identified:

➤ **B-channels (Bearer channels)**   These channels carry the digital information.

➤ **D-channels (Data channels)**   These channels are for signaling and control.

➤ **H-channels (High-speed channels)**   These channels are for channel aggregation to support bandwidth-intensive applications.

The bandwidth for an ISDN installation is determined by the number of *B-channels* carrying the digital information. Each B-channel operates at a clear channel rate of 64 kbps. The *D-channel* exists for control, device signaling, and network management. The D-channel is occasionally used for low-speed data, but this use would be unusual in a Proxy Server environment. The bandwidth of the D-Channel varies from 16 kbps for BRI to 64 kbps for PRI. The H-Channels are used to aggregate bandwidth in PRI applications. This functionality is similar to the bonding of modems I discussed in the previous section. When procuring PRI ISDN, you might run across the terms Multirate ISDN, Nx64, or Channel aggregation. Each of these terms means essentially the same thing: Your bandwidth will be dynamically allocated using inverse multiplexing over multiple B-Channels. BRI ISDN and PRI ISDN are part of a service class known as N-ISDN (Narrowband ISDN).

BRI ISDN

BRI is primarily used for residential and small business applications. The composition of BRI is two B-Channels and one D-Channel. The two 64 kbps B-Channels can be aggregated for a total of 128 kbps. MLPPP (Multilink Point to Point Protocols) typically is used for bonding BRI in Internet application where two B-channels are bonded.

five

It is also possible to bond multiple BRI for greater bandwidth. This bonding does not require the use of an H-Channel, which BRI ISDN does not have. Two BRI ISDN adapters bonded would equal a 256 kbps (4 x 64 kbps B-channels = 256 kbps).

A significant advantage of BRI is that it operates over a single pair of standard telephone wires. Most residential telephone installations are wired with a single cable that consists of two pairs of copper wire. This configuration allows a standard analog line and a BRI ISDN line in a residence. If you are considering ISDN for your residence, think twice about scrimping on an internal ISDN adapter. You might wish to use one of your B-channels for both data and voice or a fax machine. With an internal ISDN adapter, your computer would have to be turned on to make or receive phone calls or facsimiles over the B-channel.

Technically, BRI ISDN also works well for small- to medium-size businesses, particularly when you consider that BRI ISDN can be bonded together by what's called an Inverse MUX (Inverse Multiplexer). Bonding 4 BRIs together would yield a bandwidth of 512 kbps, which is quite a bit more than a modem but still less than a full T1 at 1.54 mbps (megabits per second).

Will Every Home Have A FAN?

Now you might be saying: "This is a book about Microsoft Proxy Server, why is he writing about residential telephone lines?"

Think for a moment about the number of families you know who have several members of the family who need to be online at the same time. Perhaps both parents work and need to access the Internet in the evening, while their children need Internet connectivity for researching school work and maybe even social email. The contention over a single computer could be horrifying. The scene invokes a vision similar to a single telephone line and a teenager: While it can be done, it isn't easy. Yes, you could add computers, phone lines, and modems, but a single Microsoft Proxy Server connected through ISDN would be a more economical solution.

There is a growing population implementing what is known as a FAN (Family Area Network). As computer technology converges with entertainment technology, FANs will become more common. In the United States, we have always put a priority on communications technology. A case in point: up until the mid 1980s, more homes in the United States had TVs than indoor plumbing. Is there a FAN in your future?

PRI ISDN

PRI was designed for commercial applications. It is also known as 23B+D because, in the U.S. and Japan, it has 23 B-channels and one D-channel, each operating at 64 kbps. In Europe, PRI has 30 B-channels and one D-channel. The 23 B-channels combine to give 1.472 mbps of bandwidth. Even though PRI is carried over a standard T1 trunk, it is a significant advancement over T1 in that the B-channels can be dynamically allocated. That's right, you can have bandwidth on demand to support full motion video and other bandwidth-intensive applications.

Don't get too excited about the 64 kbps D-Channel's bandwidth. In contrast to BRI, the D-Channel can only be used for signaling. On the other hand, the D-Channel can provide up to five PRI connections. This means that the first PRI is provided at standard 23 B-Channels and one D-Channel, while up to four more PRIs can be combined at 24 B-Channels each—no additional D-Channels are required. That's a lot of bandwidth!

The Reality Of ISDN

If it sounds like I'm an advocate of ISDN, you're right. ISDN has some wonderful characteristics that make it well suited for today's needs. I recall the first time I experienced an ISDN BRI connection. I replaced a 28.8 kbps modem in my home office with a 3COM Impact IQ ISDN adapter. I brought up the Microsoft Internet Explorer browser, which defaults to my intranet home page. I then went to my favorites and chose C|net to read the news—and there it was. No screeching, gurgling modem sounds and practically no wait. There was only a slight hesitation while the call was set up. I've waited on the Operating System to complete a task for longer than it took for the call to set up. Believe me, until you've experienced it, you won't understand how terrific ISDN's quick call setup is.

BRI ISDN terminal adapters are now easy for the user to configure. Manufacturers of ISDN terminal adapters have placed a tremendous amount of emphasis on making installation easy. They had to. In the United States, most carriers still don't understand how to market, deploy, and service ISDN. First, the time between placing an order and implementation is still too long. Now in all fairness, it is getting better. Waits of three to six months were commonplace in 1996. In 1997, 30 to 90 days is the reported norm and there's good reason to expect those installation times to decrease. Industry leaders such as Microsoft, 3Com, and others have put in place ISDN installation tracking services. A third party, staffed with ISDN experts and persons skilled in making installation follow-up calls, tracks your installation from beginning to end, taking the burden off the residential or small business user. Moreover, the ISDN terminal adapters now have the intelligence built in to the equipment to establish the provisioning for your ISDN line. The two biggest headaches are solved.

Why don't the carriers take the lead and market this service? I believe it's because of two factors: infrastructure costs and human resources. It is still costly for a carrier to implement ISDN. Because it is a direct digital link, lines and circuits have to be upgraded and repeaters added to the telephone infrastructure. Unlike the analog telephone system's deployment decades ago, the courts do not allow the costs of upgrading the telephone infrastructure to handle ISDN to be spread across all telephone uses or users. Instead, ISDN upgrade costs must be passed directly to the users of the ISDN service. Moreover, there is a shortage of persons trained to install, service, and support ISDN. It takes some hefty training to staff an ISDN technical services team. The carriers are unwilling to ramp up their ISDN staffs when they have an uncertainty of market viability of ISDN. So we have a chicken and egg syndrome. The market grows slowly because of high costs and poor service, and the carriers don't invest because of a slowly growing market.

ISDN Costs

The net effect is that the cost of ISDN service in most areas remains high. In addition, the costs vary widely from region to region. I am fortunate to live in an area—Columbus, Ohio—where the ISDN costs are quite reasonable. I pay a flat rate for BRI ISDN service in my home office that is very reasonable. Columbus, Ohio was one of the ISDN pilot cities, so the lower costs here can be traced to the growth and maturity of the infrastructure and subscriber base. But in other areas of the United States, ISDN costs remain astronomical. It is common for ISDN to carry a timed usage rate. This discourages the deployment of ISDN and, therefore, the rates remain high.

The computer industry's nudges seem to be working. But you still must establish a cost model to determine if ISDN is appropriate for your organization. Your cost model should cover the following topics:

➤ What are the service fees charged by your local telephone carrier?

➤ Do long distance charges apply? If so, what are the rates?

➤ What is the cost of the equipment?

➤ What does your ISP charge for ISDN services?

Local Telephone Fees

Local carrier ISDN fees vary substantially. You need to get a handle on three fee categories: installation, monthly charges, and per-minute usage charges per B-channel. Installation charges comprise all the costs associated with terminating an ISDN connection at your site. These costs include the costs of establishing the connection, repeater installation, and premise wiring. The need for a repeater is driven by your distance from the CO. There are also recurrent monthly charges for service and for the repeater, if required. In addition, per-minute connection charges are typical. These charges can rapidly mount up, so it pays to estimate your connect time carefully. Let's look at a scenario where your ISDN monthly charge was $60, your repeater charge was $26, and your online charge was 3 cents per channel per minute. In Table 5.4, I assume a small organization using both B-channels (128 kbps). This organization used the Internet for 2.5 hours every day over the course of a month that had 20 business days.

Now, let's look at the same scenario in Table 5.5, but assume you miscalculated the usage time. In the following example, your organization used the Internet for 5 hours every day over the course of a 20 business day month:

Next we will annualize the two examples in Table 5.6.

Table 5.4   ISDN usage for 2.5 hours per day for a 20-day business month.

Item	Rate	Usage (in minutes)	Monthly Charge
Basic fee			$60.00
Repeater			26.00
Usage charge (*B-1*)	.03	3000	90.00
Usage charge (*B-2*) (*3 cents per minute per B-channel*)	.03	3000	90.00
Total			$266.00

Table 5.5   ISDN usage for 5 hours per day for a 20-day business month.

Item	Rate	Usage (in minutes)	Monthly Charge
Basic fee			$60.00
Repeater			26.00
Usage charge (*B-1*)	.03	3000	180.00
Usage charge (*B-2*) (*3 cents per minute per B-channel*)	.03	3000	180.00
Total			$446.00

Table 5.6   Annual cost comparison of 2.5 hrs/day vs. 5 hrs/day ISDN usage.

Example	Monthly Estimate	Annual Charge
Budget 1 (*Table 5.1*)	266	$3192
Budget 2 (*Table 5.2*)	446	$5352
Cost of additional online time:		$2160

The increased connect time of "Budget 2" in the above example costs the organization more than $2000 per year, and your ISP charges still have to be included. If a flat-rate connection charge is offered, it might be a better choice for the small organization. If you have a larger organization and plan to bond several BRIs together, you would multiply the above by the number of BRIs. As you can see, ISDN with timed usage can quickly become expensive. Flat-rate ISDN is often a better choice. If flat-rate ISDN is not available, you might need to examine other options, such as T1, Fractional T1, and PRI.

Long Distance Charges

There is such an abundance of ISPs in most areas that you should be able to find one that does not require a toll call. If not, you will have to factor these costs into your planning. Beware, ISDN tolls for *data* connections can be substantial.

Equipment Costs

Equipment costs are a factor to consider if you are deploying ISDN. The pricing for ISDN equipment is volatile. If you are deploying BRI ISDN, you will need a terminal adapter and an NT1. The terminal adapter simply connects the computer equipment to the ISDN network. Figure 5.4 illustrates a Proxy Server connected to the Internet via an ISDN adapter. So show your ISDN savvy by never referring to an ISDN terminal adapter as a modem, *even though some manufacturers do*. ISDN is a digital connection; therefore, no MODulation and DEModulation occur.

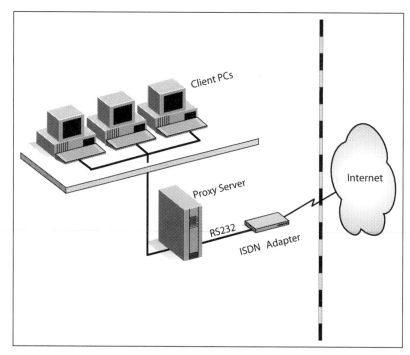

Figure 5.4 A Proxy Server connected to the Internet via an ISDN adapter.

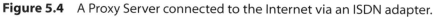

The NT1 physically connects the customer site to the carrier side of the connection. It is also responsible for the maintenance of the local loop's electrical characteristics. If you plan to use the voice capabilities of ISDN, then your NT1 should be on a battery backup unit. Lose power to your NT1 and you lose your telephone service; this, of course, is not good. NT1s are nearly always included as part of your Terminal Adapter. If you plan to use an internal TA, just remember that if your server is powered down, your NT1 will be powered down as well. No ISDN telephone services are possible.

Larger ISDN installations require a router. Figure 5.5 illustrates a Proxy Server connected to the Internet via an ISDN-capable router. Routers are available with NT1s built into them and as separate devices. Routers can work with BRI or PRI ISDN. BRI routers come in low-end and high-end models. The low-end BRI routers work with a single BRI (2-B +1-D). The high-end BRI routers work with multiple BRI connections. It's a good idea to compare these routers with the cost of PRI service and equipment. Depending on your circumstances, you might find multiple BRI connections to be more economical. PRI routers typically work best for dial-in users, while multiple BRI is best for connecting to an ISP. This is only a general rule, so examine your needs and costs carefully.

One more important issue with routers. Unfortunately, you can't pick just any router to connect with your ISP, your router must be compatible with your ISPs router. That's why it is usually a better idea to have your ISP bundle the costs of its services, a router,

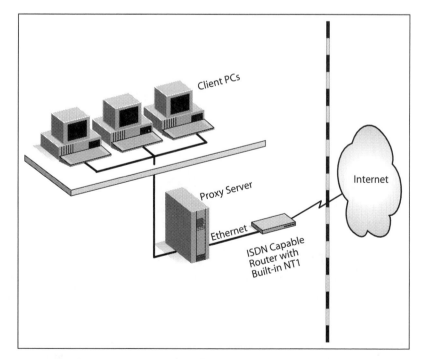

Figure 5.5 A Proxy Server connected to the Internet via an ISDN-capable router.

and an NT1 that is known to be compatible. There is a lot of finger pointing if things don't work, so minimize the variables.

Cost Of ISP Services For ISDN

Some ISPs are more predisposed to ISDN than others. Review my overall advice in the "Selecting an ISP" section, and then start shopping. Be sure to make clear the number of B-channels required and whether you need a BRI or PRI connection. The details matter and can quickly become costly. There are ISDN-friendly ISPs that offer very competitive rates. Typically, these are ISPs that invested heavily in ISDN equipment.

Reality Check

Is an ISDN Internet connection the right choice for your organization? The only way to know for sure is to carefully examine your needs and to attempt to match those needs to the available ISDN and rate structures in your area. Keep in mind that rates change often with carriers and ISPs. If you looked at ISDN a year ago and determined it was too costly, look again. There is a good chance that the ISDN prices have changed.

Switched 56 kbps

There is another service that is similar to ISDN, called switched 56 kbps. This service is only available in the United States; other parts of the globe do not have a comparable service. As with ISDN, you can call up the bandwidth when required; however, at approximately 20 seconds, the call setup time is longer than for ISDN. Another difference is that switched 56 kbps can only carry data; voice services are not available. Also, unlike ISDN, switched 56 kbps is a single channel service that requires a DSU/CSU.

Switched 56 kbps might be a viable choice if ISDN is not available in your area. But deploy ISDN if you have a choice, it is much more flexible—particularly for SOHOs (Small Office/Home Office) that can make use of the voice capabilities. Switched 56 kbps is also more expensive than ISDN. As ISDN deployments throughout North America increase, it is clear that switched 56 kbps will become obsolete.

Dataphone Digital Service (DDS)

Dataphone Digital Service (DDS) provides several benefits; the biggest is that your organization receives a persistent connection to the Internet. A 56 kbps leased line is the opening ante in the United States, while other parts of the world start at 64 kbps. Going up in bandwidth, the Fractional T1, T1, and T3 sweeten the pot. DDS provides a dedicated digital line. DDS's popularity is second only to analog access. The universal availability, combined with the ability to be configured for a variety of bandwidths, are the primary reasons for this popularity.

Typically, it is an application that drives the need for the persistent connection that DDS provides. By convention, Web Services and email through SMTP (Simple Mail

Transfer Protocol) require a persistent connection. If your Internet requirements include a large number of users who frequently access the Web, using FTP and other bandwidth-intensive applications, then a dedicated digital line is the solution. The standard for dedicated digital services is the T1.

T1

The groundwork for the T1 technology began in 1957 in Newark, New Jersey as T-carrier (the "T" stands for *trunk*). This early digital carrier was initially used for short-haul interexchange trunking. In 1977, it was first offered commercially by AT&T as part of a *special assembly* tariff. In 1983, T-carrier was sold under the name of *Accunet 1.5* by AT&T. Today, there are hundreds of thousands of T-carrier links in service. T-carrier is commonly called T1.

T1 lines are comprised of 24 64 kbps channels in the United States. The telecommunications industry term for these channels is DS-0 (Digital Signal #0). A T1 in the United States has a total bandwidth of 1.536 mbps. This grouping of 24 64 kbps channels is called a DS-1. DS-1s are media independent; DS-1s can be provisioned over twisted-pair, coaxial, microwave, satellite, infrared, or fiber optic cable. Officially, only when a DS-1 is delivered over copper wire is it a T1; nevertheless, you hear ISPs boast of their optical T1s. T1s use a 4-wire transmission path and require a DSU/CSU. Another curiosity: You will often see a T1 line specified as having a data rate of 1.544 mbps. Technically, this is correct. But don't get too excited about that extra 8 kbps, it is actually used for synchronization purposes.

The European equivalent to a T1 is called E1 and has 30 channels. The J1 is Japan's T1 equivalent and, like the T1, it has 24 channels. All over the world, channels operate at 64 kbps, but T1, E1, and J1 use different encoding, signaling, and control methods. These differences aside, the basic natures of these technologies remain quite similar.

T3

T3 is the step up in bandwidth. A T3 refers to a DS-3 delivered over copper wire. DS-3s are a collection of 672 64 kbps, DS-0 channels. Get out your calculator; that's 43.008 mbps of useable digital bandwidth. T3s are advertised as having a bandwidth of 44.736 or 45 mbps. The 1.728 mbps difference is used for synchronizing the line with the phone company and cannot be used for your data communications purposes. By the way, there is such a thing as a DS-2, but this service is not usually available to end-users; just to make you fully informed, a DS-2 consists of 4 DS-1 channels.

Fractional T1

FT1 (Fractional T1) lines allow an organization to purchase the dedicated bandwidth that it needs today, with a clear upgrade path when additional bandwidth becomes necessary. Fractional T1s are offered in increments of 1, 2, 4, 6, 8, and 12 DS-0 channels.

The idea of Fractional T1 began in Canada and was brought to the United States in 1987 by Cable and Wireless. Many ISPs offer FT1 as an entry-level solution for persistent Internet connection. FT1s are a popular option that should be weighed against ISDN if a persistent connection is not required.

Equipment Costs

Dedicated digital lines require a DSU/CSU and a router. Figure 5.6 illustrates a Proxy Server connected to the Internet via T1 using a DSU/CSU and a router. Commonly, these units are available from your ISP for lease or purchase. I would strongly urge you to obtain your DSU/CSU and router from your ISP. Compatibility, compression, and service are compelling reasons to procure this equipment from your ISP.

Frame Relay

Frame Relay is another good choice if your organization requires both outbound and inbound persistent connections. Since its commercial introduction by Wiltel in 1992 (later acquired by WorldCom), Frame Relay has become the most popular packet-switching technology for WANs (Wide Area Networks). Frame relay was designed as a replacement for the X.25 protocol. Similar to T1, Frame Relay's bandwidths range from 56 kbps to 45 mbps. The key difference between Frame Relay and X.25 is that Frame Relay does not correct errors or request retransmission. Frame Relay accomplishes this

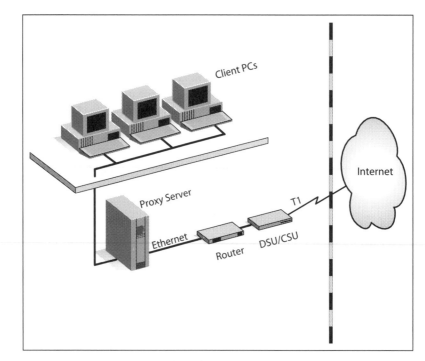

Figure 5.6   A Proxy Server connected to the Internet via T1 using a DSU/CSU and a router.

feat through the use of a quality, high-speed transport system, typically fiber optic. If errors occur, it is the responsibility of intelligent end devices to request retransmission.

Frame Relay is protocol independent. There are implementations available for both IPX and IP over Frame Relay. Of course, a Frame Relay connection to the Internet requires that IP be run over the Frame Relay connection. If you already have a Frame Relay WAN connection, you should verify that your implementation can run IP. The interoperability of different vendors' implementation of IP over Frame Relay is covered by Standard RFC 1274. By the way, you could configure WAN access using Frame Relay and the IPX protocol between two Microsoft Proxy Servers or a Proxy Server and a Proxy Server array. For large organizations, this might be less costly than using a direct Internet connection at each location.

One of the major attractions of Frame Relay is that the distance the call travels has no bearing on price—in other words, the price is distance insensitive. Usually an ISP is close enough that this benefit is not a major consideration for an Internet connection. Also, Frame Relay is not a good choice for voice or video because of the high overhead associated with frame switching. This overhead would likely provide garbled speech and jerky video images. Nevertheless, Frame Relay is the fastest growing technology of its type. If your organization already uses Frame Relay services, it might be a viable option. If not, DDS is probably a better option.

Permanent Virtual Circuits

The path through a Frame Relay network that connects two points is the *permanent virtual circuit* (PVC). A PVC is simply dedicated bandwidth for data transmission that guarantees a level of service called *committed information rate (CIR)*. A Frame Relay connection is made up of one or more PVCs. Once set up, PVCs are always active and available.

Committed Information Rate

The CIR is really a workaround to an interesting problem. Since Frame Relay has no means to control flow, theoretically, a single connection could monopolize the entire bandwidth of the Frame Relay network. So Frame Relay vendors specify a CIR: *a minimum bandwidth that is available to your PVC 24 hours a day, 7 days a week*. The CIR is completely independent of your physical connection. In other words, a 1.544 mbps physical connection might have only 128 kbps of bandwidth guaranteed. The popularity of both Frame Relay and the Internet makes the CIR a critical specification. So, scrutinize the CIR specification carefully before signing a Frame Relay service contract.

Please note that even though a vendor guarantees a CIR, delays do occur on busy Frame Relay networks. These delays can last for up to a half a second. Again, read your service contract carefully; verbiage about delays typically is buried in the agreement. If voice and video are not part of your requirements, these delays might be perfectly acceptable to you—but it's always better to know up front.

Service And Services Cost

Large ISPs have their own private Frame Relay network infrastructure. These ISPs can provide multiple PVCs access to the Internet. So, one PVC might be dedicated to SMTP mail, another to USENET newsgroups, and so on. For large organizations this provides a good way to monitor your Internet usage and requirements. You might, for example, upgrade your service by increasing your CIR for SMTP mail, but leave it as is for your Web services.

Another good use for a PVC would be to dedicate one PVC for outward-bound Internet use and another for inward-bound Internet use, perhaps for a Web site. A day of heavy hits on your Web site would have no effect on your users' ability to browse the Web themselves, or to receive their email. While it's possible to do the same thing with ISDN or DDS, it is decidedly more difficult.

Frame Relay Equipment

A Frame Relay implementation requires a FRAD (Frame Relay Assembler/Disassembler). The FRAD organizes the data to be transmitted into PDUs (Protocol Data Units) and then places the PDU into a Frame Relay frame and then encapsulates it with the necessary control information. FRADs are available in internal versions, for mounting in a PC card slot; or external, standalone units. The required DSU/CSU might be part of the FRAD or standalone. The second piece of Frame Relay equipment is the Frame Relay Switch. These are standalone units that buffer the incoming frames until the link is available. Like a router, the Frame Relay Switch contains routing tables that read the frame's control information and route the frames over the PVC.

It is possible to find a FRAD, Frame Relay Switch, and DSU/CSU as a single piece of equipment. It is generally easier to upgrade if your DSU/CSU is a standalone piece of equipment, an important consideration for a growing organization.

As with DDS, an ISP can provide you the necessary equipment for sale or lease. However, if you have an existing Frame Relay WAN in place, you need to be sure that your ISP will guarantee compatibility with your existing Frame Relay equipment.

Frame Relay Costs

The cost of Frame Relay often looks very attractive when compared to DDS or ISDN. If you can live with the limitations of Frame Relay, and many can, then it might be a good option for your organization. If your organization is large and geographically dispersed, tying Proxy Servers together with Frame Relay would work well, particularly for the common requirements of Web browsing and SMTP email.

Remember that the service is directly related to the CIR. If a quote for a Frame Relay price is substantially less than a well-respected competitor's Frame Relay price, turn right to the page that defines the CIR. It is likely that you will find the reason for the low cost. A PVC that has 128 kbps bandwidth and a CIR of zero could prove to be worthless.

SMDS, ATM, And B-ISDN

ISPs and very large organizations need huge pipes to the Internet to carry the volumes of data they move each day. Delivering applications to your user community, such as online services for your customers, CAD/CAM, video capabilities, or even hosting a very popular Web site, can drive the need for a high-bandwidth connection. SMDS, ATM, and B-ISDN offer higher bandwidth and better performance than T1, T3, and PRI ISDN for many organizations. If one of these technologies is of interest to you, you will likely be deploying multiple proxy servers to benefit from Proxy Server's distributed caching model. You also might be obtaining services from an ISP that uses one or more of these services as part of their network backbone. I will give an overview of each of these services, highlighting their strengths and weaknesses.

Switched Multimegabit Data Service (SMDS)

SMDS, first offered by Bell Atlantic in 1992, is a relatively new technology. The vendors of this packet-switched data service include major United States RBOCs and other Competitive Access Providers (CAPs), such as MCI. It is available at speeds from 1.177 mbps to 34 mbps. SMDS vendors market to organizations that wish to extend their LAN across a metropolitan or wide area. This marketing has given rise to the term MAN (Metropolitan Area Network). SMDS supports LAN-to-LAN traffic under the IEEE 802.6 standards. SMDS is sensitive to distance; the maximum serving radius is approximately 30 miles (50 Km).

Strengths. SMDS offers many advantages. It is connectionless, so setting up a physical or logical connection before sending data is not required. It has none of the latency and data loss problems that are characteristic of Frame Relay and X.25. SMDS is based on cell-switching technology and is generally delivered over a SONET (Synchronous Optical Network) ring. SMDS has stellar performance; speeds greater than T1 are offered at costs that are generally less than those for DS-3 leased lines. The biggest benefit is SMDS's smooth migration path to ATM.

Weaknesses. There are some drawbacks; the biggest is the limited availability of SMDS. This problem leads to a high-cost circle that works like this: (1) Only a few ISPs support SMDS. (2) Those ISPs that do support SMDS only offer it to a few areas, simply because it is offered by so few RBOCs and CAPs. (3) Since SMDS is such a small market, the equipment costs are astronomical. (4) The limited availability and high equipment costs keep demand for SMDS modest, so RBOCs and CAPs are slow to jump on the SMDS bandwagon. (5) Therefore, only a few ISPs support SMDS, which is where we began.

Still, SMDS is a sound way to connect to an ISP if you need more bandwidth than a T1, but less than a T3. Also notable is its smooth migration path to ATM. But check for availability and pricing in your area before you get too excited.

ATM

The concept of ATM grew out of the development of ISDN standards in the early 1980s. At that time, it was believed by the ITU (International Telecommunications Union) that a technology that offered greater bandwidth than ISDN would become a necessity because of emerging bandwidth-intensive applications, such as voice and video. The ITU was right; the rapid growth and reliance on the Internet by businesses around the globe proved the ITU's premise. In 1990, two United States government agencies, the Advanced Research Project Agency (ARPA) and the National Science Foundation (NSF), sponsored the first deployment of ATM: the *National Research and Education Network* (NREN). Since that time, ATM has been widely hailed as the future of broadband networking.

ATM is a cell-switched, connection-oriented, full-duplex, point-to-point protocol. ATM is fast. Bandwidths from 25 mbps to 622 mbps that can handle data sources as diverse as voice, facsimile, data, video, and image are part of the original design. It's really the predictable small cell size of 53 bytes that makes ATM fast and suitable for tough transmission tasks such as video. Most of the work today is with 155 mbps ATM. Unlike SMDS, ATM is not hindered by distance. Frame Relay and ATM work well together. ATM is by design a backbone technology, while Frame Relay is an access technology. ISPs will use ATM with Frame Relay in just this fashion.

Strengths. ATM is well liked for its low-error bandwidth-on-demand service. It is unique in that it works equally well in LAN, MAN, and WAN installations, handling any type of data that you throw at it. Its high speed and scalability makes it perfect for use as a backbone. It is the best choice today for high-speed applications, such as multimedia and video, over short or long distances.

Weaknesses. What are the downsides? Unfortunately, ATM is still hard to find. It is a young technology with a bright future, but it is not deployed widely in the United States and is even more difficult to find, with a few exceptions, in the rest of the world. It also has a steep learning curve. ATM's complexity is not for the faint of heart and its price requires deep pockets and a clearly identified need.

There is a threat to running ATM to the desktop; it's called Gigabit Ethernet. The standards for Gigabit Ethernet are about a year away. It's more likely that these two technologies will complement, rather than displace, one another. ATM holds the current crown for ultra high-speed bandwidth and scalability.

B-ISDN

The standards for B-ISDN (Broadband ISDN) were first introduced by the ITU in 1988. Since that time, the standards have gone through a series of revisions and additions. Basically, B-ISDN builds on the services of Narrowband ISDN (N-ISDN). The primary technical difference is that B-ISDN is based on cell-switching, while N-ISDN is based on circuit-switching. Three technologies form the foundation of B-ISDN:

➤ **SS7**   The signaling and control technology that is also used in N-ISDN.

➤ **ATM**   The backbone network switching and transport technology.

➤ **SDH/SONET**   The physical backbone network transmission technology

B-ISDN has two interfaces: User Network Interface A (UNI A) and User Network Interface B (UNI B). The data rate for UNI-A is 155 mbps and that for UNI-B is 622 mbps.

Strengths. The strength of the technologies that form the foundation for B-ISDN are so great, it is easy to see the benefits of this service. B-ISDN is fast and supports connections that are switched, permanent, semi-permanent, point-to-point, and multi-point. Like ATM, B-ISDN supports bandwidth on demand and all forms of data, including multimedia and video.

Weaknesses. B-ISDN might be a technology that will take a long time to become widely available. While standards have been proposed, they are not accepted universally. What will the cost be? Likely astronomical, because ATM switches and SONET fiber-optic transmission facilities form the foundation of this technology.

Leading Edge Access Services

It is difficult to plan for the future, even though it seems to be coming at us more quickly every day. The rush to the Internet by businesses large and small is driving a need for faster and more convenient access to your ISP. We all want more bandwidth, for less money—and we want it now. This demand leads to some creative solutions, all of which utilize some form of the existing communications infrastructure. What follow are descriptions of some services that are either here now, but in limited availability, or coming soon to an ISP near you. I would keep my eyes on all of these promising services.

DSL Services

DSL (Digital Subscriber Line) services are designed to take advantage of the local loop—that is, the twisted-pair wire infrastructure that comprises the "last mile" of the telephone system. Finding ways to wring out more bandwidth from the local loop is what DSL services are all about. The sections below describe the various types of DSL services.

ADSL

ADSL (Asymmetric Digital Subscriber Line) is now in field tests throughout the world. It is a promising service, offering downstream data rates ranging from 1.5 mbps to 9 mbps, while upstream rates reduce from 16 kbps to 640 kbps. ADSL transmissions work at distances up to 18,000 feet over a single copper twisted pair. If your organization is more of a user of Internet information, rather that a provider, then ADSL might be an alternative for the future. If providing information is important, you might consider splitting up your access services, using ADSL for Web browsing and file downloads and another service for applications such as email, which is typically an upstream and downstream service.

HDSL

HDSL is symmetrical, delivering 1.544 mbps each way. That's the same bandwidth as a T1. HDSL's distance limitation of 12,000 feet is less than that of ADSL. After 12,000 feet, repeaters need to be installed. Also, HDSL requires two twisted pairs. The primary intention of HDSL is a more cost-effective solution for providing T1 service. HDSL is a good choice for a Proxy Server for an organization that is both a provider and a user of Internet Information.

SDSL

SDSL (Single-line Digital Subscriber Line) also provides 1.544 mbps both upstream and downstream. It is different from HDSL in that, true to its name, SDSL only requires a single twisted pair. SDSL also has a shorter operating range than HDSL, with 10,000 feet as the practical limit. SDSL is a better choice for some SOHOs because it only requires a single line.

VDSL

VDSL (Very-high-data-rate Digital Subscriber Line), like ADSL, is asymmetrical. It has a rather significant distance limitation of 1,000 to 4,500 feet over a single twisted pair. What it has is lots of downstream bandwidth, 13 mbps to 52 mbps; and T1 or better bandwidth upstream, 1.5 mbps to 2.3 mbps.

IDSL

IDSL (ISDN Digital Subscriber Line) differs from regular ISDN in that it is not switched. IDSL is also called Dedicated ISDN. ISPs, such as UUNET using WorldCom's local networks, saw an opportunity when they realized that the switch that carries ISDN is costly for RBOCs. So a technology was devised that bypasses the switch and connects directly to the ISP. The RBOC saves the cost of a switch upgrade, while the ISP can offer a 128 to 786 kbps dedicated service at an attractive price. IDSL uses Standard ISDN protocols and is compatible with existing ISDN terminal adapters and routers. IDSL is available on a limited basis at this time.

Cable Modems

It's not only the telephone communications infrastructure that is serving the need for faster Internet access, the cable companies are jumping on the bandwagon too. Some cable companies, such as TCI with *@home* and Time Warner with *Road Runner*, are making plays for the home Internet access market. Also, Time Warner has plans to compete in the business market. The cable modem itself connects to the coaxial connector on the cable outlet. The PC, TV, or other devices connect to the cable modem through a 10baseT Ethernet port. Unlike a typical analog modem, the cable modem is always on. The maximum downstream bandwidth ranges from 10 mbps to 30 mbps, depending on which modulation scheme is used. That is shared bandwidth, so as cable modems are used by more households, the bandwidth goes down. Of course, the cable companies are aware of this limitation and are working to solve the problem, or at least reduce its effect.

It is difficult to know how useful SOHOs will find cable modems. It might be a violation of the cable company's contract to connect a cable modem to another device that would share the modem's bandwidth. It will be interesting to watch this technology unfold. It is probably the most significant data communications service that bypasses the telephone infrastructure.

Satellite Systems

Satellite systems, such as DirectPC, offer another high-speed connection possibility. DirectPC can beam the Internet directly into your home or office. While the initial marketing thrust was for the home market, SOHO's and larger businesses also can benefit from the bandwidth Satellite systems provide.

How much bandwidth? Up to 400kbps, one way. Yes, one way. DirectPC is a hybrid technology. The smallish 21-inch dish can receive data, but it can't transmit. Therefore, you need to use a modem or ISDN connection for upstream connectivity to complete the loop. If your needs are mostly downstream, this is an acceptable solution. But, if you are uploading files via FTP or sending email with large attachments, the enhanced bandwidth of DirectPC will not come into play.

You will also need to be sure your building offers a clear line of sight to the satellite's location and can accommodate a 21-inch satellite dish. Satellite systems are particularly useful in areas that lack the communications infrastructure of a large metropolitan area.

The Network Protocols

Most Microsoft Proxy Servers are implemented as additions to an existing network. I assume that you already have a network in place for your organization and you wish to add a Microsoft Proxy Server to the network, so I won't spend a lot of time going over the details of a full network implementation.

You do have to make sure that a Proxy Server-supported network protocol is in place. The choices are simple: TCP/IP or IPX/SPX. Microsoft Proxy Server 2.0 works with either. Practically all private networks either run one of these protocols or support them. Although IPX/SPX is much easier to implement, TCP/IP facilitates the creation of an intranet. Make your protocol choice based on your overall needs.

Name Resolution

Microsoft Proxy Server needs some way for clients to resolve the name of the server. Your choices for name resolution include: DNS (Domain Name System), WINS (Windows Internet Name Service), or DCHP (Dynamic Host Configuration Protocol). The Internet uses DNS as its native naming service; it works by simply mapping IP addresses to their domain names. The WINS naming service also maps domain names to IP addresses, but the service is specific to Microsoft Windows NT. DHCP is more comprehensive; it assigns IP addresses, allocates IP addresses dynamically, centralizes IP address management, and handles addressing conflicts.

Other services besides Microsoft Proxy Server rely on name resolution. So, your organization might already have a naming service in place. If your clients can resolve the name of the Proxy Server, that's all you need. On the other hand, implementing a name resolution system for your private network is not difficult. In fact, if you have Microsoft-based clients and servers, it's downright easy.

Microsoft Windows NT Server 4.0 includes a DNS Server that integrates with WINS and DHCP services. Consequently, it is relatively easy to implement a naming system that resolves host names to network addresses. WINS comes into play by dynamically maintaining a database that uses the NetBIOS names of the client computer in a TCP/IP environment. WINS automatically manages the dynamic updating of all host-to-address information. But WINS is a Microsoft-only protocol, so non-Microsoft clients will need a DNS entry to connect to your Proxy Server.

DHCP, on the other hand, automatically assigns an IP address for all your clients' connections, both Microsoft and non-Microsoft. Anyone who has worked with a mass of IP clients will appreciate the simplicity that DHCP's dynamic IP addressing provides. When DHCP is combined with WINS, your clients' host names and IP addresses are both assigned automatically. This saves a lot of administrative time, especially in Proxy Server environments that have large numbers of clients.

NetBIOS For Small Private Networks

A small single segment, or a single subnet private network, can use NetBIOS to provide name resolution. NetBIOS works with both TCP/IP and IPX, but there are disadvantages to this solution. For example, significant network bandwidth is used by the broadcast traffic and significant client resources are consumed, because every client must examine each broadcast datagram. Also, NetBIOS is not routable, so you can never insert a router into the private network. Consider these limitations carefully before you implement this solution.

Domain Name System (DNS)

DNS is a better solution for larger private networks. In fact, DNS must scale very well as it is the name service for the Internet. Your Proxy Server can serve a dual role and also be the DNS server for your private network using the included Windows NT DNS services. However, in this case you must confirm that the DNS service and any HOSTS files are accessible only to internal network clients. A host file contains IP addresses and their corresponding name. The entries look like this:

```
192.168.0.1        myserver.testbed1.com
192.168.0.10       myserver.client1.com
```

So, in the above example 192.168.0.1 is associated with the server named myserver. testbed1.com. Clients running TCP/IP can look up the name myserver.testbed1.com and find the host at 192.168.0.1. Using a HOSTS file typically is not a good choice if the private network includes more than a few computers. This is even truer when the private network is connected to the Internet. Substantial administrative overhead, potential for security problems, and reliance on administrators to keep the database files up to date combine to make this a poor choice in this situation.

DNS Forwarding

Your organization might already be using DNS for an intranet. If so, and you also have external DNS servers, you will need to turn off recursive forwarding for DNS searches. If DNS is running on an NT Server, you simply make an entry in the Windows NT Registry. Before attempting any change to the registry, make a registry backup. Then, to make the change, run regedt32 on the DNS server computer and add the following Registry entry:

```
HKEY_LOCAL_computer\SYSTEM\CurrentControlSet\Services\DNS
\Parameters\NoRecursion:REG_DWORD:0x1
```

Save your changes. After you complete this change, DNS searches will continue trying the other secondary DNS servers that are specified in the search list.

The above Registry entry will not work with non-NT based DNS. So if you are running a Unix DNS, you will have to review your server's documentation to turn off recursive forwarding.

The potential security threat of a HOSTS file is an important consideration. If external Internet users were to gain access to your HOSTS files and DNS service, your entire private network would be at risk. In addition, DNS must be disabled for the external network adapter. An alternative is using the HOSTS FILE alone for name resolution in a private network that does not use DNS. In any case, if you elect to use a HOSTS file, the file system security must be set to deny Internet users access.

DNS Server Location

The location of your DNS Server will differ based on its purpose. For example, the DNS services could be used for your private network only, or your organization might need to maintain a DNS service for Internet connections. The location of the DNS server depends on whether the service will be used inside the Proxy Server or outside the Proxy Server.

DNS services for Internet-only connections should be installed outside the Proxy Server and on the same segment that connects it to the Internet. An option is to place the Internet DNS services on the Proxy Server itself. Figure 5.7 illustrates the preferred method of placing the DNS server outside of the Proxy Server. Smaller organizations wishing to save money could place the DNS server on the Proxy Server; however, it is very important that the DNS service be installed only on the *external adapter*.

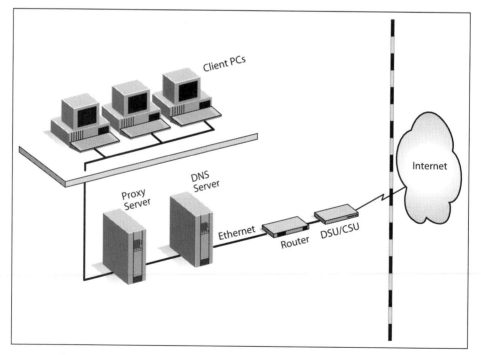

Figure 5.7   Placement of the DNS server for Internet-only connections.

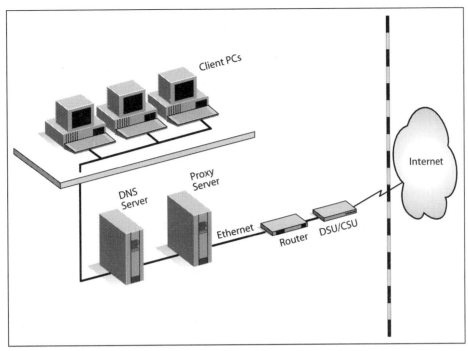

Figure 5.8   Placement of the DNS server for a private network.

Your private network DNS server should be installed inside the Proxy Server and on the segment that connects your Proxy Server to the private network. Figure 5.8 illustrates placing the DNS server inside the Proxy Server. Installing the DNS service on the Proxy Server is also an option. In this case, you must make sure the DNS service is only installed on the *internal adapter*.

DNS Using Multiple Proxy Servers

Multiple Proxy Servers that have clients configured to use all servers evenly will help balance the Internet traffic load in a large installation. For a multiple Proxy Server scenario, each client computer must have at least one DNS entry that points to the IP address of the primary DNS server. The DNS server holds the database that provides DNS resolution. The DNS server will forward all domain name requests to the correct host. For fault tolerance, a secondary DNS server is often used. The secondary DNS server provides name resolution if the primary DNS server fails.

ISPs typically place an exact copy, or *mirror*, of their content on multiple servers in order to achieve fault tolerance and load balancing. A similar technique can be used for multiple Proxy Servers. Again, each Proxy Server has at least one network adapter and at least one unique IP address. The protocol for DNS provides for multiple IP addresses' being associated with one name. For example, let's say we have two Proxy Servers associated with the name myserver.proxy.com. When a request for myserver.proxy.com occurs, the name server returns a complete list of IP addresses associated with myserver.proxy.com. There is no provision in the protocol for ordering the list. Typically, the client's software will use the first entry in the list. But Microsoft Windows NT 4.0 supports the "round-robin" feature, which works by changing the order of the list after resolving each DNS request. The round-robin feature balances the load among the available servers and provides fault tolerance.

The Microsoft Proxy Server client configuration file on each of the client computers needs to be configured appropriately to work with DNS round-robin. In Chapter 8, I'll show you exactly how to edit the mspclnt.ini file for round-robin. This is an important step if you need the load balancing and fault tolerance that round-robin provides.

Windows Internet Name Service (WINS)

WINS is a Microsoft-developed solution for medium to large networks that use Windows NT. For WINS to function correctly, the internal server adapter card must use a permanent IP address, and a default gateway cannot be specified. You wouldn't want Internet users to have access to WINS or related files. So, for security reasons, Internet users must be denied access to WINS services and the LMHOSTS files. Additionally, WINS services must be disabled on the external network adapter.

The WINS Server maintains a database that maps the IP addresses of WINS clients to their computer name, also called the NetBIOS name. WINS remains effective for large networks even though the NetBIOS name is used. This is because WINS is designed to completely eliminate the need for broadcasts to resolve computer names to IP addresses. The WINS database provides a dynamic database that maintains mappings for computer names to IP addresses.

WINS is a good choice for name resolution in a Proxy Server environment. The best implementation is to use Proxy Server as a WINS private network client. Similar to DNS, you can use the LMHOSTS file alone for name resolution in a private network that does not have WINS services. An LMHOSTS file contains IP addresses and their corresponding NetBIOS name. The entries look like this:

```
192.168.0.1       TESTBED1
192.168.0.10      CLIENT1
```

WINS Using Multiple Proxy Servers

The WINS server can be configured for a multihomed environment. In a multihomed environment, like the DNS environment, you create one entry, which contains the list of IP addresses for up to 25 Proxy Server computers. A WINS environment has three levels of name resolution:

➤ IP Address Resolution

➤ Subnet Resolution

➤ Net Resolution

Here is how it works. The WINS Server first matches a client's request with the client's IP address. Then, the WINS Server seeks a Proxy Server computer that has the same subnet as the client. The WINS Server then seeks a Proxy Server computer that has the same net as the client. If WINS cannot match a client to a gateway, it picks a gateway from the WINS list at random. While WINS does offer some degree of load balancing for the Proxy Servers, it is rudimentary when compared with DNS.

Dynamic Host Configuration Protocol (DHCP)

DHCP was designed by the Internet Engineering Task Force (IETF) to reduce the amount of configuration required when using TCP/IP. By making it easier to install TCP/IP on large networks with little user intervention or knowledge required, DHCP eliminates many of the administrative shortcomings of using TCP/IP. Clients can be dynamically assigned an IP address that is leased to them for the duration the administrator desires.

The Proxy Server can also be used as the internal DHCP server. The internal server adapter card must use a permanent IP address, and a default gateway cannot be specified. Only the internal server adapter card can have the DHCP server option enabled. You wouldn't want Microsoft Proxy Server to be a DHCP client on the private network; the Proxy Server should be assigned a permanent IP address. If you have multiple DHCP servers on your private network, Proxy Server can still be a DHCP server.

Default Gateways Using Multiple Proxy Servers

There might be good reason to use multiple Proxy Servers in a large installation. There are some issues to keep in mind as you plan a multiserver installation. For example, it is important to have only one *default gateway* in two nonconnected networks. The default gateway is defined as the intermediate network node on the network or subnet that has addresses for the network IDs of other subnets in the network. In the case of Proxy Server, the default gateway would be the IP address that points to your ISP's Internet router.

Proxy Server itself counts as one nonconnected network because of its positioning as the link between the Internet and your private network. In fact, any proxy server would be nonconnected by design as part of its security model. If two default gateways were defined, the system would be confused into believing that each gateway led to the same set of networks. So, Internet traffic would be sent to the private network and private network traffic would go to the Internet. How's that for a security nightmare? It is important to configure the IP address of the default gateway only on the Proxy Server computer.

What About Multiple Gateway Computers?

You might have multiple gateway computers. If so, you should add persistent routing to them using the Windows NT route command and the utility switch, -p. Then, the persistent routes will remain even when the computer is restarted. The routes are stored in the Windows NT Registry under:

```
HKEY_LOCAL_MACHINE\SYSTEM\CurrentControlSet\Services\TCPIP\PersistentRoutes
```

Software And NT Services

The software and services planning for Proxy Server is straightforward. Besides Proxy Server itself, you will need to be running Microsoft Windows NT 4.0, Service Pack 3 or greater. You also need the Internet Information Server installed and running the Web services, even if you do not intend to host an Internet or intranet Web site. IIS is required for the Web Proxy Services.

Proxy Server Rollout Plan

Access to the Internet usually affects many users in an organization. Carefully planning the Proxy Server rollout will smooth the transition, isolate potential problems, and ensure a successful installation. The rollout for Proxy Server consists of several distinct phases, including the following:

➤ Organize and prepare the executive and planning teams.

➤ Review the results of your needs and security assessments.

➤ Identify the preferred Proxy Server configuration.

➤ Organize and prepare the implementation, administration, and training teams.

➤ Perform lab tests of the Proxy Server client configuration.

➤ Plan the pilot rollout.

➤ Conduct the pilot rollout.

➤ Finalize the rollout plan.

➤ Roll out Internet access through Proxy Server 2.0.

This is a formal rollout plan that is appropriate for many organizations; however, all of these tasks might not be required for your organization. Still, it is wise to survey each step of this plan to determine how to scale it to your needs.

Executive And Planning Teams

In Chapter 3, you learned the importance of bringing your users into the Proxy Server implementation process. It is also important that the executives in your organization understand and support the project, hence the formation of the executive team. Business leaders regard Internet access as both a popular and sensitive topic. The implementation project manager should be an active participant of the executive team, typically acting as the technology liaison.

Internet access can involve many top-level decisions that should be made with the assistance of your executive team and planning team. The team leaders responsible for the implementation, training, and support of Microsoft Proxy Server should participate on the planning team. In a large organization, this includes participants involved in systems support, employee training, corporate standards, and the entire Proxy Server installation team. Persons from other departments in your organization, such as sales, customer support, and accounting, are assigned to this team, but only actively participate during the final rollout phase.

Later in the rollout process the Proxy Server implementation, administration, and user education teams will begin their work. It is strongly recommended that these teams be comprised of at least a few members of the executive and planning teams. A great deal of background information is assessed in the earlier phases that will be of great assistance to the Proxy Server implementation, administration, and training teams.

Review The Needs And Security Assessments

The results of the needs and security assessments assist the executive and planning teams in making informed decisions about how Internet access will benefit the organization, what levels of access are appropriate, and the security measures to put into place. Both of these teams should have a good understanding of the benefits of Microsoft Proxy Server 2.0. This book is written in such a way as to offer substantial benefit to both teams.

Identify The Proxy Server Configuration

In this phase, your planning team should now possess a good understanding of the capabilities of Microsoft Proxy Server 2.0. The needs and security assessments produced a number of criteria that your Proxy Server implementation needs to address. Now it's time to settle on the best ways to configure Proxy Server and its clients in order to meet your organization's expectations. The following questions are examples of questions you must now answer:

➤ How many Proxy Servers does our organization need?

➤ Which distributed caching model best fits our organization: arrays, chains, or a combination of both?

➤ Will access to remote Web sites be restricted? If so, which of the several methods available will be used to deny access?

➤ What kind of connection to the Internet is available? How much bandwidth is required?

It's also time to come up with the ideal client configuration and determine what Internet applications will be supported by the organization. It is likely that different groups within the organization require different configurations. Evaluate each configuration for functionality, bandwidth efficiency, and ease of support.

The Implementation, Administration, And Training Teams

There are three teams you need to organize and prepare in this phase of the rollout plan: the Proxy Server implementation, administration, and training teams. The Proxy Server implementation team includes all the technical professionals who will complete the installation. The Proxy Server administration team includes the persons who will administer and support the server and the clients. In addition, this team includes the technical professionals who will maintain the security features of Proxy Server. The duties of the Proxy Server administration team are further detailed below. Finally, the Proxy Server user education team works directly with the employees to assure an understanding of the Internet applications and how, from a user's point of view, they work with Proxy Server. The Proxy Server user education team also instructs each user on their responsibilities for safeguarding a secure environment.

There are numerous Proxy Server administrative tasks that will need to be performed periodically. Before you actually implement the Proxy Server for your organization, you need to determine who the administrator or administrators are for your Proxy Server services. This is a crucial, but often overlooked, part of any implementation plan. The benefits of Proxy Server will be decreased if you fail to plan for the administrative tasks. I've organized the Proxy Server administrative responsibilities into three major categories: server administration, security administration, and client administration.

Server Administration

The responsibility for administrating the server or servers that Proxy Server is installed on is best suited to someone who is fluent in the operation of Microsoft Windows NT 4.0, Internet Information Server, RAS (Remote Access Server), and TCP/IP concepts. The administrative tasks include setting all of the server parameters, such as:

➤ Configuring automatic dial-out.

➤ Configuring and maintaining the Local Address Table (LAT).

➤ Configuring, performance tuning, and maintaining caching.

➤ Configuring, performing, and verifying backup and restore procedures.

➤ Configuring, performance tuning, and maintaining Proxy Server arrays, chained Proxy Server computers, and integration other types of servers in your network.

➤ Monitoring server performance, including viewing service counters and logs to isolate performance problems.

➤ Troubleshooting Proxy Server.

Security Administration

Sound administration of the security policies is critical for the success of Proxy Server. These tasks are assigned to someone who understands Internet security, TCP/IP, Well-known ports, and the security features of Microsoft Windows NT 4.0 and the Internet Information Server. These administrative tasks include:

➤ Configuring password authentications.

➤ Configuring user permissions, protocol, and port permissions.

➤ Configuring domain filters, packet filters, and alerts.

➤ Configuring properties for the three service logs and the packet log.

➤ Troubleshooting security issues.

Client Administration

The Client administrator is the human interface to Proxy Server services. Good people skills are very important to carrying out these administrative responsibilities. These tasks are assigned to someone who understands Internet security, TCP/IP, Well-known ports, the security features of Microsoft Windows NT 4.0, Internet Information Server, Internet and TCP/IP applications, scripting configuration files, and the client operating system in use at your organization. These administrative tasks include:

➤ Configuring client Internet and TCP/IP applications.

➤ Configuring the client LAT properties.

➤ Creating the client configuration script.

➤ Troubleshooting clients.

Although it appears that three persons are required to administer a Proxy Server, this is not the case. In small organizations, a single person will administer the Proxy Server, while larger organizations might have several persons working on different aspects of

Proxy Server administration. The above categories simply serve as a starting point for assigning administrative duties for your staff—even if you *are* the staff. No matter what, be absolutely sure that the above responsibilities are assigned prior to the Proxy Server pilot rollout.

Proxy Server Client Configuration Tests

A series of lab tests should be performed using the client configuration previously identified. The lab test will confirm that it works as expected and is compatible with the client Internet software. If the configuration needs to be modified, tweaked, or otherwise experimented with, this is the phase in which to do it. It is also possible to do comparisons with various configurations at this time. You might find that different configurations work better for different departments in the organization. It is always best, if possible, to have a single standard configuration. So, make sure the gains of different Proxy Server client configurations are worth the added support risks and costs.

Plan The Pilot Rollout

Now, having found the most suitable Proxy Server client configurations, it's time to plan the pilot rollout. In this phase you need to test the installation if multiple servers will be deployed, settle on the pilot rollout logistics and complete the user training plan.

In multiple Proxy Server environments, a single server should be installed and tested thoroughly before you proceed with the pilot rollout. While you're testing the installation, it's a great time to construct a checklist for use during the rollout. Identify any potential problems to watch for during the pilot. Finally, document the process meticulously. Details count.

Conduct The Pilot Rollout

The idea of a pilot Proxy Server rollout is to mimic the final rollout, just on a smaller scale. The key word in this phase is *feedback*. How does the Proxy Server perform, do the users notice a difference, what problems occurred? Each problem found in this stage, as trite as it might sound, is an opportunity to make the final rollout go more smoothly. Greet the users' suggestions and complaints with that thought in mind and, whatever you do, do not become defensive. Remember that your job is to improve the system, not defend it. Also pay close attention to the time it takes to complete each task. Out of the lab, tasks can vary wildly in the time required for completion. Use the information to improve and refine the rollout plan.

Select your pilot user group wisely and train them just as you would in the final rollout. Be sure your users have time to assist with the pilot and have an active need to use the Internet. Any information gaps in the training program should be documented and filled prior to the final rollout. The complete Proxy Server administrative team should be available to assist with problems and provide support for the users. This is a valuable learning experience for the Proxy Server administrative team.

Monitor the pilot program for at least a week to be sure that the Proxy Server system is operating well. At the end of the pilot rollout, survey your users. Your goal is to find anything that might make the final rollout go better and the system operate smoothly. You will refine your final Proxy Server rollout plan from the survey information obtained during the pilot. If the pilot did not go well, be prepared to repeat the process. You should finalize the rollout plan only when you have completed a reasonably smooth pilot rollout.

Finalize The Rollout Plan

With the information provided by the pilot, you are now prepared to put the finishing touches on the rollout plan. The executive and planning teams share the responsibility for planning the final Proxy Server rollout. It's important to be sure that you have all the resources required for the final rollout. Security policies should be distributed prior to the final rollout, and user training should be scheduled. The users need a full and complete understanding of their responsibilities for security. Finally, communicate with the users about the time of the final rollout. Be sure that any inconveniences, such as client computers being down, are communicated in order to give the users an opportunity to plan their work around the down time.

Roll Out Internet Access Through Proxy Server 2.0

Your Proxy Server rollout has been planned, tested, refined, and improved. Now, you are ready to put your final plan into motion. By going through each step of the rollout planning process, you should be assured a smooth rollout. Of course, something will go wrong, but you will be organized and prepared to resolve the problems. The benefits of Microsoft Proxy Server are now ready to be used effectively by your organization.

I know the above process sounds like it would take a huge staff, but it is really scalable to any size organization. You might be part of a small organization that has only one technical support person: you. The same rollout process works, you just have to assume more roles. You also work with fewer users, so less can go wrong. The rollout process really isn't difficult, it is a good way to organize, to plan, and to confront problems before they become mission critical.

Moving On

When a Proxy Server is introduced into the organization, it heavily impacts both your organization's technology infrastructure and the people who use it. There are a lot of details to plan for, but the reward is great: easy, fast, and secure Internet access. In this chapter we covered an enormous amount of information: hardware requirements, Internet

five

service providers, bandwidth requirements, telecommunications, name resolution, and more. Each of these items represents important decisions that must be made prior to implementing Microsoft Proxy Server. But what is most important is your rollout plan, because this plan takes everything you've learned and applies it to your organization. By following my guidelines you've come up with a solid plan, and Proxy Server promises to be a substantial benefit to your organization.

In the next chapter we will go through the actual Proxy Server software installation process. Because you've planned the installation up front, the actual installation process will go smoothly and your understanding of the installation options will be clear. Now let's install Proxy Server 2.0.

Installing And Configuring Microsoft Proxy Server

This chapter guides you through the hands-on experience of installing and configuring Microsoft Proxy Server 2.0. In Chapter 5, you went through the process of planning your Proxy Server installation. Now, you put those plans to work and actually install and configure the Proxy Server computer and clients.

There are several different phases to installing and configuring Microsoft Proxy Server 2.0. First, you prepare the hardware for the installation of the server. You need to pay close attention to the details of your hardware including network adapters, modems, ISDN adapters, and the hard disk system. Next, you install and configure Windows NT 4.0, Service Pack 3, Internet Information Server (IIS), and Proxy Server 2.0. Finally, you set up the Proxy Server clients. While there are many steps, installing and configuring Microsoft Proxy Server is not particularly difficult. The collection of procedures detailed below can guide you through a successful installation on your first try.

Windows NT Server Installation

Your Proxy Server 2.0 installation begins with setting up the Windows NT server on which your Proxy Server will run. Microsoft Proxy Server is closely integrated with Windows NT Server and IIS. So, Proxy Server 2.0 requires that Windows NT Server version 4.0, service pack 3 (or greater), and Microsoft Internet Information Server 3.0 (or greater) be installed and running prior to installation. Although it is not absolutely necessary, it is a good idea to start with a fresh installation of Windows NT Server. This procedure helps isolate any problems that might occur with the installation, and it minimizes the problem of conflicting .DLL files.

A fresh installation begins with formatting the hard disk drives that will be used on the server. For security reasons, NTFS (NT File System) should be used for all volumes. If you have a multi-disk drive system where the drives have disparate performance, plan on placing the NTFS volumes that will be used for Proxy Server caching, logs, and backup configurations on the highest performance drive.

Hard Disk Drive Preparation

Caching performance is dependent on several factors, the most important being the use of fast disk drives; multiple fast disk drives are even better. Ideally, a large Proxy Server cache would be broken up into several smaller caches, thereby providing quicker access to the objects in the cache. Although not ideal, Proxy Server can use but a single disk drive for small workgroups. Allocate a large enough cache for the size of your workgroup. I recommend using 100 MB + 1 MB for each Proxy Server client. Don't struggle too much with making the Proxy Server cache the perfect size, it is a straightforward administrative task to increase the cache size at a later time.

During the Proxy Server installation you will select the disk drives to be used for caching. Proxy Server requires that NTFS be used on all cached volumes. However, I would highly recommend that only NTFS volumes be used on the entire Windows NT Server supporting Proxy Server 2.0. FAT volumes do not possess any provisions for user permissions and are therefore not secure. It makes little sense to use a Proxy Server for Internet security and then place the operating system, or anything else for that matter, on a FAT volume. Take a look at a few of the benefits of NTFS:

➤ Tight integration with Windows NT security system, permitting the control and auditing of file, share, and directory access.

➤ Support for compression on objects ranging from a directory to a single file.

➤ A recoverable file system that includes an activity log, which can be used to restore the disk in the event of a corrupted disk.

➤ A maximum file size of up to 64 GB.

NTFS provides many benefits over FAT; use NTFS on your server.

Tip

If you have a current Windows NT 4.0 server that uses FAT partitions, you can convert these partitions to NTFS by using the CONVERT utility included with Windows NT 4.0. CONVERT is a handy utility, because it does not overwrite data. To convert a FAT volume to NTFS, click Start, point to Programs, and click on Command Prompt. Then simply type:

```
CONVERT drive: /FS:NTFS
```

You cannot CONVERT the current drive or the boot drive while Windows NT is running. Also, CONVERT is a one-way process; you cannot use it to later convert back to FAT.

Upgrading From Proxy Server 1.0?

If you are upgrading from Proxy Server 1.0, you might have used FAT volumes for caching. These volumes will have to be converted to NTFS prior to Proxy Server 2.0's installation. The Quick Format command can speed up the installation process when you are upgrading from a Microsoft Proxy Server version 1.0 that used large cache on a volume separate from the operating system. Before upgrading to Proxy Server 2.0, stop the WWW service of Internet Information Server and type the following command:

```
format [drive letter] /q
```

But please be careful! The Quick Format command will delete all of the data on the disk to which it is applied, so you should only perform this operation if the volume is used for caching only.

Network Adapter Configuration

Proxy Server requires a network adapter for connection to your internal private network. You also need a network adapter, modem, or ISDN adapter connected to the external Internet for a typical single Proxy Server installation. An exception is if you are setting up multiple Proxy Server computers in a chained or cascaded configuration; then only the most upstream Proxy Server should be connected to the Internet. Also, if Proxy Server is behind a firewall, or another third-party proxy server, only a single internal network adapter is required.

So, typically at least one of your Proxy Server computers is different from most Windows NT Server installations because two network adapters are used: one for the internal private network connection, and the other for the external Internet connection. The Internet connection can use a network adapter attached to a router, an ISDN adapter, or a modem. When examining network adapter cards using the network utility in the control panel, Windows NT helps by identifying each adapter with a leading number. For example:

[1] 3Com Fast EtherLink XL Adapter (3C905)
[2] 3Com Fast EtherLink XL Adapter (3C905)

The above illustrates that two 3C905 cards are installed in the Windows NT Server. When changing a configuration, you would use the numbers [1] or [2] to distinguish between the specific physical adapters. This is particularly helpful if device conflicts occur during installation. The base I/O and IRQ settings must be unique for each physical network adapter, in addition to all other devices installed in your computer. Additionally, when you use multiple adapters in the same computer, a special configuration might be required. There are innumerable configuration variations for network adapters; so, whichever adapter you use, make a point of reading its documentation.

Your Proxy Server will require a permanent reserved IP address along with an appropriate subnet mask for your private network. Also, while you are working with the network settings, disable DHCP (Dynamic Host Configuration Protocol). DHCP will attempt to reset the default gateway you selected for Proxy Server.

Internal Network Adapter Configuration

Internal network adapters are set up much like any network adapter for a private network. You do need to pay close attention that the IP Default Gateway is *not* specified for the internal network adapter. Only the external network adapter will use the IP Default Gateway. Additionally, if your private network uses DNS, WINS, or DHCP, then your internal network adapter must be configured to work with selected naming services. Follow the suggestions made in Chapter 5 to guide your selection of a naming service.

To install the internal network adapter, follow these steps:

1. Open up the computer case and install the network adapter in an appropriate free slot on the motherboard.

2. Start the server to proceed with the network adapter's installation.

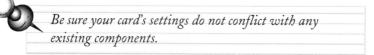

> *Be sure your card's settings do not conflict with any existing components.*

3. Click Start, point to settings, and click Control Panel.

4. Open the Network utility in the Control Panel, and then click on the Adapters tab (see Figure 6.1).

5. Click the network adapter description that matches your hardware, and then click Add.

6. Click on the Bindings tab and disable any bindings that are not used on your internal private network.

> *Network bindings are the connections between the network cards, protocols, and services that exist on your computer.*

7. In the Show Bindings For list, click All Protocols.

8. Select the protocol(s) that you will be using. For example: If you will be using the Web Proxy Service, click on the TCP/IP Protocol, and then Enable.

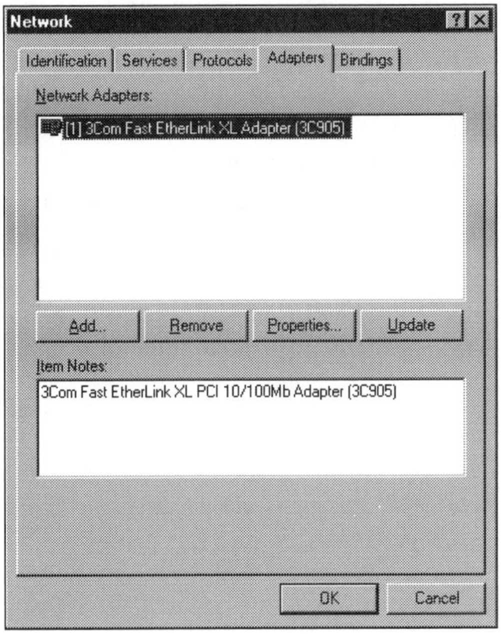

Figure 6.1   The Adapters tab in the Network utility.

Only the WinSock Proxy Service can use the NWLink IPX/SPX protocol.

9. Click on the Protocols tab, and then click Properties to select the appropriate network properties for the selected protocol.

External Network Adapter Configuration

External Network Adapters must be set up using TCP/IP. Your ISP will provide the correct settings for your connection. Make sure you obtain the following information:

➤ The IP address for your Internet Domain or your ISP's IP address as applicable.

➤ The subnet mask.

➤ The default gateway.

➤ The domain name used for DNS (Domain Name System).

➤ The IP addresses for DNS servers that are used for DNS name searches.

Also, it is possible that your ISP uses other protocols, such as DHCP or BOOTP, so check your ISP's documentation for these protocol settings if appropriate.

The IP default gateway is only configured on the external network adapter. Modems and some ISDN adapters are configured for the IP default gateway in a different way, using Dial-Up Networking (DUN). This procedure is covered later in this chapter in the section on "Modem And ISDN Adapter Configuration." Also, dial-up accounts typically use Proxy Server's Auto Dial feature. To implement this feature, you must install the Windows NT RAS (Remote Access Service) client.

To install the external network adapter, follow these steps:

1. Open up the computer case and install the network adapter in an appropriate free slot on the motherboard.

2. Start the server to proceed with the network adapter's installation.

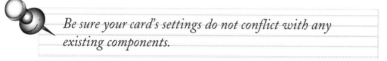
Be sure your card's settings do not conflict with any existing components.

3. Click Start, point to settings, and then click Control Panel.

4. Open the Network utility in the Control Panel, and then click on the Adapters tab.

5. Click on the network adapter description that matches your hardware, and then click Add.

6. Click on the Bindings tab and disable any bindings that are not used on your internal private network.

Network bindings are the connections between the network cards, protocols, and services that exist on your computer.

7. In the Show Bindings For list, click All Protocols.

8. Click on the TCP/IP Protocol, and then click Enable.

9. Click on the Protocols tab, and then click Properties to select the appropriate network properties for your Internet connection (see Figure 6.2).

Modem And ISDN Adapter Configuration

A dial-up connection to the Internet through Microsoft Proxy Server is a reasonable means to connect a small workgroup to the Internet. In this scenario, a modem or ISDN adapter must be configured for your Proxy Server computer. Additionally, the Windows NT RAS client must be configured as it is used by Proxy Server's Auto Dial feature.

Figure 6.2   Enabling the TCP/IP protocol.

A Proxy Server using a modem for a dial-up connection permits only minimal band-width, so use the highest common speed supported by both your modem and your ISP.

To install a modem, follow these steps:

1. Click Start, point to settings, and then click Control Panel.

2. Click on the Modem icon to run the Modem utility.

3. The New Modem Wizard runs automatically for the first modem installation.

4. Let the New Modem Wizard detect your modem by leaving Don't Detect my Modem unchecked (see Figure 6.3).

5. Click Next, and the Wizard begins a scan of your COM ports to identify your particular modem.

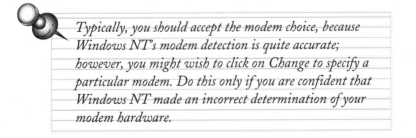

Typically, you should accept the modem choice, because Windows NT's modem detection is quite accurate; however, you might wish to click on Change to specify a particular modem. Do this only if you are confident that Windows NT made an incorrect determination of your modem hardware.

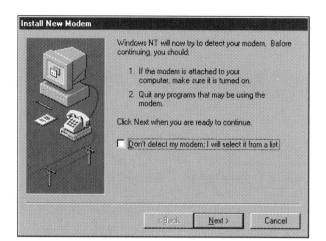

Figure 6.3 The Install New Modem wizard.

6. Click Next, to accept the selected modem.

7. When the message that Your modem has been set up successfully appears, click Finish.

ISDN adapters can be internal cards or external devices. An ISDN adapter must be installed and configured, or provisioned, to work with your computer, your telephone service, and, sometimes, your ISP. Typically, an ISDN adapter will include detailed documentation about *provisioning* the adapter to work with your telephone company. "Provisioning" is the term your telephone company will use for the configuration of your line on the telephone company's end. An ISDN line has many parameters that must be defined in accordance with your telephone company's requirements in order for the line to function, so expect some interaction with your telephone company about these details. When selecting any ISDN adapter, pay close attention to its reported ease of installation, because ISDN adapters are notorious for being difficult to install and configure. Several models on the market today offer significant advances in ease of installation over ISDN adapters in even the recent past. The leading ISDN adapter manufacturers will work with your phone company on your behalf, offering a guarantee of a swift and successful installation. These models are well worth your consideration.

External ISDN adapters are installed similarly to a modem. Typically, the manufacturer of your external ISDN adapter will have special instructions that you should follow to set up the device and to install the appropriate device driver for Windows NT. The best advice for external ISDN adapters is to follow your manufacturer's instructions carefully (see Figure 6.4).

Internal ISDN adapters are installed in a fashion similar to a network adapter. Follow the previous instructions for network adapters and follow your manufacturer's instructions for installation of the device driver for the ISDN adapter.

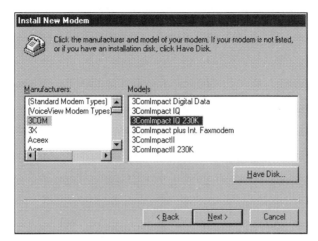

Figure 6.4   Installing an external ISDN adapter.

● ● *Tip* ● ● ● ●

You must restart the Proxy Server computer after the installation of the ISDN device drivers. Doing this ensures that all available ISDN ports are listed when you proceed to the configuration of the Remote Access Service for ISDN.

RAS Client Installation And Configuration

The Remote Access Server (RAS) client must be installed if you are using a dial-up connection to your ISP. It's best to think of RAS installation and configuration as consisting of the following phases:

➤ Hardware installation and configuration.

➤ Serial ports configuration.

➤ RAS client installation and configuration.

The successful installation and configuration of the hardware is the first phase. Follow the aforementioned procedures for installing your modem or ISDN adapter.

Next, configure your serial port, using parameters that are compatible with both your ISP and modem or ISDN adapter. External ISDN adapters that are configured for 128 kilobits per second (kbps) operation and a few high-speed external modems will benefit from an accelerated serial port card. This type of serial card will allow the higher port speed I discussed in the "Serial Ports" section in Chapter 5. These cards normally require a special device driver for their high-speed operation. In this phase, however, I would set the port speed at 57,600 or 115,000, assuring first that the modem or external ISDN adapter works properly. I would only configure and test the high-speed drivers after the RAS client is installed and you have connected successfully to your ISP. This procedure helps to isolate any accelerated driver problem that might arise.

six

Next, install the RAS client. While RAS permits dial-in or dial-out connections, only the dial-out service should be implemented for Proxy Server. A Proxy Server computer should never be used for dial-in connections, as security would be compromised.

To install the RAS client, follow these steps:

1. Click Start, point to Settings, and click Control Panel.

2. Open the Network utility in the Control Panel, click on the Services tab, and then click Add.

3. Click Remote Access Service in the Select Network Service dialog box, and then click on OK (see Figure 6.5).

4. Select a port in the Remote Access Setup dialog box, and then click Configure.

5. Click Dial Out Only in the Configure Port Usage dialog box, and then click on OK.

6. Click Network in the Remote Access Setup dialog box.

7. Click TCP/IP in the Network Configuration dialog box, and then click on OK.

8. Click Continue in the Remote Access Setup dialog box.

9. Click Close in the Network dialog box.

10. Click Yes, when prompted to restart your computer.

After your Proxy Server computer restarts, determine if RAS is working properly. Test your configuration by establishing a connection to your ISP. If for any reason this operation fails, go back to your settings for your ISP and make sure everything was entered correctly, then retest your ISP connection. Finally, when all is working well, turn your attention to the accelerated serial port card, if you will be using one. Follow the manufacturer's instructions for the installation and configuration of the card and its drivers, then retest your ISP connection.

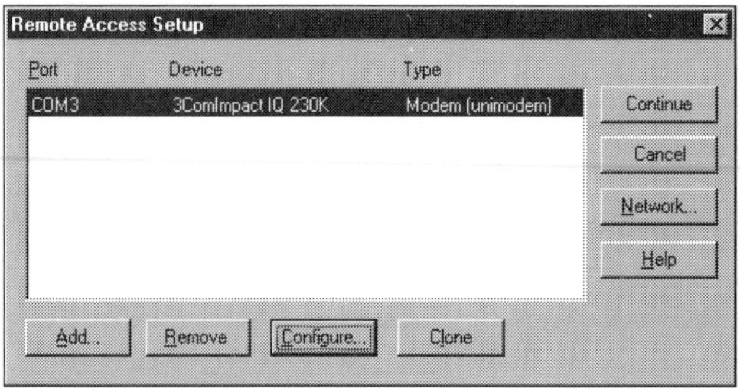

Figure 6.5 The Remote Access Setup dialog box.

Windows NT Configuration

Configuring Windows NT 4.0 correctly is an important phase of a Proxy Server instal- lation. Proxy Server 2.0 is closely integrated with Windows NT 4.0. You must have Windows NT 4.0 correctly configured for Proxy Server 2.0 to operate correctly. This section covers the configuration of Domains, Routing Tables, the IIS (Internet Infor- mation Server) Web Proxy Port, IPX/SPX network parameters, application of Service Pack 3, and other configuration issues. It is important to read this section even if you are installing Proxy Server on an existing Windows NT Server.

Windows NT Domain Configuration

Ideally, the server that is running Proxy Server 2.0 should act as a stand-alone Windows NT 4.0 server in its own domain. This will assure you the highest performance and the highest security.

A Proxy Server computer can also run as a primary domain controller or a backup do- main controller. Primary domain controllers store the master copy of the domain's users and group database; backup domain controllers store backup copies of the domain's us- ers and group database. While the server can run these services together with the Proxy Server application, a negative impact on performance might occur in large installations. Also, a security breach could result in a hacker's obtaining a copy of your domain data- base, potentially jeopardizing your entire private network. While this is unlikely, the consequences could be serious. If at all possible, configure the server that is running Proxy Server as a standalone server.

If you have multiple domains within a larger internal network, you might need to up Proxy Server as a primary domain controller (PDC) within its own domain. In this scenario, a single one-way trust relationship is established to another domain on your private network. This makes Proxy Server the trusting domain and your other private network domain the trusted domain. Therefore, a security breach would only endanger the Proxy Server computer, because no internal Windows NT server trusts the domain used for the Proxy Server. In multi-Proxy Server configurations, all Proxy Server com- puters should be added to the domain created for Proxy Server.

You should add the domain structure prior to installing Proxy Server when bringing up a new Windows NT server. Also, users and groups will have to be added; however, these accounts can be added at any time, before or after the installation of Proxy Server 2.0. See Chapter 4 for more information on using and managing Windows NT domains, users, and groups with Proxy Server.

Enabling Routing And Remote Access Service

six

You can enable both Routing and Remote Access Service (RRAS) with a little extra work. There is a hotfix for RRAS that needs to be installed. The hotfix resolves the security, reliability, and integration problems associated with using both Routing and Remote Access Service together. You will need to download a file located at http://www.microsoft.com/proxy/support/.

After you have downloaded the file, execute x86iprtr.exe to extract and expand two files: iprtrmgr.dll and readme.txt. Follow the installation instructions carefully in readme.txt. Properly installed, RRAS will provide a secure enterprise inter-networking solution.

Routing Table Configuration

There is a command-line program called the *route utility* that is used to configure the Windows NT routing table. Using the route utility allows you to specify all the static IP addresses that comprise your internal private network. Proxy Server will then be able to build its Local Address Table (LAT) correctly, allowing the network adapters that are used throughout your private network to be accessed. If the LAT is built incorrectly, or not at all, a client request for an IP address on your internal private network might be routed instead to the Internet or to the Web Proxy service. I'll discuss the specifics of LAT configuration later in this chapter in the sections titled "The LAT" and "Configuring The LAT."

Web Proxy Port Configuration

The Web Proxy service by default listens on port 80. This is the well-known port for HTTP, the protocol of World Wide Web. For security reasons, you might wish to change this port number to a less obvious one. While this change can be made after installing Proxy Server, you would also have to edit the WebProxyPort value in the client configuration file (Mspclnt.ini). So, making the change prior to Proxy Server's installation is somewhat more convenient.

You use the Internet Service Manager to change the WWW service port number. The following procedure will set the WWW service port number of IIS to the value you specify:

1. Click Start, point to programs, point to Microsoft Internet Server (common), and then click Internet Service Manager to open it.

2. Double-click the computer name next to the WWW service to open the WWW Service Properties dialog box (see Figure 6.6).

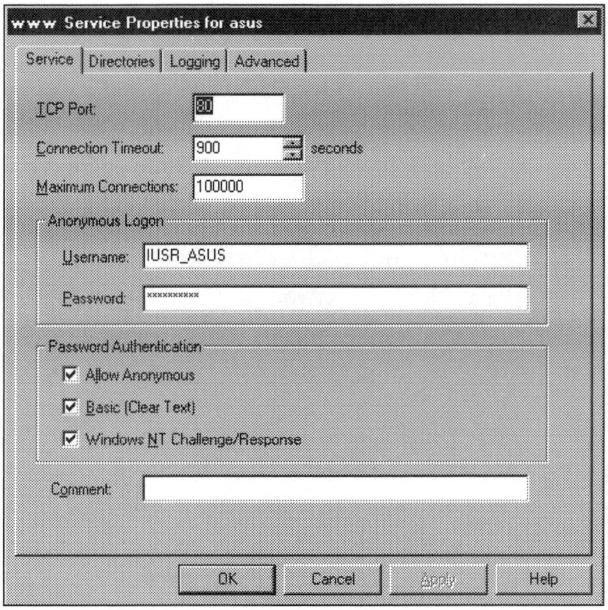

Figure 6.6   The WWW Service Properties dialog box.

3. Change the number in the TCP Port on the Service tab to the new port number, and then click on OK.

4. Stop and restart the WWW service in the Internet Service Manager.

IPX/SPX Network Configuration

IPX/SPX is a popular protocol for private networks, because it is easy to set up, fast, and routable. But, for Proxy Server to operate correctly with IPX/SPX clients, you will have to make some changes to each Windows NT server on which Proxy Server will be installed. Additionally, each Windows NT Workstation and Windows 95 client computer will require changes to allow IPX/SPX communication to work with Proxy Server. The changes that you make will vary, depending on your choice of network topology, either Ethernet or Token Ring, and on whether or not your installation uses Novell NetWare servers.

• • • *Tip* • • • •

If your installation uses Microsoft Windows 3.1 or Windows for Workgroups 3.11 clients, note that Proxy Server does not support the IPX/SPX protocols on these operating systems. In this case, you will have to use the TCP/IP protocol to successfully connect to Proxy Server. Also, only Novell's 32-bit IPX/SPX stacks are supported for Windows 95 clients. Novell's 16-bit IPX/SPX stacks are not supported.

Confused About Network Numbers?

The network number specifies the hexadecimal number that is used for a given adapter. The default network number is 0, and this number is especially important. The number 0 tells NWLink to get the network number from the network while it is running.

IPX network numbers are eight hex characters long, or four bytes. For example, ABDF1459 would be a valid IPX network number. However, you really don't need to enter a specific value, because NWLink will determine it for you if the number is left at 00000000. If your system uses specific network numbers, just be sure they all match.

The process is straightforward with Novell NetWare servers or IPX routers that provide the IPX frame type and network address. In this case, both the server and the client IPX configuration can be set to Auto. This forces Proxy Server and its clients to acquire their IPX settings automatically.

Name resolution for WinSock Proxy clients is provided by the Windows NT Service Advertising Protocol (SAP) service. Although the IPX name resolution is not required for WinSock Proxy service to operate correctly, it should be installed if you will be using the Chkwsp32 diagnostic utility from a client computer that uses the IPX/SPX protocol. The Chkwsp32 diagnostic utility simply checks to determine that the WinSock Proxy service is functioning properly.

What follows are sets of configuration procedures that are used for Windows NT Servers and Proxy Server clients. Specifically, I'll show procedures for configuring the IPX/SPX parameters for the following scenarios:

➤ Windows NT Server on a network *with* NetWare servers.

➤ Windows NT Server on an Ethernet network *with no* NetWare servers.

➤ Windows NT Server on a Token Ring network *with no* NetWare servers.

➤ Windows NT Workstation clients.

➤ Windows 95 clients.

Also, when using these procedures, pay close attention to the internal network numbers set on your server and client computers—they all must match.

The following procedure is used to configure IPX/SPX parameters for a Windows NT Server that is networked *with* NetWare servers:

1. Click Start, point to settings, and click Control Panel.

2. Double-click on the Network utility in the Control Panel, and then click on the Bindings tab.

3. Click on All Protocols in the Show Bindings For list.

4. Double-click the NWLink IPX/SPX Compatible Transport.

5. Click the appropriate external network adapter, then click the Disable button. The selected adapter will then be shown with a red "No" symbol, signifying it is disabled.

6. Click the Move Up button until the same external adapter is at the top of the list under NWLink IPX/SPX Compatible Transport.

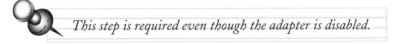

This step is required even though the adapter is disabled.

7. Click the Protocols tab in the Network utility, and then double-click NWLink IPX/SPX Compatible Transport to reveal the properties for NWLink IPX/SPX.

8. On the General tab, in the Internal Network Number field, type the appropriate 8-digit address. Also on the General tab, in the Frame Type, select Auto Frame Type Detection.

9. Click on OK, and then click Close.

10. Click Yes, when prompted to restart your computer.

The above procedures illustrate that IPX clients autoconfigure IPX settings when a Windows NT Server is networked with a Novell NetWare server. Many networks do not have a Novell NetWare server, but still use the IPX/SPX protocol for its advantages on a LAN. Unfortunately, IPX clients will not autoconfigure their IPX settings correctly without a Novell NetWare server. This is because the Windows NT Server does not respond to a client broadcast for the external network number. Defining the external network number and frame type on the Windows NT Server won't help. What follows are two procedures that you will find helpful for configuring IPX clients with no Novell Netware Servers. The first procedure is for Ethernet, and the next is for Token Ring.

The following procedure is used to configure IPX/SPX parameters on an Ethernet network topology when using a Windows NT Server that is networked *with no* NetWare servers:

1. Click Start, point to settings, and click Control Panel.

2. Double-click on the Network utility in the Control Panel, and then click on the Bindings tab.

3. Click on All protocols in the Show Bindings For list.

4. Double-click the NWLink IPX/SPX Compatible Transport.

5. Click the appropriate external network adapter, then click the Disable button. The selected adapter will then be shown with a red "No" symbol, signifying it is disabled.

6. Click the Move Up button until the same external adapter is at the top of the list under NWLink IPX/SPX Compatible Transport.

This step is required even though the adapter is disabled.

7. Click the Protocols tab in the Network utility, and then double-click NWLink IPX/SPX Compatible Transport to reveal the properties for NWLink IPX/SPX.

8. On the General tab, in the Internal Network Number field, type the appropriate 8-digit address. Then, in the Frame Type field, select Manual Frame Type Detection; in the Manual Frame Detection dialog box, in Frame Type, click Ethernet 802.3; and in Network Number, type the appropriate 8-digit address (see Figure 6.7).

9. Click Add, and then click on OK.

10. Click Yes, when prompted to restart your computer.

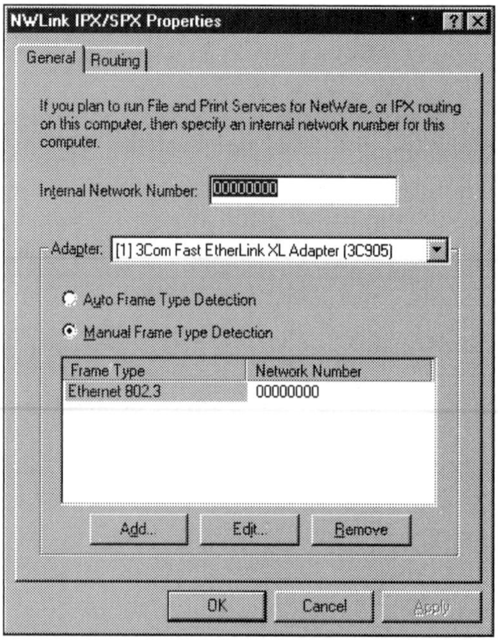

Figure 6.7   NWLink IPX/SPX Properties dialog box.

The following procedure is used to configure IPX/SPX parameters on a Token Ring network topology when using a Windows NT Server that is networked *with no* NetWare servers:

1. Click Start, point to settings, and click Control Panel.

2. Double-click on the Network utility in the Control Panel, and then click on the Bindings tab.

3. Click on All protocols in the Show Bindings For list.

4. Double-click the NWLink IPX/SPX Compatible Transport.

5. Click the appropriate external network adapter, then click the Disable button. The selected adapter will then be shown with a red "No" symbol, signifying it is disabled.

6. Click the Move Up button until the same external adapter is at the top of the list under NWLink IPX/SPX Compatible Transport.

This step is required even though the adapter is disabled.

7. Click the Protocols tab in the Network utility, and then double-click NWLink IPX/SPX Compatible Transport to reveal the properties for NWLink IPX/SPX.

8. On the General tab, in the Internal Network Number field, type the appropriate 8-digit address.

9. Click on OK, and then click Close.

10. Click Yes, when prompted to restart your computer.

The following procedure is used to configure the IPX/SPX parameters for Windows NT Workstation Client Computers (see Figure 6.8):

1. Click Start, point to settings, and click Control Panel.

2. Double-click on the Network utility in the Control Panel, and then click on the Protocols tab.

3. Double-click the NWLink IPX/SPX Compatible Transport.

4. Also on the General tab, in the Frame Type, select Auto Frame Type Detection. If necessary, on the General tab, in the Internal Network Number field, type the appropriate 8-digit address.

5. Click on OK, and then click Close.

6. Click Yes, when prompted to restart your computer.

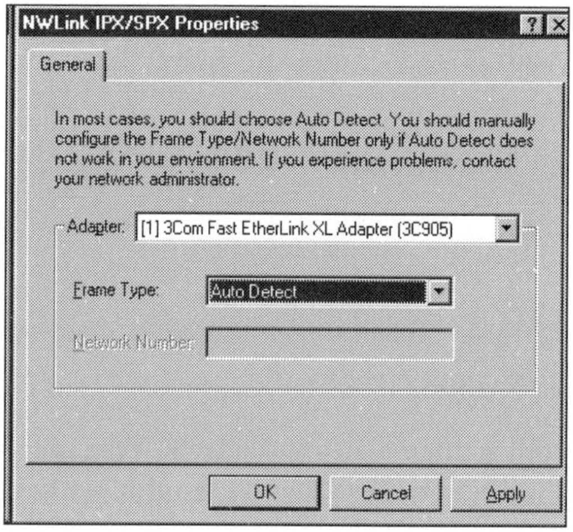

Figure 6.8 NWLink IPX/SPX Properties dialog box.

The following procedure is used to configure the IPX/SPX parameters for Windows 95 Client Computers:

1. Click Start, point to settings, and click Control Panel.

2. Double-click on the Network utility in the Control Panel, and then click the Bindings tab.

3. Double-click the NWLink IPX/SPX Compatible Protocol on the Configuration tab.

4. Click I Want to Enable Netbios Over IPX/SPX on the Netbios tab.

5. In Frame Type on the Advance tab, click Auto, in Network Address click 0, and finally, click Auto Frame Type Detection.

6. Click on OK, and then click Close.

7. Click Yes, when prompted to restart your computer.

Windows NT Service Pack Installation

Windows NT Service Pack 3 will need to be installed on the Windows NT 4.0 Server that will run Proxy Server 2.0 prior to the installation of Proxy Server. The international version of Service Pack 3 is furnished on the Proxy Server compact disc. See the sidebar "Service Pack 3 & PCT/SSL Security Provider," if you need the full 128-bit PCT/SSL Security Provider. Also, note that Windows NT Service Pack 3 must be reinstalled after Microsoft Index Server is installed on your Proxy Server computer.

Service Pack 3 And PCT/SSL Security Providers

There are two versions of Service Pack 3 for Windows NT 4.0, so you will have to make a decision regarding the PCT/SSL Security Provider. The Service Pack 3 contained on the Proxy Server compact disc is the international version, which provides the 40-bit version of the PCT/SSL Security Provider. If full 128-bit Secure Socket Layer functionality is important to your organization, and if you are located in the United States or Canada, you need to contact Microsoft to obtain the 128-bit update for Service Pack 3. Alternatively, if the 128-bit version of the PCT/SSL Security Provider is already installed on your system, you could skip the upgrade of this component when installing Service Pack 3. However, I would still order the 128-bit update. If you were to inadvertently overwrite the 128-bit version of the PCT/SSL Security Provider, it would be much easier to recover with the proper version of Service Pack 3.

The following procedure is used to install the Windows NT 4.0 Service Pack 3:

1. Go to the root directory on the Proxy Server compact disc.

2. Double-click the Ntupdate folder, and then double-click the folder that represents your computer processor (either I386 or Alpha).

3. Double-click Update.exe to run the installation for Service Pack 3.

4. Upon completion of the Service Pack installation, click Yes, when prompted to restart your computer.

5. You might be prompted to upgrade the PCT/SSL Security Provider. Make your choice as per the information in the sidebar: "Service Pack 3 & PCT/SSL Security Providers."

Windows NT Server Installation And Configuration Summary

What follows is a 12-step summary of the Windows NT Server 4.0 installation and configuration procedures that are required for Proxy Server 2.0 installation. Please note that your specific installation might not require all of the steps.

1. Format all volumes to be used for caching, logging, and configuration backup as NTFS.

2. Install and configure the internal network adapter to work with the protocol(s) used on your private network.

3. Install and configure the external network adapter, modem, or ISDN adapter using TCP/IP to connect to the Internet via your ISP.

4. If using a modem or external ISDN adapter, configure the serial port to work with your hardware and ISP.

5. Install and configure the RAS client.

6. Test the external network configuration by connecting to your ISP.

7. If an accelerated serial port is being used, install the high-speed drivers, then test again as in item 6 above.

8. Configure the Windows NT 4.0 domain, including the user and group accounts if necessary.

9. Configure the Windows NT routing table so that Proxy Server can correctly build the LAT.

10. Change the IIS service port that will be used as the Web Proxy service listen-on port to a less common value.

11. Configure Windows NT Server and its clients for IPX/SPX services if required on your network.

12. Install Service Pack 3 for Windows NT 4.0.

The LAT

It's helpful to understand the role of the LAT prior to installing Proxy Server. The Local Address Table (LAT) is Proxy Server's mechanism for isolating internal IP addresses to the private network. It consists of a series of IP address pairs that define your internal network address space. An address pair typically defines a range of IP addresses, although a single IP address might also be defined. The following is an example of defining a single IP address:

192.168.0.1 through 192.168.0.1

Tip

The LAT is meaningless if your network uses the IPX/SPX protocol *only*. In this scenario, all attempts to communicate using IP are redirected through Proxy Server. Also, if TCP/IP is running on your network and a Proxy Server client running only IPX/SPX attempts to communicate with an internal IP address, the communication request will always route through Proxy Server.

I mentioned in the "Routing Table Configuration" section earlier in this chapter that the LAT could use the Windows NT Server routing table to generate its list of internal IP

Local Client LAT Files

What if you have a specific client computer that needs access to internal IP addresses that are not defined in Proxy Server's LAT? In this case, you can create a permanent client LAT. Define your IP address pairs in a text file named Locallat.txt and place it in the client's Mspclnt directory. This allows you to add additional IP addresses that the client recognizes as part of the internal private network.

address pairs. Using the routing table for purposes of defining the LAT is convenient; however, you need to exercise caution, because your routing table might not fully define your internal private network. For example, a subnet of your internal network might be omitted. In this case, client requests for that IP address would be redirected through Proxy Server, placing a redundant load on the server. Also, the routing table list would prove problematic if it included an external IP address. In this scenario, Proxy Server would ignore client requests for that external IP address, and, even worse, it would permit unwanted external access to your internal private network. This is a serious security breach, so take the time to carefully review the generated list of IP addresses.

Proxy Server will also construct the LAT from the private IP address ranges, as defined by IANA (Internet Assigned Numbers Authority). The private IP address ranges are defined in RFC1918. Request for Comments (RFC) is a series of documents published by the Internet Engineering Task Force (IETF) covering a broad range of topics surrounding the Internet and the TCP/IP protocol suite. RFC 1918 reserves the following three blocks of the IP address space for private internets:

➤ 10.0.0.0 through 10.255.255.255

➤ 172.16.0.0 through 172.31.255.255

➤ 192.168.0.0 through 192.168.255.255

These IP addresses will never be used on the public Internet. So, knowing that these addresses will never be used on the public Internet, you can use these addresses for your internal private network without the fear that an internal address will someday become a necessary site to visit on the Internet. You might wish to visit the InterNIC at www.internic.net for more information about these private IP addresses. Search for RFC 1918.

Proxy Server allows you to add or remove a series of specific address pairs to or from the LAT. You should continue this procedure until your internal private network IP addresses are defined completely, and the list contains no external IP addresses.

The LAT can be modified after Proxy Server has been installed. You can edit the LAT through the Internet Service Manager or by using a text editor to edit the Msplat.txt file. The default location for the Msplat.txt file is C:\Msp\Clients.

Proxy Server 2.0 Installation

Now, with Windows NT 4.0 successfully installed and configured to Proxy Server requirements, it's time to install Proxy Server 2.0 itself. There are three ways to run the Proxy Server setup program:

➤ From the Proxy Server compact disk.

➤ From the command line.

➤ By running unattended server setup remotely from another computer.

The above setup procedures are covered individually in this section.

Proxy Server setup installs the basic services required for its operation, along with the administrative tools required for its management. There are three basic components that comprise a full Proxy Server 2.0 installation:

➤ The Web Proxy service.

➤ The WinSock Proxy service.

➤ The SOCKS Proxy service.

Additionally, the Proxy Server installation program sets up a collection of administrative utilities on the server. The following items are included:

➤ The setup program for the clients created in a shared directory on the Proxy Server computer.

➤ HTML-based online documentation.

➤ Additional administrative components, which become part of the Internet Service Manager tool of IIS.

● ● ● *Tip* ● ● ● ●

If your server computer's processor is based on the DEC Alpha chip, do not run the Digital FX32! X86 emulator. It will cause Proxy Server's setup program to fail. The failure occurs even if FX32! is loaded and disabled.

The Proxy Server Setup Program

You probably will be installing Proxy Server using the setup program on the compact disk. This is by far the most popular method if you have a single Proxy Server to install for your organization.

Before you install Proxy Server, log onto the server using a user account that has administrative privileges. Then locate your CD Key number; it's the product identification

The Server Setup Log

Each time you install Microsoft Proxy Server 2.0, the setup program creates a log file. This log file, named C:\Mpssetup.log, can be used to troubleshoot problems with setup. It is a standard text file and can be opened in any text editor, such as Notepad. The file is overwritten with each Proxy Server installation. This file is required if you call Microsoft for assistance with setup problems.

number located on the compact disk case. Remember also that, for security reasons, Proxy Server must be installed on a NTFS partition. Now, follow the installation procedure below, using the setup program on the compact disk.

Tip

You will receive a warning if the Windows NT SAP Agent service is not running when you install Proxy Server. Make sure to install the SAP agent prior to running Proxy Server setup if you have client computers that run only the IPX/SPX protocol. Clicking Abort will start the on-screen instructions for installation of the SAP Agent Service. You might choose to ignore this warning by clicking Continue and proceeding with Proxy Server's setup.

Starting Proxy Server Setup

1. Run setup from the root directory of the Microsoft Proxy Server 2.0 compact disk. Alternately, you can copy the contents from the compact disk to a shared folder on your network and run setup from the share.

2. Click Continue in the Welcome dialog box (see Figure 6.9).

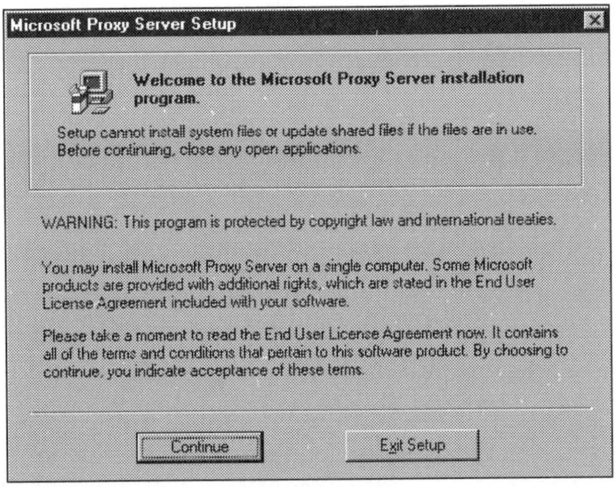

Figure 6.9   Proxy Server Setup Welcome dialog box.

3. Type your CD key number in the CD Key field, and then click on OK.

4. Click on OK to confirm the setup of Proxy Server.

5. Click on OK to accept the default folder for Proxy Server, or click Change Folder to specify a different directory.

Installing Components

The Proxy Server setup program will now list the Proxy Server components available for installation. By default, all the components are selected. Briefly, these components include:

➤ **Proxy Server**   Installs Proxy Server, the shared directory for client installations, and the files required for client installations.

➤ **The ISM Administration Tool**   Installs the administration tool as an add-on to Internet Service Manager (ISM). Also, see the sidebar: "Remotely Administering Proxy Server."

➤ **Documentation**   Installs the HTML-based Proxy Server Installation and Administration Guide, accessed via the Help menu of Internet Service Manager or from the Microsoft Proxy Server program group. A Web browser that supports frames is required, for example, Microsoft Internet Explorer (version 3.02 or greater) or Netscape Navigator (version 2.0 or greater).

Proxy Server Component Installation

1. Click Installation Options (see Figure 6.10). The Proxy Server Installation Options dialog box appears.

2. By default, all components are selected; to not install a specific component, clear its checkbox by clicking on the box. Also, you can choose not to install some of the Proxy Server options by clicking the Change Option button. For example, you may not need all the Proxy Server Client Shares for your installation (see Figure 6.11).

3. Click Continue.

Remotely Administering Proxy Server

There are circumstances where you might want to install the ISM Administration without Proxy Server. Such an installation is useful if, for example, you are setting up a workstation for remote administration of Proxy Server. The ISM Administration tool can only be run on Windows NT Server 4.0 with the Internet Information Server 3.0 installed, or on Windows NT Workstation 4.0 with the Internet Service Manager component of Microsoft Peer Web Services installed.

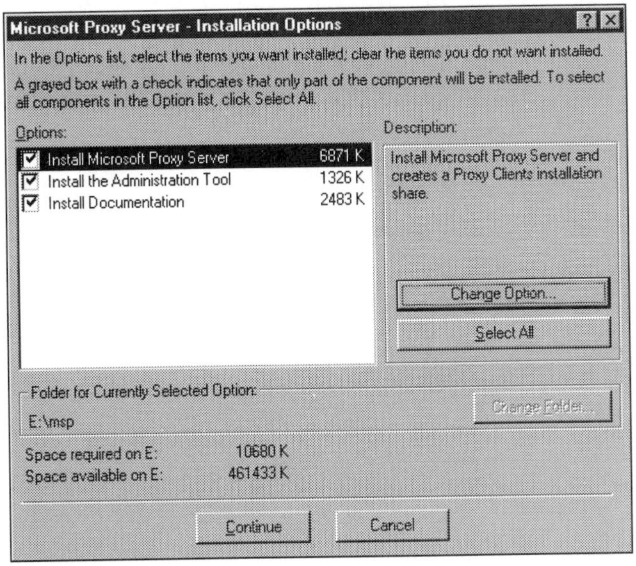

Figure 6.10   The Proxy Server Installation Options dialog box.

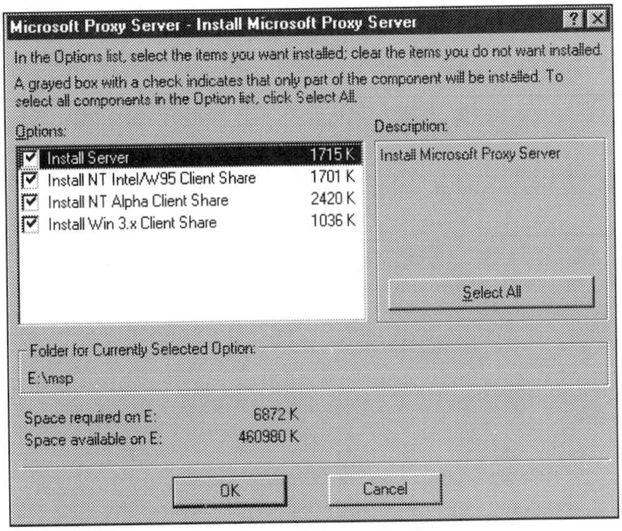

Figure 6.11   The Install Proxy Server Options List dialog box.

Configuring The Cache Drives

You will now need to select and configure a cache drive. In the planning phase, you determined the amount of disk space to set aside for the cache. Proxy Server's default is 100 MB. However, the formula I recommend is 100 MB + 1 MB for each Web Proxy service client. This is greater than Microsoft recommends, but I believe it is more realistic for most moderate-size organizations.

Setup also will ask you to select a cache drive. The Proxy Server setup program searches for your largest available NTFS drive and selects it as the default drive. You might need to change the default for the Proxy Server's cache to your fastest hard disk drive, preferably a SCSI drive that has adequate free space.

Tip

You are required to use NTFS volumes for caching. Make sure you have enough disk space on an NTFS volume for the cache size that your installation requires.

Cache Drive Configuration

1. Select a drive from the list in the Cache Drives dialog box (see Figure 6.12).

2. Type a number in the Maximum Size (MB) field.

3. Click Set.

4. Repeat steps 1 through 3 as necessary to assign additional cache drives, then click on OK.

Configuring The LAT

The next step is to include all the internal IP addresses that comprise your network, using the Local Address Table (LAT) Configuration dialog box. IP addresses not included in the LAT are considered external.

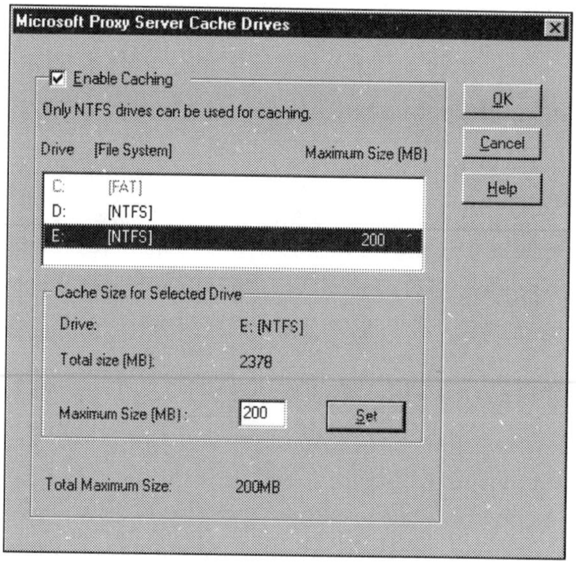

Figure 6.12   The Cache Drives dialog box.

You can have Proxy Server construct the LAT from your Windows NT Server routing table. Also, you can select the private IP address ranges, as defined by IANA in RFC 1918. These three blocks of addresses are reserved for private internets only and will never be used on the public Internet.

The setup program installs a file named Msplat.txt on the server. This file contains the specification for Proxy Server's LAT. Additionally, the setup program and associated files for Proxy Server clients are installed. By default, the Msplat.txt and the client installation files are located in the C:\Msp\Clients directory.

LAT Configuration

1. Click Construct Table in the Local Address Table Configuration dialog box. The Construct Local Address Table dialog box appears (see Figure 6.13).

2. Select the Add the Private Ranges checkbox to add the three private IP address ranges, as defined by IANA in RFC 1918.

3. Select the Load from the NT Internal Routing Table checkbox to have Proxy Server construct the LAT from your Windows NT Server routing table. Then proceed to the appropriate step below:

   ➤ If you are unsure which of the server's network adapters are connected to the internal private network and which are connected to the Internet, click Load Known Address Ranges From All IP Interface Cards. Examine the generated list of IP ranges, removing all the external Internet IP address pairs and adding all the internal IP address pairs.

   ➤ If you are sure which of the server's network adapters are connected to the internal private network and which are connected to the Internet, click Load

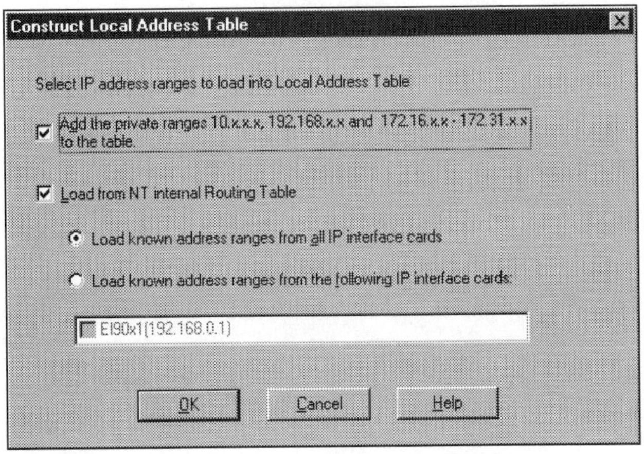

Figure 6.13   The Construct Local Address Table dialog box.

Known Address Ranges From the Following IP Interface Adapters. Next, in the list of network adapters, select the checkbox for each adapter connected to the internal private network and click to clear the checkbox for each adapter that is connected to the Internet.

4. Click on OK, then verify that the entries in the Internal IP ranges correctly identify those used on your internal network (see Figure 6.14).

5. If necessary, add or remove address pairs using the appropriate procedures from the following list:

➤ **To add a range of IP addresses to the list**   Under Edit, type a pair of addresses in From and To, and then click Add.

➤ **To add a single IP address to the list**   Under Edit, type the same address in both From and To, and then click Add.

➤ **To remove an IP address or address pair from the list**   Select the IP address or address pair from Internal IP ranges, and then click Remove.

6. Click on OK when finished defining the LAT.

Configuring Client Setup Information

Now you specify how Web browsers and WinSock Proxy client applications will connect to the Proxy Server computer. The information you place in the Client Installation/ Configuration dialog box is used by the client setup program specifically for the configuration of client computers. Although Proxy Server client configuration first occurs during Proxy Server setup, modifications are possible after Proxy Server is installed.

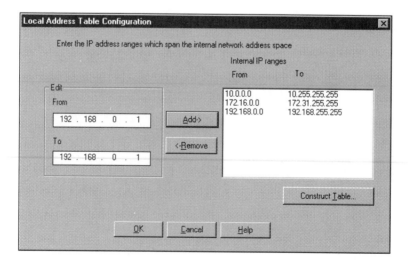

Figure 6.14   The Local Address Table Configuration dialog box.

The WinSock Proxy client provides several means for WinSock Proxy clients to connect to the Proxy Server computer. The options include by computer name, DNS name, IP address, Proxy Server array name, or group of IP addresses designating an array. You can select Manual and then edit the client configuration file named Mspclnt.ini (see Chapter 8).

Another option includes a browser configuration script that specifies how client requests are routed to Proxy Server computers. If your organization standardized on a browser that supports JavaScript, such as Microsoft Internet Explorer (version 3.02 or greater) or Netscape Navigator (version 2.0 or greater), then this is a viable selection.

You also have an opportunity to specify the routing of a Web Proxy client request. For example, you can choose whether a Web Proxy client request routes upstream to a Proxy Server computer, to a Proxy Server array, or directly to the Internet. Also, you can designate an alternate route if a Proxy Server chain is unavailable.

Client Setup Configuration

1. Click Computer Name, IP Address, or Manual under WinSock Proxy client. Edit the server name if it is incorrect.

2. Select the Automatically Configure Web Browser During Client Setup checkbox, and edit the server name if necessary, in the Proxy field (see Figure 6.15).

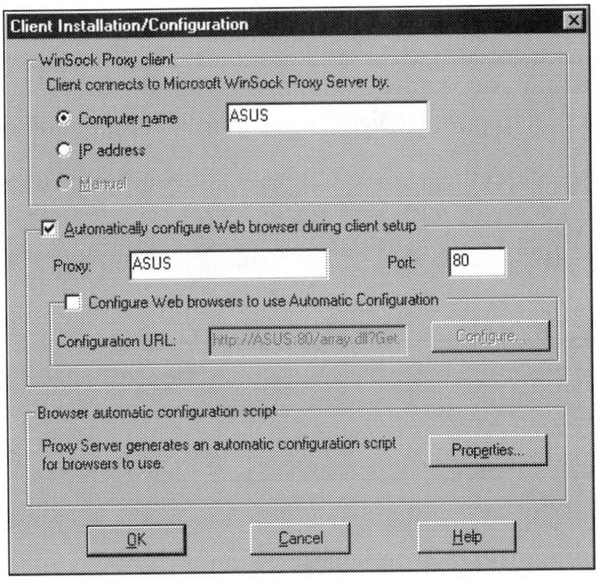

Figure 6.15 The Client Installation/Configuration dialog box.

six

Typically, you would click on OK at this point to continue the setup program. Because the Automatically Configure Web Browser During Client Setup checkbox is selected, Web browser settings are modified to forward all requests to the Proxy Server computer, instead of directly to the Internet as is normally the case. This change in the Web browser's network configuration settings actually occurs when the Proxy Server client setup is performed on the client workstation.

Additionally, if the Configure Web Browsers to Use Automatic Configuration checkbox is selected, then Proxy Server Setup places an automatically generated configuration script at the following default URL **http://servername/array.dll?Get.Routing.Script**.

In the above example, *servername* is the name of the Proxy Server computer. The configuration script parameters are automatically generated, based on the options that are set in the Advanced Client Configuration dialog box.

However, you might need to set up a Web browser to run a client configuration script located at a location other than the default URL. In this case, proceed to the section "Custom URL Configuration for Clients."

Another reason to use the procedures in the "Custom URL Configuration for Clients" section is that you do not want Web browsers to automatically download a client configuration script. For example, if you want Proxy Server clients to join an existing Proxy Server array that uses a DNS name.

Custom URL Configuration For Clients

1. Confirm that the Automatically Configure Web Browser During Client Setup checkbox is selected in the Client Installation/Configuration dialog box.

2. Confirm that the Configure Web Browsers to Use Automatic Configuration checkbox is selected in the Client Installation/Configuration dialog box.

3. Click the Configure Web Browsers to Automatically Download a Client Configuration Script checkbox if you want Web browsers to use the URL to automatically download the client configuration script. Web browsers that use this feature must support JavaScript, for example Netscape Navigator 4.0 and Internet Explorer version 3.02 and higher.

4. Click Configure. The Configuration URL For Clients dialog box appears (see Figure 6.16).

5. Proceed to the appropriate option below.

   ➤ **To use the default configuration script URL**   Click Use Default Script Supplied by Server in the Configuration URL for Clients dialog box. This

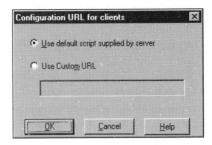

Figure 6.16   The Configuration URL For Clients dialog box.

defines the Proxy Server-generated configuration script as the URL that clients use for configuration.

➤ **To use a custom script URL**   Click Use Custom URL and then type the appropriate URL to use an alternate URL of your choice.

➤ **To clear the configuration URL so that Web browsers do not automatically download a client configuration script**   Click Use Custom URL and then delete any text in the text field below it.

6. If required, proceed to *Configuring Advanced Client Setup Information* by clicking the Properties button under Browsers Automatic Configuration Script. Otherwise, click on OK to continue with the Proxy Server Setup.

Configuring The Advanced Client Setup Information

The Advanced Client Setup Configuration screen allows you to define the following three parameters:

➤ Specify IP addresses that should not be routed through Proxy Server.

➤ Specify domains that should not be routed through Proxy Server.

➤ Configure a backup upstream route if the primary route is unavailable.

Refer to the following three sections for specific instructions about altering these Advanced Client Setup parameters.

Configuring The IP Address List

The following instructions allow you to specify IP addresses that should not be routed through Proxy Server. When you place an IP address in this list, requests for that specific IP address will bypass Proxy Server, directly routing the request to the Internet. This feature should only be used if clients have access to a DNS server that can resolve Internet names. Also, you can configure client requests to internal servers to pass through Proxy Server first. This allows Proxy Server to improve browser performance by returning cached objects.

IP Address List Configuration

1. Click the Properties button in the Client Installation/Configuration dialog box, under Browser Automatic Configuration Script.

   Select the Use Proxy for Local Servers checkbox in the Advanced Client Configuration dialog box, if you want client requests to internal servers to pass through Proxy Server first (see Figure 6.17).

2. Confirm that the Do Not Use Proxy for the Following IP Addresses checkbox is selected, then proceed to the appropriate option below:

   ➤ **Add an IP address.** Click Add in the Address Properties dialog box, then type a valid IP address in the IP Address field and type a valid subnet mask value in the Subnet Mask field, and then click on OK.

   ➤ **Edit an IP address.** Select the entry you want to change from the list, and then click Edit. Then edit the values listed in the IP Address and Subnet Mask fields.

   ➤ **Remove an IP address.** Select the entry you want to remove from the list, and then click Remove.

3. Click on OK after confirming the accuracy of your changes.

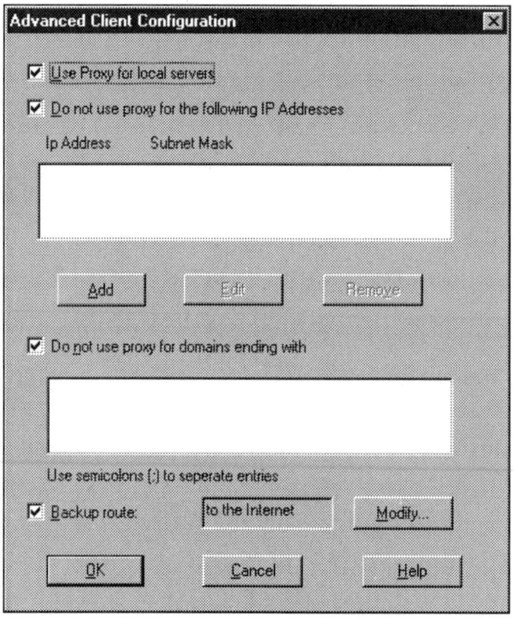

Figure 6.17 The Advanced Client Configuration dialog box.

Configuring The Domain Address List

The following instructions allow you to specify the domains that should not be routed through Proxy Server. When you place a domain in this list, requests for that specific domain will bypass Proxy Server, directly routing the request to the Internet.

1. Click Properties under Browser Automatic Configuration Script in the Client Installation/Configuration dialog box.

2. Select the Use Proxy for Local Servers checkbox in the Advanced Client Configuration dialog box, if you want client requests to internal servers to pass through Proxy Server first.

3. Select the Do Not Use Proxy for Domains Ending With checkbox.

4. Enter into the text box all the domain names that you do not want to route through Proxy Server, using semicolons to separate the domain names (see Figure 6.18).

5. Click on OK, after confirming the accuracy of your changes.

Configuring A Backup Upstream Route

The following instructions allow you to route Proxy Server to another Internet connection, if the primary route is unavailable. Authentication credentials cannot be applied to the backup upstream route, only to the primary route.

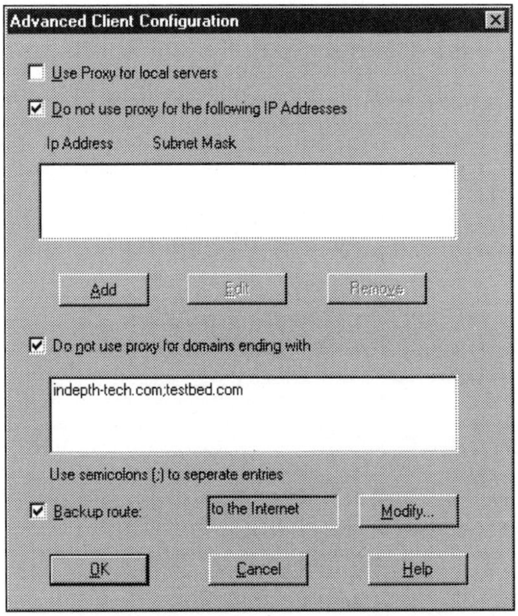

Figure 6.18   Enter domain names that you do not want to route through Proxy Server.

Using Packet Filtering With A Modem Or ISDN Adapter

Here are some special instructions if you are using a modem or ISDN adapter for a dial-out connection to the Internet and you require packet filtering. Initially, packet filtering is disabled when Proxy Server is installed. After installing Proxy Server, you must configure Auto Dial *before* you can enable packet filtering.

1. Click Properties under the Browser Automatic Configuration Script located in the Client Installation/Configuration dialog box.

2. Select the Backup Route checkbox in the Advanced Client Configuration dialog box.

3. Click Modify.

4. Proceed to the appropriate option below:

➤ **To route to a direct connection to the Internet**   Click Route to the Internet in the Configure Backup Route dialog box.

➤ **To route to an upstream Proxy Server computer**   Click Route to Web Proxy and type a valid server name in the Proxy field along with a valid port number, typically port 80, in the Port field (see Figure 6.19).

5. Click on OK, after confirming the accuracy of your changes.

Configuring Access Control

The final step in Proxy Server Setup is configuring access control for the Web Proxy and WinSock Proxy services. Access control is a means to enable security for these services through validating clients' connections. In other words, certain users or groups can be granted or denied access to the Web Proxy and WinSock Proxy services. Access control is enabled by default for both services (see Figure 6.20).

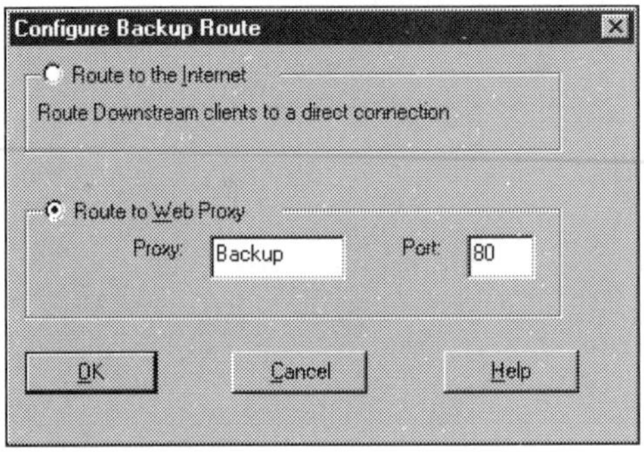

Figure 6.19   The Configure Backup Route dialog box.

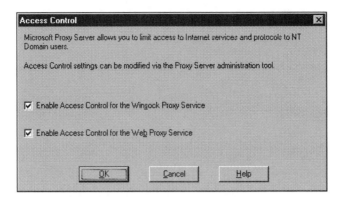

Figure 6.20   The Access Control dialog box.

1. To enable WinSock Proxy service security, in the Access Control dialog box, select the checkbox next to Enable Access Control for the WinSock Proxy service; this will enable access control for this service.

2. To enable Web Proxy service security, in the Access Control dialog box, select the checkbox next to Enable Access Control for the Web Proxy Service; this enables access control for this service.

3. Click on OK three times to complete the Proxy Server installation.

Proxy Server 2.0 Setup Installation Summary

The following are the six primary steps for a Proxy Server installation:

1. Starting Proxy Server setup.

2. Installing Proxy Server components.

3. Configuring cache drive.

4. Configuring LAT.

5. Configuring client setup information.

6. Configuring access control.

Proxy Server Command Line Installation

You can install Proxy Server by running setup from the command line. The optional parameters available on the command line are the main advantage of Command Line Server setup. These parameters speed the installation or reinstallation of Proxy Server in some circumstances.

The following defines the syntax for Proxy Server command-line setup:

```
setup [/r] [/u] [/k] "keynumber"
```

where

/r *reinstalls* Proxy Server.

/u *uninstalls* Proxy Server but leaves shared components.

/k "keynumber" provides the compact disk keynumber, which must be enclosed in quotation marks. The keynumber value is the product ID displayed on the Certificate of Authenticity provided with the product.

Tip

Do not enter a dash or a space as part of the keynumber string. Entering the key number incorrectly causes Proxy Server command-line setup to fail without indicating the cause.

Proxy Server Unattended Server Setup

Proxy Server can be installed remotely by using the Unattended Server setup command

```
stpwrapp.
```

Unattended Server setup is especially useful when multiple Microsoft Proxy Servers are being installed. Configuration information can be placed in a separate file. You must exercise care that the configuration information is entered correctly. The following is the syntax for Proxy Server unattended server setup

```
stpwrapp [/sms] /k "keynumber"
```

where

/sms is required if you use stpwrapp independent of SMS (Systems Management Server).

/k "keynumber" provides the compact disk key number, which must be enclosed in quotation marks. The keynumber value is the product ID displayed on the Certificate of Authenticity provided with the product.

Tip

Do not enter a dash or a space as part of the keynumber string. Entering the key number incorrectly causes Proxy Server unattended server setup to fail without indicating the cause.

You can also uninstall Proxy Server using Proxy Server unattended server setup. To uninstall Proxy Server from the command prompt, type "setup /qt /u".

The Unattended Setup Configuration File

The Unattended Server setup uses a file named Proxy.ini to retrieve the configuration information. The default setup value is used whenever a specific value is not specified in the Proxy.ini file. Proxy.ini has no effect on the standard Proxy Server setup program. The following information describes the entry options and values for the Proxy Server unattended server setup Proxy.ini file.

The [Install] Section

The [Install] section is used to specify the installation directory for Microsoft Proxy Server, the overwriting of previous configuration information, and if the Proxy Server computer is an array member. The following commands are available in the [Install] section.

Command:	`Install Dir`
Section:	`[Install]`
Description:	Specifies the installation directory for Microsoft Proxy Server. If not specified, defaults to the first disk drive with enough space. Syntax is drive:\directory
Example:	`Install Dir=c:\mspclnt`
Command:	`Override Existing Config`
Section:	`[Install]`
Description:	If set to 0, setup program retains existing configuration set by previous installation, ignoring data from the remaining sections of this file. The default is 0.
Example:	`Override Existing Config=0`
Command:	`Keep Array Membership If Exist`
Section:	`[Install]`
Description:	Applies to a Proxy Server computer that is configured as part of an array. If set to 1, setup program retains the existing configuration rather than setting a default configuration. The default is 1.
Example:	`Keep Array Membership If Exist =1`

The [Client Access Config] Section

The [Client Access Config] section is used to configure the Proxy Server client Setup program installed on the Proxy Server computer. Client computers can connect to the server and run client Setup using the configuration options specified in this section. The commands available in the [Client Access Config] section duplicate the options available in the Client Setup Installation/Configuration dialog box. See "Configuring Client Setup Information" earlier in this chapter. The following commands are available in the [Client Access Config] section.

Command:	`Set WinSock Proxy Access By IP Rather Than By Name`
Section:	`[Client Access Config]`
Description:	If set to 1, setup writes the IP address into the [Server IP Addresses] section in the Mspclnt.ini file. If set to 0, setup writes the computer name into that section. The default is 0.
Example:	`Set WinSock Proxy Access By IP Rather Than By Name =0`

Command:	`WinSock Proxy Access Control Enabled`
Section:	`[Client Access Config]`
Description:	If set to 1, access control for the WinSock Proxy service is enabled. The default is 1.
Example:	`WinSock Proxy Access Control Enabled=1`

Command:	`Web Proxy Access Control Enabled`
Section:	`[Client Access Config]`
Description:	If set to 1, access control for the Web Proxy service is enabled. The default is 1.
Example:	`Web Proxy Access Control Enabled=1`

Command:	`Computer Name`
Section:	`[Client Access Config]`
Description:	Specifies the computer or DNS name of the server.
Example:	`Computer Name=MYCOMPUTER`

Command:	`Set Browsers To Use Proxy`
Section:	`[Client Access Config]`
Description:	If set to 1, client setup program configures the client computer's browser to use the Proxy Server defined in the WWW Proxy field. If set to 0, prevents the client setup program from configuring clients to use a proxy server. This field has no effect on the client Mspclnt.ini file.
Example:	`Browsers To Use Proxy=1`

Command:	WWW-Proxy
Section:	[Client Access Config]
Description:	If Set Browsers To Use Proxy is set to 1, the client setup program configures client browsers to use the Proxy Server named here. This field has no effect on the client Mspclnt.ini file.
Example:	WWW-Proxy=1

Command:	WebProxyPort
Section:	[Client Access Config]
Description:	If Set Browsers To Use Proxy is set to 1, the client setup program configures client browsers to use the port specified in that field. This should be the same port number that is set for the WWW service of Internet Information Server.
Example:	WebProxyPort=80

The [Cache Config] Section

The [Cache Config] section is used to specify the disk drive, or drives, used for caching and the minimum and maximum size of the cache. See "Configuring the Cache Drives" earlier in this chapter. The following commands are available in the [Cache Config] section.

Command:	Drive
Section:	[Cache Config]
Description:	Specifies the disk drive to be used for caching. If not specified, defaults to the first NTFS partition large enough for adequate caching.

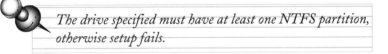

The drive specified must have at least one NTFS partition, otherwise setup fails.

Example:	Drive=D:

Command:	Size
Section:	[Cache Config]
Description:	Specifies the minimum and maximum sizes (in megabytes) to be reserved on the drive specified in the Drive field for caching. The default values are 100 100.
Example:	Size=100 100

The [LAT Config] Section

The [LAT Config] section is used to identify all internal IP addresses used on your network and to exclude all external IP addresses from network access. This information is maintained in a Local Address Table (LAT), which is used by WinSock Proxy, Web Proxy, and Socks Proxy clients. See "Configuring The LAT" earlier in this chapter. The following commands are available in the [LAT Config] section.

Command: `Include Private Ranges`

Section: `[LAT Config]`

Description: If set to 1, includes internal IP address ranges in the LAT. Syntax is 10.x.x.x. At least one entry in this section is required; otherwise setup fails.

Example: `Include Private Ranges=1`

Command: `Include Ranges From All Cards`

Section: `[LAT Config]`

Description: If set to 1, treats all network adapter IP address ranges as being on the internal network. Assumes a dial-up modem connection to the Internet. At least one entry in this section is required, otherwise setup fails.

Example: `Include Ranges From All Cards=1`

Command: `Range1,Range2`

Section: `[LAT Config]`

Description: Defines LAT IP ranges specifically. Syntax is Range1=x.x.x.x. Range2=y.y.y.y. At least one entry in this section is required, otherwise setup fails.

Example: `Range1=10.0.0.0 Range2=10.255.255.255`

 At least one entry in the [LAT Config] section is required. Setup will fail if there are no entries in this section.

Upgrading Previous Proxy Server Versions

You might be upgrading your Proxy Server from a previous version of the product. The following procedures detail the upgrade process for Proxy Server 1.0, preliminary (Beta) releases, and trial releases of Proxy Server 2.0.

Before upgrading to Proxy Server 2.0, you must log on to the server using an account that has administrative permissions. In addition, all of the preparation of the Windows

NT 4.0 server, including the installation of Service Pack 3, is required as in a regular installation.

Tip

While Microsoft Proxy Server 2.0 does support WinSock Proxy version 1.0 clients, WinSock Proxy 2.0 clients require Microsoft Proxy Server 2.0.

Upgrading From Proxy Server Version 2.0 Beta

1. Uninstall the Beta release by running setup from the root directory of the Beta compact disk or from the directory where the setup files were copied.

2. Click Remove All and follow the on-screen instructions.

3. Restart the server after the setup program removes the Beta release.

4. Delete the cached directory (Urlcache) if it was not removed.

5. Upgrade the server to Version 2.0 by running setup from the root directory of the Proxy Server 2.0 compact disk or from the directory where the setup files were copied.

6. Follow the on-screen instructions.

Upgrading From Proxy Server Version 1.0

Run setup.exe from the root of the Microsoft Proxy Server 2.0 compact disk or from the directory where the setup files were copied. Then follow the on-screen instructions. Do not run setup from the Proxy Server version 1.0 compact disk.

Reinstalling Proxy Server

There are several reasons to become familiar with the Proxy Server reinstallation process. For example, you might need to reinstall Proxy Server if files are missing or have become corrupted. Either the Proxy Server 2.0 setup program or the Control Panel is used for reinstallation of the server. Additionally, changes in your organization or Proxy Server requirements might necessitate the addition or removal of Proxy Server components. The Proxy Server 2.0 reinstallation procedures follow.

Tip

Is the Proxy Server computer that you are reinstalling part of an array? If so, accept the default parameters for the array. This forces the computer to synchronize automatically to the array.

Proxy Server Reinstallation Using Setup

1. Exit the Internet Service Manager if it is running.

2. Run setup from the root directory of the Microsoft Proxy Server compact disk or from the directory where the setup files were copied.

3. Click Reinstall in the Setup dialog box.

4. Proceed with the on-screen instructions.

Proxy Server Reinstallation Using The Control Panel

1. Exit the Internet Service Manager if it is running.

2. Click Add/Remove Programs on the server, in Control Panel.

3. Click the Install/Uninstall tab in the Add/Remove Programs Properties dialog box (see Figure 6.21).

4. Click Microsoft Proxy Server, and then click Add/Remove.

5. Proceed with the on-screen instructions.

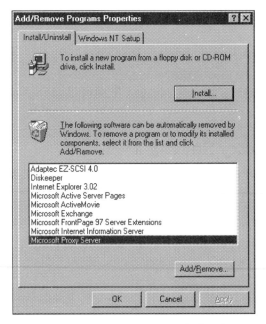

Figure 6.21 The Add/Remove Programs Properties dialog box.

Addition Or Removal Of Selected Proxy Server Components

1. Exit the Internet Service Manager if it is running.

2. Run setup from the root directory of the Microsoft Proxy Server compact disk or from the directory where the setup files were copied.

3. Click Add/Remove in the Setup dialog box.

4. Proceed with the on-screen instructions.

Uninstalling Proxy Server

You might need to uninstall your Proxy Server at some point in time. For example, when you upgrade to a new server computer you decide to use the old server computer for another purpose. The Proxy Server 2.0 Program Group, setup program, or the Control Panel can be used for uninstallation of the server. If desired, you can save the cache, log, and backup files. Also, because the deletion of the cache files can take a long time, you can halt this action during the uninstallation process.

Uninstallation From The Proxy Server Program Group

1. Click Uninstall in the Microsoft Proxy Server program group.

2. Click Yes in the Uninstall Proxy Server dialog box.

3. You now are presented with the option to delete the cache, log, and backup files. To delete these files, click Yes in the Setup Information dialog box; to save these files, click No.

4. Click Skip Cache Cleaning if you want to halt the deletion of the cache files.

5. Uninstallation is complete when you get the message that *Proxy Server Setup was completed successfully*.

Uninstallation Using The Proxy Server Setup Program

1. Run setup from the root directory of the Beta compact disk or from the directory where the setup files were copied.

2. Click Remove All in the Setup dialog box.

3. Click Yes, to confirm that Proxy Server should be removed.

4. You now are presented with the option to delete the cache, log, and backup files. To delete these files, click Yes in the Setup Information dialog box; to save these files, click No.

5. Click Skip Cache Cleaning if you want to halt the deletion of the cache files.

6. Uninstallation is complete when you get the message that *Proxy Server Setup was completed successfully*.

Uninstallation Using The Control Panel

1. Click Start, point to Settings, and click Control Panel.

2. Click on the Add/Remove Programs utility.

3. Click the Install/Uninstall tab in the Add/Remove Programs Properties dialog box.

4. Click Microsoft Proxy Server.

5. Click the Add/Remove button.

6. Click Remove All, in the Microsoft Proxy Server Setup screen.

7. Click Yes, to confirm that Proxy Server should be removed.

8. You now are presented with the option to delete the cache, log, and backup files. To delete these files, click Yes in the Setup Information dialog box; to save these files, click No.

9. Click Skip Cache Cleaning if you want to halt the deletion of the cache files.

10. Uninstallation is complete when you get the message that *Proxy Server Setup was completed successfully*.

Proxy Server Client Installation

You need to install the Proxy Server clients after the server itself is installed. Recall the Client Installation/Configuration dialog box you completed during Proxy Server setup? The options you specified in this dialog box are used to configure the client. During client setup, each Proxy Server client receives a copy of the configuration information, along with other Proxy Server client components. The components that clients receive from the server include:

➤ A shared client configuration file named Mspclnt.ini.

➤ A shared client Local Address Table (LAT) file named Msplat.txt.

➤ The WinSock Proxy client application.

The default settings for all these components can be changed after client installation. Later, I'll discuss how this file can be edited to create a custom client configuration file.

The Client Setup Log

The Microsoft Proxy Server Client Setup program creates a log file on the client each time the client software is installed. This log file, named C:\Mpcsetup.log, can be used to troubleshoot problems with setup. It is a standard text file and can be opened in any text editor, such as Notepad. The file is overwritten with each Proxy Server client installation. If you call Microsoft for assistance with setup problems, you will need this file.

You can perform client setup using the following methods:

➤ Running the setup program on the server computer.

➤ Running setup from a Web browser.

➤ Running the setup program using the command line, with or without optional parameters.

➤ Running unattended client setup using Systems Management Server (SMS).

What follows are the procedures required for installing, upgrading, reinstalling, and uninstalling Proxy Server clients using each of the above methods.

Tip

Do you need to install Proxy client software on a dual-boot computer? You can; however, you need to run client setup for each operating system. Additionally, you must specify a different client directory for each installation. For example, the Windows NT and Windows 95 client software must be installed in different directories.

Client Installation By Running Setup On The Server

1. Connect to the Mspclnt share on the Proxy Server from the client computer.

2. Run setup.exe on the Mspclnt share.

3. Follow the on-screen instructions.

Client Installation Using A Web Browser

1. Type http://*servername*/Msproxy in the Address field of the Web browser, where servername is the name of the Proxy Server computer.

2. Wait for the client installation page to load (see Figure 6.22).

3. Follow the on-screen instructions to run setup and install client components.

WinSock Proxy Client 2.0 Installation - Microsoft Internet Explorer

File   Edit   View   Go   Fa▸ | Links   ⏋Best of the W ▸ | Address ⏋ http://asus/msproxy/

WinSock Proxy Client Installation For Microsoft Proxy Server

The WinSock Proxy service provides secure and transparent access to Internet resources for applications that use the Windows Sockets API. Microsoft Proxy Server version 2.0 supports applications that use Windows Sockets version 1.1. Some examples of supported applications include:

- RealPlayer for streaming real-time audio and video
- Enliven Viewer for streaming real-time audio and video
- VDOLive for streaming real-time video
- SMTP mail readers for Internet mail
- NNTP news readers for Internet newsgroups
- IRC clients for Internet chat sessions

Install the WinSock Proxy 2.0 client for Microsoft Proxy Server version 2.0.

Once you install the WinSock Proxy client, no further changes are needed for your applications to work with the WinSock Proxy service.

If you are viewing this page with Netscape Navigator, you need to save the Setup.bat file to your local hard disk first. After you save Setup.bat to your hard disk, you can use the following procedure to install the WinSock Proxy 2.0 client.

Local intranet zone

Figure 6.22   Client installation using a Web browser.

Tip

Occasionally, the browser settings configured by client setup are not appropriate for a particular client computer. If this is true for one of your clients, then use the Web browser's own configuration interface to specify the server name and the protocol port number.

Client Installation From The Command Line

You can install Proxy Server client software by running setup from the command line. The optional parameters available on the command line are the main advantage of Command Line Client Setup. These parameters speed up the installation or reinstallation of Proxy Server clients in some circumstances.

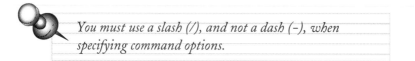

You must use a slash (/), and not a dash (-), when specifying command options.

The following defines the syntax for Proxy Server Command Line Setup:

```
setup [/r] [/u] [/q[1, t]]
```

where

/r reinstalls Proxy client software.

/u uninstalls the WinSock Proxy client application, but leaves shared components.

> *The /r and /u options cannot be used with 16-bit clients—for example, computers running the Microsoft Windows 3.1 or Microsoft Windows for Workgroups operating systems.*

/q runs client setup in quiet mode. The screen displays progress windows and a Setup Completion dialog box, but does not prompt the user to approve or modify installation settings. Quiet setup always installs the client software into the default Mspclnt directory.

/q1 is the same as the /q option, but also hides the Setup Completion dialog box.

/qt is the same as the /q option, but also hides the progress windows and the Setup Completion dialog box.

> *After installation completes, the client computer is restarted if required by the setup program. This option is not available for 16-bit clients. You can use quiet mode only for an initial setup. If a client is already installed, you cannot reinstall or uninstall it by using the /q option.*

Unattended Client Installation Examples

You can install or uninstall Proxy Server clients from a remote computer by using the unattended client setup command. The following are command syntax examples for installing and uninstalling clients.

Installation example for 32-bit clients:

```
setup /qt
```

Installation example for 16-bit clients:

```
setup /q1
```

Uninstallation example for 32-bit clients:

```
setup /qt /u
```

Uninstallation example for 16-bit clients:

```
setup /q1 /u
```

Unattended Client Setup With Microsoft SMS

The Microsoft Systems Management Server (SMS) offers a means of centrally managing computers distributed across many locations. It integrates an extensive collection of management functions into a single product. Systems Management Server is an effective solution for managers of distributed systems who are concerned with the cost and complexity of building, maintaining, and managing a mission critical network.

Microsoft Proxy Server 2.0 is designed to operate with SMS. The file Mspver.txt enables the SMS Admin Inventory mechanism to acknowledge the existence of Proxy Server on computers that have the SMS client application installed. The Mspver.txt file is installed by Proxy Server setup.

The following procedure describes the configuration of SMS for unattended client setup.

SMS Configuration

1. Start the SMS Administration Agent.

2. Click New from the File menu.

3. Click Import in the Package Properties dialog box.

4. Navigate to the root in the dialog box that appears, and then click mspsrvr.pdf.

5. Click Workstation.

6. Type the path to the installation tree in the Source Directory field, located in the Setup Package for Workstations dialog box.

7. Double-click Setup32.

8. In the Command Line Properties dialog box, replace the string "write your compact disk key here" with the actual compact disk key number in quotation marks. For further information, consult your SMS documentation.

Proxy Server SMS Support Files

Microsoft Systems Management Server (SMS) can be used with Proxy Server to automate the installation of client software. The support files required for SMS are installed by default in C:\Msp\Clients. You also must import the Mspclnt.pdf file, using the SMS Administrator program to add SMS support for Proxy Server clients. The Smssetup program automates the installation and uninstallation of client software. SMS manages automatic system restarts after the installation or uninstallation of 32-bit Windows clients. Only automatic installing is supported for 16-bit clients.

Unattended setup relies on a file named Proxy.ini for configuration of the client's default installation directory. This file is located in the Mspclnt share on the server and has no effect on the standard Proxy Server client setup program. The shared directory is created upon installation of Proxy Server 2.0. The client Proxy.ini consists of a single section and entry.

The following illustrates the default contents of the Proxy.ini file:

```
[Proxy Setup Install]
Install Dir=C:\Mspclnt
```

The following defines the syntax for installing clients using SMS:

SMS Example for 32-bit client installation:

```
setup /l smssetup.lst /qt
```

SMS Example for 16-bit client installation:

```
setup /l smssetup.lst /q1
```

where

/l specifies the file to be used with the setup command (in the example's case, smssetup.lst), rather than the default file (setup.lst).

The following defines the syntax for uninstalling clients using SMS:

SMS Example for 32-bit client uninstallation:

```
setup /l smssetup.lst /qt /u
```

SMS Example for 16-bit client uninstallation:

```
setup /l smssetup.lst /q1 /u
```

The Mspclnt share on the server must be copied from, or used directly as, the distribution source for the client setup and client uninstall packages.

Upgrading Clients

Proxy Server clients can be upgraded from Version 2.0 Release Candidate, Version 2.0 Beta, or Version 1.0 product using the following procedure:

1. From the client computer, connect to the Mspclnt share on the server that has Microsoft Proxy Server 2.0 installed.

2. Run setup.exe from the Mspclnt share.

3. Follow the on-screen instructions.

Client Reinstallation

Reinstalling Proxy Server client software is a rather common need. For example, upgrading a client computer's operating system, including the application of an operating system service pack, can cause the WinSock Proxy client components to be overwritten. The solution is to reinstall the Proxy Server client software. You can use the Proxy Server client setup program, the Mspclnt share, or Control Panel to reinstall Proxy Server client software.

Client Reinstallation Using The Proxy Server Program Group

1. Open the Microsoft Proxy client on the client computer program group, and click Setup.

2. Click Reinstall in the Client Setup dialog box.

3. Follow the on-screen instructions.

Client Reinstallation Using The Mspclnt Share

1. Connect to the Mspclnt share on the server.

2. Run client setup.

3. Click Reinstall in the Client Setup dialog box.

4. Follow the on-screen instructions.

Client Reinstallation Using The Control Panel

1. Open the Control Panel on the client computer.

2. Click the Add/Remove Programs utility.

3. Click the Install/Uninstall tab in the Add/Remove Programs Properties dialog box.

4. Click on the Microsoft Proxy Client (see Figure 6.23).

5. Click Add/Remove.

6. Click Reinstall in the Client Setup dialog box.

7. Follow the on-screen instructions.

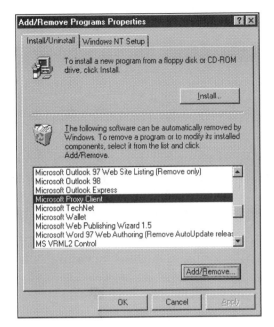

Figure 6.23   Client reinstallation from the Control Panel.

Uninstalling Clients

Proxy Server 2.0 clients can be uninstalled using the Microsoft Proxy Client program group, the Proxy Server client setup program, or the Control Panel.

Client Uninstallation Using The Proxy Server Program Group

1. Click Uninstall in the Microsoft Proxy Client program group.

2. Click Yes in the Uninstall Proxy Client dialog box.

Client Uninstallation Using The Mspclnt Share

1. Connect to the Mspclnt share on the server.

2. Run client setup.

3. Click Remove All (see Figure 6.24).

4. Follow the on-screen instructions.

Client Uninstallation Using The Control Panel

1. Open the Control Panel on the client computer.

2. Click Add/Remove Programs utility.

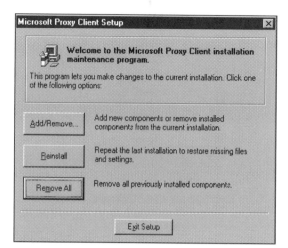

Figure 6.24   Client uninstallation using the MspcInt share on the server.

3. Click the Install/Uninstall tab in the Add/Remove Programs Properties dialog box.

4. Click on the Microsoft Proxy client.

5. Click Add/Remove.

6. Click Uninstall in the Client Setup dialog box.

7. Follow the on-screen instructions.

Moving On

Proxy Server 2.0 is installed and configured along with the client computers that use Proxy Server for their connection to the Internet. The reach of your organization, through the Internet service that is available to your organization through Proxy Server, now encompasses the world—yet, your work isn't over.

There is still more to learn about keeping Proxy Server running the way you want. In the next chapter we will cover the details of Proxy Server Administration. No doubt, your requirements will change over time: You will add new users, and your system will grow. You'll need to back up your Proxy Server configuration in the event that your changes or additions are unsuccessful. Understanding Proxy Server administration will help you keep your system up-to-date and running. Also, don't forget that security is an ongoing administrative challenge. For example, you might need to restrict access to certain users or services. I'll cover all these issues and more in the next chapters.

PART IV

Administering The Server, Clients, And Security

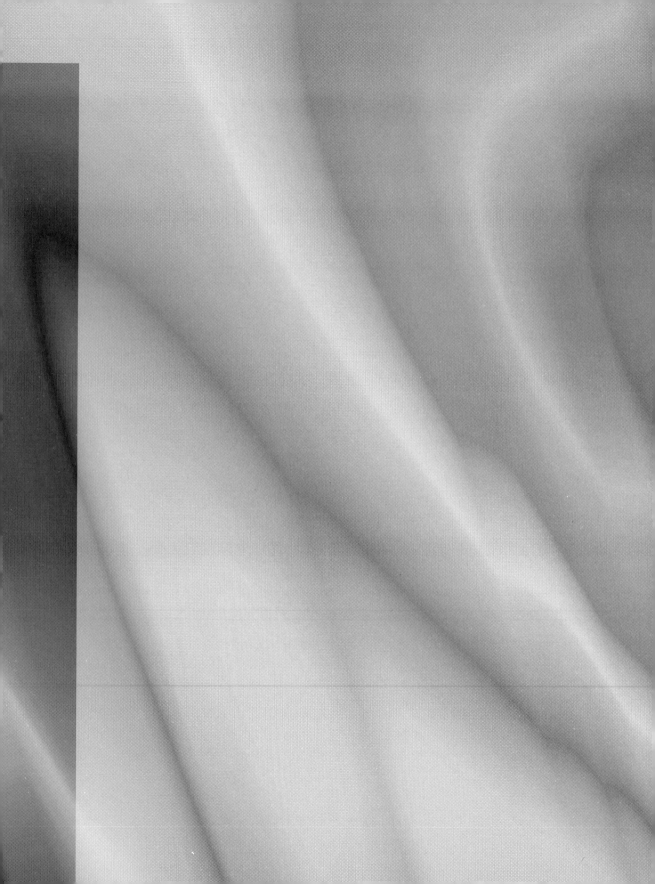

Administering Microsoft Proxy Server

When you installed Microsoft Proxy Server, you used many of the same dialog boxes that are used in the administration of the Proxy Server computer. So, you've already been exposed to several of the basic administrative concepts for Proxy Server. In this chapter, we will take an in-depth look at Proxy Server administration, giving you detailed procedures and examples for administering your Proxy Server computer.

Proxy Server Administration can be accomplished using the Internet Service Manager (ISM) or the Command Line. ISM is included with the Internet Information Server (IIS) version 3.0, which is contained in Microsoft Windows NT 4.0 Service Pack 3. ISM is a menu-based administration utility also used for IIS. Command-line administration of Proxy Server allows the use of configuration scripts. Configuring multiple Proxy Server computers identically is very efficient when using command-line scripting.

●●● *Tip* ●●●●

You *cannot* mix versions of Proxy Server and its associated client software. You must use Proxy Server 2.0 client software with the Proxy Server 2.0 services running on a server computer. Additionally, you cannot mix Proxy Server 2.0 Beta software versions with the released version of Proxy Server 2.0.

Internet Service Manager (ISM)

The ISM Administrative tool is included with Internet Information Server 3.0. When Proxy Server 2.0 is installed, ISM is modified to show the Socks Proxy, WinSock Proxy, or Web Proxy services along with the WWW, FTP, and Gopher services that comprise the standard services of IIS (see Figure 7.1). Although at first you might be a little disconcerted with the relationship of Proxy Server to ISM, you will find that sharing the same administrative interface with IIS enhances your ability to learn both services. You can administer Proxy Server with ISM running on the computer that Proxy Server is

![Microsoft Internet Service Manager window showing computer asus with services: Socks Proxy (Stopped), WinSock P... (Running), Web Proxy (Running), WWW (Running), Gopher (Stopped), FTP (Stopped). Status bar reads Ready, 1 Server(s), 3 Service(s) Running.]

Figure 7.1   Microsoft Internet Service Manager.

installed on, or you can administer Proxy Server remotely. The ISM Administration tool requires Windows NT Server 4.0 with the Internet Information Server 3.0 installed, or on Windows NT Workstation 4.0 with the Internet Service Manager component of Microsoft Peer Web Services installed.

To use ISM to administer Proxy Server from the computer it is running on, follow these steps:

1. To display the Internet Service Manager window, click Start, point to Programs, point to Proxy Server, and then click Internet Service Manager.

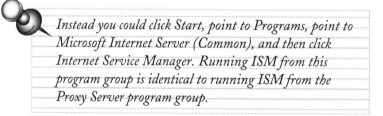

> *Instead you could click Start, point to Programs, point to Microsoft Internet Server (Common), and then click Internet Service Manager. Running ISM from this program group is identical to running ISM from the Proxy Server program group.*

2. To administer a Proxy Server service, double-click the server name next to the Socks Proxy, WinSock Proxy, or Web Proxy service.

To use ISM to administer Proxy Server from a remote computer, follow these steps:

1. To display the Internet Service Manager window, click Start, point to Programs, point to Proxy Server, and then click Internet Service Manager.

> *Instead you could click Start, point to Programs, point to Microsoft Internet Server (Common), and then click Internet Service Manager. Running ISM from this program group is identical to running ISM from the Proxy Server program group.*

2. On the Properties menu, click Connect to Server to specify a particular Internet server, or click Find All Servers and ISM will connect to all Internet Servers on your private network.

3. To administer a Proxy Server service, double-click the server name next to the Socks Proxy, WinSock Proxy, or Web Proxy service.

The WinSock Proxy service exhibits some confusing characteristics. For example, you will not see the WinSock Proxy service if you use Find All Servers. To show the WinSock Proxy service, click Connect to Server and specify the server name for the connection. Also, when you stop the WinSock Proxy service the configuration settings can be changed, but the changes do not take effect until you restart the service.

Another confusion surrounds starting or stopping the Web Proxy service or the WWW service. When you start or stop either service, the other service is started or stopped simultaneously. Unfortunately, ISM will not report the change in the other service's state unless you press the F5 key to refresh the ISM's screen.

Command Line Administration

Two command-line utilities are available to administer and configure Proxy Server. These utilities are markedly superior to ISM if you need to configure several Proxy Server computers identically. Because configuration commands can be placed in script files, the command-line utilities are much more efficient than ISM when you are administering several Proxy Servers uniformly. The two command-line utilities included with Proxy Server 2.0 are:

➤ **RemotMsp**   Used to administer and configure a remote Proxy Server computer.

➤ **WsProto**   Used to add, edit, and delete the WinSock Proxy service protocol definitions.

The appropriate use of command-line utilities requires an adequate understanding of the syntax of the utilities. What follows is an explanation of each command's syntax.

The RemotMsp Utility

You use the RemotMsp utility (remotmsp.exe) to administer and configure a remote Proxy Server computer. There are many options available to RemotMsp, several of which include a [*common options*] section that uses the following syntax:

```
[-c:server name [ -v -h ]]
```

where:

➤ **-c** specifies a remote Proxy Server computer.

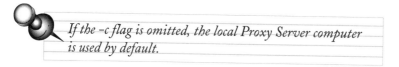

If the –c flag is omitted, the local Proxy Server computer is used by default.

➤ **-v** specifies verbose output.

➤ **-h** returns help for usage.

Where pertinent, these options are global across the entire script. For example, if a remote Proxy Server computer is specified, all the commands in the script file will be applied to that particular Proxy Server computer. Also, don't expect too much from the help option, it's rather terse.

Configuring The Server Service With RemotMsp

You can specify the Proxy Server service that the RemotMsp starts or stops. In addition, you can request the status of Proxy Server services using the **RemotMsp** command.

```
RemotMsp [common options] START | STOP |
        STATUS-SERVICE:service name
```

where **service name** is one of the following:

➤ **All** For all Proxy Server services

➤ **Admin** For Proxy Server administrative or security functions

➤ **WSP** For the WinSock Proxy service

➤ **WP** For the Web Proxy service

➤ **SOCKS** For the Socks Proxy service

The following examples illustrate the use of the **RemotMsp** command for starting, stopping, and displaying the operational status of a Proxy Server service.

Example 7.1

Examine the following command:

```
RemotMsp -v -c:proxy1 STATUS -SERVICE:All
```

In this case, the **RemotMsp** command is flagged for verbose output (**-v**) on the Proxy Server computer named proxy1 (**-c:**) to return the operating status (**STATUS**) for all services (**-SERVICE:All**). Executing this command will indicate which Proxy Server services are running or stopped.

Example 7.2

Executing this command stops the WinSock Proxy service:

```
RemotMsp -v -c:proxy1 STOP -SERVICE:WSP
```

Example 7.3

Executing this command starts the WinSock Proxy service:

```
RemotMsp -v -c:proxy1 START -SERVICE:WSP
```

 Tip

There is an anomaly in the initial release of Proxy Server 2.0 that appears when you start or stop the Proxy Server SOCKS service with RemoteMSP. The utility incorrectly indicates that the Web Proxy service (W3svc) was started or stopped. Performing a refresh (F5) in ISM will indicate the correct operating status.

Performing Server Backup And Restore With RemotMsp

The **RemotMsp SAVE** command permits you to perform a backup of the server configuration information to a file. That backup file can then be used for a later restore using the **LOAD** command. The following describes the syntax for the **SAVE** and **LOAD** commands.

The SAVE Command

The following is the syntax for the **SAVE** command:

```
RemotMsp [common options] SAVE -FILE:filename
```

Example 7.4

Executing this command saves the configuration of the Proxy Server computer proxy1 to a file in the current directory named mpscnfg.mcp:

```
RemotMsp -c:proxy1 SAVE -FILE:mpscnfg.mcp
```

The LOAD Command

The following is the syntax for the **LOAD** command:

```
RemotMsp [common options] LOAD -FILE:filename -LEVEL:level
```

where **level** is one of the following:

➤ Global

➤ Computer

You use the level **Computer** to restore the machine-specific configuration parameters for your Proxy Server computer.

> *The -LEVEL:level parameter must be used with the LOAD command. But, never use the -LEVEL:level parameter with the SAVE command.*

Example 7.5

The following is an example of the **LOAD** command:

```
RemotMsp -c:proxy1 LOAD -FILE:mpscnfg.mcp
    -LEVEL:Computer
```

RemotMsp Server Configuration Options

You can set several Proxy Server configuration options with **RemotMsp** using the **SET** command. The following is the syntax for using the **SET** command with **RemotMsp**:

```
RemotMsp [common options] SET option=value
```

where **option** is one of the following:

➤ **WSPAccessControl** Use a value of 1 to enable WinSock Proxy service access control and 0 to disable.

➤ **W3PaccessControl** Use a value of 1 to enable Web Proxy service access control and 0 to disable.

➤ **EnableDiskCache** To enable disk caching, use a value of 3 for FTP only, 5 for HTTP only, or 7 for both FTP and HTTP. Use a value of 0 to disable disk caching.

➤ **ResolveInArray** Use a value of 1 to enable your Proxy Server computer resolve to an array and 0 to disable.

➤ **EnableSynchronization** Use a value of 1 to enable synchronization of Proxy Server computers, thereby allowing common configuration maintenance to be performed for all of the Proxy Server computers in an array. Use a value of 0 to disable synchronization.

➤ **LoadFactor** Used to adjust the load factor for a Proxy Server computer that is a member of an array. The load factor setting can only be modified using the **RemotMsp**. See Chapter 10 for an explanation of the **LoadFactor** command.

WinSock Proxy Protocol Administration Using The WspProto Utility

You use the WspProto (*wspproto.exe*) command-line utility to add, delete, and edit WinSock Proxy service protocol definitions. The protocol definitions are placed in a text file organized with section and entry information. While the structure of this text file is similar to an initialization (.ini) file, a protocol definition filename must have an extension of .wsp. The following illustrates the format of the text file used by the WspProto utility to define a protocol:

```
[ProtocolName]
PrimaryPort=port, direction, type
SecondaryPorts=sub; sub
```

● ● *Tip* ● ● ●

Adding a protocol definition is easy if you associate the .wsp extension with wspproto.exe; then you can simply double-click the file name.

Each protocol has its own section in the protocol definition file. For example, the section name for the FTP protocol is [FTP]. You can have any number of sections in the protocol definition file, each section defining a different protocol. Upon execution of the WspProto utility, the program scans the protocol definition file, adding each protocol definition it finds. The following defines the parameters you use with the command entries when defining a protocol:

```
PrimaryPort=port, direction, type
```

where:

➤ **port** Is any valid port number.

➤ **direction** Can be equal to In or Out.

➤ **type** Can be equal to Tcp or Udp.

```
SecondaryPorts=sub; sub
```

➤ **sub** Defines a range, direction, or type. Range defines a port number or a port range of the form port number, or port number—port number, respectively. For example, the following defines a RealAudio protocol:

seven

[RealAudio (7070)]

PrimaryPort=7070,OUT,UDP

SecondaryPorts=6770,OUT,UDP;6970-7170,IN,UDP

In this example, the SecondaryPorts command has two sub parameters. In the first sub, the range parameter (6770) is a single outbound UDP port. In the second sub the range parameter (6970-7170) is a range of outbound UDP ports.

Example 7.6

The Network News Transfer protocol (alias=usenet) would be defined in the protocol definition file as follows:

```
[NNTP]
PrimaryPort=119,OUT,TCP
```

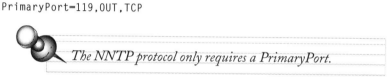

The NNTP protocol only requires a PrimaryPort.

Example 7.7

The MS NetShow protocol would be defined in the protocol definition file as follows:

```
[MS NetShow]
PrimaryPort=1755,OUT,TCP
SecondaryPorts=1025-5000,IN,UDP
```

The MS NetShow protocol requires a PrimaryPort and SecondaryPorts.

The [@MSP_WSP Protocols] Section

By placing the [@MSP_WSP Protocols] section in the protocol definition file, you can provide a list of protocol names. This helps to better organize the protocols contained in the file. The following illustrates the format of the [WSP Protocols] section:

```
[WSP Protocols] Proto1=xxx Proto2=yyy
```

where:

xxx and yyy refer to the various protocol definition sections.

Example 7.8

The AlphaWorld and AOL protocols would be defined in the protocol definition file as follows:

```
[WSP Protocols]
Proto1=AlphaWorld
Proto2=AOL
[AlphaWorld]
PrimaryPort=5670,OUT,TCP
SecondaryPorts=80-80,OUT,TCP;3000-3050,IN,UDP;3000-3050,OUT,UDP;7000-
7999,OUT,TCP;7000-7999,OUT,UDP
[AOL]
PrimaryPort=5190,OUT,TCP
```

WspProto Utility Syntax

The following illustrates the syntax of the WspProto utility:

```
WspProto [-f] filename.wsp
WspProto -l
```

 Tip

You can use the optional **-c:server** name entry with all WspProto utility options. If you omit the **-c:server** name entry, the local Proxy Server computer is used.

where:

➤ **-f** forces, or overwrites, an existing protocol definition.

 WspProto forces a protocol update, even if -f is omitted.

➤ **-l** lists the current protocol definitions. This parameter uses the WSP file format so it can later be loaded to another Proxy Server computer.

Tip

Deleting and renaming protocol definitions can only be accomplished through the WspProto utility. There is no equivalent action using ISM administration.

Example 7.9

```
WspProto -l
```

This command lists the current WinSock Proxy protocol definitions on the Proxy Server computer.

Example 7.10

```
WspProto -f newproto.wsp
```

This command creates new WinSock Proxy protocol definitions from the entries contained in the newproto.wsp file.

● ● ● *Tip* ● ● ● ●

The Proxy Server documentation lists additional command-line flags for executing wspproto.exe. These flags suggest that you can add, delete, and modify WinSock Proxy protocol definitions by placing protocol parameters on the command line, thus negating the need for a protocol definition file (.wsp). Don't bother with these flags, it's much simpler and safer to use a definition file.

Custom HTML Error Messages

Proxy Server returns error messages to your browser in HTML. You can create HTML error messages that are customized for your organization. The default HTML error file (default.htm) is located in an \ErrorHtmls directory. By default, this directory is placed as a subdirectory under the \Winnt directory. The file default.htm should not be deleted. You can use default.htm to create additional HTML error message pages. Error message pages are named using an errorcode.htm naming convention. For example, Proxy Server error #11001 denotes the host was not found. When Proxy Server returns the #11001 error condition, the page 11001.htm is called and displayed in the browser. The default.htm page is returned for any error condition that does not have a corresponding error message page.

You can use inline graphics in the form of GIF or JPEG files in your custom HTML error messages. However, these files must be stored in a separate shared directory on the Proxy Server computer and fully qualified URLs must be used in the HTML error message files to point to inline graphics. In other words, the URLs must consist of their host names and their domain names. For example, a computer that has the host name of proxy1 and the domain name of mycompany.com has the fully qualified URL of proxy1.mycompany.com. Also, any arrayed or chained Proxy Server configurations must include the fully qualified URL name of the Proxy Server computer that serves the HTML error messages.

You can edit the default.htm file just as you would any HTML page. Notepad works fine for simple pages, though you might be more comfortable using a full-fledged HTML editor such as Microsoft FrontPage. The following illustrates the syntax of HTML error messages.

➤ **[ERRORNUM]** Replace with the appropriate error code value.

➤ **[ERRORTEXT]** Replace with the appropriate error message text.

➤ **[SERVERNAME]** Replace with the name of the server that returns the HTML page.

➤ **[VIAHEADER]** Replace with the "via" header message string that the Proxy Server computer receives.

Example 7.11
The following is an example of a custom HTML error message:

```
<!DOCTYPE HTML PUBLIC "-//IETF//DTD HTML//EN">
<html>

<head>
<title>Proxy Server Report: Default</title>
</head>

<body bgcolor="#000000" topmargin="0" leftmargin="0"
   text="#FFFFFF">

<table border="0" width="100%">
  <tr>
    <td width="100%" bgcolor="#000000"> 
       <p align="right">
    </td>
  </tr>
</table>
<div align="center"><center>

<table border="0" width="85%" height="454" bgcolor="#808080">
  <tr>
    <td width="100%" colspan="2" height="26"
       bgcolor="#FFFF00"><h2><font color="#000000">Proxy
    Reports an error:</font></h2>
    </td>
  </tr>
  <tr>
    <td width="50%" height="12"><font color="#FF0000">
       <strong>[ERRORNUM]</strong></font></td>
       <td width="50%" height="12"><font color="#FF0000"><strong>[ERRORTEXT]</
       strong>
</font></td>
```

```
    </tr>
    <tr>
      <td width="100%" height="209" colspan="2"
          align="left"> <p> </p>
      <p><em>An error occurred while trying to retrieve your URL.
          </em></p>
      <p><em>This error could have been caused by:</em><ul>
        <li><em>Bad / misspelled URL</em></li>
        <li><em>Your access permissions</em></li>
        <li><em>Your network connection and/or transient
            conditions on the Internet</em></li>
        <li><em>An error on the source Web server</em></li>
      </ul>
      </td>
    </tr>
    <tr>
      <td width="50%" height="133"> <p><a href="http://www.microsoft.com/
proxy"><em>Microsoft
      Proxy Server v2.0</em></a></p>
      <p><strong>Proxy Server : [SERVERNAME]</strong></p>
      <p><strong>Via : [VIAHEADER]</strong></td>
      <td width="50%" height="133">Contact your
          <a href="mailto:proxyadmin@indepth-tech.com">
          Proxy Server Administrator</a> for help.</td>
    </tr>
    <tr>
    <td width="100%" height="19" colspan="2" bgcolor="#FFFF00"></td>
    </tr>
  </table>
</center></div>
</body>
</html>
```

LAT Administration

When you installed Proxy Server the Local Address Table (LAT) was created. The LAT consists of all the IP addresses that comprise your private network. The parameters for the LAT are contained in the file Msplat.txt that was created during installation. You might need to change these parameters from time to time as your private network changes. This is a relatively straightforward task, because the server maintains the master copy of the LAT and downloads a copy of the LAT to Proxy Server clients. Keep in mind that the LAT must not contain any IP addresses of external adapter cards installed on Proxy Server computers. You typically modify the LAT by simply adding or removing IP address pairs.

Modifying The LAT Using ISM

The following procedure uses the Internet Service Manager (ISM) to modify the LAT:

1. Open the Internet Service Manager.

2. Double-click the computer name next to the Web Proxy, WinSock Proxy, or Socks Proxy service.

3. Click Local Address Table in the Service Properties dialog box (see Figure 7.2).

4. You can now analyze the Internal IP ranges in the Local Address Table Configuration dialog box for appropriateness. Proceed to the appropriate action below once you determine the type of change necessary.

   ➤ **Add a Range of IP Addresses** Under Edit, type a pair of IP addresses in From and To, and then click Add.

   ➤ **Add a Single IP Address** Under Edit, type the identical IP address in both From and To, and then click Add.

   ➤ **Remove an IP Address or Address Pair** Under Internal IP Ranges, select the IP address or address pair no longer needed, and then click Remove.

5. Click on OK when you are finished making changes.

6. For the changes to take effect on the server, you must Stop and then restart the Web Proxy, WinSock Proxy, or Socks Proxy service.

For most purposes, the above procedure works fine. However, network routing changes could be so vast as to require a complete replacement of the LAT. In this case, you can generate a new LAT from the Windows NT Routing Table for your internal private network. It is crucial that the Windows NT Routing table is functioning properly before attempting to completely replace the LAT.

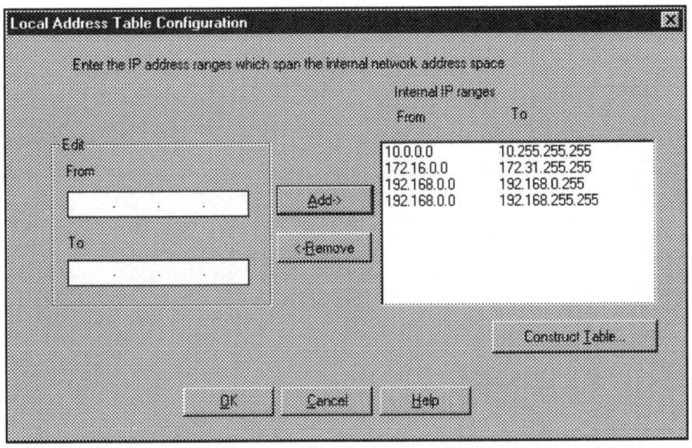

Figure 7.2 The Local Address Table Configuration dialog box.

Replacing The LAT Using ISM

You can use the following procedure to generate a new LAT from the Windows NT Routing Table using ISM:

1. Open the Internet Service Manager.

2. Double-click the computer name next to the Web Proxy, WinSock Proxy, or Socks Proxy service.

3. Click Local Address Table in the Service Properties dialog box.

4. Click Construct Table in the Local Address Table Configuration dialog box (see Figure 7.3).

5. Select the Add the Private Ranges checkbox to add the IP address ranges reserved for internal use by RFC 1918.

6. Select the Load from NT Internal Routing Table checkbox, then proceed to the appropriate action below.

   ➤ **IP Addresses of Internal Network Adapter Cards are Known**   Click Load Known Address Ranges from the following IP interface cards; then select only the internally connected cards, and click to clear any externally connected cards.

   ➤ **IP Addresses of Internal Network Adapter Cards are Unknown**   Click Load Known Address Ranges from all IP interface cards.

7. Click on OK when you are finished.

8. You can now analyze the entries' Internal IP ranges in the Local Address Table Configuration dialog box for appropriateness. Proceed to the appropriate action below after you determine the type of change necessary.

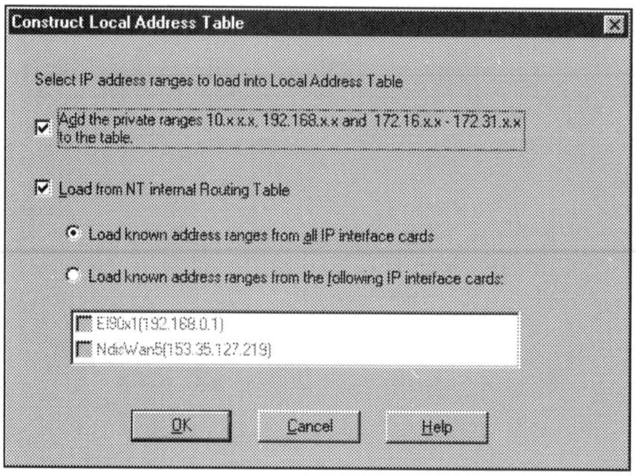

Figure 7.3   The Construct Local Address Table dialog box.

> ➤ **Add a Range of IP Addresses**   Under Edit, type a pair of IP addresses in From and To, and then click Add.

> ➤ **Add a Single IP Address**   Under Edit, type the identical IP address in both From and To, and then click Add.

> ➤ **Remove an IP Address or Address Pair**   Under Internal IP Ranges, select the IP address or address pair no longer needed, and then click Remove.

9. Click on OK when you have finished making changes.

10. To have the changes take effect on the server, you must stop and then restart the Web Proxy, WinSock Proxy, or Socks Proxy service.

Cache Administration For Single Proxy Servers

Caching is an important performance feature of the Web Proxy service. Your Proxy Server will continue to store local copies of your HTTP and FTP objects up to the specified size of the Proxy Server cache. The first request for a URL will cache any object type that is associated with that URL. This includes GIF and JPEG objects. All subsequent requests for the URL will return its associated objects from the cache. Because the cache is located on the Proxy Server computer, the objects do not need to be returned from the Internet; the performance gain is clear.

You have a great deal of control over what, when, and how much data is cached on Proxy Server. There are four primary configuration options for Proxy Server caching:

➤ Passive caching parameters and General Object Expiration Policy

➤ Active caching parameters

➤ Cache location and size

➤ Advanced caching policy parameters

The following sections describe the steps required for each of these cache configuration procedures.

Configuring Passive Caching Parameters And General Object Expiration Policy

Passive caching allows all objects returned to Proxy Server by Internet servers to be stored in the cache. It's important to note that for security reasons a few objects, such as Internet objects that require authentication or the Secure Sockets Layer (SSL), cannot be cached. Yet, the vast majority of objects are cached. Also, Proxy Server calculates a Time-To-Live (TTL) for each object in the cache. When an object's TTL expires, the next request for that object is transferred to the client from the Internet instead of from

Proxy Server's cache. The following procedure is used to set passive caching and an expiration policy. For additional information on configuring Proxy Server's cache expiration policy, see Decision Tree 7.1.

1. Open the Internet Service Manager.

2. Double-click the computer name next to the Web Proxy service.

3. Click the Caching tab in the Web Proxy Service Properties dialog box, and confirm that the Enable Caching checkbox is selected (see Figure 7.4).

4. Set the parameters for maintaining the freshness of objects in the cache. Proceed to the appropriate action below after you determine the cache expiration policy required:

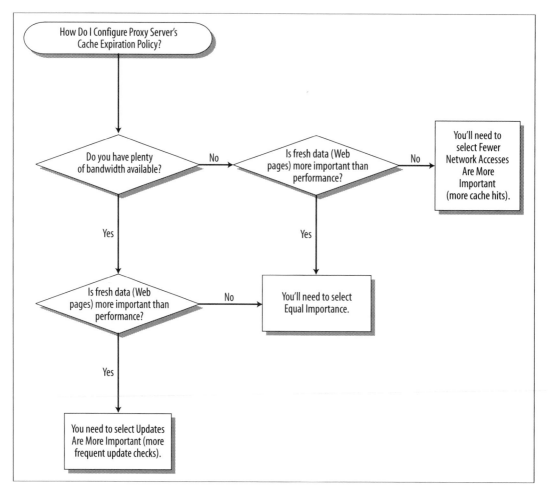

Decision Tree 7.1   How do I configure Proxy Server's cache expiration policy?

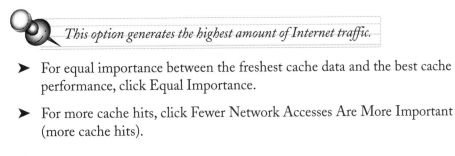

Figure 7.4   The Caching tab in the Web Proxy Service Properties dialog box.

➤ For the freshest cache data, click Updates Are More Important (this choice gives you more frequent update checks).

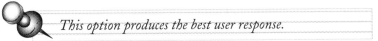

This option generates the highest amount of Internet traffic.

➤ For equal importance between the freshest cache data and the best cache performance, click Equal Importance.

➤ For more cache hits, click Fewer Network Accesses Are More Important (more cache hits).

This option produces the best user response.

Configuring Active Caching Parameters

Proxy Server will retrieve data from the Internet automatically through a process called active caching (see Decision Tree 7.2). This process further enhances performance because it retrieves the data that is most often requested by your users and then stores it in the Proxy Server cache, before a user makes the next request for the data. The following procedure is used to set active caching:

1. Open the Internet Service Manager.

2. Double-click the computer name next to the Web Proxy service.

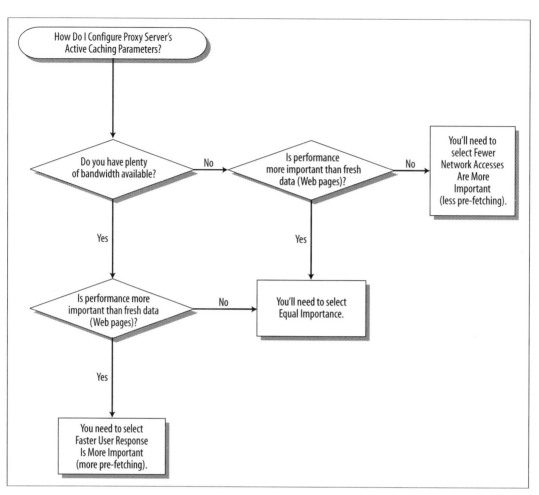

Decision Tree 7.2   How do I configure Proxy Server's active caching parameters?

3. Click the Caching tab in the Web Proxy Service Properties dialog box, and click the Enable Active Caching checkbox (see Figure 7.5).

4. Set the parameters for active caching. Proceed to the appropriate action below once you determine the level of active caching required:

➤ For the best cache performance and therefore the best user response, click Faster User Response Is More Important (more pre-fetching).

➤ For equal importance between the freshest cache data and the best cache performance, click Equal Importance.

➤ For the least Internet traffic on your Proxy Server and the least fresh cache data, click Fewer Network Accesses Are More Important (less pre-fetching).

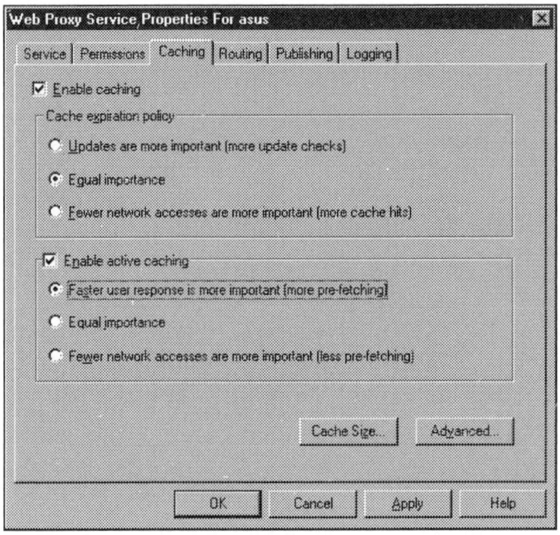

Figure 7.5 The Caching tab in the Web Proxy Service Properties dialog box.

● ● *Tip* ● ● ● ●

Using Auto Dial? Proxy Server will not actively cache during the times that Auto Dial is disabled. However, if a connection is established prior to the disabled time period and Proxy Server begins its active caching, it will continue its caching into the disabled time. Active caching will continue until Proxy Server stops caching for a time greater than the Idle Seconds parameter before hanging up. This parameter is set in Dial-Up Networking by selecting More and clicking on Logon Preferences.

Configuring Cache Location And Size

You originally assigned the disk drives for caching and the size of the cache during Proxy Server setup. When you execute the procedure below, a screen will display all of the local disk drives installed on the Proxy Server computer and the amount of space allocated for each drive's Proxy Server cache.

Note that when you reduce the size of the cache, you risk losing some of the cached data. Increasing the size of the cache on a drive has no effect on the cached data. The following procedure is used to configure the Proxy Server cache location and size:

1. Open the Internet Service Manager.

2. Double-click the computer name next to the Web Proxy service.

3. Click the Caching tab in the Web Proxy Service Properties dialog box, and then click Cache Size (see Figure 7.6).

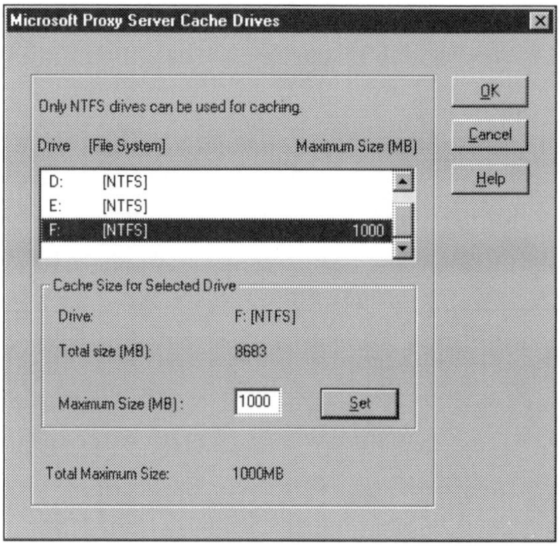

Microsoft Proxy Server Cache Drives

Only NTFS drives can be used for caching.

Drive [File System]   Maximum Size (MB)

D:	[NTFS]	
E:	[NTFS]	
F:	[NTFS]	1000

OK
Cancel
Help

Cache Size for Selected Drive

Drive: F: [NTFS]

Total size (MB):   8683

Maximum Size (MB):   1000   Set

Total Maximum Size: 1000MB

Figure 7.6   The Microsoft Proxy Server Cache Drives dialog box.

4. Configure the Proxy Server cache location and size. Proceed to the appropriate action below once you determine the change required in the size or location of the Proxy Server cache:

➤ To increase the cache size, type a larger value in Maximum Size (MB) under Cache Size for Selected Drive, and then click Set.

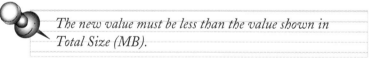

The new value must be less than the value shown in Total Size (MB).

➤ To decrease the cache size, type a smaller value in Maximum Size (MB) under Cache Size for Selected Drive, and then click Set.

➤ To stop storing cached data, type 0 in Maximum Size (MB) under Cache Size for Selected Drive, and then click Set.

5. For each cached drive you need to change, repeat step 4.

6. Click on OK when finished.

Tip

Try this procedure if you ever need to clear the Proxy Server cache: First, use the above procedure to reduce the size of the drive's cache to zero. This deletes all of the cached data. Then repeat the above procedure, increasing the size of the cache to meet your requirements. You now have a fresh Proxy Server cache.

Configuring Advanced Caching Policy

Proxy Server 2.0 allows you considerable flexibility in determining the size, age, and origin of cached objects. You can set an advanced caching policy by setting specific caching parameters; for example, you can configure:

➤ a limit to the size of cached objects

➤ the use of expired cached objects

➤ the TTL for HTTP & FTP objects

➤ a cache filter list

The following sections describe the procedures for each of the above advanced caching policy configurations.

Configuring A Limit To The Size Of Cached Objects

By default, the size of a cached Internet object is unlimited. However, you can impose a size limitation on the caching of requested Internet objects. Subsequently, Proxy Server will not cache any object that is larger than the size limit you specified. You limit the maximum size of cached objects by using the following procedure:

1. Open the Internet Service Manager.

2. Double-click the computer name next to the Web Proxy service.

3. Click the Caching tab in the Web Proxy Service Properties dialog box, and then click Advanced.

4. Select the Limit Size of Cached Objects checkbox and enter a size in KB (see Figure 7.7).

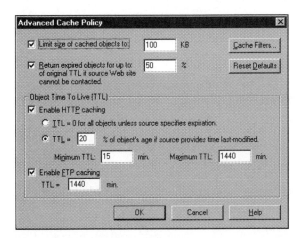

Figure 7.7   The Advanced Cache Policy dialog box.

seven

Configuring The Use Of Expired Cache Objects

Proxy Server can keep and use expired objects in the cache for a specified amount of time if the source Internet site for an object is unavailable. An expired object is an object whose Time-to-Live (TTL) has run out. You can specify the time beyond an object's expiration that the object can remain active in the Proxy Server cache. This procedure is particularly useful if you have an Internet connection that is unavailable during certain periods, or if your users need to access Internet servers that repeatedly are unavailable. Not only will the object still be returned to a client even though the object has expired or the Internet server is unavailable, but in addition your users will experience fast response time for all objects through this procedure. This feature is enabled by default and can be "tweaked" using the following procedure:

1. Open the Internet Service Manager.

2. Double-click the computer name next to the Web Proxy service.

3. Click the Caching tab in the Web Proxy Service Properties dialog box, and then click Advanced.

4. Select the Return Expired Objects for Up To checkbox, and in %, type a number that represents a percentage of the object's TTL (Time-to-Live).

Configuring The TTL For HTTP And FTP Objects

You can change the Time-to-Live (TTL) settings for both HTTP (Web) and FTP objects, thereby overriding the cache expiration policy set in the previous procedure. Note that Proxy Server always sets a TTL value even if an Internet server did not set the TTL. Specify the TTL for HTTP (Web) or FTP by using the following procedure:

1. Open the Internet Service Manager.

2. Double-click the computer name next to the Web Proxy service.

3. Click the Caching tab in the Web Proxy Service Properties dialog box, and then click Advanced.

4. The TTL for HTTP (Web) objects is specified by selecting the HTTP check-box under Object Time-To-Live (TTL), then proceeding to the appropriate action below:

   ➤ To set a time limit for object expiration, click TTL=, then enter a value in minutes.

   ➤ To set a time span between object updates, click TTL=, then type a value that is a percentage of an object's age. In both Minimum TTL and Maximum TTL, type a value in minutes.

5. The TTL for FTP objects is specified by selecting the FTP checkbox, then in TTL=, typing a value in minutes.

Configuring A Cache Filter List

You might need to exercise control over which specific Internet sites are cached. You do this by creating a list of cache filters. Once created, the entries in your cache filter can be edited or deleted.

Cache filters are made up of URL entries that use the format of **www.domain.com/path**. *Domain* is the Internet domain name, and *com* can be any valid suffix. For example, **www.internic.net/ds/** specifies the ds (directory services) page at **www.internic.net**.

Proxy Server permits the use of a wildcard character, an asterisk. You can use the wildcard character in several different ways. For example, you can specify all pages under a path. So **www.internic.net/ds/*** specifies all pages under the /ds path at **www.internic.net**. Placing the wildcard in front of the domain specifies sites that have similar domain names. For example, *.internic.net includes **www.internic.net**, **rs.internic.net**, and **ftp.internic.net**. Additionally, you could use the format domain.com/path to include all sites that have similar domain names and all pages under that path. For example, internic.net/ specifies all pages at internic.net.

What if you need to cache a specific page at a domain, but only that page? You can accomplish this feat by first setting an overarching filter policy and then creating exceptions to that policy. For example, you could set *.internic.net as a caching filter and then specify **www.internic.net** as an exception. All pages at **www.internic.net** are then cached, but only those pages. Pages at **rs.internic.net**, for example, are not cached.

The cache filter list is built by using the following procedure:

1. Open the Internet Service Manager.

2. Double-click the computer name next to the Web Proxy service.

3. Click the Caching tab in the Web Proxy Service Properties dialog box, click Advanced, and then click Cache Filters (see Figure 7.8). Then proceed to the appropriate action below:

   ➤ To create a new cache filter, click Add.

   ➤ To edit an existing cache filter, select the appropriate filter in the list, and then click Edit.

   ➤ To delete a cache filter, select the appropriate filter in the list, and then click Remove.

4. Next, type a URL to be filtered in the Cache Filter Properties dialog box.

You must use one of the required URL formats, as explained above.

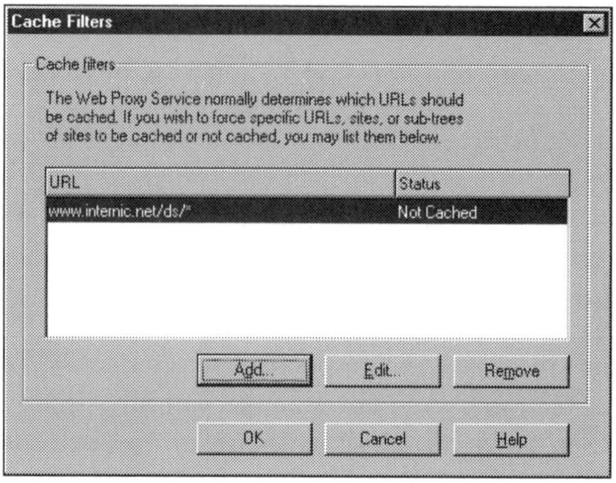

Figure 7.8   The Cache Filters dialog box.

5. Under Filtering Status, proceed to the appropriate action below, depending on your requirements:

➤ To always cache Internet objects returned from the URL entered, click Always Cache.

➤ To prevent caching of Internet objects returned from the URL entered, click Never Cache.

6. Click on OK to return to the Cache Filters dialog box.

7. Continue building the cache filter list by repeating steps 5 through 6 as necessary.

8. Click on OK when finished.

Performing Server Backup And Restore With ISM

You can back up and restore Proxy Server configuration parameters using ISM (Internet Service Manager). These parameters are stored in a text file, which is placed by default in C:\Msp\Config directory. While you can change the directory where the backup configuration files are kept, you should always place these files in a secure NTFS directory. You should perform a backup of the Proxy Server configuration before changing any of the Proxy Server configuration parameters.

The configuration file is named automatically using the following convention:

MSPyyyymmdd.mpc

where:

➤ yyyy is the year.

➤ mm is the month.

➤ **dd** is the day.

As you can see, the above naming convention for the backup configuration file integrates the computer's system date with the file name, thereby assisting the rolling back of a configuration to a specific date.

Backing Up The Server Configuration

The following procedure is used to back up a server configuration using ISM:

1. Open the Internet Service Manager.

2. Double-click the computer name next to any Proxy Server service.

3. Click Server Backup in the Service Properties dialog box on the Service tab Size (see Figure 7.9).

4. Type a valid path for the new server configuration backup file.

Alternately, you can click Browse to display a listing of the local file system and then select an existing path and file name from the list.

Restoring The Server Configuration

Once your Proxy Server configuration has been backed up, you can restore the server from the configuration file. You can either fully or partially restore a server. The full restore consists of both computer-specific and non-computer-specific parameters, while the partial restore consists of only the non-computer-specific parameters. Table 7.1 illustrates the parameters rolled back using either the full or partial restore process.

Use the following procedure to restore a Proxy Server configuration:

1. Open the Internet Service Manager.

2. Double-click the computer name next to any Proxy Server service.

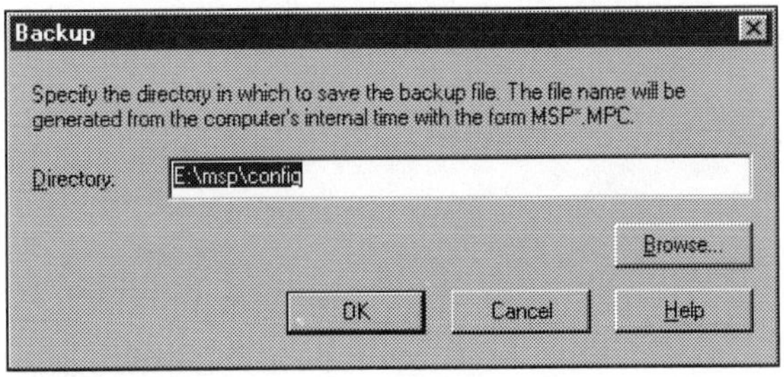

Figure 7.9   The Backup dialog box.

Table 7.1   Configuration parameters rolled back using full or partial restore process.

Parameters Restored	Full Restore	Partial Restore
Non-Computer-Specific Parameters		
User Permissions	✔	✔
Array Membership information	✔	✔
Computer-Specific Parameters		
Web Proxy service cache size and disk location	✔	✘
Disk location for all service logs and the packet filter log	✔	✘
Packet filter configuration information	✔	✘
Auto Dial configuration information	✔	✘
Server alias used in the "HTTP Via" header for routing	✔	✘
Server intra-array IP address	✔	✘
Registry keys that cannot be configured through the Internet Service Manager user interface	✔	✘

✔ = yes   ✘ = no

3. Click Server Restore in the Service Properties dialog box on the Service tab Size (see Figure 7.10).

4. Proceed to the appropriate action below after determining the type of restore required:

➤ To restore all server configuration parameters, click Full Restore.

➤ To restore only non-computer-specific server configuration parameters, click Partial Restore.

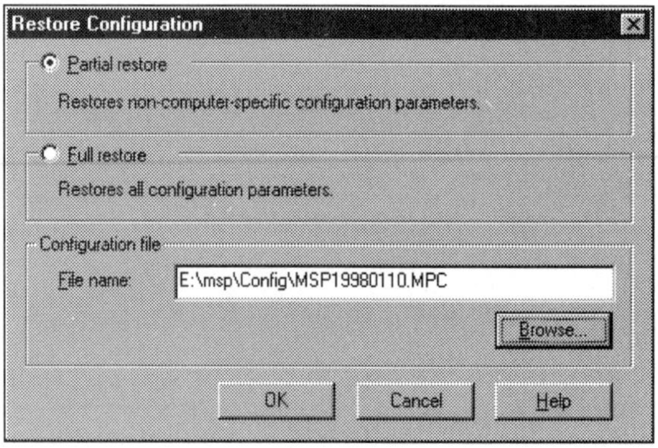

Figure 7.10   The Restore Configuration dialog box.

5. Type a valid path for the location to the server backup file under Configuration file.

Alternately, you can click Browse to display a listing of the local file system and then select an existing path and file name from the list.

Configuring Auto Dial

Small workgroups can use Proxy Server's Auto Dial feature to connect to an ISP through a modem or a dial-up ISDN connection. For Auto Dial to initiate a dial-out connection request as a RAS client, a valid Remote Access Service (RAS) Phonebook entry must be installed and configured to work with your modem or ISDN adapter. Typically, your ISP will furnish the Domain Name System (DNS) parameters required for your connection. Check your ISP's documentation for these specific details, and see Decision Tree 7.3 for more information on configuring Proxy Server to auto dial your ISP.

Once properly configured, Proxy Server will auto dial your ISP whenever the following circumstances occur:

➤ A client requests an object through the Web Proxy service and the object cannot be located in the Proxy Server cache.

➤ Active caching is automatically refreshing cached objects for the Web Proxy service.

➤ A client request routes through the WinSock Proxy or Socks Proxy services.

There are several tasks that must be completed for Auto Dial to function properly. Use the following list as a guide for completing all the tasks required for configuring Proxy Server to Auto Dial your ISP:

➤ Confirm the proper installation of a RAS client on the Proxy Server computer. (See Chapter 6.)

➤ Create a RAS Phonebook entry for your ISP for use with the Proxy Server Auto Dial feature.

➤ Configure Windows NT Remote Access service properties for use with Proxy Server's Auto Dial feature.

➤ Unbind the WINS client from external network adapters.

➤ Enter logon credentials as required by your ISP.

➤ Enable or restrict dial-out services and time periods as appropriate for your user community.

➤ If necessary, stop and restart the Proxy Server services.

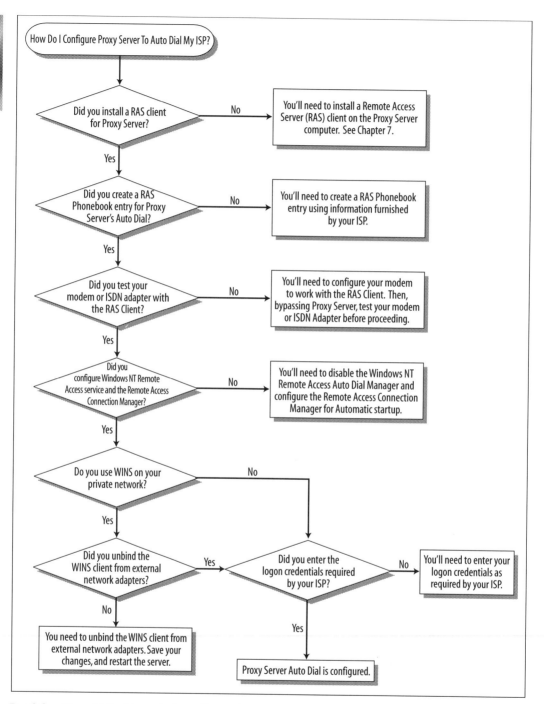

Decision Tree 7.3   How do I configure Proxy Server to auto dial my ISP?

Configuring The RAS Phonebook

You learned how to install and configure the RAS client in Chapter 6. Now you use Dial-Up Networking (DUN) to create an entry in the RAS Phonebook for your ISP. Your ISP must supply you with the access number and the specific parameters for establishing a dial-up connection. Note that Proxy Server's Auto Dial does not support multiple RAS phonebook entries, so you can not automate the dialing of multiple ISPs.

Tip

Do you need to add an extra digit to use an outside line? You must add the digit directly to the RAS Phonebook entry. *Adding the digit in the Dialing Properties dialog box in the Modem's application under Control Panel will not work.*

Use the following procedure to create a RAS Phonebook entry:

1. Click Start, point to Programs, point to Accessories, and click Dial-Up Networking.

2. If this is the first time you are running Dial-Up Networking, the following information will have to be placed in the Dialing Properties Dialog Box:

   ➤ The country in which the server is installed.

   ➤ The area or city code for the local phone exchange.

   ➤ The number used, if any, to dial an outside line.

   ➤ The type of dialing your phone system uses, either Tone or Pulse.

3. Click on OK in the Dial-Up Networking dialog box if the Phonebook is empty, or click the New button if other entries exist in the Phonebook.

4. In the New Phonebook Entry Wizard dialog box, give the new Phonebook entry a name.

5. Select the checkbox associated with the following information, as appropriate:

   ➤ **I Am Calling The Internet**   Select this box.

   ➤ **Send My Plain Text Password If That's The Only Way To Connect**   Typically your ISP will specify this box to be selected.

   ➤ **The Non-Windows NT Server That I Am Dialing Expects Me To Type Login Information After Connecting, Or To Know TCP/IP Addresses Before Dialing**   Select as appropriate.

6. Next, select the modem or adapter that this entry will use from the list presented.

7. Enter the country code, area code, and phone number of the dial-up server.

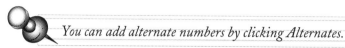

You can add alternate numbers by clicking Alternates.

8. Click Finish to add the new Phonebook entry.

9. Next, select the new Phonebook entry from the drop-down list in the Dial-Up Networking dialog box, click the More button, and then select User Preferences.

10. In the User Preferences dialog box, make the following selections as appropriate:

   ➤ **Enable Auto Dial By Location**   Click to clear the New Location (the current location) check box.

   ➤ **Number of Redial Attempts**   Type a value for the number of times you want to redial if a connection cannot be established.

   ➤ **Seconds Between Redial Attempts**   Type a value for the number of seconds between each of the above redial attempts.

   ➤ **Idle Seconds Before Hanging Up**   Type a value representing the number of seconds the connection can be inactive before an automatic disconnection occurs. For example, 300.

   ➤ **Redial on Link Failure**   Select this checkbox.

11. Click on OK, and then click Close.

The remaining parameters for your RAS Phonebook entry, such as TCP/IP settings and passwords, will be specific to your ISP. Be sure to enter this information as furnished by your ISP before proceeding.

Configuring RAS Auto Dial

You can verify that the RAS client is installed properly by dialing your ISP. You do this by bringing up the Dial-Up Networking Utility and clicking the Dial button. The RAS client is properly installed if an Internet connection is then established. Next, you configure the Remote Access Auto Dial Manager and Remote Access Connection Manager services to use the Proxy Server Auto Dial service instead of RAS auto-dial service. Use the following procedure to configure Remote Access properties for Auto Dial:

1. Click Start, point to Settings, and click Control Panel.

2. Double-click the Services utility.

3. Select Remote Access Auto Dial Manager in the Services dialog box, and then click Startup.

4. Click Disabled in the Service dialog box under Startup Type, and then click on OK (see Figure 7.11).

5. Select Remote Access Connection Manager in the Services dialog box, and then click Startup.

6. Click Automatic in the Service dialog box under Startup Type, and then click on OK.

7. Click Close.

Unbinding The WINS Client From External Network Adapters

Next, you need to unbind the WINS client from the external Network Adapters using the following procedure:

1. Click Start, point to Settings, and click Control Panel.

2. Double-click the Network utility.

3. Click the Bindings tab in the Network dialog box.

4. Click the down arrow for the drop-down list box that is located next to Show Bindings For, and then select all adapters.

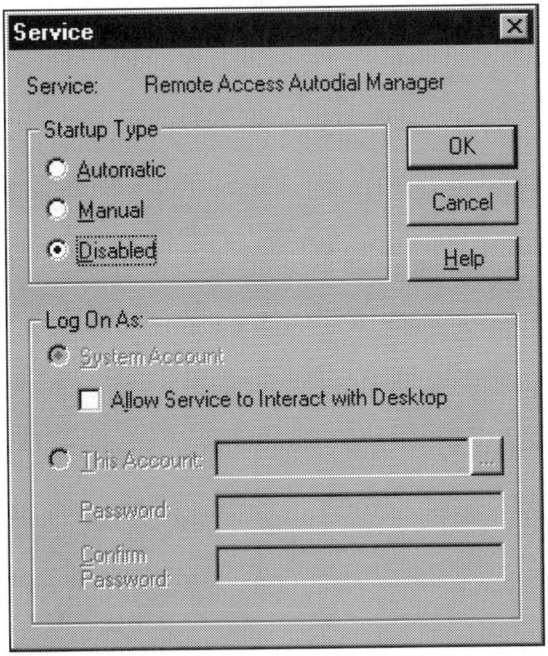

Figure 7.11   Services dialog box for the Remote Access Auto Dial Manager.

5. Click the plus sign that is next to Remote Access WAN Wrapper in the Adapter list. This expands the view.

6. Click once to highlight the WINS client (TCP/IP) under Remote Access WAN Wrapper and then click the Disable button (see Figure 7.12).

7. Click on OK when finished.

Entering Your Logon Credentials

Most ISPs will require you to log on to their service with a username and password each time a dial-up connection is established. The following procedure allows you to associate these credentials in a RAS Phonebook entry:

1. Open the Internet Service Manager.

2. Double-click the computer name next to any Proxy Server service.

3. Click Auto Dial in the Service Properties dialog box on the Service tab.

4. Click the Credentials tab (see Figure 7.13).

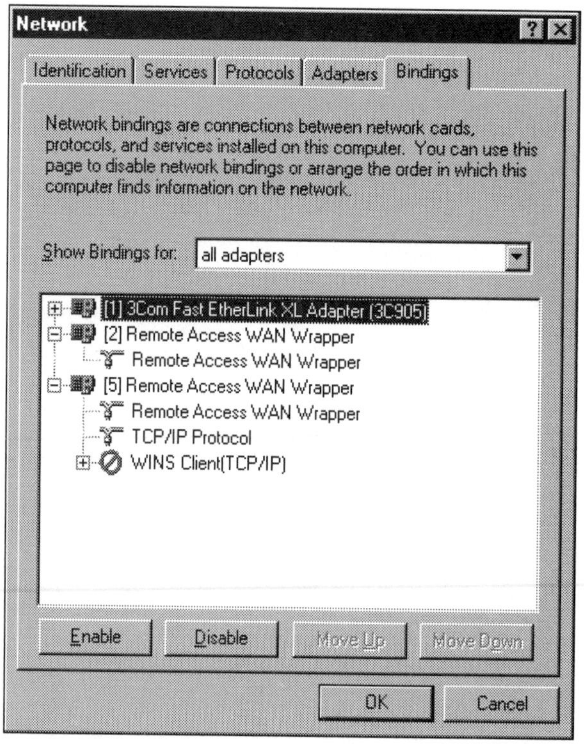

Figure 7.12   The Bindings tab in the Network dialog box.

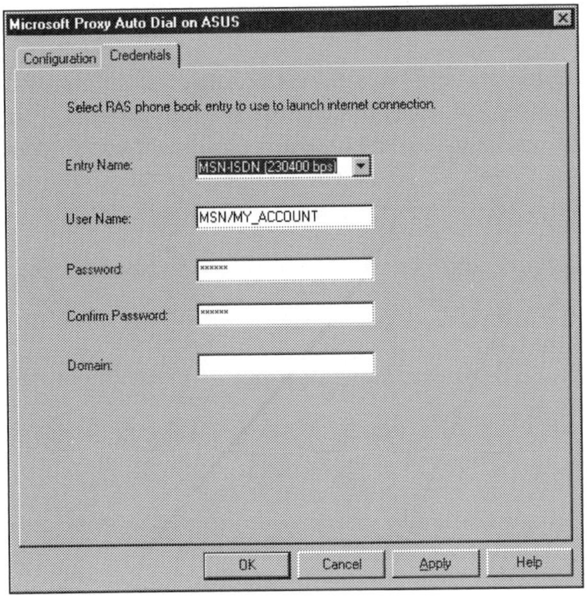

Figure 7.13   The Credentials tab in the Microsoft Proxy Auto Dial dialog box.

5. In the Entry Name field, select the name of the RAS Phonebook entry to use with Proxy Server's Auto Dial feature.

6. In the User Name field, type the username to log on to your ISP account.

7. In the Password field, type the password required to log on to your ISP account.

8. In the Confirm Password field, retype the password you entered above.

9. In the Domain field, type the domain name required, if any, to log on to your ISP account.

10. Click Apply, and then click on OK to finish.

Configuring Dial-out Services And Time Periods

By default, Proxy Server enables dial-out Internet access for all hours. You might be billed for your connection time or you might want to restrict your user community from dial-out Internet access during certain periods. You can enable or restrict Auto Dial for the following services and times:

➤ The WinSock Proxy and Socks Proxy services.

➤ The Web Proxy service primary route.

➤ The Web Proxy service backup route.

➤ Specified hours of the day or specified days of the week.

Tip

Do you need to automate your Proxy Server dial-up connection? While this feature is absent in Proxy Server Auto Dial, you can use the RAS dial-out scripting options to achieve the same result. Just set the parameters within the RAS scripting file named Switch.inf. See your Windows NT Server 4.0 documentation or query RAS Help for more information.

Use the following procedure to enable or restrict dial-out services and time periods:

1. Open the Internet Service Manager.

2. Double-click the computer name next to any Proxy Server service.

3. Click Auto Dial in the Service Properties dialog box on the Service tab (see Figure 7.14).

4. Click the Configuration tab, then proceed to the appropriate action below, as required:

   ➤ To enable Auto Dial for the WinSock Proxy and Socks Proxy services, select the Enable Dialing for WinSock and SOCKS Proxy checkbox under Dialing Services.

   ➤ To enable Auto Dial for the primary route of the Web Proxy service, select the Enable Dialing for Web Proxy Primary Route checkbox under Dialing Services.

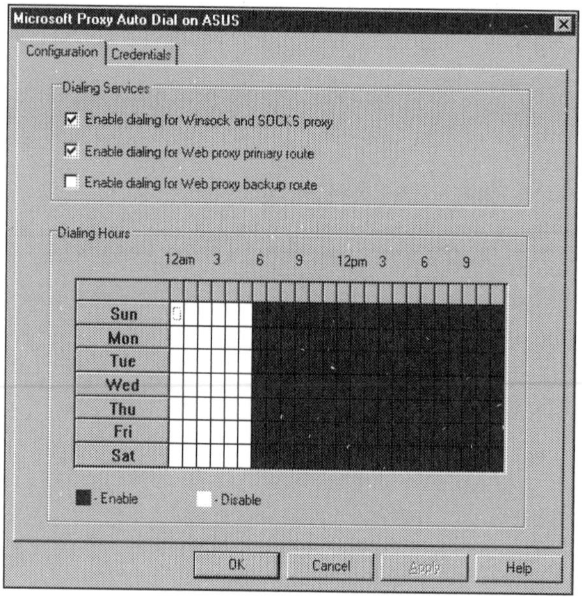

Figure 7.14   The Microsoft Proxy Auto Dial dialog box.

➤ To enable Auto Dial for the backup route of the Web Proxy service, select the Enable dialing for Web proxy backup route checkbox under Dialing Services.

➤ To disable dialing during specified hours of the day or for specified days of the week, click the appropriate table grid cells under Dialing Hours.

5. Click Apply when you have enabled or disabled the dial-out services or time periods you require.

6. Click on OK to finish.

Restarting Services

The following circumstances necessitate the restarting of *all* Proxy Server services when using Auto Dial to establish a dial-up connection to an ISP:

➤ **The first time Auto Dial is used.** To initialize Proxy Server's use with Auto Dial, *all* services must be restarted.

➤ **The clearing of current Auto Dial settings.** When Auto Dial settings are cleared, *all* services must be restarted for the new parameters to take effect.

Once used, additional changes to Auto Dial settings do not require the restarting of Proxy Server services—unless, of course, the Auto Dial settings are cleared. You can start and stop the services using ISM or the command Prompt. Use the following procedure to stop services using ISM:

1. In ISM, right-click the computer name next to any Proxy Server service.

2. Click Stop Service.

3. Repeat steps 1 and 2, stopping the Web Proxy, WinSock Proxy, and Socks Proxy services.

4. In ISM, right-click the computer name next to any Proxy Server service.

5. Click Start Service.

6. Repeat steps 4 and 5, starting the Web Proxy, WinSock Proxy, and Socks Proxy services.

Alternately, you can use the following procedure to stop and restart the Proxy Server services by typing the following commands from a command prompt:

For the Web Proxy service:

```
net stop | start w3svc
```

For the WinSock Proxy service:

```
net stop | start wspsvc
```

For the Socks Proxy service:

```
net stop | start spsvc
```

Configuring RAS Server

Typically, the Windows NT Remote Access Server (RAS) should be configured for Dial Out Only. The Proxy Server computer is considered a RAS client if only dial out is permitted. Only in rare instances should a Proxy Server computer be configured as a RAS server. To become a RAS server one of the following conditions must exist:

➤ The Windows NT computer is configured to dial out and receive calls.

➤ The Windows NT computer is configured to receive calls.

Your Proxy Server computer *should not* be configured as a RAS server. Use the following procedure if your Proxy Server computer was previously a RAS server and you wish to reconfigure it as a RAS client:

1. Click Start, point to Settings, and click Control Panel.

2. Double-click the Network utility.

3. Click the Services tab in the Network dialog box.

4. Click Remote Access Service under Network Services, and then click Properties.

5. Select a port in the Remote Access Setup dialog box and then click Configure (see Figure 7.15).

6. Click Dial Out Only in the Configure Port Usage dialog box, and then click on OK (see Figure 7.16).

7. Click Continue in the Remote Access dialog box, and then click the Protocols tab.

8. Click TCP/IP Protocol under Network Protocols, and then click Properties.

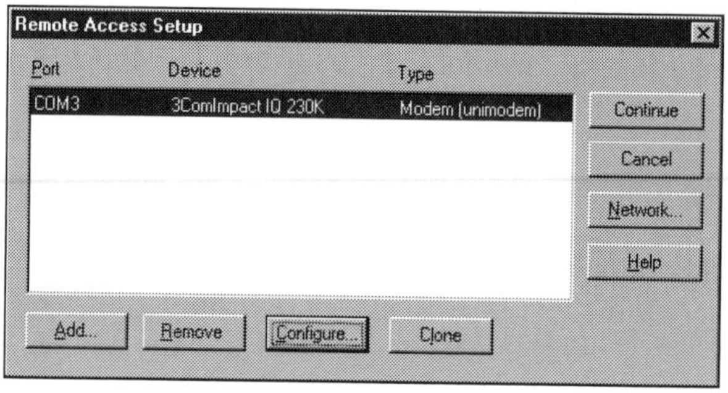

Figure 7.15   The Remote Access Setup dialog box.

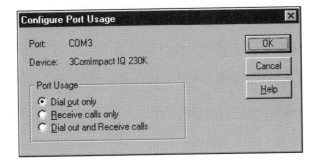

Figure 7.16   The Configure Port Usage dialog box.

9. Click the Routing tab in the Microsoft TCP/IP Properties dialog box; then click once, if required, to clear the Enable IP Forwarding checkbox, click Apply, and then click on OK.

10. Click Close in the Network dialog box, and then click Yes when prompted to restart your computer.

Moving On

You should now have a basic understanding of how to administer the Proxy Server computer. One of the benefits of Proxy Server is that you can reconfigure it at any time through the ISM or the command-line utilities. Therefore, reinstallation—or even rebooting—is seldom required. With the rapidly changing Internet environment, this ease of configuration is a real aid to the busy network administrator.

Your Proxy Server clients will also need to be kept up-to-date with your server changes. In the next chapter, we'll examine the tools and techniques used to administer Proxy Server clients.

Proxy Server Client Administration

Proxy Server automatically creates the files needed to configure your clients, and your clients might work fine with these automatically generated files. Nevertheless, any private network, particularly one connected to the Internet, is subject to change, and these changes might necessitate changes in your Proxy Server clients. This chapter gives you the information you need to administer Proxy Server clients.

Even if you have no need to make changes at this time, understanding Proxy Server client administration now will be helpful if client problems should arise. Moreover, reviewing the structure of the Client Configuration file will further your understanding of how Proxy Server works. Let's begin by examining the Client Configuration dialog box.

The Client Configuration Dialog Box

You enter the configuration parameters for clients by using the Client Installation/Configuration dialog box. This dialog box is accessible from the main dialog box for any Proxy Server service. Use the following procedure to access the Client Installation/Configuration dialog box:

1. Click Start, point to Programs, point to Microsoft Proxy Server, and click on Internet Service Manager.

2. Click on the computer name next to the SOCKS Proxy, WinSock Proxy, or Web Proxy service.

3. Click on Client Configuration; under Configuration, bring up the Client Installation/Configuration dialog box.

Figure 8.1 illustrates the Client Installation/Configuration dialog box. Notice that it is identical to the dialog box used initially to configure clients during setup. Although the dialog box is organized into three major sections, it is typically easier to understand by breaking it into two sections:

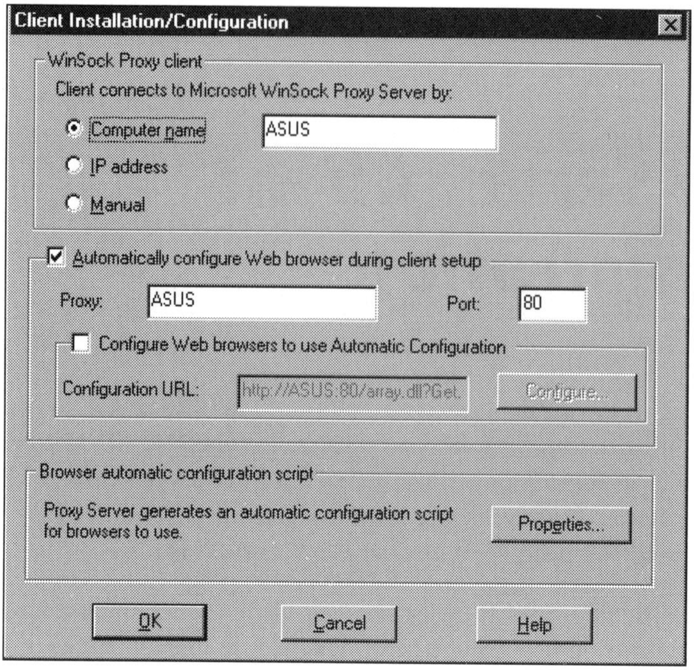

Figure 8.1   The Client Installation/Configuration dialog box.

➤ WinSock Proxy Client Parameters

➤ Web Browser Configuration Parameters (including automatic configuration and advanced properties)

The Client Installation/Configuration dialog box displays several client parameters that are available for editing. You can change any or all of these parameters during an editing session. Each of these client configuration parameters is explained in detail in the text that follows. Once you are satisfied that you've made the appropriate changes, simply click on OK.

WinSock Proxy Client Parameters

Using the Client Installation/Configuration dialog box you can specify that WinSock Proxy clients connect to the Proxy Server computer using:

➤ A computer or DNS name

➤ An IP address

➤ A manually entered array name or group of IP addresses for an array

See Decision Tree 8.1. WinSock Proxy clients, by default, connect using a computer or DNS name. If you decide to use an IP address, you enter the IP address of the Proxy Server computer. If your private network runs IPX/SPX as its only internal protocol to

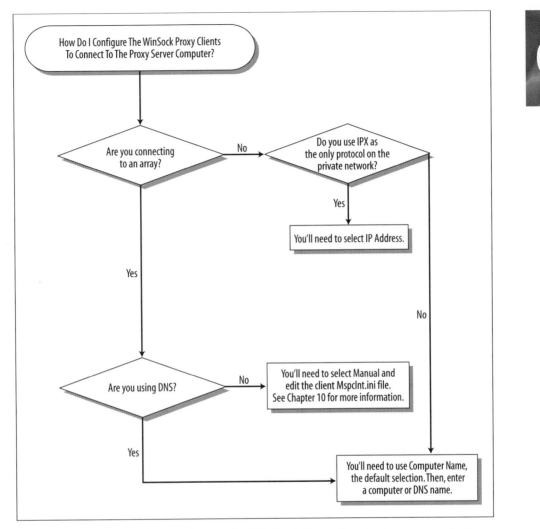

Decision Tree 8.1   How do I configure the WinSock Proxy Service to connect to the Proxy Server computer?

connect clients, you must use an IP address to connect to the Proxy Server computer. The third option is viable for an array of Proxy Server computers and requires you to edit the client configuration file, Mspclnt.ini.

Web Browser Configuration Parameters

The following Web browser configuration options are available using the Client Configuration dialog box:

➤ **Automatically Configure Web Browser During Client Setup**   Proxy Server will set up your Web browsers automatically when you select the Automatically Configure

eight

Web Browser During Client Setup checkbox. If this information is not already entered, you must specify the Proxy Server computer name in the Proxy field and the Web Proxy service port in the Port field. You cannot change the service port value by using this dialog box. This default value is the TCP port number that is set for Internet Information Server. To change the service port value, you must use Internet Service Manager to administer the WWW service.

➤ **Configure Web Browsers to Use Automatic Configuration**   This option specifies how the client setup program updates Web browsers. Recent Web browsers, such as Internet Explorer version 3.02 and later and Netscape Navigator, have the ability to use JavaScript. The automatic configuration JavaScript works with your browser to locate the Proxy Server computer at the IP address you specify. When you select Configure Web Browsers to Use Automatic Configuration, your Web browser is configured using this JavaScript. Proxy Server creates a default URL during setup that points to the location of the automatic configuration JavaScript. Clicking Configure allows you to change the location of the Automatic Configuration URL. Typically, you only change this location if you are using an array or hierarchical chain of Proxy Server computers. The primary purpose of the script is to locate cache objects in a Proxy Server array. The JavaScript determines which computer in the array contains the cached object and returns the object to the client. If the requested object is not cached, the Proxy Server computer chosen by the script retrieves the object from the Internet.

Using a Client Configuration Script can improve browser performance and assure Web browser configuration parameters are up-to-date. This JavaScript is downloaded each time the user opens the Web browser. The JavaScript is executed again on every URL that the browser requests. The purpose is to lessen the work performed by the Proxy Server array by moving the routing request to the Web browser. Therefore, the only real benefit to using a Client Configuration Script is if the Web Proxy client points directly to a Proxy Server array.

➤ **Browser Automatic Configuration Script**   Clicking the Properties button under Browser automatic configuration script brings up the Advanced Client Configuration dialog box (see Figure 8.2).

The Advanced Client Configuration Dialog Box

When you click the Properties button under Browser automatic configuration, the following Advanced Client Configuration options are available:

➤ **Use Proxy For Local Servers**   Select this option if you want client requests to internal servers to first pass through Proxy Server. Using this option with Proxy Server caching turned on would place an increased load on the Proxy Server computer, while decreasing the load on the internal Web servers.

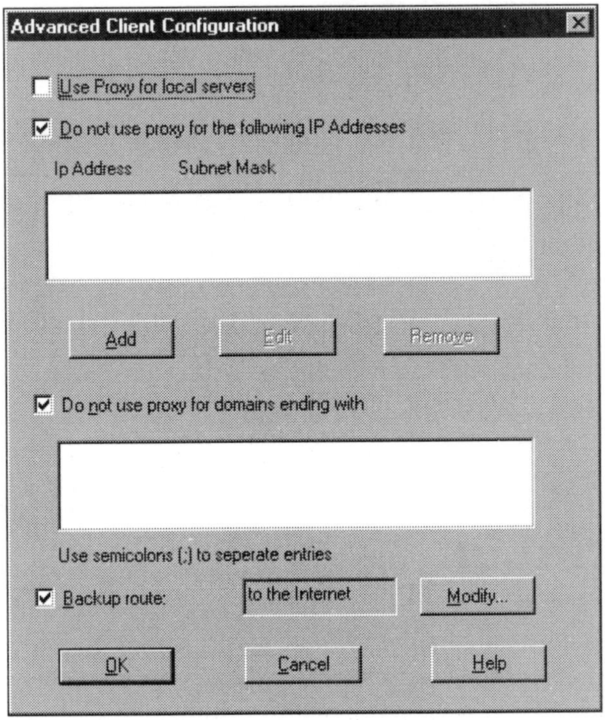

Figure 8.2   The Advanced Client Configuration dialog box.

➤ **Do Not Use Proxy For The Following IP Addresses**   Selecting this option will allow client computers to bypass Proxy Server and access the Internet directly for the IP addresses specified in the list. Even if Proxy Server caching is turned on, no caching will occur for the IP addresses that are specified in this list.

➤ **Do Not Use Proxy For Domains Ending With**   Selecting this option will allow client computers to bypass Proxy Server and access the Internet directly for the domains specified in the list. Even if Proxy Server caching is turned on, no caching will occur for the domains specified in this list.

➤ **Backup Route**   Selecting this option allows you to specify an alternate route to the Internet if the Proxy Server computer is unavailable. Thus, the failure of a single Proxy Server computer is unlikely to bring down the entire Proxy Server chain. You can route Web Proxy client requests to the following locations:

• To an upstream Proxy Server computer or a Proxy Server array.

• Directly to the Internet.

• When you Click Modify, the above options are available under the Configure Backup Route dialog box (see Figure 8.3).

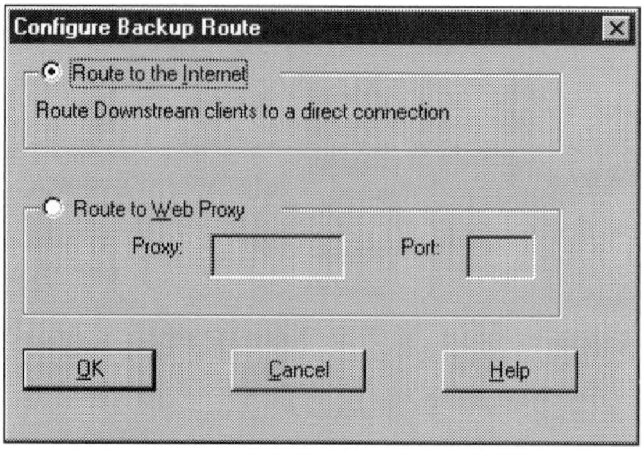

Figure 8.3   The Configure Backup Route dialog box.

Understanding The Client Configuration File: Mspclnt.ini

The key to understanding the details of Proxy Server client configuration is through examining the client configuration file. The master copy of the client configuration file, Mspclnt.ini, is located by default in the C:\Msp\Clients directory on the Proxy Server computer. This file contains the configuration information for Proxy Server clients. The Mspclnt.ini file is created automatically during Proxy Server setup. When Proxy Server clients are set up on Microsoft Windows computers, they receive a copy of Mspclnt.ini, which by default is stored in the Mspclnt directory on the client computer.

The client configuration file can be modified at any time using a text editor or by again running Proxy Server setup and specifying new information in the Client Installation/ Configuration dialog box. After you successfully install the WinSock Proxy client, the client configuration file is downloaded and updated on the client computer every time it is started and, by default, every six hours after the initial refresh is made. You can also change the client's copy of the client configuration file by using a text editor or by re-freshing the client's copy of the file by downloading the current file version from the server. However, if you use a text editor to modify the client's copy of Mspclnt.ini, it will be overwritten upon the refresh by the server. Therefore, it is a good idea to only change the Mspclnt.ini file on the server.

Examine the following example of a Mspclnt.ini:

```
[Internal]
scp=9,10
Build=2.0.372.12
[wspsrv]
Disable=1
[inetinfo]
```

```
Disable=1
[services]
Disable=1
[spoolss]
Disable=1
[rpcss]
Disable=1
[kernel32]
Disable=1
[mapisp32]
Disable=0
[exchng32]
Disable=0
[outlook]
Disable=0
[raplayer]
RemoteBindUdpPorts=6970-7170
LocalBindTcpPorts=7070
[rvplayer]
RemoteBindUdpPorts=6970-7170
LocalBindTcpPorts=7070
[net2fone]
ServerBindTcpPorts=0
[icq]
RemoteBindUdpPorts=0
ServerBindTcpPorts=0,1025-5000
NameResolutionForLocalHost=P
[Common]
WWW-Proxy=ASUS
Set Browsers to use Proxy=1
Set Browsers to use Auto Config=0
WebProxyPort=80
Configuration Url=http://ASUS:80/array.dll?Get.Routing.Script
Port=1745
Configuration Refresh Time (Hours)=6
Re-check Inaccessible Server Time (Minutes)=10
Refresh Give Up Time (Minutes)=15
Inaccessible Servers Give Up Time (Minutes)=2
Setup=Setup.exe
[Servers Ip Addresses]
Name=ASUS
[Servers Ipx Addresses]
[Master Config]
Path1=\\ASUS\mspclnt\
```

This client configuration file is used for a single Proxy Server computer. It contains many, but not all, of the parameters that are typically set in the Mspclnt.ini file. The following section describes the various command entries that are possible in the

Mspclnt.ini file, with an example for each. Where possible, those examples relate to the above Mspclnt.ini file. Of course, no Mspclnt.ini file would contain all of the possible entries. Therefore, some of the examples here are in addition to those contained in the above Mspclnt.ini file.

The [Master Config] Section

Entry:	`Path1`
Section:	`[Master Config]`
Description:	A Universal Naming Convention (UNC) path pointing to the shared network directory on the server that contains the master copy of the client configuration files. If the Proxy Server computer is participating in an array, the paths to the shared network directories of all array members. This section is required for backward compatibility with Microsoft Proxy Server version 1.0 clients.
Example:	`Path1=\\ASUS\Mspclnt\`

The [Servers IP Addresses] Section

The command entry provided here must correspond with the addressing scheme that you use on your private network. Two types of address forms are possible: the computer or DNS names, or specific IP addresses.

Entry:	`Name`
Section:	`[Servers IP Addresses]`
Description:	The computer or DNS name (if a DNS server is available) for the Proxy Server computer used by the client. If the computer is participating in an array, the DNS name for the array. (This entry does not appear if the client uses an IP address to connect with the Proxy Server computer.)
Example:	`Name=ASUS`

Entry:	`Addr1`
Section:	`[Servers IP Addresses]`
Description:	The IP address of the Proxy Server computer used by the client. If the computer is participating in an array, the IP address of each array member. (This entry does not appear if a computer or DNS name is used.) Additional entries are shown as Addr2, Addr3, and so on. This entry can be used if there is not a DNS server available on your internal network.
Example:	`Addr1=192.168.0.1`

● ● *Tip* ● ● ● ●

A Proxy Server array will resolve to a single DNS name, but not a single IP address. This is because if you're using DNS, you can create an array name, using your DNS Server, which resolves the names of the individual array members. When you create the DNS array name, it includes the IP address of each array member. Subsequently, your client computers, or downstream Proxy Server computers, can be configured to use the array name. In this way, your DNS server provides resolution to multiple IP addresses. IP Addressing alone does not have this capability. See the "Array Addressing" section in Chapter 10 for more information.

The [Common] Section

Entry:	Port
Section:	[Common]
Description:	The port Proxy Server uses for the control channel. This value is rarely changed. If you need to change it, edit the server's master copy of the Mspclnt.ini file.

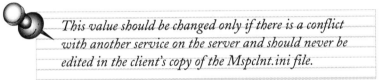

This value should be changed only if there is a conflict with another service on the server and should never be edited in the client's copy of the Mspclnt.ini file.

Example:	Port=1745

Entry:	Configuration Refresh Time (Hours)
Section:	[Common]
Description:	After this interval, specified in hours, the client asks the server to download a fresh copy of the Local Address Table (Msplat.txt).
Example:	Configuration Refresh Time (Hours)=6

Entry:	Re-check Inaccessible Server Time (Minutes)
Section:	[Common]
Description:	For this interval, specified in minutes, the WinSock client does not try to redirect a request by using the specific inaccessible server. Default value is 10 minutes.
Example:	Re-check Inaccessible Server Time (Minutes)=10

Entry:	Refresh Give Up Time (Minutes)
Section:	[Common]

Description:	After this interval, specified in minutes, the WinSock client attempts to refresh the configuration if a previous refresh attempt has failed. Default value is 15 minutes.
Example:	`Refresh Give Up Time (Minutes)=15`

Entry:	`Inaccessible Servers Give Up Time (Minutes)`
Section:	`[Common]`
Description:	For this interval, specified in minutes, the WinSock client does not try to redirect a request if all servers are marked as inaccessible. After this interval, the client tries one of the servers even if the Refresh Give Up Time has not expired. Default value is 2 minutes.
Example:	`Inaccessible Servers Give Up Time (Minutes)=2`

Entry:	`Set Browsers To Use Proxy`
Section:	`[Common]`
Description:	In the Proxy.ini file, set this value to 1 to have the client setup program configure the client computer's browser to use the Proxy Server computer defined in the WWW Proxy field. Set the value to 0 to prevent the client setup program from configuring clients to use a Proxy Server computer. This field has no effect on the client's version of the proxy.ini file.
Example:	`Set Browsers to use Proxy=1`

Entry:	`Configuration URL`
Section:	`[Common]`
Description:	The location of the configuration script that is downloaded to a client browser to use for routing into a particular Proxy Server computer in an array. The URL has the form http://servername/array.dll?Get.Routing.Script, where servername is the name of the Proxy Server computer that stores the script.
Example:	`Configuration Url=http://ASUS:80/array.dll?Get.Routing.Script`

Entry:	`LocalDomains`
Section:	`[Common]`
Description:	A list of suffixes for names that are resolved locally and separated by commas. Domain names that end in the listed strings are resolved at the client.
Example:	`LocalDomains=mydomain.com,www.localdomain.com`

Entry:	WWW-Proxy
Section:	[Common]
Description:	In the Proxy.ini file, if Set Browsers to Use Proxy is set to 1, the client setup program configures client browsers to use the Proxy Server computer named here. This field has no effect on the client's version of the file.
Example:	WWW-Proxy=ASUS

IPX Client Configuration Entries

Proxy Server 2.0 supports IPX clients with certain restrictions. For example, IPX clients running Windows 3.1 or Windows for Workgroups 3.11 are not supported by Proxy Server 2.0. These clients must use TCP/IP. Even if Windows 3.1 clients use TCP/IP, they cannot use the WinSock Proxy service. As a workaround, you could use the Socks Proxy service, but you would also have to install the appropriate Socks client applications on the Windows 3.1 clients.

Proxy Server 2.0 does support Windows 95 and Windows NT clients using the IPX protocol. In fact, the Novell Client32 (32-bit) IPX stack is supported on Windows 95 clients. If you're using the IPX/SPX protocol for clients on your network, you should verify that the following entries exist in your Mspclnt.ini file:

```
[Services]
Disable=1
[Spoolss]
Disable=1
[Rpcss]
Disable=1
```

The above settings prevent the configuration from refreshing or redirection by particular Windows NT services that are running on WinSock Proxy IPX clients. The Mspclnt.ini file uses 1 to symbolize yes, and 0 to symbolize no. So, **Disable=1** means that the service called in the section is disabled. Conversely, **Disable=0** means that the service is enabled. Looking back to our initial example of a complete Mspclnt.ini file, we see that these entries are reversed. This is because the particular client configuration file used for the example is running on a TCP/IP-only network.

Additionally, a **[Servers IPX Addresses]** section is required if your network contains Novell NetWare servers or IPX routers to provide the network with the IPX frame type and a network address. The format for the entry is:

```
Addr1=(Internal Network Number)-(MAC Address)
```

Configuring this parameter is actually simpler than it looks, because no matter what your NIC card's actual MAC Address is, Proxy Server requires you to use 000000000001. Look at the following as an example of a valid **[Servers IPX Addresses]** section for an IPX-based network:

```
[Servers Ipx Addresses]
Addr1=55555555-000000000001
```

> On a Novell NetWare network, this section is created automatically during your client installation; however, if no Novell NetWare servers exist on your Ethernet or Token Ring network, you must add the entry manually.

The [Servers IPX Addresses] Section

This section would be used to specify an address for a Proxy Server computer on a private network using the IPX protocol.

Entry:	Addr1
Section:	[Servers IPX Addresses]
Description:	The IPX address of the Proxy Server computer. If the computer is participating in an array, the IPX address of each array member. (This entry does not appear if a computer or DNS name is used to connect with the Proxy Server computer.) Additional entries are shown as Addr2, Addr3, and so on. This entry can be used if there is not a DNS server available on your internal network.
Example:	Addr1=55555555-000000000001

WinSock Proxy Client Application Configuration

Proxy Server's WinSock Proxy service supports Windows Sockets version 1.1 applications. The proper configuration of the WinSock Proxy client is important if you intend to use Windows Socket applications. You configure WinSock Proxy clients when you initially run the client setup program. Alternately, you can run the WSP client utility that is installed in the control panel after running Proxy Server clients setup. The client setup program installs a number of WinSock Proxy client components that replaced the Windows Sockets DLL file that is typically used by WinSock applications. In effect, this forces all Windows Socket applications to use the WinSock Proxy service for Internet access.

Some WinSock Proxy Client Configuration Tips

- While many Windows Sockets client applications have configuration Parameters for using a Proxy Server, you should not select this option with Microsoft Proxy Server 2.0.

- When running the IPX/SPX protocol on your private network, you must enter the Proxy Server computer's IP address instead of the computer name. This restriction also applies to Web browsers.

- When running 16-bit WinSock client applications, you might need to enter additional information during a client logon procedure.

- Be careful of incompatibilities when running SOCKS client applications through the SOCKS Proxy service. You should disable the WinSock Proxy client application if you're running a SOCKS client application through the SOCKS Proxy service.

Windows Sockets applications use a number of different protocols on many different service ports. Therefore, it is very important to make sure that the WinSock Proxy service has been configured appropriately for your WinSock applications. Configuration of the protocols and ports used by the WinSock Proxy service is discussed in the Configuring Security Parameters section.

Tip

You must reinstall the WinSock Proxy client software if you upgrade a Windows NT client computer.

Windows For Workgroups 3.11 Clients

If you have client computers running Windows for Workgroups 3.11, you'll see a user credentials dialog box appear the first time an application is redirected through the WinSock Proxy client application. To correct this behavior, set a domain name for client logon using the following procedure:

1. Click on the network utility in the Control Panel.
2. Click Startup.
3. Select Log On on the Windows NT or LAN Manager Domain checkbox found in the Options for Enterprise Networking dialog box.
4. Enter the applicable domain name.
5. Click on OK when finished.

eight

Configuration Entries For Microsoft Outlook And Exchange Clients

If you're running Microsoft Outlook, Exchange, or other email applications, you might have to edit the client configuration file on the Proxy Server computer for these applications to run properly. Locate the following entries in the Mspclnt.ini file:

```
[Mapisp32]
Disable=1
[Exchng32]
Disable=1
```

Change these entries to:

```
[Mapisp32]
Disable=0
[Exchng32]
Disable=0
```

After you refresh the client configuration file on your Proxy Server client computers, your email client applications should work properly.

Updating The Client Configuration File

You can update the client configuration file, Mspclnt.ini, any time by using the following procedure:

1. Click Start, point to Settings, point to Control Panel, and then double-click WSP Client to bring up the WinSock Proxy Client dialog box.

2. Click Update Now.

3. Click on OK, and then click on OK again.

4. Click Restart Windows Now to restart the computer.

WinSock Application Configuration

Most common Windows Sockets applications do not require special configuration settings, because the default settings for the WinSock Proxy service work in most instances. Yet, it sometimes is necessary to customize the configuration settings in order for specific Windows Sockets applications to work properly. For example, Microsoft Exchange requires additional configuration settings to work properly with the WinSock Proxy service. For more information on discovering where a WinSock Proxy client application is getting its configuration settings.

The configuration settings for WinSock applications can be stored in two places: either in the global client configuration file, Mspclnt.ini, or in an application-specific configuration file, named Wspcfg.ini, that is created for a specific WinSock application. An important difference between these files is that the Mspclnt.ini file is updated periodically from the Proxy Server computer. This is usually an advantage, because the automatic update overwrites the client's old version of the file, so the Mspclnt.ini file can be changed once and the settings will be downloaded automatically to all client computers. However, making changes in the Mspclnt.ini file on a single client computer is futile because the file will be overwritten when the next update occurs.

On the other hand, a Wspcfg.ini file is not overwritten by the Proxy Server computer. Therefore, you can tune your configuration settings for specific client computers using a Wspcfg.ini file. Another important difference in the Wspcfg.ini file is that it is located in the same directory as the client application. This means that it is possible to create configuration settings that apply only to a specific WinSock Proxy application on a specific client computer. In addition, because many WinSock applications can exist in different directories on a single client computer, many Wspcfg.ini files can exist on the same client computer—one for each WinSock application.

When you create a Wspcfg.ini file to be stored on a client computer, the settings contained in the file are called *Application-specific*. However, if the settings are to be applied to all WinSock applications, then the entries are made in the Mspclnt.ini file and are called *Global*. The following definitions illustrate the differences between *Application-specific* and *Global* settings:

➤ **Application-specific**   Application-specific settings are customized for each specific Windows Sockets application and are configured by adding a section called **[WSP client]** in the client configuration file, where WSP client is the name of the Windows Sockets application.

➤ **Global**   Global settings are created by adding a section called **[Common Configuration]** in the client configuration file, Mspclnt.ini. The settings entered under the **[Common Configuration]** section are used for all Windows Sockets applications that do not have application-specific configuration settings.

Take a moment to examine the following procedure, which follows a WinSock Proxy client application through its search for configuration settings (see Decision Tree 8.2).

1. Upon execution, the WinSock Proxy client application first looks for the disable entry under the **[Common Configuration]** section in the Mspclnt.ini file. If the setting is **Disable=1**, then the WinSock Proxy service is disabled and no further WinSock Proxy processing occurs. However, if the setting is **Disable=0** the WinSock Proxy client application then looks for a Wspcfg.ini file in the directory holding the Windows Sockets application.

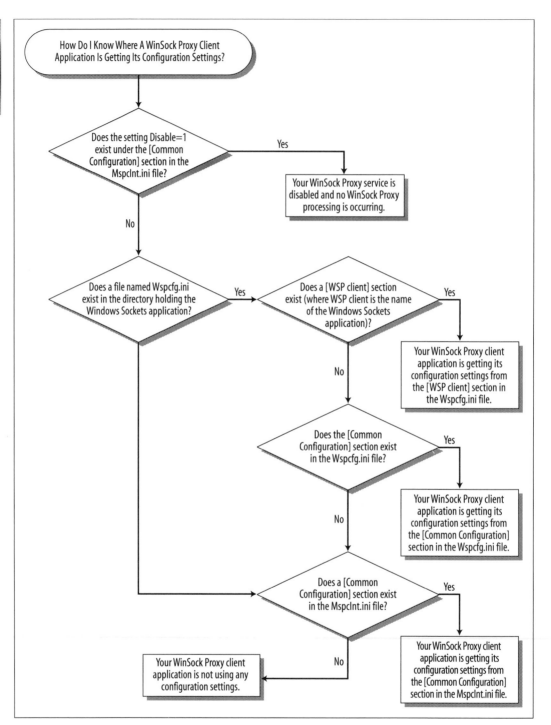

Decision Tree 8.2 How do I know where a WinSock Proxy client application is getting its configuration settings?

2. If the Wspcfg.ini file is found, the client application then looks for a [WSP client] section where WSP client is the name of the Windows Sockets application. If this section doesn't exist, the WinSock Proxy client application then looks for the [Common Configuration] section in the Wspcfg.ini file.

3. If the [WSP client] and the [Common Configuration] sections were not found in the Wspcfg.ini file, the WinSock Proxy client application then looks for the same sections in the Mspclnt.ini file.

It is important to note that the first section found by this search is used to apply the application-specific configuration settings. No other application-specific configuration settings are used.

The following section describes the command entries that can be placed in a configuration file for Windows Sockets application.

The [Common Configuration] Or [WSP client] Section

Notice that a specific port declaration can only appear in one of the following command entries, either as Local, Remote (redirected), or Server (redirected).

Entry:	Disable
Section:	[Common Configuration] or [WSP client]
Description:	This setting disables the WinSock Proxy service for all WinSock Proxy client applications when the value is set to 1 and the entry is placed in the [Common Configuration] section. This setting overrides any other settings that might be placed in a [WSP client] section. If this entry is found in a [WSP client] section, the setting only applies to that specific WSP client.
Example:	Disable=1

Entry:	NameResolution
Section:	[Common Configuration] or [WSP client]
Description:	By default, resolution for all dot-convention names (www.anydomain.com) is redirected. Forces name resolution to local (L) or redirected (R), as specified.
Example:	NameResolution=R

Entry:	LocalBindTcpPorts
Section:	[Common] or [WSP client]
Description:	Specifies a TCP port, list, or range that is bound locally.
Example:	LocalBindTcpPorts=7777

Entry:	`LocalBindUdpPorts`
Section:	`[Common]` or `[WSP client]`
Description:	Specifies a UDP port, list, or range that is bound locally.
Example:	`LocalBindUdpPorts=7000-7022, 7100-7170`

Entry:	`RemoteBindTcpPorts`
Section:	`[Common]` or `[WSP client]`
Description:	Specifies a TCP port, list, or range that is bound remotely.
Example:	`RemoteBindTcpPorts=30`

Entry:	`RemoteBindUdpPorts`
Section:	`[Common]` or `[WSP client]`
Description:	Specifies a UDP port, list, or range that is bound remotely.
Example:	`RemoteBindUdpPorts=3000-3050`

Entry:	`ServerBindTcpPorts`
Section:	`[Common]` or `[WSP client]`
Description:	Specifies a TCP port, list, or range used by a server application, so an accept operation on these ports is intended to serve clients both locally and on the Internet. Requires that the port is available on both the client and the Proxy Server computer.
Example:	`ServerBindTcpPorts=100-300`

Entry:	`ProxyBindIp`
Section:	`[Common]` or `[WSP client]`
Description:	Specifies an IP address or list that is used when binding with a corresponding port. Used by multiple servers that use the same port and need to bind to different ports on the Proxy Server computer. The syntax of the entry is:
	`ProxyBindIp=[port] : [IP address], [port] : [IP address].`
	The port numbers apply to both TCP and UDP ports.
Example:	`ProxyBindIp=80:110.52.144.103, 82:110.51.0.0`

Entry:	`KillOldSession`
Section:	`[Common]` or `[WSP client]`
Description:	When the setting for this entry is 1, it specifies that if Proxy Server holds a session from an old instance of an application, that session is

terminated before the application is granted a new session. This option solves the problem of restarting an application. For example, if an application crashes or for some reason fails to close the socket on which it is listening, it might take up to 10 minutes before Proxy Server discovers that the application's session should be terminated. During this period, you are unable to restart the application because the port on which it is listening remains in use. Setting **KillOldSession=1** solves this problem.

Example:	`KillOldSession=1`

Entry:	`Persistent`
Section:	`[Common]` or `[WSP client]`
Description:	When the setting for this entry is 1, it maintains a specific server state on the Proxy Server if a service is stopped and restarted and if the server is not responding. The client sends a keep-alive message to the server periodically during an active session. If the server is not responding, the client tries to restore the state of the bound and listening sockets upon server restart.
Example:	`Persistent=1`

Entry:	`ForceProxy`
Section:	`[Common]` or `[WSP client]`
Description:	Used to force a specific Proxy Server computer for a specific Windows Sockets application. The syntax of the entry is:

`ForceProxy=[tag] : [entry]`

where tag equals **i** for an IP address, **x** for an IPX address, or **n** for a name.

Example:	`ForceProxy=i:172.23.23.23`

Tip

Entry is the address of the name. If the **n** flag is used, the WinSock Proxy service works over IP only.

Entry:	`ForceCredentials`
Section:	`[Common]` or `[WSP client]`
Description:	This entry is used when running a Windows NT service or server application as a WinSock Proxy client application. When the setting

for this entry is 1, it forces the use of alternate user authentication credentials that are stored locally on the computer running the Windows NT service. The user credentials are stored on the client computer using the Credtool.exe application that is provided with Proxy Server. *User credentials must reference a user account that can be authenticated by Proxy Server, either local to Proxy Server or in a domain trusted by Proxy Server.* The user account is normally set not to expire; otherwise, user credentials need to be renewed each time the account expires.

Example: `ForceCredentials=1`

Entry: `NameResolutionForLocalHost`

Section: `[Common] or [WSP client]`

Description: This entry is used to specify how the "LocalHost" computer name is resolved. This entry assists Windows Sockets applications that rely on the IP addresses to which the local host computer resolves. Such applications call **gethostbyname("LocalHost")** to find their local IP address and send it to an Internet server. When this option is set to **L** (the default), **gethostbyname()** returns the IP addresses of the local host computer. When this option is set to **P**, **gethostbyname()** returns the IP addresses of the Proxy Server computer. When this option is set to **E**, **gethostbyname()** returns only the external IP addresses of the Proxy Server computer (those IP addresses that are not in the LAT).

Example: `NameResolutionForLocalHost=L`

*The "LocalHost" computer name is resolved by calling the Windows Sockets API function **gethostbyname()** using the "LocalHost" string, an empty string, or a NULL string pointer.*

Tip

Proxy Server does not make any provisions for client applications that require connections both on the internal private network and on the Internet. All private network WinSock applications will be directed through Proxy Server.

Configuring Laptop Computers As WinSock Proxy Clients

Configuring laptop computers as WinSock Proxy clients can be challenging. Typically, the problem is that laptop computers need to use the WinSock Proxy service while connected to the private network and also need to access an alternate Internet Service Provider (ISP) through a modem connection. Actually, you might have desktop computers that meet the same criteria.

Under these circumstances, the WinSock Proxy client application must be disabled before the computer can be used to access the alternate ISP. When you turn off the WinSock Proxy Server client application, an alternate route to the Internet becomes possible.

Use the following procedure to *disable* the WinSock Proxy Client application:

1. Click Start, point to Settings, point to Control Panel, and then double-click WSP Client to bring up the WinSock Proxy Client dialog box.

2. Click to clear the Enable WinSock Proxy Client checkbox, if necessary.

3. Click to clear the Select the Force IPX/SPX Protocol checkbox if necessary (see Figure 8.4).

4. Click on OK, and then click Restart Windows Now to restart the computer.

When the laptop computer needs to connect back to the private network, use the following procedure to *enable* the WinSock Proxy Client application:

1. Click Start, point to Settings, point to Control Panel, and then double-click WSP Client to bring up the WinSock Proxy Client dialog box.

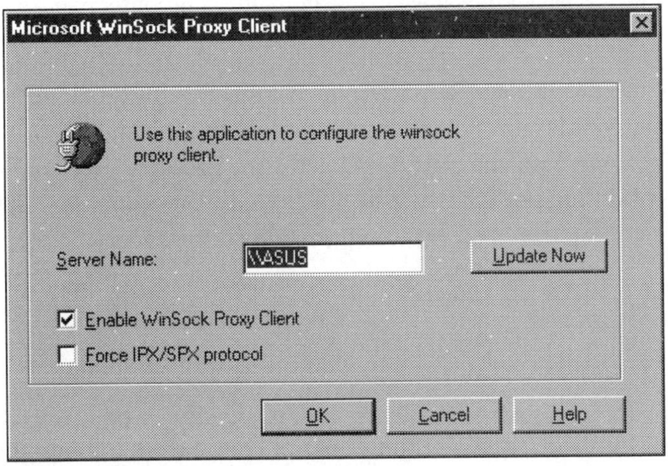

Figure 8.4   The Microsoft WinSock Proxy Client dialog box.

2. Click to select the Enable WinSock Proxy Client checkbox, if necessary.

3. Click to select the Force IPX/SPX protocol checkbox if the client computer uses the IPX/SPX protocol for network communications and also has TCP/IP installed.

4. Click on OK, and then click Restart Windows Now to restart the computer.

Web Proxy Client Application Configuration

The most common type of Web Proxy client application is the Web browser. The Web browser, or any Web Proxy client application, must be configured properly to use the Web Proxy service of Proxy Server. Typically, this is straightforward because Web Proxy clients are configured automatically by the client setup program.

Yet, it is possible that the Web browser settings that are automatically configured by the client setup program are inappropriate for a particular client installation. It is also possible that a well-meaning user will change the settings for his Web Proxy client, rendering the application unusable until the next refresh of the client configuration file. Therefore, it's a good idea to have a solid understanding of what the configuration options are for Web Proxy clients. This understanding not only will help when you need to configure a particularly difficult Web Proxy application, but also will assist you in your trouble-shooting.

Tip

If your clients connect to the network using the IPX protocol, the Web browser uses the WinSock Proxy service instead of the Web Proxy service. In addition, your application must specify an IP address instead of a domain or computer name to establish a connection to the Proxy Server computer.

Configuring most Web Proxy applications to connect with Proxy Server is simple. Usually, you simply specify either the computer or the domain name of the computer running Proxy Server, along with the port number for the protocol use; for Web browsers you usually use port 80. In the following section, specific procedures are detailed for configuring the most popular Web browsers—Microsoft Internet Explorer and Netscape Navigator.

Tip

"Helper" applications, such as RealPlayer clients, should not be configured as Web Proxy clients. These applications connect to the Proxy Server through the WinSock Proxy service. Also, do not configure the application to connect through a Proxy Server computer.

SOCKS Web Browsers

You can run a Web browser as a SOCKS client on a non-Windows client platform. However, you'll need to provide a DNS (Domain Name System) proxy server to your SOCKS clients for name resolution. The DNS proxy server resolves names by forwarding client requests to a server on the Internet.

Web Browser Configuration

When your default browser is either Microsoft Internet Explorer or Netscape Navigator, the Proxy Server client setup program configures your browser automatically. These browsers are configured as a Web Proxy client application that accesses the Internet using a proxy server. Both Microsoft Internet Explorer and Netscape Navigator are designed in such a way that the browser's own configuration interface also can be used to set up a connection to your Proxy Server computer.

Microsoft Internet Explorer

The following procedure configures Microsoft Internet Explorer 3.x or 4.x to use the Web Proxy service:

1. Open the Microsoft Internet Explorer browser.

2. Click View on the menu bar, then click Internet Options (click Options in Microsoft Internet Explorer 3.x).

3. Click the Connection tab on the dialog box (see Figure 8.5).

4. Select the Access the Internet Using a Proxy Server checkbox (or select the Connect Through a Proxy Server checkbox in Microsoft Internet Explorer 3.x).

5. Click the Advanced button (click the Settings button in Microsoft Internet Explorer 3.x).

6. Under Address of Proxy to Use (see Figure 8.6), in the HTTP field, type "http://*name*" (where *name* is the computer or domain name for your Proxy Server computer), then in the Port field, type a valid port number (typically 80).

7. Select the Use the Same Proxy Server for All Protocols checkbox.

8. Click on OK, then click on OK again to finish.

Netscape Navigator Version 3.x

The following procedure configures Netscape Navigator Version 3.01 Gold to use the Web Proxy service:

1. Open the Netscape Navigator browser.

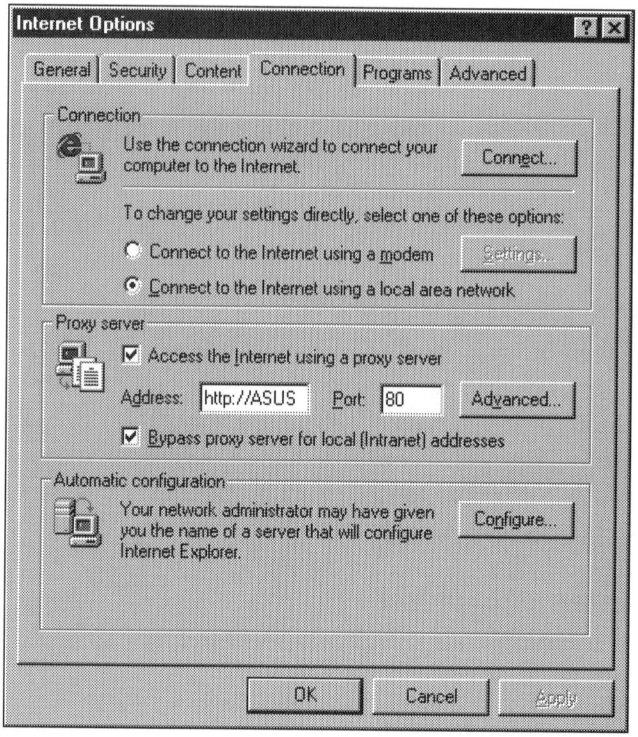

Internet Options   ? X

General | Security | Content | **Connection** | Programs | Advanced

Connection
Use the connection wizard to connect your computer to the Internet.

[Connect...]

To change your settings directly, select one of these options:

○ Connect to the Internet using a modem   [Settings...]

◉ Connect to the Internet using a local area network

Proxy server
☑ Access the Internet using a proxy server

Address: http://ASUS   Port: 80   [Advanced...]

☑ Bypass proxy server for local (Intranet) addresses

Automatic configuration
Your network administrator may have given you the name of a server that will configure Internet Explorer.

[Configure...]

[OK]   [Cancel]   [Apply]

Figure 8.5   The Connection tab under the Internet Options dialog box in Microsoft Internet Explorer 4.x.

Proxy Settings   ? X

Servers

Type	Address of proxy to use	Port
HTTP:	http://ASUS	: 80
Secure:	http://ASUS	: 80
FTP:	http://ASUS	: 80
Gopher:	http://ASUS	: 80
Socks:		:

☑ Use the same proxy server for all protocols

Exceptions
Do not use proxy server for addresses beginning with:

Use semicolons (;) to separate entries.

[OK]   [Cancel]

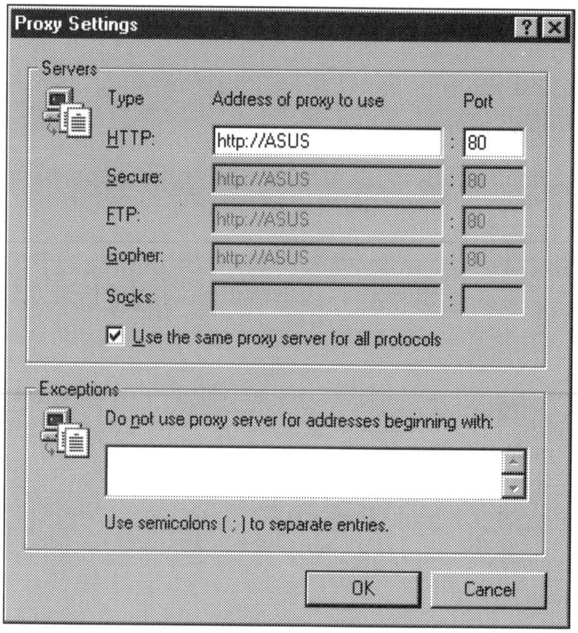

Figure 8.6   The Proxy Settings dialog box in Microsoft Internet Explorer 4.x.

2. Click Options on the menu bar.

3. Click Network Preferences.

4. Click on the Proxies tab.

5. Click on the Manual Proxy Configuration.

6. Click View.

7. In the HTTP Proxy field, type the computer or domain name for your Proxy Server computer, then in the Port field, type a valid port number (typically 80).

8. Click on OK twice.

Netscape Navigator Version 4.x

The following procedure configures Netscape Navigator Version 4.x to use the Web Proxy service:

1. Open the Netscape Navigator browser.

2. Click Edit on the menu bar.

3. Click Preferences.

4. Click on Advanced.

5. Click on the Manual Proxy Configuration radio button.

6. Click View.

7. In the HTTP Proxy field, type the computer or domain name for your Proxy Server computer, then in the Port field, type a valid port number (typically 80).

8. Click on OK twice.

• • • *Tip* • • • •

You can run a Web browser on the computer running Proxy Server. However, the browser on the Proxy Server computer must be configured to use the IP address of the Proxy Server network adapter card that is connected to the private network. In this case, you should not use the computer or domain name of the Proxy Server computer.

Creating A Custom Client LAT File

The LAT (Local Address Table) is made up of all the IP addresses used on your private network. Running Proxy Server client setup will install a file named Msplat.txt into the Mspclnt directory on the client computer. This is a text file containing all the IP addresses that comprise the LAT. The refreshing of the Msplat.txt file occurs at a frequency prescribed by the **Configuration Refresh Time (Hours)** entry in the Mspclnt.ini file (every six hours by default). The LAT file is used whenever a Windows Sockets application attempts to establish a connection to an IP address. If the IP address is found in the LAT, a direct connection is made to the private network; however, when the IP address is not found in the LAT, a connection is made through the WinSock Proxy service on the Proxy Server computer. Usually, the Msplat.txt file is not changed on a client computer. Instead, changes in the LAT are made at the Proxy Server computer, and those changes are propagated to all clients as Mspclnt.ini refreshing occurs.

It is possible, however, that the LAT table provided by the Proxy Server computer does not completely define all the IP addresses that a specific client requires on a private network. Simply editing the Msplat.txt file on the client computer is ineffective, because the file is overwritten at regular intervals from the Proxy Server computer. However, you can create a custom LAT file for the client computer. You do this by opening a text editor, entering the additional IP address ranges required by the client, and then saving the file as Locallat.txt in the Mspclnt directory. The Msplat.txt file then will be used along with the Locallat.txt file to determine which IP addresses comprise the private network and which IP addresses should be directed to the WinSock Proxy service.

As with the Msplat.txt file, IP addresses are entered in pairs into the locallat.txt file. An IP address pair defines either a range or a single IP address located on the private network. Examine the following example to better understand this convention. The first entry defines an IP address range; the second entry defines a single IP address.

```
192.168.56.1 192.168.56.100
192.168.57.1 192.168.57.1
```

Tip

The LAT does not require entries for subnet masks.

Moving On

Accessing Proxy Server is what client administration is all about. Whether you need to configure a Web browser, configure a laptop computer, or create a custom Client Configuration File for Proxy Server access, your users simply want access to the Internet. This chapter gave you the information you need to administer Proxy Server 2.0 clients and keep your users connected.

However, while your users want access, security is a tremendous concern for network administrators and the organizations they serve. In the next chapter, you'll learn how to make the most out of the vast security features of Microsoft Proxy Server 2.0.

Security Administration And Configuration

A major justification for a Proxy Server installation is the robust security it provides between your private network and the Internet. You can configure Proxy Server to meet your specific security needs through the appropriate implementation of the many security configuration parameters available to the network administrator. The result is that Proxy Server provides a secure gateway to the Internet for your organization.

Some essential security measures, designed to shield your private network from unwanted Internet access, were implemented when you first installed Proxy Server. For example, *IP forwarding* was disabled on the server so IP packets could not be forwarded through Proxy Server to the private network. Additionally, the ability to *listen on* inbound service ports was denied; therefore, Internet users cannot initiate a connection on a service port unless inbound access is enabled on that specific service port. While these measures are a good start, Proxy Server allows the configuration of even more robust and flexible security. This chapter will give you the information you need to grant or deny access to users, services, ports, or domains as required—and as appropriate—for your particular installation.

Configuring Access Control And Permissions

Access control allows the network manager to determine exactly which Internet services are available to the entire organization, members of specific groups, or individual users. Access control is a crucial feature of Proxy Server security and *should always be enabled*. Running Proxy Server with access control *disabled* creates security holes and is considered a non-secure operating condition. In addition, when access control is disabled, password authentication settings are unavailable. Both the Web Proxy and the WinSock Proxy services have access control features.

Proxy Server's Permissions Tabs

You enter permissions parameters by using the Permissions tab in one of the Proxy Server services dialog boxes. Each service—Web Proxy, WinSock Proxy, and SOCKS Proxy—has its own Permissions tab, allowing you to set the permissions associated with that specific service. The Permissions tab uses the Windows NT user and group accounts and is a good example of Proxy Server's close integration with the operating system. As illustrated in Figure 9.1, the Permissions tab is accessible from the main dialog box for any Proxy Server service.

Use the following procedure to access the Permissions tab for a specific Proxy Server service:

1. Click Start, point to Programs, point to Microsoft Proxy Server, and click Internet Service Manager.

2. Double-click on the computer name next to the SOCKS Proxy, WinSock Proxy, or Web Proxy service.

3. Click on the Permissions tab to bring up the permissions options for the service.

The following sections describe the permissions parameters available for the Web Proxy, WinSock Proxy, and SOCKS Proxy services.

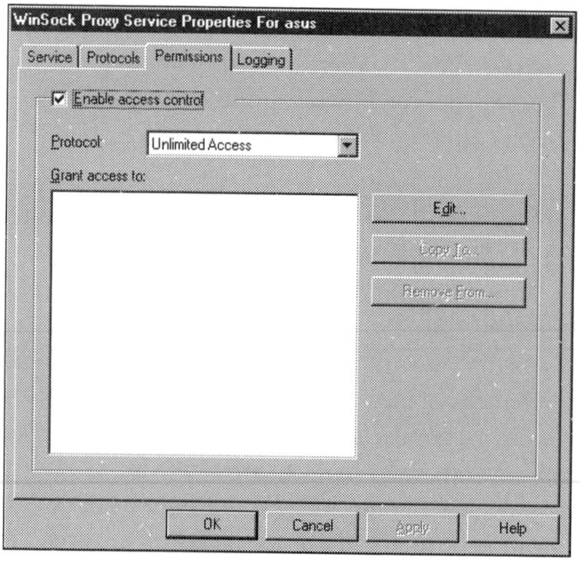

Figure 9.1   The Permissions tab is available for any Proxy Server service (shown here is the WinSock Proxy service main dialog box).

The Web Proxy Permissions Tab

You use the Web Proxy permissions tab to select which users or groups of users are allowed to access FTP Read, Gopher, WWW (HTTP and HTTPS), and Secure protocols through the Web Proxy service. The following list describes the options available in the Web Proxy Permissions tab (see Figure 9.2):

➤ **Enable Access Control**   This checkbox enables the Web Proxy service security. When the checkbox is selected, the Web Proxy service attempts to validate connections from clients. You set the authentication options used by the Web Proxy service through the WWW service of the Internet Information Service (IIS).

➤ **Protocol**   The Protocol list box provides the Internet protocols available to users who connect through the Web Proxy service on a Proxy Server computer. The protocols available include: FTP Read, Gopher, WWW (HTTP and HTTPS), and Secure, which allows various secure socket layer connections. You can permit a user or group to use a protocol by selecting that protocol in the Protocol list box, clicking Add, and then completing the Add Users and Groups dialog box.

➤ **Grant Access To**   This is a list of the users and groups permitted to use the specific protocol selected in Protocol.

➤ **Edit**   Click this button to grant or deny a user or group the right to use a specific protocol. Rights are changed by first selecting the protocol, clicking the Edit button, and then completing the Permissions dialog box for that specific protocol.

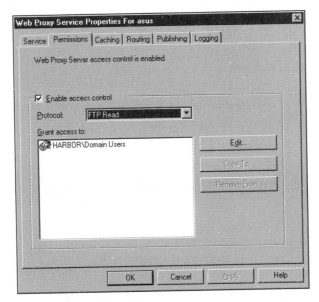

Figure 9.2   The Web Proxy Permissions tab.

➤ **Copy**   Click this button to copy or add protocols to a user or group from the Services Selection dialog box.

➤ **Removed From**   Click this button to remove protocols from a user or group from the Service Selection dialog box.

The Web Proxy Permissions Dialog Box

Clicking the Edit button on the Web Proxy Permissions tab calls a Permissions dialog box for the protocol selected in the Protocol list. For example, if the FTP protocol is selected, the FTP Permissions dialog box is called when you click the edit button.

The Permissions dialog box (see Figure 9.3) allows you to determine which users or groups of users are allowed access to the Internet via specific protocols. For example, to grant FTP Read access to a user or group, use the following procedure:

1. Select FTP Read in the Protocol list, then click Edit.

2. In the FTP Read Permissions dialog box, click Add.

3. In the Add Users and Groups dialog box, select the user or group you wish to add and click Add. The group's name will then appear in the Add Names list.

4. When you've added all the names you require, click on OK, click on OK again, and then click Apply.

Use the following procedure to remove FTP Read access for user or group:

1. Select FTP Read in the Protocol list, then click Edit.

2. In the FTP Read Permissions dialog box, select the user or group you wish to remove, then click Remove.

3. Click on OK and then click apply.

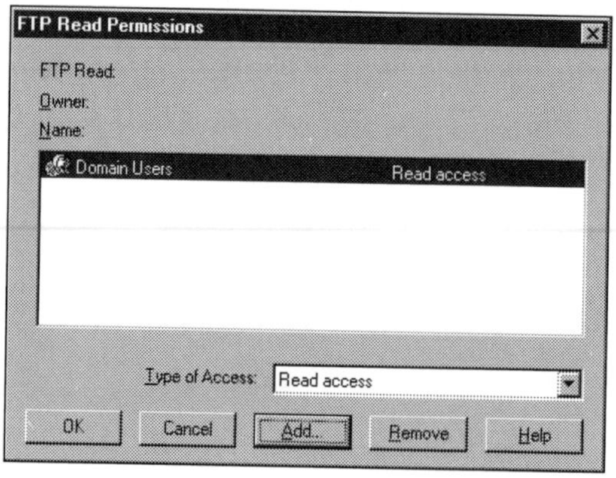

Figure 9.3   The Web Proxy Permissions dialog box.

The Web Proxy Service Selection Dialog Box

Clicking the Copy To or Delete From buttons on the Web Proxy Permissions tab calls the Services Selection dialog box. The Copy To or Delete From buttons are only available if a user or a group of users is selected in the Grant Access To list.

The Service Selection dialog box (see Figure 9.4) allows you to grant or remove user access permissions for one or more Web Proxy protocols. Use the following procedure to add user access permissions for a Web Proxy protocol:

1. Select one or more users or groups in the Permissions dialog box, then click Copy To. This brings up the Service Selection dialog box.

2. In the Service Selection dialog box, select the protocol for which you want to grant permissions.

3. Click on OK.

Use the following procedure to revoke user access permissions for a Web Proxy protocol:

1. Select one or more users or groups in the Permissions dialog box, then click Remove From.

2. In the Service Selection dialog box, select the protocol for which you want to revoke permissions.

3. Click on OK.

The WinSock Proxy Permissions Tab

You use the WinSock Proxy Permissions tab to determine which users or groups of users can access the Internet through the WinSock Proxy service when using a particular

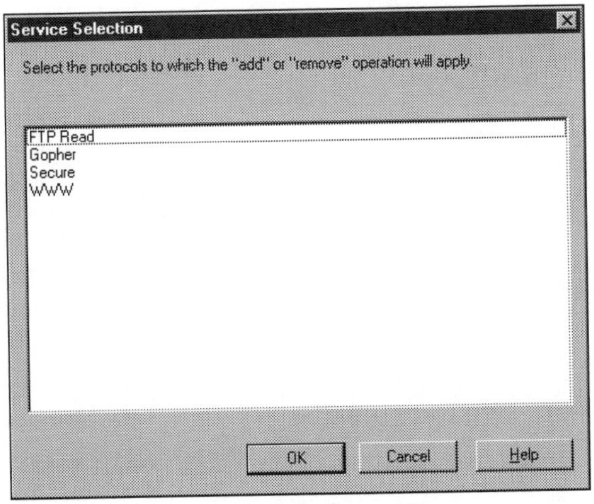

Figure 9.4 The Web Proxy Service Selection dialog box.

protocol configuration. For example, MS NetShow is accessed through the WinSock Proxy service using TCP port 1755 outbound for an initial connection and using inbound UDP ports ranging from 1025-5000 for subsequent connections. These parameters are pre-configured for the WinSock Proxy service and can be viewed under the Protocols tab in the WinSock Proxy Service dialog box. Under the WinSock Proxy Permissions tab, you can grant or revoke permissions for the MS NetShow protocol using the WinSock Proxy Permissions tab (see Figure 9.5).

The following list describes the options available in the WinSock Proxy Permissions tab:

➤ **Enable Access Control**   This checkbox specifies if access control is enabled or disabled. When you enable access control, only the users who are granted WinSock Proxy permissions can use the WinSock Proxy protocols to access the Internet through the WinSock Proxy service. If you disable access control, any WinSock client can access the Internet through the WinSock Proxy service. It might help to regard disabling access control as the WinSock Proxy service equivalent of Anonymous access.

Using the WinSock Proxy service without access control enabled is considered a non-secure operating condition.

➤ **Protocol**   This is a complete listing of the protocol configurations available to users of the WinSock Proxy service. While all the well-known ports—the most popular Internet protocols—are predefined, you can add, remove, and modify the

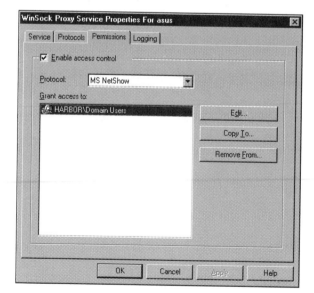

Figure 9.5   The WinSock Proxy Permissions tab.

protocol definitions using the Protocols tab for the WinSock Proxy service. The first selection in the Protocol list box is Unlimited Access; this selection is a special option that allows access to all protocols and all ports of the server, including ports not defined in any protocol configuration. Additionally, users granted Unlimited Access are unaffected by WinSock Proxy domain filtering. Be very careful when granting permission to Unlimited Access.

➤ **Grant Access To**   This is a list of the users and groups permitted to use the specific protocol that is selected in Protocol.

➤ **Edit**   Using the Edit button, you can change the protocol permissions for a user or group on the Proxy Server computer. To grant or deny a user or group the right to use a specific protocol, select the protocol in Protocol, click Edit, and then complete the Protocol Permissions dialog box.

➤ **Copy To**   Using the Copy To button, you can grant permissions for more than one protocol at a time. To grant users access permission for several protocols, select a protocol in Protocol, select one or more users and groups under Grant Access To, click Copy To, and complete the Protocol Selection dialog box.

➤ **Remove From**   Using the Remove From button, you can revoke permissions for more than one protocol at a time. To deny users permission for several protocols, select a protocol in Protocol, select one or more users and groups under Grant Access To, click Remove From, and complete the Protocol Selection dialog box.

Protocol Permissions Dialog Box

The Edit button under the WinSock Proxy Permissions Tab calls a Permissions dialog box for the protocol selected in the Protocol list box. Figure 9.6 illustrates the Permissions dialog box. You add or remove user or group access permissions for specific protocols by using the Permissions dialog box. It greatly simplifies Proxy Server administration to grant permissions to groups, rather than to single users.

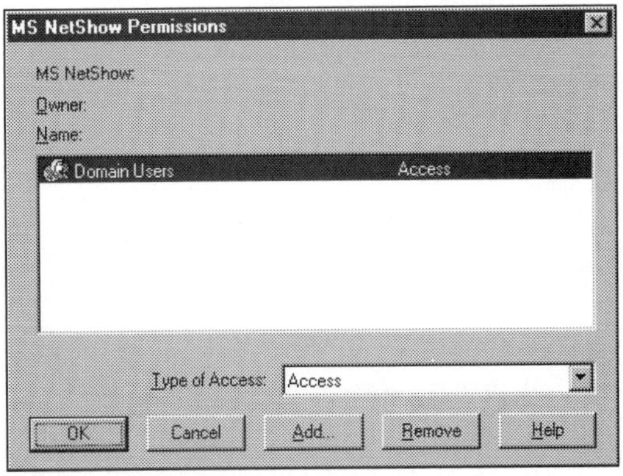

Figure 9.6   The Permissions dialog box.

Tip

You can use the Windows NT User Manager for Domains application to create groups and add users to those groups.

The following list describes the actions of the Add and Remove buttons in the permissions dialog box:

➤ **Add**   Clicking Add brings up the Add Users and Groups dialog box. Using the Add Users and Groups dialog, you can grant permission for a user or group to use the selected protocol configuration to access the Internet through the WinSock Proxy service on the server. You can grant access to users and groups from this server, from the local Windows NT domain, and from trusted Windows NT domains.

➤ **Remove**   Using the Remove button, you can remove protocol permissions from a user or group. To remove protocol permissions, select the applicable entry in the list and then click Remove.

Protocol Selection Dialog Box

You use the Protocol Selection dialog box to grant or remove user access permissions for one or more WinSock Proxy protocols. Figure 9.7 illustrates the Protocol Selection dialog box. Use the following procedure to grant or remove WinSock Proxy protocol permissions:

1. Select one or more users or groups on the Permissions tab.

2. To add protocols, click Copy To; to remove protocols, click Remove From.

3. Select the protocol or protocols you wish to add to, or remove from, the selected users or groups.

4. Click on OK.

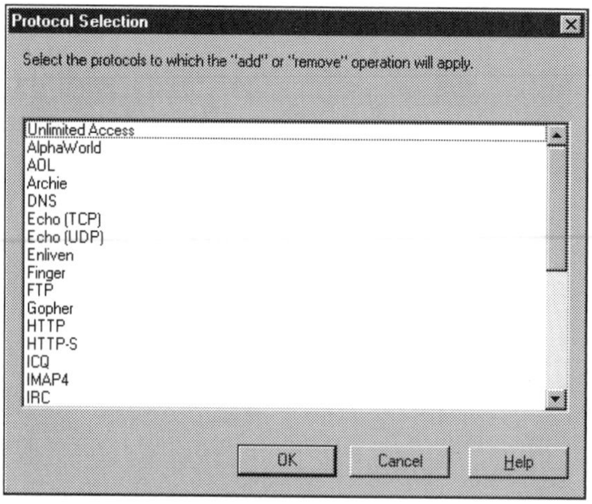

Figure 9.7   The Protocol Selection dialog box.

Configuring WinSock Proxy Service Protocols

No discussion of administering Proxy Server security would be complete without examining the WinSock Proxy service protocol definitions. Protocol definitions allow you to determine which Windows Sockets applications are available to Proxy Server clients when accessing the Internet. In addition, you can specify, within each protocol definition, which specific ports are used for outbound and inbound connections. Both the WinSock Proxy and the SOCKS Proxy services use application service ports.

Tip

There is a special selection in the Protocol list that functions independently of the WinSock Proxy Protocols tab: *Unlimited Access.* This selection *allows access to all protocols and all ports of your Proxy Server computer, not just the ones defined under the Protocols tab.* If Unlimited Access is assigned to a user or group, full control is available to use any protocols or ports with WinSock Proxy. So, exercise extreme caution when assigning this option to users or groups. In addition, keep in mind that users who are granted Unlimited Access are not affected by WinSock Proxy domain filtering.

The WinSock Proxy Service Protocols Tab

The WinSock Proxy service Protocols tab is illustrated in Figure 9.8. You use the Protocol tab to manage the list of protocol definitions that specify which Windows Sockets applications are permitted to access the Internet. Furthermore, for each protocol definition, you can specify which TCP or UDP ports are available for outbound and inbound

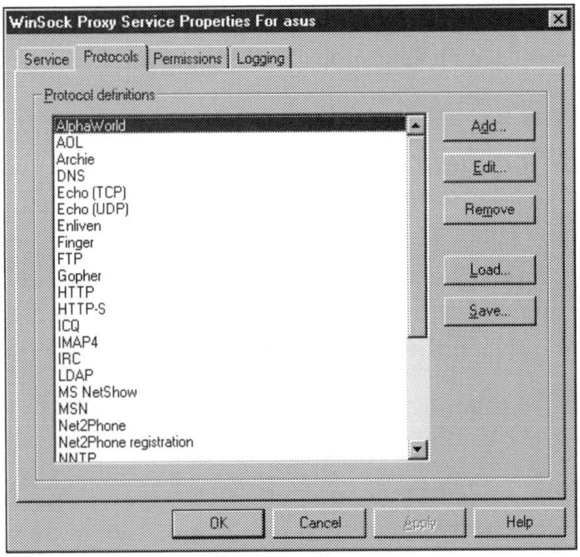

Figure 9.8   The WinSock Proxy service Protocols tab.

connections. Windows Sockets-based applications use these UDP or TCP ports in combination with IP addressing to form a "socketed" connection between hosts. Additionally, the WinSock Proxy service can redirect a listen() call. This allows Proxy Server to listen to and redirect Internet requests on behalf of a server-based Internet application, such as an internal Exchange mail server.

Using the Protocols tab, you can add to, remove from, or modify the WinSock Proxy service protocol definitions. In addition, you can save the protocol definitions to a file to be loaded at another time. There is no limit to the protocol options available to the WinSock Proxy service.

The following list describes the actions of the Add, Edit, Remove, Load, and Save buttons on the WinSock Proxy service Protocols tab:

➤ **Add**   You use the Add button to call the Protocol Definition dialog box (*see below*), which allows you to configure a new WinSock protocol. This process will add the protocol to the list that defines all the protocols available for access to the Internet through the WinSock Proxy service.

➤ **Edit**   Using the Edit button, you call the Protocol Definition dialog box (*see below*), which allows you to modify the settings for a configured protocol.

➤ **Remove**   By selecting a protocol under Protocol definitions and then clicking Remove, you delete a protocol definition.

➤ **Load**   By clicking Load and completing the Load Protocol Definition dialog box (*see below*), you can restore all protocol definitions previously saved from a network share or a local hard drive.

➤ **Save**   By clicking Save and completing the Save Protocol Definition dialog box (*see below*), you can back up all protocol definitions to a network share or a local hard drive.

Protocol Definition Dialog Box

You will find that the predefined protocol definitions included when Proxy Server was first installed will suit most, if not all, of your needs. But you are not limited to Proxy Server's predefined protocol definitions. You can create a protocol definition for any Windows Sockets application by using the Protocol Definition dialog box (see Figure 9.9). The actions available in the dialog box are described below:

➤ **Protocol Name**   In this space, you must type the name of the protocol definition you are adding to the WinSock Proxy service.

➤ **Initial Connection**   Enter the connection parameters for the WinSock Proxy service, including the port number used for the initial connection, the transmission type (either TCP or UDP), and the direction (either Inbound or Outbound).

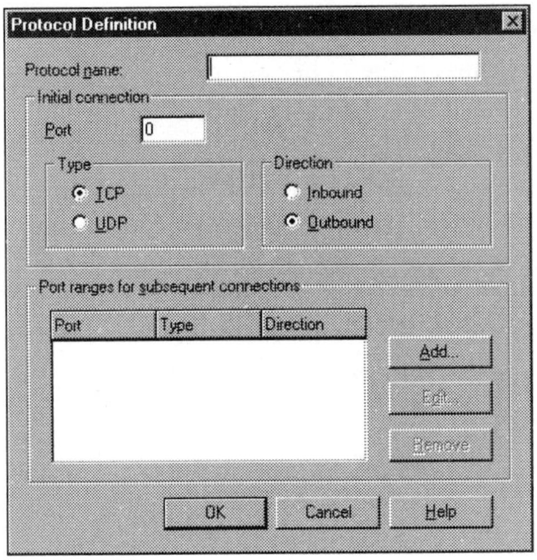

Figure 9.9   The Protocol Definition dialog box.

Notice the differences between TCP and UDP when selecting the port direction. Clicking Outbound when selecting TCP allows clients to initiate connections to external sites through the port. Clicking Outbound when selecting UDP allows the port to pass packets sent from a client to an external site. Clicking Inbound when selecting TCP allows external sites to initiate connections to clients through the port. Clicking Inbound when selecting UDP allows the port to pass packets sent from an external site to a client.

➤ **Port Ranges For Subsequent Connections**   This option defines the handling of additional connections or packets that follow the initial connection. The subsequent connection parameters include the port number or range, the protocol type, and the direction for each existing subsequent connection. You configure these values by clicking Add or Edit and completing the Port Range Definition dialog box. A port range setting of 0 for inbound connections indicates Port_Any, which allows the server to select the port from the range 1024 through 5000. Examine the pre-defined Real Audio protocol using the Protocol Definition dialog box for an example of using Port Ranges for Subsequent Connections.

➤ **Remove**   Select the port or port range under Port Ranges for Subsequent Connections, and then click Remove to delete.

Load Protocol Definition Dialog Box

The Load Protocol Definition dialog box provides a space for you to type the name of the protocol definitions file to load (see Figure 9.10). The default directory for protocol definitions is \msp\config\. Alternately, you can click Browse Files to locate protocol definition files stored on another network share or a local hard drive.

Save Protocol Definition Dialog Box

The Save Protocol Definition dialog box provides a space for you to type the new name of the protocol definitions file to save (see Figure 9.11). The default directory for protocol definitions is \msp\config\. Alternately, you can click Browse Files to save the protocol definition file on another network share or a local hard drive.

Configuring SOCKS Permissions

The SOCKS Proxy service is similar to the WinSock Proxy service in that both operate by redirecting API calls to a remote site. The SOCKS Proxy service uses TCP and must use applications that are designed specifically for the SOCKS protocol. These applications are linked with SOCKS network interface libraries. Then, using the SOCKS protocol, a data channel can be established between the client and server computers. Telnet, FTP, Gopher, and Web browsers are typical of Internet applications that have SOCKS versions. Internet applications that use UDP, such as RealPlayer and NetShow, are not supported by the SOCKS Proxy service.

Tip

You must disable the WinSock Proxy client application on the client computer when running a SOCKS client application through the SOCKS Proxy service. To disable the WinSock Proxy client, click on the WSP client in the Control Panel on the client computer. In the Microsoft WinSock Proxy dialog box, click the Enable WinSock Proxy Client check box to remove the check. Then restart the client computer.

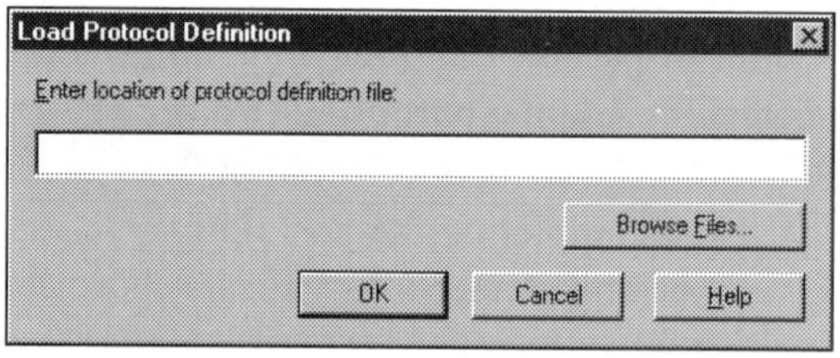

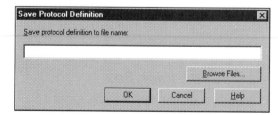

Figure 9.10 The Load Protocol Definition dialog box.

Figure 9.11 The Save Protocol Definition dialog box.

There are some differences between the WinSock Proxy service and the SOCKS Proxy service. For example, the WinSock Proxy service uses global domain filters that support DNS names in addition to IP addresses, while the SOCKS Proxy service only defines filters on destination IP addresses. In addition, while the WinSock Proxy service can open primary and secondary ports for an application, the SOCKS Proxy service is restricted to primary ports only. Another difference is that the SOCKS Proxy service is dependent on the Web Proxy service running. Therefore, if you stop the Web Proxy service, the SOCKS Proxy service also stops running. Because the SOCKS Proxy service supports the SOCKS 4.3a protocol, the service can use IP addresses and the Identification (Identd) protocol to identify and authenticate Proxy clients.

The SOCKS Permissions Tab

You click on the Add button under the Permissions tab (see Figure 9.12) to configure new permissions, use the Edit button to change existing permissions, and use the Remove button to delete SOCKS permissions. You can change the order in the Permissions list by clicking on Move Up or Move Down.

The SOCKS Permissions Dialog Box

Permissions must be configured when you add or edit them. You configure the SOCKS Proxy service permissions by using the Socks Permissions dialog box. Once a permission is entered, it is visible in the SOCKS Proxy Service Properties dialog box. The following list describes the options available in the SOCKS Permissions dialog box (see Figure 9.13).

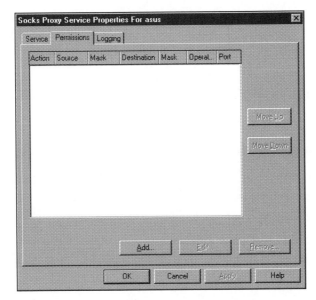

Figure 9.12   The Socks Permissions tab.

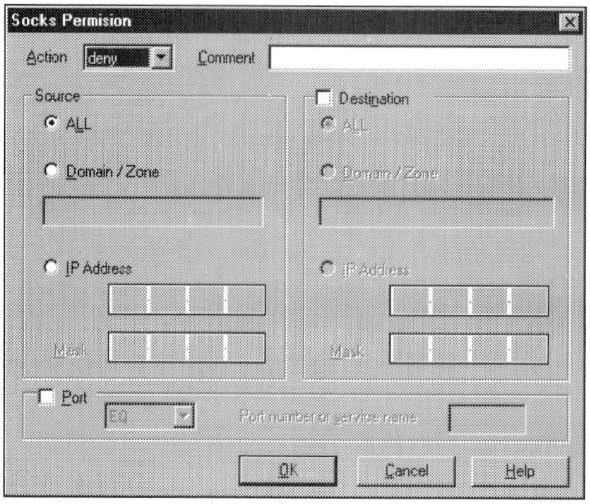

nine

Figure 9.13   The Socks Permissions dialog box.

➤ **Action** The Actions drop-down list box is used to specify whether a request is denied or permitted, based on the configured specifications.

➤ **Comment** The Comment field is optional and provides a space for you to type the name for the permission that is being created.

➤ **Source** Under Source, you can specify the origin of the request as:

- All of the computers by clicking All.

- A domain of computers by clicking Domain/Zone.

- A single computer by clicking IP Address and typing a valid IP address. Additionally, type a valid subnet mask in *Mask* if one is required.

➤ **Destination** Under destination, you can specify the allowed or denied destination of the permission entry. The destination can be specified as:

- All of the computers by clicking All.

- A domain of computers by clicking Domain/Zone.

- A single computer by clicking IP Address and typing a valid IP address. Additionally, type a valid subnet mask in Mask if one is required.

➤ **Port** Selecting the Port checkbox allows you to specify the relative range of the port number. The port range can be defined as equal (EQ), not equal (NEQ), greater than or equal (GE), or less than or equal (LE). You use the Port Number or Service Name field to type a valid TCP service name.

The Identd Simulation Service

The Identd Simulation Service is used by the SOCKS Proxy service and occasionally by other Internet servers that require users to identify themselves before allowing access. For example, an FTP service frequently requires a unique identifier for each user. You will find the Identd.exe file on the Proxy Server compact disk. Once installed, the Identd Simulation Service provides a random, false username when one is required for server access.

Follow these steps to install and run the Identd Simulation Service:

1. Create a directory named Identd on the Proxy Server computer.

2. Use Windows NT Explorer to open the Identd directory on the Proxy Server compact disk. Then, open the appropriate subdirectory for the server's processor architecture.

3. Copy Indentd.exe to the Identd directory on the Proxy Server computer.

4. Change to the Identd directory on the server, and type "identd –install".

5. Using the command prompt, type "net start identd".

6. Open the dialog box for the Web Proxy service.

7. Click Security, then under the Packet Filters tab, click Add.

8. In the Packet Filter Properties dialog box under Allow this Windows NT Server to Exchange Packets of Type, click Custom Filter.

9. In Protocol ID select TCP, and in Direction select Both.

10. Under Local Port, click Fixed Port and type "113".

11. Under Remote Port, click Fixed Port and type "113".

12. Click on OK three times, then restart the server.

The Identd Simulation Service appears in Control Panel under Services after installation. The service will start automatically after the server computer is restarted.

Firewall Configuration

Proxy Server has a number of security features that typically are found in full-featured Internet firewall products. For example, you can automatically filter packets, set up security alerts, and create logs. These features allow you to personalize the control of flow of information to and from Proxy Server. While you cannot specify packet filtering on a user-level basis, you can configure different Proxy Server computers on your private network to offer access to different protocols and ports for different users. The following sections describe the configuration of these firewall security features in Proxy Server 2.0.

Configuring Packet Filters

You can configure individual packet filters to block unwanted packets from being passed through Proxy Server, while allowing the desired packets to pass through unencumbered. Both inbound and outbound packet filtering are supported by Proxy Server. Proxy Server's packet filtering only affects external network adapters. Therefore, all Windows NT security measures, including password authentication and user permissions, remain available to the private network.

Packet filtering works by intercepting and evaluating packets prior to passing them through to the Proxy Server services. This provides a significant level of security and protection for your private network. For example, Proxy Server can reject packets that originate from a specific Internet host and can even reject address spoof and FRAG attacks. In addition, Proxy Server can be configured to determine automatically which IP packet types are allowed to pass through the internal networks circuit and application layer services. Previously, such advanced packet-filtering services were only found in dedicated Internet firewall products.

Proxy Server provides two modes of packet filtering: *dynamic* and *static*. Both of these methods control which TCP and UDP ports are open for communication. Dynamic packet filtering is sometimes called automatic packet filtering because it is not necessary to explicitly unbind specific services from the external network adapter of Proxy Server. Instead, the Web Proxy, WinSock Proxy, and SOCKS Proxy services perform the filtering on an as-needed basis. For example, when you use dynamic packet filtering, packets can be automatically blocked and ports are automatically opened for both transmitting and receiving. Then, after any Proxy Server service terminates the connection, the ports are immediately closed. The result is that a minimal number of ports are open and only for a limited time. Thus, dynamic packet filtering offers a reasonable degree of security while requiring little administration. Even tighter security, albeit with increased administrative requirements, is available by manually configuring static packet filters. Note that, for security reasons, it is highly recommended that you configure static filters if you intend to access the Internet using the same computer that is running Proxy Server. For more information on determining when you should use static packet filtering, see Decision Tree 9.1.

Tip

Packet filtering is disabled by default during Proxy Server installation. An external network interface must be installed and set up on your Proxy Server computer before packet filtering can be enabled. When you use a modem or ISDN adapter for a dial-out connection to the Internet, Proxy Server's Auto Dial feature must be configured before you can enable packet filtering.

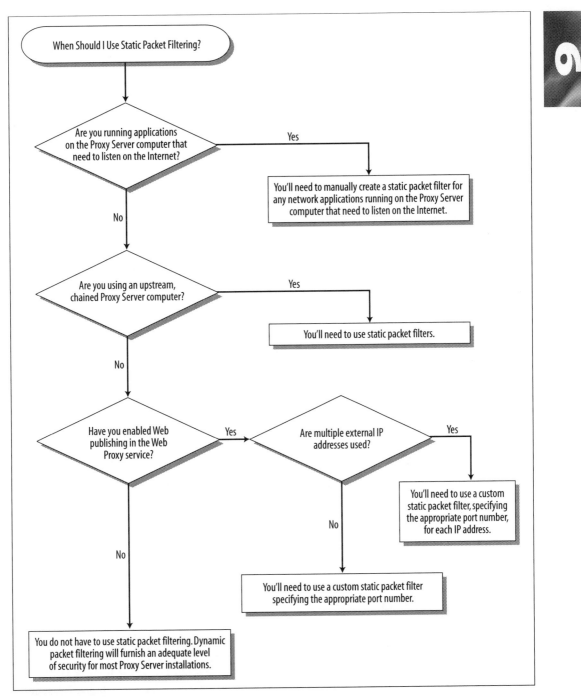

Decision Tree 9.1   When should I use static packet filtering?

When using packet filtering, keep in mind the following facts:

➤ The Enable Dynamic Packet Filtering of Microsoft Proxy Server Packets checkbox is selected by default when the Enable Packet Filtering on External Interface is selected. Typically, this furnishes an adequate level of security for most Proxy Server installations. It's advisable to keep this feature enabled unless you have a specific need to create packet filter exceptions and you thoroughly understand the process.

➤ On the other hand, you *must* disable dynamic packet filtering and manually create a static packet filter for network applications that are running on the Proxy Server computer and that need to listen on the Internet. Such applications include Microsoft Exchange, Microsoft Routing, and Remote Access Service. It's advisable not to have these applications running on the Proxy Server computer if possible.

➤ Static packet filters also are required, when using an upstream, chained Proxy Server computer, to allow packet exchange with a downstream Proxy Server computer.

➤ A custom static packet filter is required if you enable Web publishing in the Web Proxy service. If multiple external IP addresses are used, each IP address must have a custom static packet filter that specifies the appropriate port number.

➤ If you enable Web publishing in the Web Proxy service, you need to create a custom static packet filter for each external IP address used that specifies the applicable port number.

➤ When creating or editing a custom static packet filter using the ICMP protocol, you enter the "Code" field value in Local Port, and the "Type" field value in Remote Port.

➤ When creating or editing protocols other than TCP, UDP, or ICMP, you must enter dummy values in Fixed Port under Source Port and Remote Port in the Packet Filter Properties dialog box.

➤ Unless you're using DHCP or RAS to automatically assign your IP addresses, you should specify a default gateway for at least one of the network interfaces on the Proxy Server computer.

➤ Don't forget to verify that no external network IP addresses are contained in the Local Address Table (LAT).

The Packet Filters Tab

The Packet Filters tab on the Security dialog box (see Figure 9.14) is used to configure packet filtering. A number of predefined packet filter exceptions are installed by default during Proxy Server setup. All packet types will be blocked except those contained in the exceptions list. Therefore, if a packet filter is not enabled for a specific port, that port is disabled. While this assures the maximum security, it can also be a potential source of

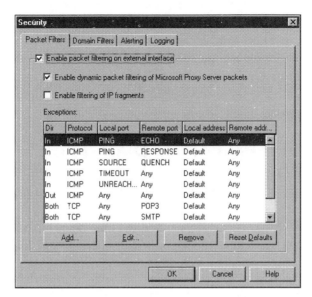

Figure 9.14   The Packet Filters tab on the Security dialog box.

problems. For example, if an Internet application requires a specific port to communicate, that port must be specified properly in the exceptions list. Additionally, the exceptions list applies to all requests issued to the server, regardless of whether the request originated from the Internet or from an internal private network client.

The following list describes the options available using the Packet Filters tab on the Security dialog box:

➤ **Enable Packet Filtering On External Interface**   Selecting this checkbox enables the packet filtering feature on the external network adapter. Additionally, the Enable Dynamic Packet Filtering of Microsoft Proxy Server Packets checkbox is selected automatically. Both checkboxes must remain selected as long as packet filtering is enabled.

➤ **Enable Dynamic Packet Filtering Of Microsoft Proxy Server Packets**   Selecting this checkbox enables the WinSock Proxy, Web Proxy, and SOCKS Proxy services to create dynamic filters as needed; therefore, Proxy Server will automatically open and close ports as requested by internal and external Internet applications. Conversely, clearing this checkbox grants the administrator detailed control over which ports Proxy Server can use for external communication. This results in tighter security, but with a greater possibility that configuration problems will arise.

➤ **Enable Filtering Of IP Fragments**   Selecting this checkbox allows the Web Proxy, WinSock Proxy, or SOCKS Proxy services to filter datagram or packet fragments. See Appendix B for information about TCP/IP datagrams.

> **Exceptions**   This is a list of packet filters allowed to pass through the Proxy Server computer. Packet filters contain the following parameters: the direction of data flow, the transport protocol, the remote IP address of the host, the remote service port, and the local service port. You must create exceptions to the packet filters when running other types of services on the Proxy Server computer, such as Microsoft Exchange or the Identd service.

The Packet Filter Properties Dialog Box

You add or edit packet filters using the Packet Filter Properties dialog box (see Figure 9.15). You must exercise caution when specifying protocols that require multiple filters; two entries in the exceptions list are required for these protocols. For example, the Point-to-Point Tunneling Protocol (PPTP) requires multiple filters. In this case, PPTP requires two bi-directional filter entries using port 1723: one for a call filter and another for a receive filter.

The following list describes the options available in the Packet Filter Properties dialog box:

> **Predefined Filter**   Select this checkbox to specify one of Proxy Server's predefined filters. The protocol packets included are ICMP, DNS, PPTP, SMTP, and POP3. You are required to use the predefined protocols for DNS, PPTP, SMTP, and POP3 packets, and it's recommended that you use the predefined protocol for ICMP packets.

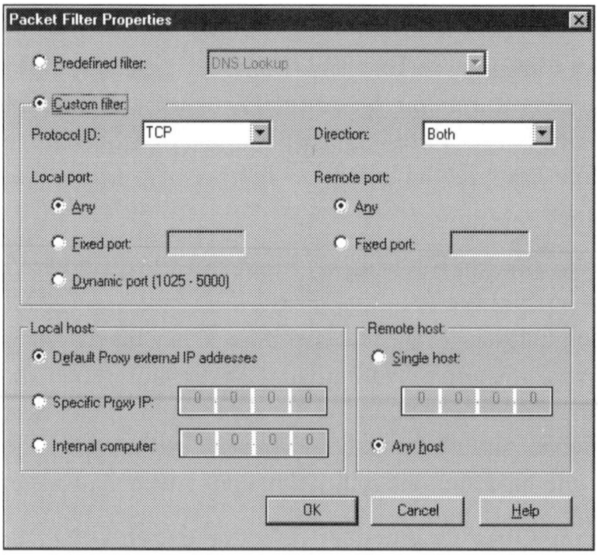

Figure 9.15   The Packet Filter Properties dialog box.

➤ **Custom Filter**   Selecting Custom Filter allows you to define the packet filtering parameters for ICMP, TCP, or UDP packets and requires you to provide the protocol ID, direction, source port, destination port, and host parameters. When creating or editing a custom static packet filter using the ICMP protocol, you enter the "Code" field value in Local Port, and the "Type" field value in Remote Port.

➤ **Protocol ID**   Use this list box to select the protocol ID.

➤ **Local Port**   Enter the port number required for the Proxy Server computer under the Local Port. Three options are available: Any, Fixed Port, and Dynamic Port (1025-5000). Any enables any local or remote port to transmit or send the data packet. Fixed Port enables only the port specified to send or receive the packet. Dynamic Port (1025-5000) reduces the load on the ports by allowing Proxy Server to route the packet using the most efficient route. Any port between the range of 1025 through 5000 can be used by Proxy Server to route the packet.

➤ **Remote Port**   Enter the port number required for the remote host computer under Remote Port. Two options are available: Any and Fixed Port. Any enables any local or remote port to transmit or send the data packet. Fixed Port enables only the port specified to send or receive the packet.

➤ **Local Host**   You must specify the computer in your private network that exchanges packets with a remote Internet host. You have three options under Local Host: Default Proxy External IP Addresses, Specific Proxy IP, and Internal Computer. If your local host is the Proxy Server computer, select Default Proxy External IP Addresses, because this option allows the default IP address for each external interface of the Proxy Server computer to exchange packets. Select Specific Proxy IP to enter a single IP address as the external interface of the Proxy Server computer permitted to exchange packets. Select Internal Computer and enter a single IP address to permit a specific internal computer located behind Proxy Server to exchange packets.

➤ **Remote Host**   You can specify the remote Internet host computer that is allowed to exchange packets with the Proxy Server computer. Under Remote Host you have two options: Single Host or Any Host. Select Single Host to specify the IP address of the one remote host computer that will always be used to send or receive a packet. Select Any Host to allow the packet to be sent or received to any remote host computer on the Internet.

Configuring Domain Filters

You can restrict which Internet sites are accessible through Proxy Server by using domain filters. There are two basic options available when using domain filtering: granting access to all Internet sites, except specific sites that you list; or denying access to all

Internet sites, except specific sites that you list. The exceptions list that you create is processed for each Internet request submitted to Proxy Server. If a Proxy Server client issues a request for a restricted domain, an error message is returned to the client.

In multi-Proxy Server environments, each Proxy Server can be configured to offer access to different sites for different groups of users. However, Proxy Server does not offer domain filtering on a per-user basis. If you use a chained or cascaded configuration of Proxy Servers, the most upstream Proxy Server in the chain must have direct Internet access in order for domain filtering to function successfully. Domain filtering requires the ability to access Internet Domain Name System (DNS) servers. If a chained Proxy Server computer does not have access to DNS, domain filtering is ineffective.

The Domain Filters Tab

Domain filtering is configured using the Domain Filters tab (see Figure 9.16) on the Security dialog box. An entry in the domain exceptions list can be configured in three different ways: as an IP address, as an IP subnet, or as a domain name. In addition, using domain names in the exceptions list is quite flexible because domain names can take a variety of forms. For example, entering **mydomain.com** restricts access to **ftp.mydomain.com** and **www.mydomain.com**, while entering **www.mydomain.com** restricts access only to **www.mydomain.com**. Also, if you deny access to a site by IP address and the site has more than one IP address registered, access is denied to all IP addresses for that site.

You use domain filters to grant or deny access to the Internet sites you specify. You can filter WWW, FTP, and Gopher sites. The following list describes the options available using the Domain Filters tab on the Security dialog box:

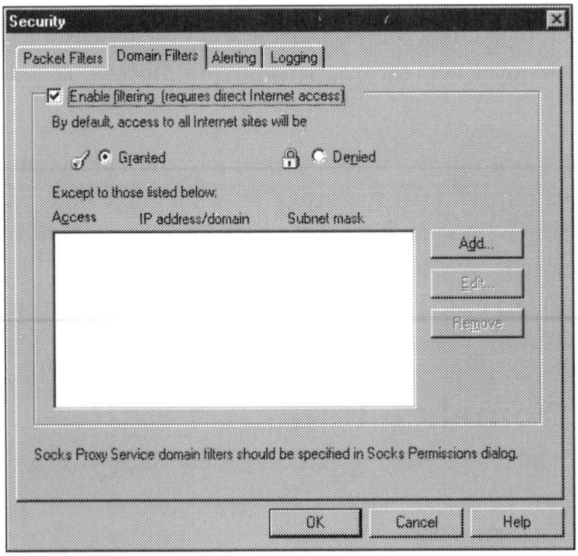

Figure 9.16 The Domain Filters tab.

➤ **Enable Filtering**   Select this checkbox to enable domain filtering, thus controlling access to Internet sites by Proxy Server clients. All users who access the Internet through the Proxy Server computer on which you enable filtering are affected by this setting. With domain filtering enabled, you have two access options: Granted and Denied. Selecting Granted specifies that users are granted access to all Internet sites, except those that are listed. Selecting Denied specifies that users are denied access to all Internet sites, except those that are listed.

➤ **Except To Those Listed Below**   This window shows the exceptions list for the Granted or Denied option selected above. The exceptions list can be modified by using the Add, Edit, or Remove buttons. The Access field displays whether client access to Internet sites is granted or denied. The IP Address/Domain field displays the IP address or domain name of the address where client access to Internet sites is granted or denied. The Subnet Mask field displays the subnet mask where client access to Internet sites is granted or denied.

➤ **Add**   The Add button adds an item to the exceptions list.

➤ **Edit**   The Edit button allows editing of a selected item on the exceptions list.

➤ **Remove**   The Remove button removes a selected item from the exceptions list.

The Grant Access To And Deny Access To Dialog Boxes

The Grant Access To or Deny Access To dialog box is called by pressing the Add or Edit button. If you selected Granted in the domain filters tab, the Grant Access To dialog box is called (see Figure 9.17). Conversely, if you selected Denied in the Domain Filters tab, the Deny Access To dialog box is called (see Figure 9.18). The options available in either dialog box are identical. The following list describes the options available in both the Grant Access To and the Deny Access To dialog boxes:

➤ **Single Computer**   Select this radio button option to grant or deny access to a single computer. If you select this option, you must also enter the computer's IP address.

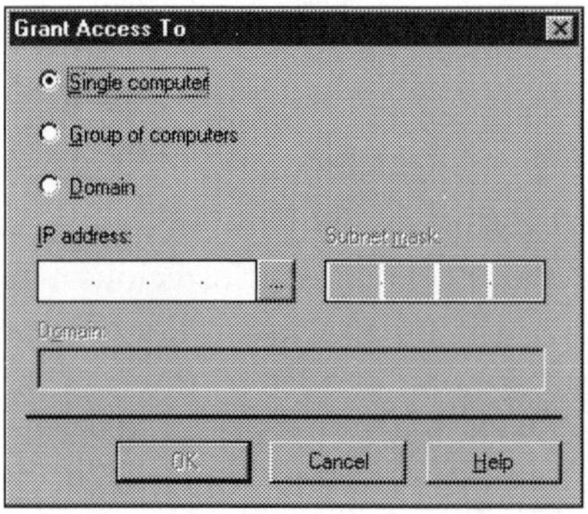

Figure 9.17   The Grant Access To dialog box.

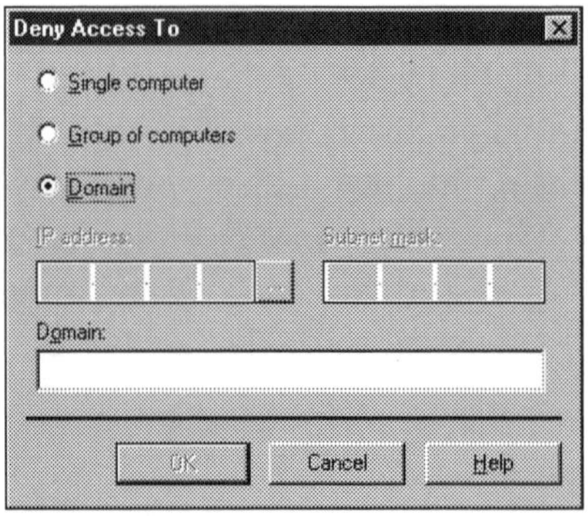

Figure 9.18   The Deny Access To dialog box.

➤ **Group of Computers**   Select this radio button option to grant or deny access to a group of computers. If you select this option, you must also enter an IP address and a subnet mask.

➤ **Domain**   Select this radio button option to grant or deny access to a domain. If you select this option, you must also enter a domain name in Domain.

➤ **IP Address**   When selecting the Single Computer or Group of Computers option, you can type the appropriate IP address in the space provided. Clicking the ellipsis (. . .) button to the right of IP Address allows you to search for an IP Address by typing a DNS name in the DNS Lookup dialog box.

➤ **Subnet Mask**   When selecting the Group of Computers option, you can type the subnet mask.

➤ **Domain**   If you selected the Domain radio button option, you can type the domain name, including a path if desired, in the space provided.

Tip

You can use Domain filtering to control WinSock Proxy access to Internet sites. Just create a filter for both the domain and the IP address of the site.

Configuring Alerts

You might not think of alerts as a security feature, yet alerts are just as important as the other security options previously discussed. Suspicious network events, such as frequent protocol violations, SYN or FRAG attacks, or dropped packets, can signal an attack. A prompt alert can give you the time needed to thwart a security breach. Moreover, you could discover an offense by sending alerts to a log file or the Windows NT system event log and analyzing suspicious patterns. To use alerts, you must turn on packet filtering.

The Alerting Tab

The following list describes the options available under the Alerting tab (see Figure 9.19):

➤ **Event**   You use the Event drop-down list box to select whether to send alerts for Rejected Packets, Protocol Violations, or Disk Full errors. Rejected Packets and Protocol Violations events are recorded in the packet filtering log, the Proxy Server logs, and, if selected, the Windows NT System event log. It is advisable to review the logs, so that you can determine what is generating the events.

➤ **Rejected Packets**   This option instructs Proxy Server to generate an alert after the number of rejected packets you specify. A high frequency of rejected packets might indicate an attack on your internal network. Included in the analysis of rejected packets are the frequency of filtered frame anomalies and protocol violations. You could be experiencing a network attack if an error condition is repeated at a high rate over a given time span.

➤ **Protocol Violations**   This option allows Proxy Server to recognize some rejected packets as being illegal and, therefore, potentially malicious. An alert is generated when the frequency of rejected packets exceeds the number specified. See "Generate System Event" below.

➤ **Disk Full**   This option instructs Proxy Server to generate an alert when a failure is caused by a full disk.

➤ **Generate System Event**   When this option is selected, an event is recorded if the events per second exceed the number specified. The default is 20 events per second.

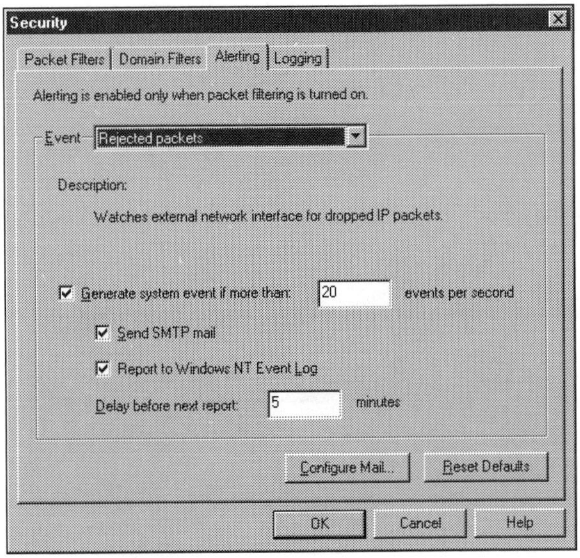

Figure 9.19   The Alerting tab.

> **Send SMTP Mail**   When this checkbox is selected, Proxy Server will send a notification email message of the event to the mail server and administrator.

> **Report To Windows NT System Event Log**   Selecting this checkbox instructs Proxy Server to record the event in the Windows NT system event log.

> **Delay Before Next Report**   You type the time desired between event reports in this field. The default is 5 minutes.

> **Configure Mail Alerting**   Click this button to direct email event reports to the desired location. See the next section for more information.

The Configure Mail Alerting Dialog Box

Proxy Server can send notification of alert events to designated recipients as an email message using SMTP. However, you should be careful where you route email alerts because it is unwise to send an email alert through an Internet path that might be under attack. In fact, it is advisable to send these notifications to an internal mail server instead of a mail server on the Internet, although the specified internal mail server must be capable of receiving SMTP mail. Proxy Server automatically adds a default message in the subject line of the email message, indicating the nature of the alert.

The following list describes the options available in the Configure Mail Alerting dialog box (see Figure 9.20):

> **Mail Server**   Type the name of the mail server that will receive the email message. Because the SMTP protocol is used to exchange mail, you must furnish the name of a server capable of receiving SMTP.

> **Port**   Type the port number of the mail server to which the email message is sent.

> **Send Mail To**   Type the email account name of the individual who is to receive Proxy Server email alert messages.

> **From Address**   Type the originating address of the email message. You can use the name of the Proxy Server computer or the administrator's account on the Proxy Server computer.

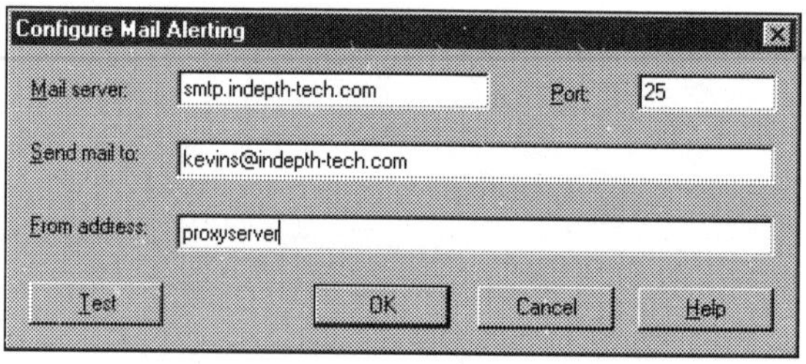

Figure 9.20   The Configure Mail Alerting dialog box.

➤ **Test**   Click this button to send a test message using the information entered. Proxy Server returns a message confirming whether the mail server and port configuration are correct or incorrect.

Configuring Logs

It's important, for security reasons, to enable Proxy Server logging and to review the log data frequently. In fact, running Proxy Server with logging disabled is considered a non-secure operating condition. Proxy Server includes event logs for the Web Proxy, WinSock Proxy, and SOCKS Proxy services. In addition, Proxy Server uses a separate log to record network packet traffic-related events.

Log information is stored by default in a text file. However, log information also can be stored in an ODBC-compliant database table, such as Microsoft Access or Microsoft SQL Server. I recommend using the default text files for log information rather than an ODBC database table, unless you have specific requirements that necessitate using ODBC. This is because using an ODBC-compliant database table can degrade your system performance significantly. You should also store Proxy Server logs on a local disk drive for maximum performance. Ideally, the log data is kept on a different volume than the Proxy Server cache.

Logging Proxy Server services generates a considerable amount of data. Fortunately, you can choose between two different log formats: *regular* or *verbose*. The regular log format is considerably smaller and can be used if disk space is limited. The verbose format contains all available log information for each service and, consequently, is large and densely packed. Nevertheless, if you suspect a problem with Proxy Server, use the verbose format for troubleshooting.

The Logging Tab

You use the Logging tab (see Figure 9.21) to set the logging options for the WinSock Proxy, Web Proxy, and SOCKS Proxy services. Although the logging tab appears identical for each Proxy Server service, you must enable logging for each service separately. Logging is set for each Proxy Server service by clicking on the WinSock Proxy, Web Proxy, or SOCKS Proxy service tab in the Internet service manager, and then clicking on

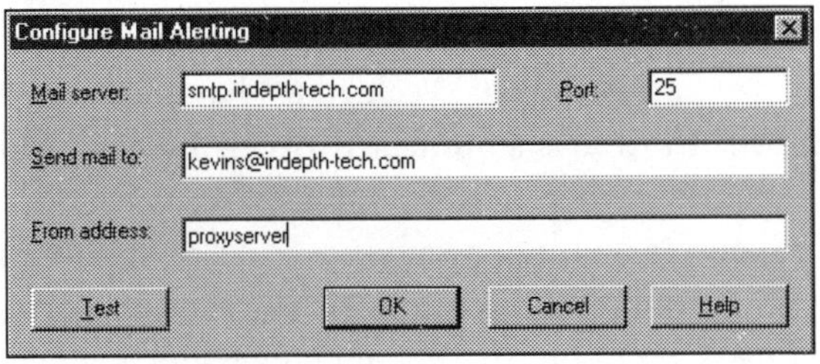

Figure 9.21   The Logging tab.

the Logging tab. You can also set logging for packet filtering. The following list describes the options available for all services and packet filtering under the Logging tab:

➤ **Enable Logging Using** Select this checkbox to log Internet accesses to a text file, or to a table in an SQL- or ODBC-compliant database. Use the drop-down list box to select Regular Logging or Verbose Logging. Selecting Regular Logging records a subset of all available information for each Internet access. Selecting Verbose Logging records all available information for each Internet access.

➤ **Log To File** Select this option to save log information to a text file that can be viewed using a text editor, such as Notepad.

➤ **Automatically Open New Log** Select this option to specify how often to begin a new log file. Available options include: daily, weekly, or monthly intervals. Each time a new log file is started, the old log file is closed. It's a good idea to archive closed files for future reference.

➤ **Limit Number of Old Logs To** Selecting this checkbox allows you to set the number of log files that are stored on the hard drive. By default, this checkbox is not selected, permitting storage of an unlimited number of logs.

➤ **Stop Service If Disk Full** This checkbox is located on the Logging tab for either the WinSock Proxy, SOCKS Proxy, or Web Proxy service. If the hard drive is full, Proxy Server stops the service. Before you can restart the service, you need to remove files from the hard drive.

➤ **Stop All Services If Disk Full** When this checkbox is selected, all Proxy Server services are stopped if the hard drive becomes full. Before you can restart the Proxy Server services, you must free space by deleting files on the volume that contains the log files.

➤ **Log File Directory** You can specify the path where log files are written and stored in this field. To change this location, type a new path or click Browse. The default path for all of the logs for WinSock Proxy, Web Proxy, SOCKS Proxy, and packet filtering is C:\Winnt\System32\msplogs.

➤ **Log File Name** This is the filename of the log. Log files are named automatically by Proxy Server. Daily log filenames have the format WSyymmdd.log, where *yy* is a number representing the year, *mm* is a number representing the month, and *dd* is a number representing the day of the month. Weekly logs have the format WSWyymmw.log, where the third *w* is a number between 1 and 5. Monthly logs have the format WSMyymm.log, where *mm* is a number between 1 and 12. Finally, when the Automatically Open New Log checkbox is selected, a new log file is opened each time the log file reaches a specified size; the filename takes the format WSBnnnn.log, where *nnnn* is a number that increments with each new log.

The first two letters of a log filename identify the service it originated from:

- WS = WinSock Proxy service
- W3 = Web Proxy service
- SP = Socks Proxy service
- PF = Packet filters

➤ **Log To SQL/ODBC Database**   Select this checkbox to write all Internet accesses to a table in an SQL- or ODBC-compliant database. Writing log data to a database is slower than writing to a text file, but data querying and reporting are enhanced. Log files are stored in a single table, and each Internet transaction generates one record in the table. The database can exist on a Proxy Server computer or on another computer on your internal network.

➤ **DBC Data Source Name (DSN)**   Use this field to type the ODBC Data Source Name (DSN) for the database to which Proxy Server is logging.

➤ **Table**   Use this field to type the name of a table in the database to which Proxy Server logs information.

➤ **User Name**   Use this field to type a valid username for the database table.

➤ **Password**   If the table is password protected, you use this field to type the password.

Moving On

It's a good idea to review this chapter often, because Proxy Server's robust security features can take some time to learn. In addition, as your Internet needs change over time, your security requirements also change. The dynamic nature of the Internet necessitates frequent review of Proxy Server security parameters to keep your private network shielded from attack. When Proxy Server is properly configured, many organizations will find that its advanced security model is an effective safeguard for their private network.

You might find that your organization is growing and additional Proxy Servers are required. Fortunately, Proxy Server is highly scalable. In the next chapter, we'll examine configuring multi-server environments.

Administering And Configuring Multiple Server Environments

Proxy Server is highly scalable, offering the ability to grow with your organization's Internet access needs. You can use Proxy Server with other server computers in your private network in several different ways. For example, you can create Proxy Server arrays, chains of Microsoft Proxy Servers, or a Microsoft Proxy Server chained with third-party CERN-based proxy servers or other firewall products. You can even configure Proxy Server to listen and respond on behalf of Web servers or other servers, such as Microsoft Exchange, that are located behind the Proxy Server. You can use any or all of these configurations to provide the Internet access and security your organization requires. While many different multiple server configurations are possible, the foundation for this extensibility is Proxy Server's caching models. So let's start with Proxy Server's distributed and hierarchical caching.

Distributed And Hierarchical Caching

Proxy Server supports two basic models of multiserver caching: distributed and hierarchical. Linking multiple Proxy Server computers in an array results in *distributed caching*. In an array, a single Proxy Server computer is called an *array member*. Some points to remember about arrays include:

➤ An array of Proxy Server computers effectively creates one large Internet objects cache, distributed evenly among the array members.

➤ The Cache Array Routing Protocol (CARP) is the mechanism for routing requests for Internet objects within the array.

➤ Array members communicate among themselves using peer-to-peer communications and HTTP remote procedure calls (RPCs).

➤ Each Proxy Server computer maintains a local copy of its own array membership table.

Distributed caching provides several benefits, including increasing caching performance, allowing simultaneous administration of each array member, load balancing, and fault tolerance. Chapter 2 contains detailed information about the architecture of arrays and the CARP mechanism.

Linking Proxy Server computers with other Proxy Server computers in a chained configuration results in *hierarchical caching*. Chained computers communicate in an upstream hierarchy. The server that is connected to the Internet is the most upstream computer, and the server that is closest to the client is the downstream computer. Here are some points to remember about Proxy Server chains.

➤ While Proxy Server computers that are linked with other third-party products are called chains, only Proxy Server computers that are linked with other Proxy Server computers perform hierarchical caching.

➤ A Proxy Server chain uses CARP to forward HTTP requests from one Proxy Server computer to another Proxy Server computer. In this way, caching can be distributed both across an array and hierarchically in a chain, with the client load evenly balanced among all array members and chain members.

Distributed and hierarchical caching are closely related features because of their reliance on CARP. From an administrative standpoint, you need to properly configure the routing and caching for each Proxy Server computer in the array or hierarchical chain. However, the caching and routing services are transparent to the user.

Configuring Proxy Server Arrays

All Proxy Server services work with arrays, but the greatest performance gains are provided to the Web Proxy clients through distributed caching. Proxy Server's caching model allows the cache load to be distributed evenly among all array members. Each member of an array independently maintains an array membership table that contains configuration and status information for all members of the array. The array membership table is modified whenever a Proxy Server computer joins, or is removed from, an array. Not only is the load evenly distributed among the array members, but also, if one array member is unavailable, the other members of the array detect the problem automatically and avoid routing requests to that member until it becomes available.

You create or join an array by first logging into the Proxy Server computer using an account that has administrative permissions on each array member. It's important to perform a server backup before you join an array, because if you decide to leave—or to remove the server from—an array, the server computer's pre-array state is not restored automatically. By performing a server backup prior to joining an array, you can simply restore the Proxy Server configuration after the server is no longer an array member. The same steps are involved whether you are creating a new array or joining an existing array. A new array is created by just joining together two standalone Proxy Server computers. You join an existing array by joining a standalone Proxy Server computer to any other Proxy Server computer that is already a member of an existing array.

Tip

Leaving an array and *removing from* an array are slightly different operations. *Leaving* an array involves executing the process from the computer being deleted from the array. The process of *removing* a Proxy Server computer from an array is executed remotely from another Proxy Server array member. Remember to save the Proxy Server configuration prior to joining an array and to restore the Proxy Server configuration after deleting a server from an array.

Automatic Synchronization

It's not too difficult to configure and administer arrays because you can perform maintenance simultaneously for all array members when the default *automatic synchronization* option is left enabled. In this way, you simply administer a single member of an array and allow the array synchronization to perform updates across the array. Even if automatic synchronization is disabled, the array membership table remains synchronized at all times. Therefore, think of automatic synchronization as an administrative feature.

When you create a new array, the Proxy Server computer you're joining is synchronized automatically to the computer you are administering. However, when you join an existing array, the checkbox for *Synchronize Configuration of Array Members* must be selected in order for the new array member to be synchronized automatically to the existing array. If you attempt to join an unsynchronized array, a warning message box is displayed, stating that you should directly administer the array members.

All array members are required to belong to the same Windows NT domain when access control is enabled. The array member on which you're performing the administration is always updated first. The array membership tables for the other Proxy Server computers in the array are updated when array members periodically query each other. When a Proxy Server computer joins an array, you might receive a Proxy Server message stating that the IIS authentication settings do not match. If this occurs, you can change the settings in the WWW service by using ISM.

Tip

The anonymous IUSR_computername account will not correctly replicate across an array. Instead, when configuring an array you should grant user permissions to the "Everyone" account in the Web Proxy service if you have the following needs:

1. You have multiple Proxy Server computers configured as an array.

2. You want to allow "anonymous" access to Web publishing from the local IIS computer.

3. You want to authenticate users for client requests that pass through the Web Proxy service.

Table 10.1 illustrates which parameters are replicated throughout the array when automatic synchronization is enabled.

The Array Dialog Box

Arrays are created or configured from the Service Properties dialog box of any Proxy Server service by clicking the Array button to bring up the Array dialog box (see Figure 10.1).

The following list describes the options available in the Array dialog box:

➤ **Join Array**   Pressing this button allows you to create or join an array by bringing up the Join Array dialog box. In the Join Array dialog box, type the name of the Proxy Server computer you want to form the array with, and click on OK. If the server detects that this is a new array, you need to complete the New Array dialog box; this dialog box appears automatically.

➤ **Array Name**   Use this field to specify the name of the array.

Table 10.1   Parameters replicated when automatic synchronization is enabled.

Parameters Replicated Throughout the Array	Parameters Not Replicated Throughout the Array
Domain filters	Web Proxy service enable caching flag
Web Proxy service caching options, including advanced caching options such as cache filters	Web Proxy cache size
Web Proxy service protocol access control information	Web Proxy cache disk location
Web Proxy service upstream routing options	Web Proxy service directory information
Web Proxy service publishing (reverse proxying) information	Logging directories for each service
WinSock Proxy service protocol definitions	Packet filters
WinSock Proxy service access control information	Microsoft Internet Information Server (IIS) WWW service password authentication settings
SOCKS Proxy service permissions	
Logging configuration for each service, including packet filter logging	
Packet filter alerting information	
Local Address Table (LAT) information	
Client configuration information	

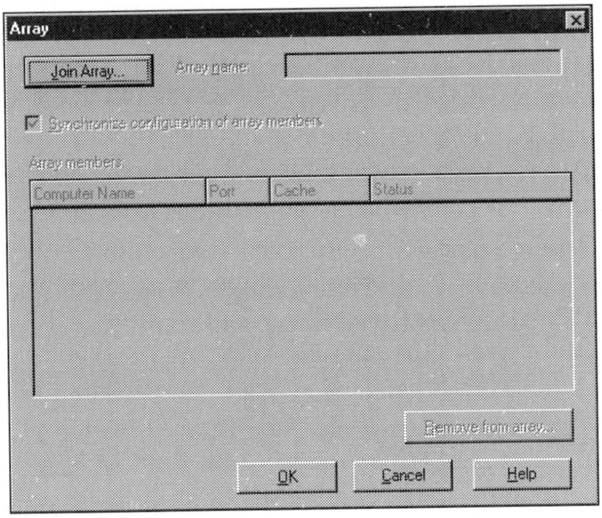

Figure 10.1   The Array dialog box.

➤ **Synchronize Configuration of Array Members**   Selecting this checkbox allows configuration changes to be replicated to other array members. Note that this checkbox is not available if there are pending changes in the join, leave, or remove from options.

➤ **Array Members**   This list box shows the member computers of the array, the port number the Web Proxy service is listening to, the maximum cache size, and the status of the Mspadmin service.

➤ **Remove From Array**   To remove an array member, select the member from the list in Array Members, and then click Remove From Array.

Tip

You must complete and apply certain configuration changes before you can execute other changes. For example, you must apply Proxy Server computer configuration changes before you can execute array membership changes. Also, you cannot perform a server backup or restore operation if you have pending changes that have not yet been applied.

Creating Or Joining An Array

You use the following procedure to create or join an array:

1. Double-click the computer name next to any of the Proxy Server services in the Internet Service Manager.

2. Click Array in the Service Properties dialog box on the Service tab, and then click Join Array. The Join Array dialog box appears.

Want To Increase Array Performance?

Proxy Server array members maintain a client configuration script that is written in JavaScript. The script defines how Web browsers connect to a Proxy Server array. Whenever possible, client computers should use this configuration script. In this way, you can have the configuration script directly route the client computer's Web browser request to a specific Proxy Server computer in an array. This technique relieves the processing burden of the array by reducing routing calculations that need to be performed by the array itself. By using the client configuration script, the Web browser connects to the specific array member that most likely holds a cached copy of the URL requested by the client. Just by using the client configuration script, you will improve routing performance. See Chapter 8 for more information.

3. Type the name of the server you want to join with in the Computer Name to Form an Array With text box, and then click on OK.

4. Click on OK once more, and then click Apply.

Leaving An Array

You must perform the leave array procedure from the array computer you want to delete from the array. It is possible that you are leaving a two-member array. In this case, both array members will become standalone Proxy Server computers and will need to be administered appropriately. You use the following procedure to leave an array:

1. Double-click the computer name next to any of the Proxy Server services in the Internet Service Manager.

2. Click Array in the Service Properties dialog box on the Service tab, and then click Leave Array.

3. Click on OK, and then click Apply.

Removing An Array Member

You use the following procedure to delete an array member computer remotely from another member computer:

1. Double-click the computer name next to any of the Proxy Server services in the Internet Service Manager.

2. Click Array in the Service Properties dialog box on the Service tab.

3. In the list of array members, select the array member you want to remove, and then click Remove From Array.

4. Click on OK, and then click Apply.

Arrays, Winsock Proxy, And The Mspclnt.Ini File

You need to manually add new sections and command entries to the Mspclnt.ini file located on the Proxy Server computer when configuring an array for WinSock Proxy clients. The sections and procedures for editing the Mspclnt.ini file were detailed in Chapter 8.

When configuring the WinSock Proxy service to connect to an array, you should check the manual option in the Client Installation/Configuration dialog box (see Figure 10.2). You bring up this dialog box by clicking the Client Configuration button under the WinSock Proxy Service tab. When the manual option is enabled, it will protect any changes you make manually to the Mspclnt.ini file.

Array Addressing

Proxy Server clients can access the Proxy Server array members by using DNS, IP addresses, or IPX addresses. Use the following procedures, as appropriate, to configure your array addressing:

➤ **Using DNS**   If you're using DNS, you must create an array name, using your DNS Server, that resolves the names of the individual array members. When you create the DNS array name, it should include the IP address of each array member. Then your client computers, or downstream Proxy Server computers, can be configured

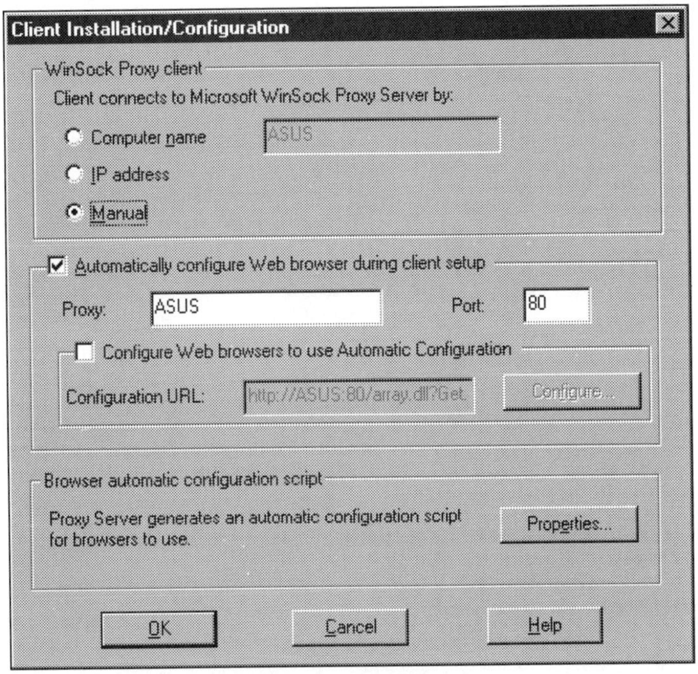

Figure 10.2   The Client Installation/Configuration dialog box.

to use the array name. The advantage to this approach is that you can later change the names of individual array members without making changes to each client or downstream computer.

► **Using IP or IPX**   If you are using IP or IPX addresses, then your WinSock Proxy clients must access the array using IP or IPX addresses. There is a file, named local-address.dump, that lists all of the IP and IPX addresses that are assigned to a specific Proxy Server computer. By default, this file is located in the C:\Msp\Clients directory on the Proxy Server computer. The information contained in this file should be combined with the information contained in every other array member's local-address.dump file and transferred into the **[Servers IP Addresses]** and **[Servers IPX Addresses]** sections of the client Mspclnt.ini file. Next, you must manually copy the edited Mspclnt.ini file to the other members of the array.

For more information on what kind of addressing to use for your Proxy Server array, see Decision Tree 10.1.

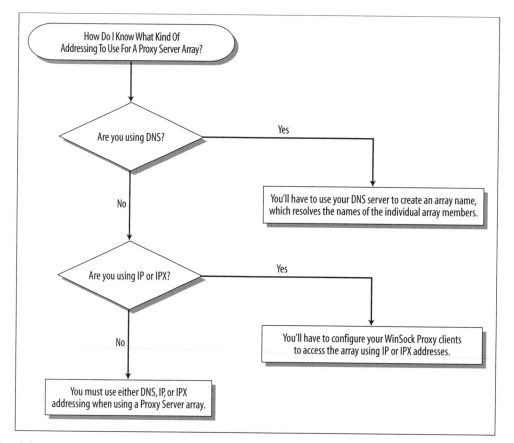

Decision Tree 10.1   How do I know what kind of addressing to use for a Proxy Server array?

Array Synchronization Conflicts

Array synchronization conflicts can occur if more than one person is administrating an array. For example, problems will arise if an administrator applies a configuration change to an array while another administrator applies a configuration change to the same array from a different array member. Depending on the exact sequence of events, different problems could occur, as illustrated below.

Scenario 1

1. *Administrator 1* makes and applies a configuration change to a Proxy Server computer that is a member of *Array 1*.

2. The Proxy Server *Array 1* replicates the changes to one or more array members.

3. *Administrator 2* makes a configuration change to a Proxy Server computer that is a member of *Array 1*, but the change is not applied.

4. The Configuration Changed message box is displayed on *Administrator 2's* computer. He or she is presented with two options:

   ➤ **Click Refresh**   If *Administrator 2* clicks Refresh, all changes pending on the array member that the administrator is changing are discarded. However, the array member that *Administrator 2* is changing remains synchronized. This is the preferred option.

   ➤ **Click Overwrite**   If *Administrator 2* clicks Overwrite, the changes made by *Administrator 1* are overwritten by *Administrator 2's* changes. *Administrator 2's* changes are replicated throughout the array, with the exception of *Administrator 1's* Proxy Server array member. This creates a synchronization conflict.

Scenario 2

1. *Administrator 2* makes configuration changes to a Proxy Server computer that is a member of *Array 1*.

2. *Administrator 2* applies the configuration changes to the Proxy Server computer, and the changes begin to replicate to other members of *Array 1*.

3. *Administrator 2's* array member detects configuration changes from *Administrator 1's* array member and displays the Array Configuration Conflict message box with a notification that the array is out of synchronization. *Administrator 2* is presented with two options:

   ➤ **Click Synchronize Now**   If *Administrator 2* clicks Synchronize Now and selects an array member with which to synchronize from the list displayed, all configuration parameters from the array member he or she chooses to synchronize with are replicated throughout all other members of *Array 1*. This is the preferred option, because it maintains the synchronization of the array.

➤ **Click Cancel** If *Administrator 2* clicks Cancel, the changes he or she made are applied only to the array member that the administrator is currently administering. No replication throughout the rest of Array 1 occurs. Then an Array Update Errors dialog box appears, displaying the other members of *Array 1* that are unsynchronized with the array member being administered.

Viewing The Array Membership Table

A Proxy Server array membership table is an important part of CARP, because it determines which array member receives an object request. The array membership table can be viewed using a Web browser. For example, if you wanted to check the status of an array member named "Proxy2" in an array named "PrxArray," you would use the following procedure:

1. Type **http://PrxArray/array.dll?Get.Info.v1** in the address field of your Web browser.

2. The above URL returns the Proxy Array Information/1.0 membership table.

```
ArrayEnabled:1
ConfigID: 305419896
ArrayName:PrxArry
ListTTL: 3000

Proxy1 192.168.0.1 80 http://Proxy1:80/array.dll MSProxy/2.0
   63572 Up 100 100
Proxy2 192.168.0.10 80 http://Proxy2:80/array.dll MSProxy/2.0
   63572 Up 100 100
Proxy3 192.168.0.100 80 http://Proxy3:80/array.dll MSProxy/2.0
   713 Down 100 100
```

Table 10.2 defines, from left to right, how the above fields are interpreted:

Table 10.2 Definitions of fields in a Proxy Server membership table.	
Server (Array Member) Name	**Proxy1**
Server IP address used for communication within the array	192.168.0.1
Port number used for communication within the array	80
URL for Array.dll	http://Proxy1:80/array.dll
Proxy Server version	MSProxy/2.0
	Continued

Table 10.2   Definitions of fields in a Proxy Server membership table (Continued).

Server (Array Member) Name	Proxy1
Number of seconds the server has been in the current state	63572
The current server state (Up means available, Down means unavailable)	Up
Load factor of server expressed as a relative percentage of normal load	100
Cache size of server in megabytes (MB)	100

Array Administration Using The Command Line

You can use the **RemotMsp** command-line utility to administer Proxy Server arrays. In fact, the only way the load factor can be modified is with **RemotMsp**. Additional information about the **RemotMsp** command line utility, including a description of the common options, is found in Chapter 7. The following is the syntax used to administer Proxy Server array membership:

```
RemotMsp [common options] JOIN | REMOVE | SYNC
    | STATUS -MEMBER:array member name
```

The SYNC Command

Executing the **SYNC** command synchronizes configuration among all array members. The Proxy Server computer that you are administering becomes the owner of the master copy of the array configuration information for the duration of the procedure, and all other array members are synchronized to it. If the **MEMBER** parameter is present, only that member is synchronized.

The STATUS Command

The **STATUS** command simply lists all array members and the configuration date stamp. The following is the syntax of the **STATUS** command:

```
RemotMsp [common options] STATUS -MEMBER:array member name
```

The LOADFACTOR Command

Executing the **LOADFACTOR** command sets the array member's load factor, where X is expressed as a relative percentage. The term **LOADFACTOR** needs a little explanation. The **LOADFACTOR** is expressed as a *relative percentage*. For example, if **LOADFACTOR=50** for Proxy1 and **LOADFACTOR=150** for Proxy2, the normal load is the sum of the **LOADFACTOR**s of Proxy1 and Proxy 2, or 200. Proxy1 is set to 50 percent relative to the normal load (200) and Proxy2 is set to 150 percent relative to the normal load (200). This means that Proxy1 receives 25 percent and Proxy2 receives 75 percent of the total load. If this parameter is not set, all array members are set to **LOADFACTOR=100.** The following is the syntax of the **LOADFACTOR** command:

```
RemotMsp [common options] SET LOADFACTOR=[X] -MEMBER:array member name
```

The JOIN And REMOVE Commands

Executing the following command joins an array:

```
RemotMsp [common options] JOIN -MEMBER:array member name
```

where

array member name refers to the name of the Proxy Server computer or array to join with.

Executing the following command removes the current Proxy Server computer from an array:

```
RemotMsp [common options] REMOVE -MEMBER:array member name
```

where

array member name refers to the name of the Proxy Server computer or array to remove the current Proxy Server computer from.

Tip

Need to modify the load factor setting? You must use the command-line option to modify this setting. There is no equivalent setting option available through the Internet Service Manager (ISM).

Registry Entries For Arrays

There are two undocumented registry keys for Proxy Server that are useful under certain circumstances. Using these keys, you can change the default ping timeout value and the number of communication attempts use in an array. The following defines the entry names, data types, and default values:

➤ **MaxPingTries** is type **REG_DWORD.** The default value when this entry is absent is three.

➤ **PingTimeout** is type **REG_DWORD.** The default value when this entry is absent is 500 (milliseconds).

Use the Registry Editor to create these entries. The entries must be installed to the following Windows NT Registry key path:

```
HKEY_LOCALMACHINE\SYSTEM
  \CurrentControlSet
    \Services
      \Mspadmin
        \Parameters
```

As always, you should exercise caution when making any changes to the Windows NT Registry.

Configuring Web Proxy Routing

You can route Web Proxy client requests within an array, to an upstream Proxy Server, to a Proxy Server array, or directly to the Internet. In addition, you can resolve client requests within an array prior to routing the request upstream. You administer Proxy Server routes from the Web Proxy service, because only Web Proxy client requests can be routed through chained Proxy Server computers or Proxy Server arrays. The WinSock Proxy and SOCKS Proxy services do not support chained requests. Therefore, if the Web Proxy service is not used in your installation, upstream routing should be disabled.

Upstream Routing

Web Proxy client requests can be routed upstream to a Proxy Server computer, to a Proxy Server array, or directly to the Internet. User authentication is available when routing to an upstream Proxy Server computer or Proxy Server array. As mentioned in Chapter 6, you can specify a backup route to the Internet if a chained computer is unable to process a request. The backup route provides the same features and functionality as the primary route. Once requests are directed through the backup route, the unavailable Proxy Server computer continues to be queried until it is again available. At that time, the primary route is reactivated automatically. This eliminates the possibility of a single point of failure.

Routing Within An Array

Once you have created or joined a Proxy Server array, you can configure routing Web Proxy client requests within an array, before routing them to an upstream Proxy Server computer or a Proxy Server array. This option offers continued high performance even if an array member goes down. For example, consider an array that consists of four array members: proxy1, proxy2, proxy3, and proxy4. If proxy2 becomes inaccessible, new client requests are no longer routed to this Proxy Server computer. However, if you have enabled Routing Within an Array, the load and the Web Proxy service caching are evenly distributed among proxy1, proxy3, and proxy4 computers during the downtime. Proxy1, proxy3, and proxy4 will continue to periodically query proxy2 until it becomes available. The Routing Within an Array option is found on the Web Proxy service's Routing tab.

You also can set the array membership table Time-to-Live (TTL). This option allows you to specify the frequency with which array members can update their internal membership tables. The array membership Time-to-Live also specifies how often a downstream Proxy Server computer queries the upstream array for the membership table. Additionally, you can set user credentials for upstream routing. This enables Proxy Server-to-Proxy Server authentication credentials from one Proxy Server computer to another Proxy Server computer within an array. The IP address that is used for communicating with other array members can be specified, which is beneficial when Proxy Server has multiple IP addresses—for example, if a Proxy Server computer has multiple internal network adapter cards. These options are available under the Advanced Array Options dialog box.

The Routing Tab

The Routing tab (see Figure 10.3) is used to direct client requests for Internet objects within arrays. Requests for Internet objects can be routed through an array, to upstream Proxy Server computers, or directly to the Internet. The following list describes the options available in the Routing dialog box for configuring routing for Web Proxy clients:

➤ **Upstream Routing** The options available under Upstream Routing allow you to determine whether a Web Proxy client request is sent directly to the Internet or to another Web Proxy server or array. The options are Use Direct Connection or Use Web Proxy or Array. If you select Use Direct Connection, client requests are sent directly to the Internet. If you select Use Web Proxy or Array, client requests are

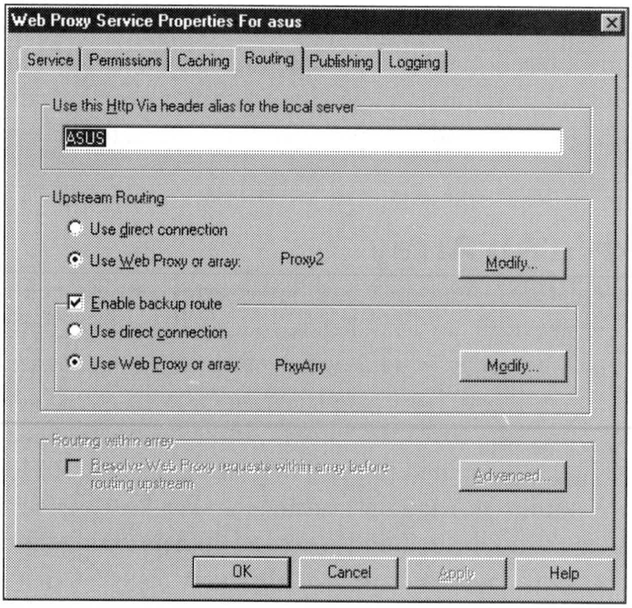

Figure 10.3 The Routing tab.

sent upstream to another Proxy Server computer or array. To configure the up-stream route, click the Modify button and complete the Advanced Routing Options dialog box.

> *If you are routing through a Proxy Server computer or array, you can configure a backup route if the primary route is unavailable. The backup routing option is available when Use Web Proxy or Array is selected. When you are routing upstream traffic through an array, you must configure the array prior to configuring routing.*

➤ **Enable Backup Route**   Selecting this checkbox makes available the Use Direct Connection or Use Web Proxy or Array options. If you select Use Direct Connection, client requests are sent directly to the Internet if the primary upstream Proxy Server computer or array is inaccessible. If you select Use Web Proxy or Array, client requests are sent upstream to another Proxy Server computer or array if the primary upstream route is inaccessible. You also can configure the backup route if you use an array for the backup route by clicking the Modify button and completing the Advanced Routing Options dialog box.

➤ **Routing Within Array**   This option routes Web Proxy clients within an array before sending the request upstream to another Proxy Server computer or the Internet. It is available only if the Proxy Server computer is a member of an array.

➤ **Resolve Web Proxy Requests Within Array Before Routing Upstream**   When this checkbox is selected, the Web Proxy resolves cached object requests within the array before routing upstream. If an array member computer is inaccessible, other member computers can accept the request. This option provides load balancing and caching between the array members.

➤ **Advanced**   Clicking this button will display the Advanced Array Options dialog box, which allows you to configure advanced array options.

The Advanced Routing Options Dialog Box

You use the Advanced Routing Options dialog box to configure both the primary and backup Proxy Server computer routes. The following list describes the options available in the Advanced Routing Options dialog box:

➤ **Upstream Web Proxy Server**   Web Proxy client requests are routed to the Proxy Server computer or array you identify. You must specify the name of the upstream Proxy Server computer or array and the port number where the Web Proxy service is listening for incoming Web requests in the Proxy and Port text boxes respectively.

As you enter the Proxy Server computer name in the Proxy text field, the name is automatically entered, using HTTP format, in Array URL under Auto-poll Upstream Proxy for Array Configuration.

➤ **Auto-poll Upstream Proxy For Array Configuration**   When this checkbox is selected, upstream Proxy Server computers are automatically polled for the latest information about the array properties of the upstream server. If the upstream Proxy Server computer is a member of an array, array properties include the most recent member server list.

➤ **Array URL**   This text box is filled in automatically with a Proxy Server computer name, in HTTP format, as the information is entered in the Proxy box under Upstream Web Proxy Server (for example, **http://proxy2:80/array.dll**, where proxy2 is the Proxy Server computer name and 80 is the port number). This URL is used by the Array Manager if the upstream computer is running Proxy Server.

➤ **User Credentials To Communicate With Upstream Proxy/Array**   When this checkbox is selected, you can specify the authentication parameters that are used between member Proxy Server computers and upstream Proxy Server computers or arrays. Type the *username* and *password* in the appropriate text box for the account that allows access to the upstream Proxy Server computer. Using authentication is optional and must be configured by the administrator of the upstream Proxy Server computer.

➤ **Allow Basic/Clear Text Authentication**   When this option is selected, the username and password are sent in clear text.

➤ **Allow Encrypted Authentication (NT CR)**   When this option is selected, the username and password are sent encrypted.

The Advanced Array Options Dialog Box

The Advanced Array Options dialog box is used to specify the amount of time between membership queries and to set the credentials to use within the array. This dialog box is displayed by clicking Advanced under Routing Within Array on the Web Proxy Routing tab. The following list describes the options available in the Advanced Array Options dialog box:

➤ **Table TTL**   Allows you to specify the maximum length of time between queries of member computers in an array. It also sets the frequency used by downstream Proxy Server computers to check for configuration changes in the array. The default is 50 minutes.

➤ **Use Credentials To Communicate Within Array**   This option provides a space to enter a username and password to identify the request to the array. Using an administrator account for the username and password is recommended. This account must have permission to use HTTP.

➤ **Intra-array Communication**   Allows you to specify the internal IP address used for multiple Proxy Server computers to communicate with each other. You can accept the default internal IP address or change it to another internal IP address. This feature is beneficial if you have multiple network cards on a computer, have multiple Proxy Server computers, or want to direct communications through a specific IP address.

For example, the Proxy Server computer you are administering might have three network cards: a network card connecting externally to the Internet, a network card connecting internally to the private network, and another network card connecting internally between Proxy Server computers. It is possible that the auto-detect feature, or Setup, is unable to differentiate between the two internal cards and uses the wrong IP address. You can choose to either enter the correct IP address manually, or use *Auto-detect* to search your internal IP addresses.

➤ **Publishing**   This option allows computers downstream from the Proxy Server computer to use Proxy Server to publish to the Internet. Proxy Server supports reverse proxying and reverse hosting. Therefore, any computer on your internal network can publish to the Internet. Security is maintained because all incoming and outgoing requests are filtered through the Proxy Server computer. In addition, Proxy Server can also cache incoming requests from the Internet, which provides safe, easy access. There is more information on publishing later in this chapter in the section titled "Configuring Proxy Server For Internet Publishing."

Tip

Proxy Server's Routing script does not work properly with the Internet Explorer version 3.02 when using NTLM authentication. Internet Explorer version 4.x does not exhibit this problem.

Using Proxy Server With A Single Network Adapter

You might want to use a Proxy Server computer that has a single network adapter to chain with a downstream Proxy Server or for caching only. In this case, the Proxy Server computer would only have a single IP address. While you can operate Proxy Server in this configuration, you must disable packet filtering. In addition, if the Proxy Server computer is connected to the Internet, you should either disable the WinSock Proxy service, or disable access control for the WinSock Proxy service.

Configuring Proxy Server For Internet Publishing

The classical use for any proxy server is to provide outbound Internet service for users of your private network. Because the proxy server is limited to servicing only outbound connections, your private network is not continually visible to Internet users. Of course, this one-way-street approach provides a measure of security for your private network. Yet, many organizations need to maintain a Web presence and choose the convenience of hosting their own Web server. Without careful planning and appropriate firewall protection, this Internet Web server can seriously expose your private network to attacks from external Internet users. Microsoft Proxy Server 2.0 provides security enhancements that allow you to safely publish to the Internet from any machine on your private network, other than Proxy Server itself.

Reverse Proxying And Reverse Hosting

Proxy Server offers two features that allow you to securely host Web services on a server that is located behind the Proxy Server computer: reverse proxying and reverse hosting.

Reverse proxying works by listening to an incoming request for an internal Web server and responding on behalf of that server. Proxy Server "impersonates" the Web server, while providing caching services to Internet users who request objects from the Web server. It's convenient to think of reverse proxying as "inverse chaining," because external requests for Internet objects are forwarded downstream to a Web server that is located behind the Proxy Server computer. Therefore, reverse proxying works in the opposite direction of the Proxy Server chaining mentioned previously in this chapter. However, similar to Proxy Server chaining, reverse proxying works only with Web servers.

Reverse hosting works by maintaining a list of internal server computers that have permission to publish to the Internet. Using a mapping table, Proxy Server listens for responses on behalf of multiple servers that are located behind it and redirects requests to the appropriate server. In this way, the servers can use a single IP address to publish to the Internet. It's important to note that with reverse hosting the servers don't necessarily have to be Web servers. Internet clients receive no indication the request is being passed through the Proxy Server computer.

Tip

You should not host Internet Web services on the same computer that is running Proxy Server. Although Proxy Server can be operated in this configuration, to do so is unwise. *Intranet* publishing hosted on the Proxy Server computer, on the other hand, does not affect Internet security.

The reverse proxying and hosting features are not only secure, but also highly flexible. Any computer on your private network that is running an HTTP application can publish to the Internet with Proxy Server. Because all incoming requests and outgoing responses are passed through the Proxy Server first, your security is not compromised. Furthermore, it is entirely possible that the Proxy Server will enhance performance because of its caching features. For example, a single Web server, such as IIS, can host a Web site anywhere on your private network. A Proxy Server computer is configured to provide reverse proxying for the Web server. The first hit the Web server receives for its home page results in Proxy Server's caching that page. The next time an Internet user requests that home page, Proxy Server returns the object from its cache. This not only reduces the load on the Web server, but also reduces the traffic on the private network. If your needs include running multiple Web servers throughout your organization, the enhanced performance can be substantial. Some downsides include potential problems with new Web pages being unavailable until the TTL expires on the cached object and the ability of your Proxy Server computer to be up to the task. However, the required computer performance is easily accomplished through the creation of a Proxy Server array.

Tip

Be sure to test all Web publishing content and links for compatibility with Proxy Server 2.0. Proxy Server is compatible with most Web publishing content. However, if your content is authored with redirect (HTTP 302) messages, the following mappings might not work:

➤ Computer name mapped to computer name/path. For example:

http://proxy1.yourdomain.com

mapped to:

http://yourdomain.internal/path1

➤ Computer name/path mapped to computer name. For example:

http://proxy.yourdomain.com/user1

mapped to:

http://user1

➤ Computer name/path mapped to computer name/path. For example:

http://proxy.yourdomain.com/user1

mapped to:

http://yourdomain.internal/user1

If your tests reveal a content problem that is difficult to change, you can use server proxying instead.

The Publishing Tab

You use the Publishing tab (see Figure 10.4) in the Web Proxy Service Properties dialog box to configure computers downstream from the Proxy Server computer to publish to the Internet. By using reverse proxying and reverse hosting, you filter all incoming and outgoing requests through the Proxy Server computer. This provides a secure method for Web hosting and enhanced performance through Proxy Server caching. The following list describes the options available for publishing to the Internet using the Publishing tab.

➤ **Enable Web Publishing**   By selecting this checkbox you enable computers downstream from the Proxy Server computer to publish to the Internet. When you enable Web publishing, the remaining options on the Publishing tab become available.

➤ **Discarded**   If you select this option, Proxy Server refuses the requests it cannot map by using the mapping table.

➤ **Sent To The Local Web Server**   If you select this option, Proxy Server will then listen for incoming Web server requests and forward those requests to the local Web publishing server.

➤ **Sent To Another Web Server**   If you select this option, you enable reverse proxying or reverse hosting. Proxy Server will then listen for incoming Web server requests and forward the requests to the server or servers used for Internet publishing. To

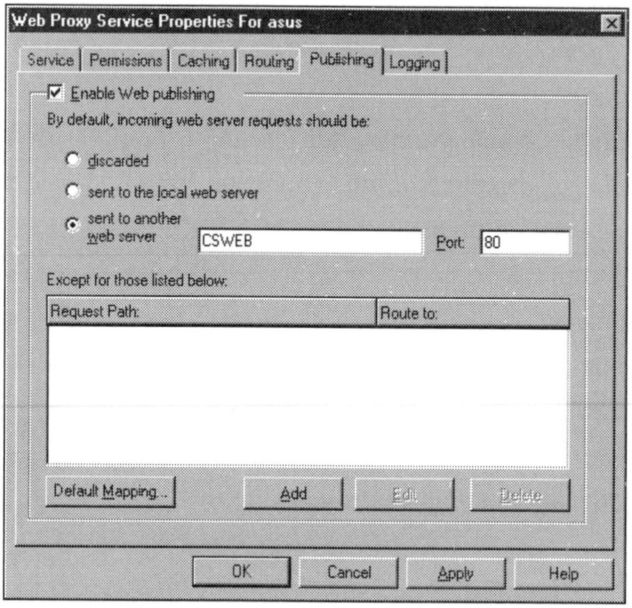

Figure 10.4   The Publishing tab.

Need To Restrict Access From The Internet To FTP And Gopher?

You need to use other security measures if you need to restrict access from the Internet to FTP and Gopher services, because these services do not distinguish between internal and external publishing. For example, you can set access control list (ACL) permissions for FTP or Gopher files. Better yet, if FTP or Gopher services are not used, you can stop these services using Internet Service Manager. Note that, beginning with IIS version 4.0, the Gopher service is not included.

enable reverse proxying, type a valid server name and port number in the text box provided. To enable reverse hosting, first type a valid server name and port number in the text box provided, and then create a mapping table using the Add button. (See the next option, "Except for Those Listed Below".)

➤ **Except For Those Listed Below**   This option allows you to create and modify the mapping table for reverse hosting. It is used to reroute incoming Internet requests to a different downstream computer, other than the one specified in the request. This is accomplished by mapping the host name and the path specified in the request to a path that points to a URL on your private network. You use the Add, Edit, or Delete buttons on the Publishing tab to create or modify the mapping table.

For example, suppose you need to route a request that has the URL **http://www.yourhost.com/** from the Internet to a downstream computer that has the URL **http://www.privatenet.com/**. You would enter this mapping by clicking Add, entering the original path, **http://www.yourhost.com/**, and then typing in a mapped URL, such as **http://www.privatenet.com/**, in the Mapping dialog box (see Figure 10.5). Note that you must enter URLs with the http:// prefix.

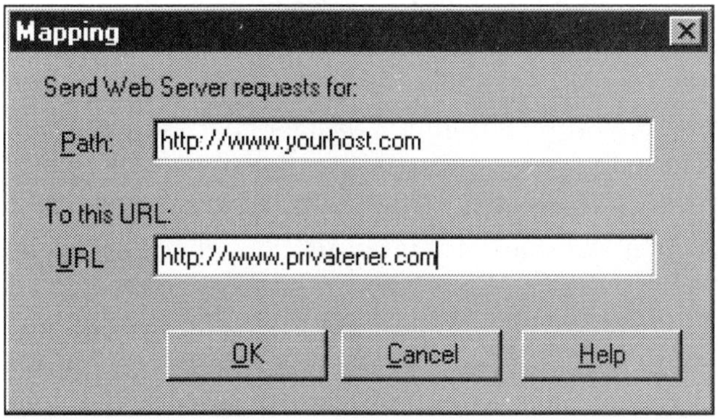

Figure 10.5   The Mapping dialog box.

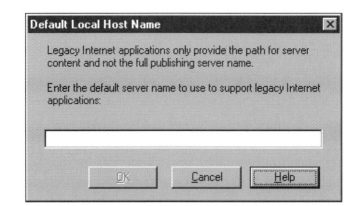

Figure 10.6   The Default Local Host Name dialog box.

➤ **Default Mapping**   Use this button to set the default Web server host in the
Default Local Host Name dialog box (see Figure 10.6). Older Web clients might
not supply a path and host header to create a URL for incoming requests to a Web
server. Typing the default server name in Default Local Host Name allows the
default host name to be substituted if the Internet client does not supply this
information. Note that newer Web browsers—such as Internet Explorer 3.0 and
higher and Netscape Navigator 3.0 and higher—do supply the required information.

Configuring Proxy Server For Server Proxying

Proxy Server has the ability to listen for inbound packets destined to a server computer
that is connected behind the Proxy Server computer. The incoming requests are then
forwarded by Proxy Server to the server on the private network. This process is called
server proxying. For example, using server proxying, you can direct incoming mail to your
Microsoft Exchange Server computer without compromising your network security.

Ideally, the server application is installed on a computer located behind the Proxy Server
computer; however, the server application can be installed on the same computer that
runs Proxy Server if necessary. Running a server application on a computer located behind Proxy Server permits the packet filtering features of Proxy Server to protect the
server application. While most Windows Sockets server applications are able to use the
server proxy feature, additional advanced settings might be required of your internal
server.

To configure server proxying, you must first bind the server applications or services to
the external network adapter on the Proxy Server computer using your Winsock Proxy
client application. This will make your server application available to Internet clients.
Proxy Server will then listen for and forward the incoming Internet requests to the

appropriate server on the private network. In addition, you need to verify that dynamic packet filtering is enabled for any server applications that run as WinSock Proxy clients by using the WinSock Proxy service. Once configured, Internet clients simply contact the internal server by connecting to the Proxy Server's external IP address. This process is completely transparent to an Internet client.

Step 1: Install The Winsock Proxy Client Application

The first step is to configure the server application on the private network as a Proxy client application. You accomplish this task by installing the Winsock Proxy client application on the private network computer that is running the server application.

Step 2: Edit Wspcfg.ini File

You will also need to add various entries in the Wspcfg.ini file to configure the application to work with Proxy Server. The Wspcfg.ini entries were explained in Chapter 8. For example, you might use internal FTP servers binding to port 21 that need their own IP address. This results in more than one IP address on the Proxy Server computer's network adapter that is connected externally to the Internet. In this case, two different IP addresses for the external network adapter of the Proxy Server computer are required, each binding to port 21. You would use the ProxyBindIp entry in the Wspcfg.ini file to allow each internal FTP server to bind to a single IP address.

 ## *Tip*

When using a Proxy Server array, you should designate an array member to always be used for a specific internal server application. You use the ForceProxy entry to force redirection by means of the same Proxy Server computer. Then Internet clients will always look for the same IP address of the same Proxy Server computer to connect with the server application.

Step 3: Configure Account Credentials

You need to consider the implications of the system credentials required to run your server application or service. If the application or service requires a local system account, you need to place the following entry in the appropriate section in the Wspcfg.ini file:

```
ForceCredentials=1
```

When the setting for this entry is 1, it forces the use of alternate user authentication credentials that are stored locally on the computer that is running the Windows NT service. You use the Credtool.exe application to set and store the user credentials on client computers. This tool is provided with Proxy Server. The user credentials must reference a user account that can be authenticated by Proxy Server either locally or in a domain trusted by Proxy Server. When the user account for an application is set up, the credentials typically are set so as not to expire.

ten

You need to store the user credentials on each computer that is running a Windows NT service or server application. You use the **credtool** command-line utility that is provided with Proxy Server to store alternative user authentication credentials in local security storage. The syntax for **credtool** is as follows:

```
credtool [-r | -w | -d] -n servicename
  [-c username domain password]
```

where

-r reads the credentials.

-w writes, or stores, the credentials.

-d deletes the credentials.

-n servicename specifies the Windows NT service or server application, where servicename is the filename (without the .exe extension) of the service or server application.

-c username domain password stores user authentication credentials, where username domain password specifies the user name, domain, and password.

You need to create a dependency on the Windows NT LM Security Support Provider (NtLmSsp) service if you are running the service on a computer that uses the IPX/SPX protocol, and the service requires redirection. If the service does not require redirection, you need to add an entry to the Wspcfg.ini file to disable redirection for that service.

You use the Service Controller Command-line utility (sc.exe) to create a dependency on NtLmSsp. Once the dependency is created, the WinSock Proxy application is dependent on having the NtLmSsp service running first. The SC.EXE utility is included in the Windows NT Resource Kit. Its purpose is to make a service that you want to run remotely to be dependent on the NtLmSsp service.

To create a service dependency, use the following command:

```
SC \\MyMchineName CONFIG MyServiceName DEPEND= ntlmssp
```

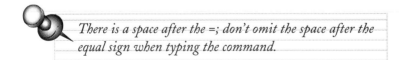

There is a space after the =; don't omit the space after the equal sign when typing the command.

To query a service dependency:

```
SC \\MyMachineName QC MyServiceName
```

Configuring FTP Service With Proxy Server

The following procedure describes configuring an internal FTP service for use with Proxy Server. In this case, the configuration is specifically for the FTP Service that is provided with Microsoft Internet Information Server (IIS).

1. Create a Wspcfg.ini file in the directory where the ftp.exe file is located (usually \Winnt\system32\). Place the following configuration settings in the Wspcfg.ini file (see Chapter 8 for definitions of these entries).

```
[Inetinfo]
ServerBindTcpPorts=21
LocalBindTcpPorts=20
Persistent=1
KillOldSession=1
ForceCredentials=1
```

2. Use the **credtool** utility to specify the user credentials for the account that is used for **Inetinfo**.

3. Create a protocol definition on the Proxy Server computer that uses the WinSock Proxy service, using the following parameters:

   ➤ Protocol name: **FTP Server**

   ➤ Initial connection: **21 TCP Inbound**

   ➤ Subsequent connection: **0 TCP Inbound, 1025-5000 TCP Outbound**

Additionally, you can use the **ForceProxy** and **ProxyBindIp** entries if necessary.

Configuring Microsoft Exchange With Proxy Server

The following procedure describes configuring Microsoft Exchange for use with Proxy Server:

1. Install and configure Microsoft Proxy Server.

2. Install and test the WinSock Proxy (WSP) client on the Exchange Server computer by running a WinSock client application, for example, FTP. When you're assured that the WinSock Proxy client is working properly, you need to create Wspcfg.ini files for the Exchange applications.

3. Place the Wspcfg.ini file in the directory where the application's .exe file is installed. There is more than one .exe file for Exchange Server's Internet mail. Each .exe file needs to be bound to the proxy server with the appropriate entries in its own Wspcfg.ini file. Therefore, you will create more than one Wspcfg.ini file.

4. Create a Wspcfg.ini file for use with the Exchange SMTP service, adding the entries below to this file. Place this file in the directory where Msexcimc.exe is located.

```
[MSEXCIMC]
ServerBindTcpPorts=25
Persistent=1
KillOldSession=1
```

The command ServerBindTcpPorts=25 binds the SMTP port (TCP port 25) on the Exchange Server to the proxy server's port 25.

5. Next, create a second Wspcfg.ini file for the Exchange store (Store.exe), adding the entries below to this file. Place this file in the directory where Store.exe is located.

```
[STORE]
ServerBindTcpPorts=110,119,143
Persistent=1
KillOldSession=1
```

The command ServerBindTcpPorts=110,119,143 is binding three ports to Proxy Server. Internet mail needs port 110 for POP services. Since Store.exe also provides Network News Transfer Protocol (NNTP) services, ports 119 and 143 are added to the entry.

6. Proxy Server's dynamic packet filtering should be enabled so that Proxy Server will dynamically open all necessary ports as they are requested. No other special configuration is needed.

7. Reboot the Exchange Server, or stop and start the Exchange services, for the new settings to take effect.

8. Exchange Server is now set up for server proxying with Proxy Server. To test your configuration, attempt to contact the Exchange server by connecting to the proxy server's Internet IP address using SMTP, NNTP, or POP.

Configuring DNS For Server Proxy With Exchange Server

Next, you need to configure DNS for server proxying with Exchange Server.

1. First, verify that any MX and A resource records used by remote mail servers on the Internet refer to the proxy server's external network adapter IP address and not the internal IP address of the Exchange Server or SMTP server. For example, suppose your registered Internet domain name is mydomain.com, and your internal Exchange Server uses a DNS host name of exchange1. In this case, you need to use a MX (mail exchanger) record in order to give other Internet hosts the name of your internal Exchange Server. Therefore, you would add a MX record in the mydomain.com zone with the following information:

```
mydomain.com IN MX 10  exchange1.mydomain.com
```

2. Next, you need to create an A (address) record for exchange1.mydomain.com that uses an external IP address of the proxy server. If the external IP address of your proxy server were 127.43.52.89, you would add the following A record to the mydomain.com zone:

```
exchange1.mydomain.com  IN A 127.43.52.89
```

3. In addition, you should add or create a PTR, or pointer, record to the mydomain.com zone to provide reverse lookup. For example, a valid PTR record to do this would be:

```
89.52.43.127.in-addr.arpa  IN PTR exchange1.mydomain.com
```

4. The Exchange/SMTP server computer must be configured to resolve external (Internet) names by directly accessing an external DNS server. You should specify a DNS server on the DNS server search listing of your Exchange/SMTP server computer that can resolve Internet DNS addresses.

The location of this DNS server is not critical. It can be located on your network, located on your Proxy Server gateway computer, or located externally on the Internet. However, the IP address of this DNS server must be listed on the same machine that is running Exchange Server and is used to route mail from your network to the Internet.

You can use either static assignment or dynamic assignment to assign the DNS server's IP address to the Exchange Server. For *static assignment*, set the IP address by adding it to DNS Service Search Order in TCP/IP Protocol Properties. For *dynamic assignment*, configure your DHCP server to provide this address by using the standard DHCP assigned option code 6 (DNS Server List) on your Exchange Server machine. If your

Exchange Server uses DHCP to obtain its IP address, you should reserve this address with the DHCP server for permanent assignment to the Exchange Server computer.

Tip

Microsoft Exchange Server runs using a user account on the Proxy Server computer. Therefore, you must set the appropriate security parameters for the Exchange Server "user." For example, for the SMTP service, you should define the Protocol and Port Definitions used by the SMTP server protocol as 25 TCP IN. Other Winsock applications also will require appropriate security parameters.

Moving On

Arrays, routing, Internet publishing, and server proxying are all examples of the flexibility that Proxy Server offers, while maintaining robust security and high performance. The flexibility of Microsoft Proxy Server 2.0 puts it in the league of a true firewall.

So, with your Proxy Server up and running and providing a secure connection to the Internet, it's time to broaden your horizons. As you've discovered in this chapter, Proxy Server works well with Microsoft Exchange. For example, reading *Microsoft Exchange Server 5.5 On Site*, also from The Coriolis Group, will give you the background you need to provide easy-to-implement solutions for managing, collaborating, and analyzing your organization's information using Microsoft Exchange Server. But before you do that, why not take some time out to surf the Web from your secure Proxy Server connection. You deserve it!

Appendix A
Troubleshooting

Although Proxy Server is relatively easy to set up, problems can and do occur. Fortunately, Proxy Server error events are logged and usually can be resolved swiftly. The information contained in this appendix serves as a basic guide to troubleshooting Proxy Server. For more information, check the following sources:

➤ The Microsoft Proxy Server Web site at *http://www.microsoft.com/proxy/*

➤ The Microsoft Proxy Server newsgroup *microsoft.public.proxy*

Server Troubleshooting

Proxy Server uses the *Windows NT system event* log to record events for active services. These logs provide useful information if a problem occurs with Proxy Server. Each log entry lists a source name to indicate the Proxy Server service that logged the event. This information aids in monitoring server performance or troubleshooting server problems.

Table A.1 lists Proxy Server event source names that appear in the Windows NT system event log and the services that correspond to each source name.

Table A.1   Proxy Server event source names and services.

Source Name	Description
MSProxyAdmin	Proxy Server administrative events
PacketFilterLog	Packet filter alert events (filtered frames)
SocksProxy	Socks Proxy service events
SocksProxyLog	Socks Proxy logging events
WebProxyCache	Web Proxy caching events
WebProxyLog	Web Proxy logging events
WebProxyServer	Web Proxy service events
WinSockProxy	WinSock Proxy service events
WinSockProxyLog	WinSock Proxy logging events

Additionally, if you use the Web Proxy service's reverse hosting feature to publish to an internal Web publishing server, then all publishing requests are recorded in the Internet Information Server's WWW service log. Of course, this logging also occurs when the Proxy Server computer itself is running as a Web publishing server.

● ● ● *Tip* ● ● ● ●

When a packet filter event occurs in a Proxy service, then that specific Proxy service logs the event. Only packet filter *alert* events are logged in the Windows NT system event log with the PacketFilterLog event source name.

Windows NT Event Viewer

You use the Windows NT Event Viewer to read information about events. The Windows NT Event Viewer displays the event's source, including a description of the message and additional details generated by a logged event.

Use the following procedure to view event messages from Event Viewer:

1. Click Start, point to Programs, point to Administrative Tools (Common), and then click Event Viewer.

2. Click Log on the menu bar, then System for the current view.

3. Double-click the event you want to view from the list of events (see Figure A.1).

Date	Time	Source	Category	Event	User	Computer
3/23/98	9:53:40 PM	WinSockProxy	None	142	N/A	ASUS
3/23/98	8:05:56 PM	WinSockProxy	None	142	N/A	ASUS
3/23/98	7:25:48 PM	WinSockProxy	None	142	N/A	ASUS
3/23/98	3:32:05 PM	BROWSER	None	8015	N/A	ASUS
3/23/98	3:32:03 PM	BROWSER	None	8015	N/A	ASUS
3/23/98	3:32:00 PM	BROWSER	None	8015	N/A	ASUS
3/23/98	3:31:34 PM	Wins	None	4097	N/A	ASUS
3/23/98	3:31:31 PM	MSFTPSVC	None	101	N/A	ASUS
3/23/98	3:30:24 PM	AccelePort	None	2	N/A	ASUS
3/23/98	3:30:24 PM	AccelePort	None	2	N/A	ASUS
3/23/98	3:30:24 PM	AccelePort	None	2	N/A	ASUS
3/23/98	3:30:20 PM	EI90x	None	3	N/A	ASUS
3/23/98	3:30:20 PM	EI90x	None	3	N/A	ASUS
3/23/98	3:30:20 PM	EI90x	None	3	N/A	ASUS
3/23/98	3:30:15 PM	EventLog	None	6005	N/A	ASUS
3/23/98	3:30:20 PM	EI90x	None	0	N/A	ASUS
3/23/98	3:26:36 PM	BROWSER	None	8033	N/A	ASUS
3/23/98	3:26:36 PM	BROWSER	None	8033	N/A	ASUS
3/23/98	3:26:36 PM	BROWSER	None	8033	N/A	ASUS
3/22/98	8:27:21 PM	WebProxyServer	None	142	N/A	ASUS
3/19/98	7:53:31 PM	WinSockProxy	None	142	N/A	ASUS
3/18/98	10:40:06 PM	WinSockProxy	None	142	N/A	ASUS
3/18/98	9:49:21 PM	WinSockProxy	None	142	N/A	ASUS
3/18/98	8:47:58 PM	WinSockProxy	None	142	N/A	ASUS
3/18/98	8:17:43 PM	WinSockProxy	None	142	N/A	ASUS
3/18/98	7:47:16 PM	WinSockProxy	None	142	N/A	ASUS
3/17/98	10:08:03 PM	WinSockProxy	None	142	N/A	ASUS
3/17/98	9:22:55 PM	WinSockProxy	None	142	N/A	ASUS
3/17/98	8:54:17 PM	WebProxyServer	None	142	N/A	ASUS

Event Viewer - System Log on \\ASUS
Log View Options Help

Figure A.1   The Event Detail dialog box.

Proxy Server Service Logs

Proxy Server uses other logs, besides the Windows NT Event Log, that can be helpful when isolating problems. For example, there are three service logs that record events generated by the Web Proxy, WinSock Proxy, and Socks Proxy services. Additionally, there is a separate packet log that records network packet traffic-related events. These logs by default are stored in a text file format. However, an ODBC-compliant database, such as Microsoft Access or Microsoft SQL Server, can also be used. Proxy Server will perform best, however, when logging to a text file.

The Server Diagnostic Utility

You can use the *Mspdiag utility* to detect common Windows NT configuration problems on the computer that Proxy Server runs on. This utility is automatically installed and placed in the \Msp directory when you first set up Proxy Server. Alternately, you can copy the utility from the Proxy Server compact disk prior to installing Proxy Server. In this way, you can pre-configure Windows NT to work properly with Proxy Server. You will find Mspdiag.exe in the \Msproxy directory on the Proxy Server compact disk.

Following are some of the various conditions that the Mspdiag utility checks:

➤ What version of Proxy Server is installed, if any? Also, if Proxy Server is installed, it reports the status of the Proxy Server services.

➤ That Internet Information Server (IIS) 3.0 or later is installed; if so, it reports the status of the IIS WWW service.

➤ That Windows NT Server 4.0 or later is installed.

➤ That Windows NT Service Pack 3 or later is installed.

➤ That the SAP (Service Advertising Protocol) agent is installed, if the IPX/SPX protocols also are installed and configured.

➤ That valid IP addresses are assigned in the LAT.

➤ That you have administrator privileges on the server computer.

➤ That IP forwarding is disabled.

➤ That there is only one CD default gateway specified.

➤ That the settings in the Mspclnt.ini file agree with the server computer's configuration settings.

Use the following procedure to run the server diagnostic utility:

1. Click Start, point to Programs, and then click Command Prompt.

2. Change to the Msp directory, or the directory in which you placed *mspdiag.exe*.

3. Type **mspdiag**.

Proxy Server Error Messages

While not all error messages follow this format, Microsoft Proxy Server 2.0 returns the majority of messages in the following general format:

```
Messagetext Errornumber
```

where:

Messagetext is the explanatory message.

Errornumber is a Windows NT error code number.

Usually, the message text will indicate the nature of the error and a possible solution.

Server Setup Troubleshooting

The Proxy Server setup program can fail if the installation instructions are not followed carefully. Before installing Proxy Server, be sure the following conditions are met:

➤ **Administrator privileges**   Make sure you are using a Windows NT account that has administrator privileges.

➤ **Stop all Internet services**   Use Internet Service Manager (ISM) to manually stop all other Internet services.

➤ **Disk drive configuration**   Make sure your disk drives are configured properly.

➤ **Upgrading Proxy Server**   When upgrading from a previous version of Proxy Server, it's best to start clean by running setup and selecting Remove All to completely remove all components from the previous version before installing again. Additionally, you should manually delete any remaining Proxy Server files from the \msp directory before installing Proxy Server 2.0.

If the Proxy Server setup program fails, it returns server setup event messages. Close all other applications and restart the computer before running setup.

The Mpssetup.log File

Microsoft Proxy Server Setup automatically creates a log file when Proxy Server is installed. This file, named *Mpssetup.log*, contains valuable information that goes beyond the error messages that are displayed to users. If you call Microsoft Technical Support for assistance, you must have access to this file.

The Web Proxy Service

The Web Proxy service is integrated tightly with IIS (Internet Information Server) and Windows NT. When the Web Proxy service fails, Proxy Server records event messages in the Windows NT system event log. Proxy Server uses the source names WebProxyServer and WebProxyLog for Web Proxy service events, including events for Proxy Server arrays and chains.

Troubleshooting The Web Proxy Service

You can correct most Web Proxy service errors by verifying the following conditions:

➤ **Authentication**   Make sure that the Windows NT challenge/response authentication is set up correctly. Proxy Server uses the password authentication specified by the WWW service to validate Web Proxy clients. You can troubleshoot the Web Proxy service by temporarily selecting Basic (clear-text) authentication.

➤ **IIS scripts directory**   Verify the location of your IIS scripts directory and make sure there is a Proxy subdirectory under this directory location.

➤ **Adjust time and date**   Reset the time and date for the server to the correct date, using the Date/Time application.

Also, if you are using a release candidate version or 60-day evaluation version of Proxy Server, the product is date-sensitive and will expire. At that time, you must either remove Proxy Server from your system or upgrade to the final release version of Proxy Server 2.0.

The Web Proxy Cache

Proxy Server places the Web Proxy service cache event messages in the Windows NT system event log under the source name WebProxyCache. The first thing to check if caching fails is that the available disk space on the cache drive is sufficient and that the disk drive allocated for caching is not full. You might need to increase the disk cache space or delete cached objects from the hard disk.

Troubleshooting The Web Proxy Cache

You can resolve most Web Proxy service caching errors by correcting the cache settings in the Web Proxy service using the following procedure:

1. Use Internet Service Manager to stop the Web Proxy service.

2. Click Advanced on the Caching tab, and then click Reset Defaults.

3. Use Internet Service Manager to restart the Web Proxy service.

If the error message reoccurs, you can type **chkdsk /r** at the command prompt to locate disk errors and recover readable information for the disk drive. If caching still fails, you might have to run setup and select the Reinstall option.

The Web Proxy Array And Chain

Proxy Server array and chain features are functions of the Web Proxy service. Therefore, the error events for Proxy Server arrays and chains are recorded in the Windows NT system event log as Web Proxy service events. As previously mentioned, Proxy Server uses the source names *WebProxyServer* and *WebProxyLog* for these events. Most array and chain errors occur because of proxy-to-proxy communication problems.

Troubleshooting Web Proxy Arrays And Chains

The most common errors and troubleshooting techniques include the following:

➤ **Unavailable Proxy Server**   If an upstream Proxy Server computer or array member computer is unavailable, you can use the Internet Service Manager to determine the reason; restart the server, if necessary.

➤ **Authentication problems**   If there is an array of Proxy Server computers, or if they are chained, they must authenticate communication between servers. Verify that you are using the correct proxy-to-proxy authentication.

The WinSock Proxy Service

The WinSock Proxy service has more configuration options than any other Proxy Server service. There is a high potential for having a configuration problem arise. Proxy Server records error events for the WinSock Proxy service in the Windows NT system event log under the source names WinSockProxy and WinSockProxyLog. What follows are some likely scenarios and troubleshooting advice.

Troubleshooting The WinSock Proxy Service And Third-Party TCP/IP Stacks

You might have problems if you try to use the WinSock Proxy service with a *third-party TCP/IP stack*. Because Proxy Server has not been tested with other third-party TCP/IP implementations, you should avoid the use of a third-party stack.

Troubleshooting The WinSock Proxy Service And Protocol Administration

You also might experience that a user is unable to access or administer different protocols for the WinSock Proxy service. This is because the *Administrator user logon account* is the only account that, by default, can access any port, regardless of port configuration.

You can allow other users to access or administer protocols or assigned ports by using the following procedure:

1. Check the LAT to make sure that the user computer's IP address is included.

2. Use Internet Service Manager to check that the protocol has been added.

3. Use Internet Service Manager to check that the user (or a group the user belongs to) has been granted permission to use the protocol.

Troubleshooting The WinSock Proxy Service With Ping And Tracert

You might find that Ping and Tracert fail to work reliably with the WinSock Proxy service. Ping and Tracert are standard utilities for troubleshooting TCP/IP-related problems on your network, but using these utilities with Proxy Server can be problematic. The Ping and Tracert utilities do most of their work at the transport layer, using Internet Control Message Protocol (ICMP). Because ICMP does not use Windows Sockets, the Ping and Tracert utilities cannot be redirected by the Proxy Server computer. So using Ping or Tracert to test Proxy Server connections might produce invalid results.

Ping will use Windows Sockets when looking up the domain host name of the server you are trying to ping. But once the Domain Name System (DNS) host lookup is complete, Ping switches to ICMP for connection. Here are a couple of things you can check:

➤ **Internal DNS server**   If you are using an internal DNS server, make sure the IP address of the DNS server is contained in the Local Address Table (LAT). You can check this in the file \Msp\Msplat.txt.

➤ **Ping utility**   Check your Ping utility program. If you are using an application to ping that requires the use of a third-party Windows Sockets DLL, ICMP ping results are unpredictable.

Troubleshooting The WinSock Proxy Service And DNS

Finally, you might find that *server domain name lookups* fail on the local network. This is because the WinSock Proxy service redirects all DNS lookups to the computer that is running Proxy Server. As mentioned previously, you need to make sure its IP address is contained in the LAT if you use an internal DNS server. Another point: Domain names that do not contain dots are considered internal names by Proxy Server.

You can correct some Web Proxy service errors by verifying the following conditions:

➤ **Local Address Table**   Check that the LAT is configured correctly.

➤ **The Security.dll file**   Check that Security.dll is located in the Windows NT system directory, usually Winnt\System32, and then restart the WinSock Proxy service.

➤ **The Wspsperf.dll file**   Confirm that Wspsperf.dll is in the Windows NT system directory, usually \Winnt\System32. If it is missing, run setup and select Reinstall to restore the missing DLL file and reinitialize service settings.

Socks Proxy Service

The Socks Proxy service records both successful connections and error conditions. Proxy Server records an event when the Socks Proxy service connection is first established. Another event, detailing the number of bytes sent and received, is recorded when the connection is terminated. Proxy Server also records aborted connections, so that you can determine the reason for the termination. Proxy Server places the Socks Proxy service event messages in the Windows NT system event log under the source names SocksProxy and SocksProxyLog.

Packet Filtering Event Messages

Proxy Server records packet filtering event messages in the Windows NT system event log under the source name PacketFilterLog. You might receive an error stating that the proxy Packet Filter log cannot allocate memory. Usually, this is simply a low memory condition. You should check for available memory and memory usage on the server by using the following procedure:

1. Click Start, point to Administrative Programs (Common), and click Windows NT Diagnostics.

2. Click the Memory tab on the Windows NT Diagnostics dialog box.

3. Check if the available memory is low.

It might be possible to reallocate memory on the server by closing all applications that are not required. Alternately, you can add memory to the Proxy Server computer.

RAS And Auto Dial Event Messages

Proxy Server dial-out connection failures can be fairly common. Sometimes the errors are benign; for example, the connection to your Internet service provider (ISP) is unavailable due to a busy condition. When these errors occur, Remote Access Service (RAS) and Proxy Server Auto Dial error event messages are placed in the Windows NT system event log. If you suspect a more serious problem, check that Auto Dial and RAS are configured properly. It's also possible that a chained Proxy Server computer is unavailable.

Client Troubleshooting

Proxy Server clients' errors also are recorded in the Windows NT system event log. It is convenient to group client errors into the following categories: client setup problems, Web Proxy client problems, WinSock Proxy client problems, IPX client problems, and client performance problems. Each is covered in the following sections.

Client Setup Troubleshooting

The Proxy Server Client setup program can fail if the installation instructions are not followed carefully. If setup problems arise, be sure the following conditions are met:

➤ **Multiple copies of Winsock.dll**   Only one copy of the winsock.dll file can be located within the Windows or System directory of a Proxy Server client computer. If the Proxy Server Client setup program finds more than one copy, then you must delete or rename the additional copies of this file from the Windows and System directories and rerun setup.

➤ **The Local Address Table (LAT) file**   Verify that the Proxy Server Client setup program placed this file on the client computer. It must be present for the Proxy Server client to operate correctly. The file is named Msplat.txt and is typically installed in C:\Wspclnt. Also, this file must contain at least one valid range of address pairs that identify internal IP network clients.

➤ **Adequate disk space**   Prior to running the Proxy Server Client setup program, make sure you have adequate disk space and that the logon account you are using is permitted to write to C:\Wspclnt\Msplat.txt.

➤ **Browser configuration**   You might need to manually configure some browsers for use with the Web Proxy service.

➤ **The System.ini file**   Verify that the System.ini file exists.

➤ **The Wsock32.dll file**   Verify that the Wsock32.dll file exists on your system. For Windows NT clients, verify that the Wsock32.dll file is located in C:\Winnt\System32.

➤ **Upgrading Proxy Server clients**   When upgrading clients from a previous version of Proxy Server, it's best to start clean by running setup and selecting Remove All to completely remove all components from the previous version before installing again. Additionally, you should manually delete any remaining Proxy Server client files before installing the new client software. Typically, these files are placed in the \mspclnt directory on the client computer.

➤ **Manually rename files**   You might be required to manually rename _msrws32.dll to Wsock32.dll for Windows 95 or Windows NT clients, or to rename _msrws16.dll

to Winsock.dll for Windows 3.1 clients. After renaming the appropriate file, run setup again.

➤ **Verify Windows NT files** When running Windows NT clients, you might need to verify that the following files are present in the System directory: Router.exe, Lodctr.exe, and Unlodctr.exe. These are system files that setup uses.

The Web Proxy Client

Web Proxy clients receive error event messages from the Internet Information Server (IIS) services. These event messages can be returned during Web Proxy connections to FTP, Gopher, or World Wide Web (WWW) services. Some messages are general in nature and are common to all IIS services. The service that returns the message is noted with each entry in brackets, as shown in Table A.2.

HTTP browser client messages are displayed in the following form

```
The Proxy Server has encountered an error. MessageText
```

where

MessageText is a brief explanation of the error message.

Web Proxy Client Troubleshooting

Web Proxy client errors are generally non-destructive. The error messages returned are descriptive and point the system administrator to the problem's likely cause and solution. The following list describes some common Web Proxy client problems:

➤ **Gopher version** Verify that the server supports the same version of Gopher protocol used by the client. In some cases, protocol errors can occur between a server that supports only standard Gopher and a client that uses Gopher Plus.

➤ **Protocol support** Verify that the protocol is a supported type, such as HTTP, FTP, or Gopher.

Table A.2 IIS service error categories.

Source Name	Description
[IIS - All Services]	The message is non-specific to a Web Proxy connection accessing either WWW, FTP, or Gopher services for IIS.
[WWW Service]	The message is specific to a Web Proxy connection accessing WWW services for IIS.
[FTP Service]	The message is specific to a Web Proxy connection accessing FTP services for IIS.
[Gopher Service]	The message is specific to a Web Proxy connection accessing Gopher services for IIS.

► **Authentication**   Clients must have the appropriate security or permissions to access secure URL sites.

► **Empty FTP directories**   When using a Web browser to access an empty FTP directory on a remote computer, the Web Proxy client will receive an error message.

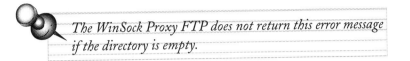

The WinSock Proxy FTP does not return this error message if the directory is empty.

The WinSock Proxy Client

You can use the *WinSock Proxy diagnostic utility* to detect common WinSock Proxy configuration problems on the computer that the Proxy Server client software runs on. This utility is automatically installed and placed in the Mspclnt directory when you first set up the Proxy Server client. For computers running 32-bit operating systems, the utility is named *Chkwsp32*. For computers running 16-bit operating systems, the utility is named *Chkwsp16*.

WinSock Proxy Client Troubleshooting

You use the following procedure to run the WinSock Proxy diagnostic utility:

1. Change to a command prompt on the client computer.

2. Change to the Mspclnt directory.

3. Type **chkwsp32 -f** (or **chkwsp16 -f** for computers running 16-bit operating systems).

The diagnostic utility will proceed to check connectivity with the Proxy Server computer. If the connection succeeds, the message "Client control protocol matches the server control protocol" is displayed. Further testing is possible by using FTP or Telnet to connect to a site on the Internet. However, you might receive a message stating that the client is not installed properly. Usually, this is because the configuration information or the winsock.dll file is missing. The following details some common WinSock Proxy configuration problems:

► **Missing configuration information**   The configuration information is missing in the System.ini file in the [Microsoft Proxy Service] section, "Configuration Location" key.

► **Missing winsock.dll file**   The winsock.dll file was not found, or it was found to be the original system DLL rather than the one installed by the Proxy Server Client setup program. Check that you have only one copy of the winsock.dll file and that it is located in the Windows directory.

IPX Clients

Most Proxy Server IPX client problems involve troubleshooting connectivity issues. The two most common problems encompass issues with the WinSock Proxy client and the TCP/IP protocol installed on an IPX client. These problems and their solutions are detailed below. Also, the IPX protocol is supported only for Windows 95 and Windows NT clients, so clients running operating systems such as Windows for Workgroups are unable to use the WinSock Proxy service over an IPX network.

➤ **WinSock Proxy problems**   When a WinSock Proxy client is set up to use the internal private network and you need to connect with another Internet service provider (ISP), Windows Sockets applications will not be available. This is a common problem with mobile computers that need to connect to the Internet via a dial-up connection and, also, to the corporate network. You can solve this problem simply by turning off the WinSock Proxy client in the Control Panel. Be careful, though: You still must avoid using a third-party TCP/IP stack.

➤ **TCP/IP protocol installed on an IPX client**   For various reasons, you might have the TCP/IP protocol installed on a client computer that uses IPX to connect to the private network. Yet, the TCP/IP protocol is not enabled on the computer's internal network adapter for the Proxy Server computer. In this case, you can either remove TCP/IP from the client computer, or force the client to use only the IPX protocol for all WinSock Proxy connections. The latter can be done by editing the Mspclnt.ini file on the Proxy Server computer. You do this by removing the [Servers IP Addresses] section. This is even a good solution if you have multiple clients with this problem, because Proxy Server clients refresh their configuration automatically. So, you don't need to refresh multiple clients manually.

IPX Client Troubleshooting

Use the following procedure to diagnose Windows NT clients by showing the client IPX settings:

1. Change to a command prompt on the client computer.

2. Type **ipxroute config**.

Use the following procedure to diagnose Windows NT clients by showing the client TCP/IP settings:

1. Change to a command prompt on the client computer.

2. Type **ipxconfig /all**.

...procedure to diagnose Windows 95 IPX clients:

...he Network icon in the Control Panel.

...figuration tab in the Network dialog box, and double-click the ...SPX Compatible Protocol icon.

... frame type on the server and the client match. If this is okay, ... are set to Auto Frame Type Detection.

... Internal Network Number is 00000000. If you change this setting, ...oblems with connectivity to other IPX-enabled servers on your

...y that the client can connect to a share on the server with only IPX ...e client.

...spclnt.ini file on the server. Verify that this file contains one IPX ...he IPX address is for the network adapter on the *internal (private)* ...twork. If there is more than one IPX address in your Mspclnt.ini file, ...t one of them is for the external adapter. You must then disable the ... on the external adapter and reinstall Proxy Server, so that the ...ile is set correctly.

...ting Client Performance Problems

...nvolving the performance of Proxy Server clients are related to name or ...n. If Internet connections appear to be slow, first check the configura- ...WINS or DNS server in use on the private network. Next, check that ... of all private network computers, and in particular the one you are ...t with, are defined in the Local Address Table (LAT). The client LAT ...he file C:\Mspclnt\Msplat.txt.

On Site

Appendix B
TCP/IP Basics

Your mastery of Proxy Server is incomplete without a basic understanding of TCP/IP. The TCP/IP protocol suite comprises the key protocols that drive the Internet. Moreover, TCP/IP is rapidly becoming the standard protocol suite for LANs and WANs. There are multi-volume books devoted to TCP/IP, so this introduction to the protocols is far from complete. Instead, it is focused on the knowledge that will make implementing Microsoft Proxy Server 2.0 easier and more logical.

What Is A Protocol?

What is a protocol? It is simply a set of rules governing the behavior or method of operation of something. In TCP/IP, protocol refers to the rules that allows computers to communicate over a network. All protocol definitions are made up of two basic parts:

➤ A message format written as a formalized *textual description* that allows humans to understand its proper use.

➤ A message format written as *technical rules* and implemented by programmers as code that allows two or more machines to exchange messages.

Whenever we want to exchange data with another machine, we need a protocol. For example, a standalone computer that has a printer connected to it needs a protocol to communicate with the printer. When we exchange email, whether within a LAN or across the Internet, we need a protocol. Often, many protocols are used simultaneously. Clear definitions and faithful implementations of protocols are what keeps everything working well.

TCP and IP work together as the basic protocols for communicating on the Internet. It's no secret that the Internet is popular and growing more so every day. Its popularity stems from its ability to connect a worldwide network of diverse machines. TCP/IP is the most basic ingredient to this universal interconnectivity.

TCP/IP was first developed by the RAND Corporation, in conjunction with the Massachusetts Institute of Technology and the University of California, Los Angeles, to

provide high-speed communication between networked devices for the United States Department of Defense. It was designed to continue to work, even if some of the connecting links failed. Sounds perfect, doesn't it?

Not quite. Like all technology, the Internet and TCP/IP are far from perfect. Both the strengths and weaknesses of the TCP and IP protocols are best understood by delving into why they were developed originally.

A Short History Of The Internet

You will better grasp the reasoning that produced the deployment of TCP and IP as the key protocols for Internet communication by understanding the heritage of the Internet. What is now known as the Internet began as a United States Defense Department project in 1969. So, much of the science that produced the Internet was the result of experts' trying to solve problems that are far different from those produced by the way the Internet is used today and might be used in the future. Electronic commerce, commercial email services, and cyber-entertainment were never part of the original vision of the Internet.

The United States Defense Department's project was to find a solution for the weakness of the telephone system as a digital communication system during wartime. The telephone system relies on centralized switching stations for its communications. These switching stations easily could be targeted during an attack, thereby immobilizing vital digital communications links throughout the world during a crisis.

In theory, it was possible to design a network that could quickly reroute digital traffic around failed nodes. This looked like a good solution. So, the Advanced Research Projects Agency (ARPA) was put in charge of turning this theory into practice. Subsequently, it launched ARPAnet. The fundamental principle that drove ARPAnet was delivery of message packets over an unreliable network. In other words, a system of computers that could recognize data loss and then retransmit the lost data created an effective, if not efficient, network infrastructure.

Throughout the 1970s, academic and military researchers primarily used the ARPAnet, allowing it to exist in relative obscurity. In 1972, ARPA became known as the Defense Advanced Research Projects Agency (DARPA). In 1973, TCP and IP were first proposed as transport protocols for ARPAnet. DARPA, deeming the project a success, turned ARPAnet's management over to the Defense Communications Agency in 1975. TCP and IP, along with many of the core Internet protocols that are popular today, were adopted throughout ARPAnet in 1983. This was due in a large part to the University of California at Berkeley's releasing in the same year a version of Unix that incorporated TCP/IP as a transport protocol.

IP—The Internet Protocol

The IP protocol provides the ability for machines, called *hosts*, to transmit blocks of data, called *datagrams*, from a source host to a destination host. This transmission is accomplished through a fixed-length addressing scheme that identifies each host. Datagrams can become fragmented; IP allows for this and reconstructs fragmented datagrams that are transmitted through networks that only handle small packets. So, at the most basic level the two key functions of IP are:

➤ Addressing

➤ Fragmentation

The functionality of addressing and fragmentation is built into each datagram package. Fundamentally, the datagram is an IP package of bits; it contains the Internet header and the data being transmitted. The Internet header contains a variety of information about the datagram, including the source and destination addresses.

IP Addressing

IP addresses ensure that data is transmitted to and from the intended hosts. This is similar to how the front of a letter's envelope has an address and a return address. To carry this analogy a little further, think of the datagram as the envelope and the front of the envelope as the Internet header. So, on an envelope we have an address and a return address that look like Figure B.1.

You might be baffled when you first look at an IP address. For example, here is a typical IP address:

```
192.168.0.1
```

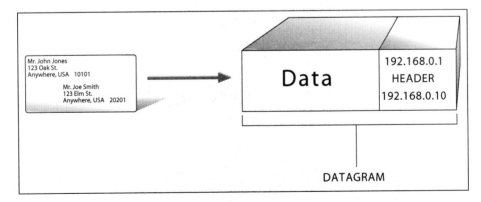

Figure B.1   The addresses on the front of a typical letter envelope can be likened to the addressing scheme found in the Internet header of a datagram.

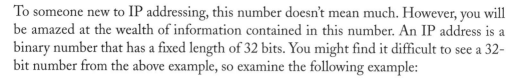

To someone new to IP addressing, this number doesn't mean much. However, you will be amazed at the wealth of information contained in this number. An IP address is a binary number that has a fixed length of 32 bits. You might find it difficult to see a 32-bit number from the above example, so examine the following example:

11000000101010000000000000000001

The above number is the same address as the first example, expressed in *binary notation*. However, you seldom see an IP address written this way. While binary is the base language of most computers, it is simply too difficult for humans to work with. Instead, we break the IP address apart for clarity. So, IP addresses are expressed as four octets, or four eight-bit sets, translated into decimal numbers from 0 through 255. For organizational clarity, each octet is separated by a period. Please review carefully the following process of converting the same number to *dotted-decimal notation*:

1. A pure 32-bit binary string:

   11000000101010000000000000000001

2. The same 32-bit binary string separated into four octets (8 bits):

   11000000

   10101000

   00000000

   00000001

3. The four binary octets converted to decimal:

Binary		Decimal
11000000	becomes	192
10101000	becomes	168
00000000	becomes	0
00000001	becomes	1

4. Dotted-decimal notation of the original 32-bit binary number:

   192.168.0.1

It's a little easier to work with dotted-decimal notation, isn't it? But, please don't forget what the number represents. If IP addressing problems creep into your network, you will often find understanding the 32-bit number helpful in sorting out the problems. In fact, we will use the 32-bit numbering scheme to understand IP address classes and subnets in the following sections.

● ● *Tip* ● ● ● ●

Are you having trouble converting binary to decimal? Windows 3.1, Windows 95, and Windows NT have a calculator applet that is very helpful. When the applet is started, follow these instructions:

1. Change the view to scientific by selecting the View|Scientific options on the menu bar.

2. Then select Dec and enter the decimal number.

3. Next, select Bin; the number is translated to binary.

Other than padding the result with up to seven leading zeros, that's all there is to it—and you thought decimal to binary conversion was difficult!

IP Address Classes

Networks fall into three basic classes for the purpose of IP addressing. Each IP Address class is based on the maximum number of nodes in a given network. The three IP Address classes are as follows:

➤ **Class A**   Large network with up to 16,777,216 nodes

➤ **Class B**   Medium-sized network with less than 65,534 nodes

➤ **Class C**   Small network with less than 254 nodes

Remember all the trouble we went to in order to understand binary IP addresses? Now that knowledge really starts to come in handy. Recall that the message format of a protocol is written as a formalized textual description that allows humans to understand its proper use. In the case of IP address classes, you must work with binary in order to understand the message format. IP addresses are placed into classes by examining the high-order bits of the first octet of a binary address in the following way:

➤ **Class A**   The first bit is zero. The first bit, counted from left to right, is referred to as the high-order bit.

➤ **Class B**   The first two bits are one-zero. The first two bits, counted from left to right, are referred to as the high-order two bits.

➤ **Class C**   The first three bits are one-one-zero. The first three bits, counted from left to right, are referred to as the high-order three bits.

Let's take a look at the following examples of IP address classes.

➤ **Class A Example**   The first octet of the IP address 109.0.0.0 is 109. When 109 is translated into binary, the first octet becomes 01101101. The first bit of the octet is zero; therefore, this is a *class A IP address.*

➤ **Class B Example**   The first octet of the IP address 131.0.0.0 is 131. When 131 is translated into binary, the first octet becomes 10000011. The high-order two bits are one-zero; therefore, this is a *class B IP address.*

➤ **Class C Example**   The first octet of the IP address 192.0.0.0 is 192. When 192 is translated into binary, the first octet becomes 11000000. The high-order three bits are one-one-zero; therefore, this is a *class C IP address.*

You now should have a clear understanding of what high-order bits represent in an IP address. But there are 32 bits in an IP address and, obviously, the remaining bits have a purpose. Let's take a look at what these additional bits mean. To do that, I will once again break the address apart by class, because what the remaining bits mean depends on the class. Here are some new terms: the *network address* and *local address*. The *network address* is the logical network address to the subnet to which the computer is attached. The *local address* defines the logical device address for each host (computer) on a subnet.

Study the following examples:

➤ **Class A**   The high-order bit is zero, the next 7 bits are the network, and the last 24 bits are the local address (see Figure B.2).

➤ **Class B**   In a Class B address, the high-order two bits are one-zero, the next 14 bits are the network, and the last 16 bits are the local address (see Figure B.3).

➤**Class C**   In a Class C address, the high-order three bits are one-one-zero, the next 21 bits are the network, and the last 8 bits are the local address (see Figure B.4).

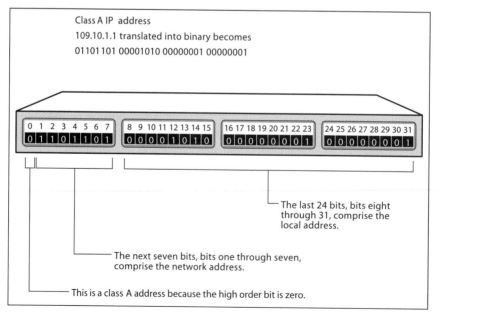

Figure B.2   Class A IP address.

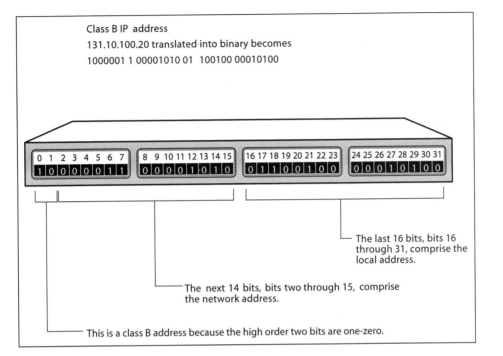

Class B IP address
131.10.100.20 translated·into binary becomes
1000001 1 00001010 01 100100 00010100

The last 16 bits, bits 16 through 31, comprise the local address.

The next 14 bits, bits two through 15, comprise the network address.

This is a class B address because the high order two bits are one-zero.

Figure B.3   Class B IP address.

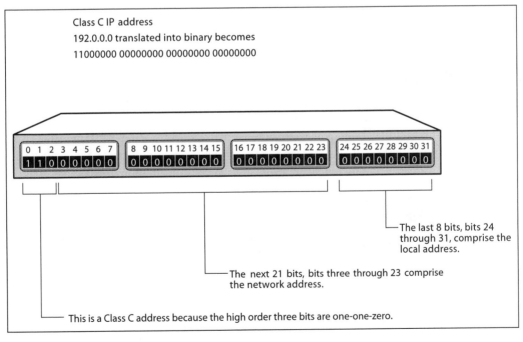

Class C IP address
192.0.0.0 translated into binary becomes
11000000 00000000 00000000 00000000

The last 8 bits, bits 24 through 31, comprise the local address.

The next 21 bits, bits three through 23 comprise the network address.

This is a Class C address because the high order three bits are one-one-zero.

Figure B.4   Class C IP address.

Table B.1   IP address classes.

Class	Class Definition	First Octet Binary Addresses	First Octet Decimal Addresses
A	The first bit, referred to as the high-order bit, is zero. The next 7 bits are the network, and the last 24 bits are the local address.	00000001 through 01111110 **Note:** 01111111 is reserved as a local loopback address.	1 through 126 **Note:** 127 is reserved as a local loopback address.
B	The high-order two bits are one-zero. The next 14 bits are the network, and the last 16 bits are the local address.	10000000 through 10111111	128 through 191
C	The high-order three bits are one-one-zero. The next 21 bits are the network, and the last 8 bits are the local address.	11000000 through 11011111	192 through 223

Table B.1 summarizes IP address classes, the class definition, and the numbering of the first octet in both binary and decimal notation.

One more important point: Any binary local address comprised of all ones or all zeros is invalid. For example, the Class C addresses of 192.168.0.0 and 192.168.0.255 are invalid as local addresses because binary 0 is 00000000 and binary 255 is 11111111. The Class C address 192.168.0.0 defines the network.

Subnets Masks

You can further divide, or subnet, a Class A, B, or C IP address using a subnet mask. A subnet mask is a bit pattern that defines which part of the IP address represents a subnet address. The default subnet mask is comprised of ones, which define the binary network address component of the address and zeros, which in turn define the binary local address component. Therefore, the following are the default subnet masks for the Class A, B, and C IP addresses:

➤ Class A Default Subnet Mask.

11111111 00000000 00000000 00000000

or

255.0.0.0

➤ Class B Default Subnet Mask.

11111111 11111111 00000000 00000000

or

255.255.0.0

➤ Class C Default Subnet Mask.

11111111 11111111 11111111 00000000

or

255.255.255.0

Subnets exist to help you organize the physical networks in your organization using the logical addressing scheme of the Internet. For example, consider an organization whose network uses the Class C network address of 192.168.0.0 for its private network. Suppose the organization needed to connect to four other locations geographically separated from the "home office." By extending the subnet mask into the local address octet, you can assign a unique subnet mask to each location, thereby simplifying the TCP/IP routing and network administration.

How far you extend the subnet mask into the local address will determine how many subnets are available. For example, to create two subnets you extend one place, to create four subnets you extend two places, and so forth. Confused? The following will help; it details how to divide your Class C network address into four subnets by using a subnet mask:

1. The default subnet mask for a Class C address is:

    11111111 11111111 11111111 00000000

    or

    255.255.255.0

2. Next, change the last octet of the default subnet mask to:

    11111111 11111111 11111111 110000

    or

    255.255.255.192

3. By borrowing the first two bits from the local address, you created four subnets:

00000000	(Decimal 0)
01000000	(Decimal 64)
10000000	(Decimal 128)
11000000	(Decimal 192)

4. The last six digits of the IP address's last octet then can be used for the local address. Therefore, the following addresses are valid:

192.168.123.1 *through* 192.168.123.62

192.168.123.65 *through* 192.168.123.126

192.168.123.129 *through* 192.168.123.190

192.168.123.193 *through* 192.168.123.254

5. Also, the following are the network addresses for the four subnets:

192.168.123.0

192.168.123.64

192.168.123.128

192.168.123.192

Do you recall that binary local addresses comprised of all ones or all zeros are invalid? This is a little tricky, so read carefully. In the above example, you cannot use addresses with the last octet of 0, 63, 64, 127, 128, 191, 192, or 255. The last octets (0, 64, 128, and 192) are used to define the subnet networks, and the remaining (63, 127, 191, and 255) are unusable as local addresses. This is because only the last six digits of the octet are used. The pattern is seen clearly when converting the above numbers to binary, as shown in Table B.2.

IP Fragmentation

Internet datagrams fragment by design. This is because to reach its destination on the Internet, a datagram might start in a network that allows large packet sizes and then pass through another network that limits packets to a smaller size. Without IP fragmentation,

Table B.2   Defining a subnet.

Last Octet	Binary	Last Six Digits of the Last Octet
0	00000000	000000
63	00111111	111111
64	01000000	000000
127	01111111	111111
128	10000000	000000
191	10111111	111111
192	11000000	000000
255	11111111	111111

the datagram might never make it to its destination. The IP fragmentation procedure permits the breaking of a datagram into an almost arbitrary number of pieces that can be reassembled later.

Microsoft Windows NT's implementation of IP does not fragment datagrams. However, a router connected to Windows NT might provide IP fragmentation. Also, because a datagram could arrive fragmented, Microsoft Windows NT's implementation of IP will reassemble Internet datagrams.

Probably the most important thing to know about IP fragmentation is that to the user—and the system administrator—it is completely transparent.

TCP—The Transmission Control Protocol

The previous sections concentrated on the Internet Protocol (IP). Fundamentally, IP is a mechanism for addressing and reassembling fragmented Internet datagrams. Of course, these are important functions, but to complete the package you need a protocol that, unlike IP, ensures end-to-end reliability. That's the role of TCP (Transmission Control Protocol), the reliable transport protocol for Internet datagrams.

TCP is built on the assumption that IP is unreliable. TCP is a connection-oriented, end-to-end reliable protocol that can operate over networks ranging from hard-wired LANs to packet-switched WANs. So, just what is a connection-oriented protocol? It means that the receiving host must acknowledge receipt of the data sent within a specific period. TCP views data as a stream of bytes called segments. The following procedure illustrates the connection-oriented aspect of TCP:

1. A TCP/IP host (Host 1) sends a data segment.

2. Another TCP/IP host (Host 2) receives the data.

3. Host 2 returns an acknowledgement (ACK).

4. Host 1 receives the ACK within a specified time, and then sends the next data segment.

Notice that the receiving host must return an ACK within the time specified by the sending host. If the sending host does not receive the ACK, the data is retransmitted. In addition, if the data is received damaged, the receiving host will discard the damaged data but does not send an ACK. The sending host waits the specified time for an ACK, and then retransmits the segment. In Windows NT, the TcpMaxDataRetransmissions registry parameter holds the value for the ACK timer.

TCP accomplishes end-to-end reliability by assigning a *sequence number* to each byte transmitted and a *checksum* to each segment. The *sequence number* guarantees that all the bytes were received. Sometimes bytes are received out of sequence, but these bytes signal the receiving host that other bytes are still to come. The *checksum* contains information about the data that should have been captured by the receiving host. If the checksum fails, the segment is discarded and an ACK is not sent. The sending host will wait the specified time and then retransmit the data segment.

UDP—The User Datagram Protocol

UDP (The User Datagram Protocol) is a connectionless transmission protocol. While it does not guarantee the reliable transmission of data, it does have special benefits that make it a valuable member of the TCP/IP protocol suite. For example, UDP is a multipoint connectionless service. This means UDP can send the same data to multiple clients simultaneously. Also, since UDP is connectionless, UDP does not have the house-keeping overhead of TCP. Its simple, "best-effort" delivery mechanism allows much faster transmission rates than TCP. This is why real-time voice and video applications, such as RealAudio and VDOLive, use UDP. When speed is more important than guaranteeing both the arrival of datagrams and the correct sequencing of delivered packets, applications use UDP.

The following procedure illustrates the connectionless aspect of UDP:

1. A TCP/IP host (Host 1) initiates a connection to a server by sending a request for an explicit application through UDP to an Internet host.

2. The Internet host (Host 2) immediately sends or receives the data to the IP address and port specified by the client.

Contrast the UDP connectionless communication process to TCP's. It is much simpler and faster.

Ports

TCP/IP uses ports to allow its transmission protocols, TCP and UDP, to connect and communicate with multiple hosts. Ports allow the communication between hosts and applications to be uniquely identified and controlled. For example, Proxy Server's WinSock Proxy service uses ports to redirect Windows sockets applications. Your understanding of ports is critical for the proper administration of Proxy Server's WinSock Proxy security.

Well Known Ports

The Well Known Ports are controlled and assigned by the Internet Assigned Numbers Authority (IANA). Ports are used in TCP to name the ends of logical connections that carry long-term conversations. Ports can be designated to use either TCP or UDP. On Microsoft Proxy Server, port assignments are enabled separately for inbound ports and outbound ports. Inbound ports are used to listen for client requests from Internet clients, and outbound ports are used to listen for requests from clients on the private network.

Well Known Ports comprise only a small portion of the possible port numbers. Currently, the range for Well Known Ports includes port numbers from 0 through 1023. There are also Registered Ports that range from 1024 through 49151. This still leaves 49152 through 65535 as dynamic or private ports. These ports can be used if the initial port is unavailable, or used for new custom server applications.

Because Well Known Ports and Registered Ports are pre-defined, they provide services to unknown callers. For example, an application used with the WinSock Proxy service will specify a specific port number as the initial contact port on the server for a Windows sockets application. Once a connection is established, the WinSock Proxy service can dynamically assign ports. In some ways, these same port assignments are used with UDP; however, a UDP application must supply the IP address and port number of the destination application.

For the most up-to-date information on Well Known Ports and Registered Ports, point your browser to **http://www.isi.edu/div7/iana/**. This is the home page for Internet Assigned Numbers Authority (IANA).

Appendix C
Windows Sockets
API Support

Proxy Server 2.0 supports the following Windows Sockets API calls:

➤ accept()

➤ acceptex()

➤ bind()—Unless explicitly requested for the proxy IP, heuristics are used to determine whether to proxy the request or not.

➤ closesocket()

➤ connect()—Proxied according to the LAT.

➤ getacceptexsockaddrs()

➤ gethostbyaddr()—Proxied according to the LAT.

➤ gethostbyname()—Proxied according to whether the name is dotted or not.

➤ gethostname()—For IP, this is passed to the original Winsock DLL; for IPX, the name is taken from the INI file. The default name is anonymousIPX.

➤ getpeername()

➤ getprotobyname()—Always passed to the original Winsock DLL.

➤ getprotobynumber()—Always passed to the original Winsock DLL.

➤ getservbyname()—Proxied only for an IPX environment.

➤ getservbyport()—Proxied only for an IPX environment.

➤ getsockname()—For a proxied connection, you get the proxy IP/port pair.

➤ getsockopt()

➤ ioctlsocket()—This is a local operation, only the FIONBIO option is relevant.

➤ listen()—Proxied only if the bind was proxied.

➤ recv()

➤ recvfrom()

➤ send()

➤ sendto()

➤ setsockopt()—Not all options are proxied (in fact, only TCP_NODELAY is passed to the proxy, but all are supported locally).

➤ socket()—This is a native call, but in an IPX environment (or forced IPX environment) the client DLL uses an IPX socket when an IP socket is requested.

➤ transmitfile()

➤ WSAasyncgethostbyname()—see gethostbyname().

➤ WSAasyncgethostbyaddr()—see gethostbyaddr().

➤ WSAasyncgetprotobyname()—Proxied only for an IPX environment.

➤ WSAasyncgetservbyname()—Proxied only for an IPX environment.

➤ WSAasyncgetservbyport()—Proxied only for an IPX environment.

➤ WSAasyncselect()

Proxy Server 2.0 *does not* support the following Windows Sockets API calls; instead, these calls are passed to the renamed copy of the original WinSock DLL:

➤ arecv()

➤ asend()

➤ closesockinfo()

➤ enumprotocolsA()

➤ enumprotocolsW()

➤ getaddressbynameA()

➤ getaddressbynameW()

➤ getnamebytypeA()

➤ getnamebytypeW()

➤ getserviceA()

➤ getserviceW()

➤ gettypebynameA()

➤ gettypebynameW()

➤ setserviceA()

➤ setserviceW()

➤ WSHEnumprotocols()

The WinSock Proxy service does not support Out-Of-Band (OOB) data transfer. Typically, OOB is dependent on a specific implementation and might not work between different network stacks. Also, Proxy Server 2.0 cannot redirect the following APIs:

➤ duplicatehandle()

➤ getsockopt ()—This API returns the local information, which is usually equal to the remote information.

Appendix D
Online Information Sources And Bibliography

Official Microsoft Information Sources

Microsoft maintains an up-to-date Proxy Server Web site filled with valuable information and free downloads. Check out these official Microsoft Proxy Server online information resources shown in Table D.1.

TCP/IP, Internet Security, And Firewalls Online Information Sources

Of course, there is a lot of information about TCP/IP, Internet security, and firewalls sprinkled on Web sites around the world. You will find some of the best of these sites in Table D.2.

Table D.1   Official Microsoft Proxy Server information resources.

Resource	URL
Microsoft Proxy Server 2.0 Home Page	http://www.microsoft.com/proxy/
Case Studies	(Available from the above URL)
Reviewer's Guide	(Available from the above URL)
Proxy Server 2.0 Technical Papers	(Available from the above URL)
Proxy Server News Group	http://www.backoffice.microsoft.com/bbs/ (select microsoft.public.proxy)
Microsoft Developer Forum	http://www.backoffice.microsoft.com/Dev/ (select Proxy Server 2.0 in the related technologies box)
Microsoft Proxy Server 2.0 Download and Trial Center	http://backoffice.microsoft.com/downtrial/

Table D.2 TCP/IP, Internet security, and firewalls online information sources.	
Resource	**URL**
The InterNIC is the official site for domain name registration and IP network number assignment. It also offers a wealth of information about the Internet, including: Directory and Database Services, Information and Education Services, and Net Scout Services (help in finding the best information resources on the Internet).	http://www.internic.net/
The Internet Assigned Numbers Authority (IANA) contains up-to-date information about Well-Known Ports and Registered Ports.	http://www.isi.edu/div7/iana/
WWW Security References (Rutgers University Network Services)	http://www-ns.rutgers.edu/www-security/reference.html
National Computer Security Association (Firewalls and Internet Security)	http://www.ncsa.com/catalog/catfirerity.html
The CERT Coordination Center studies Internet security vulnerabilities and publishes a variety of security alerts.	http://www.cert.org/
WGC Classroom (Click on Security to review some good information, then to WWW Security FAQ.)	http://wgc.chem.pu.ru/educate/
Chernicoff, David. "NT Server, Watching the Gate," *Windows Sources*, February 1998.	http://www.zdnet.com/wsources/content/0298/nts_splash.html

Proxy Server Third Party Plug-ins And Other Tools

There is a growing list of Proxy Server 2.0 plug-ins and other complementary software packages, including: firewalls, anti-virus, content-filtering, and reporting tools. The compact disk that accompanies this book includes trial versions of several of the products from the companies listed in Table D.3.

Table D.3 Proxy Server third party plug-ins and other tools.	
Resource	**URL**
InDepth Technology offers information about Microsoft Proxy Server, security issues, relevant downloads, and an online security bookstore.	http://www.indepth-tech.com
TELEMATE.Net by TELEMATE Software is a reporting tool.	http://www.telemate.net/
Hit List by Marketwave is a reporting tool.	http://www.marketwave.com/

Continued

Table D.3 Proxy Server third party plug-ins and other tools (Continued).	
Resource	**URL**
Crystal Reports by Seagate Software is a reporting tool.	http://www.img.seagatesoftware.com/
WebSENSE by NetPartners Internet Solutions is a content-filtering tool.	http://www.websense.com/
Cyber Patrol Proxy by Microsystems Software is a content-filtering tool.	http://www.microsys.com/
SmartFilter by Secure Computing is a content-filtering tool.	http://www.smartfilter.com/
InterScan WebProtect 2.0 byTrend Micro, Inc. is an antivirus tool.	http://www.antivirus.com/
Checkpoint Software Technologies, Ltd. is the maker of a variety of Internet security products, including FireWall-1.	http://www.checkpoint.com/
FireWall/Plus 4.0 by Network-1 Software & Technology, Inc. is a multiprotocol firewall.	http://www.network-1.com/
Stalker 3.0 by TIS is an intrusion-detection firewall.	http://www.tis.com/

Bibliography

Amoroso, Edward. *PC Week Intranet and Internet Firewall Strategies.* Emeryville, CA: Ziff-Davis Press, 1993.

Cheswick, William R. *Firewalls and Internet Security.* Reading, MA: Addison-Wesley Publishing Co., 1994.

Horak, Ray. *Communications Systems and Networks.* New York: M&T Books, 1997.

Martin, James. *TCP/IP Networking Architecture, Administration, and Programming.* Englewood Cliffs, NJ: PTR Prentice Hall, 1994.

Orfali, Robert. *The Essential Client/Server Survival Guide,* Second Edition. New York: John Wiley & Sons, 1996.

Taylor, Ed. *Demystifying TCP/IP.* Plano, TX: Wordware Publishing, Inc., 1993.

Glossary

10Base2   An Ethernet term referring to a maximum transfer rate of 10 megabits per second, using baseband signaling, a maximum contiguous cable segment length of 100 meters, and a maximum of two segments.

10Base5   An Ethernet term referring to a maximum transfer rate of 10 megabits per second, using baseband signaling, a maximum contiguous cable segment length of 100 meters, and a maximum of five segments.

10BaseT   An Ethernet term referring to a maximum transfer rate of 10 megabits per second, using baseband signaling and twisted-pair cabling.

Accept System Call   A socket system call used by the server process in a connection-oriented application protocol employing TCP to cause the server to wait for a connection request to arrive from a client.

Access Control   A process that defines each user's privileges on a system. Firewalls are often referred to as access control devices between networks.

Access Control Entry (ACE)   An entry in an Access Control List (ACL). The entry contains a security ID (SID) and a set of access rights. A process that has a matching SID is either allowed access rights or denied them.

Access Control List (ACL)   A level of Windows NT permission that can be set on a file or a directory allowing specified users access within an NTFS directory. An Access Control Entry (ACE) is an entry in the list.

Acknowledgment (ACK)   A positive response returned from a receiver to the sender, indicating success. TCP uses acknowledgments to indicate the successful reception of a packet.

Active Caching   A method used to automatically initiate requests to update objects in a cached file without user intervention. Requests can be activated based on the length of time an object has been cached or the date and time that the object was last retrieved from its source location. This type of caching is used to assure the freshness of specified data within the cache. *See also Passive Caching, Fresh Data.*

Active Open   An operation performed by a client to establish a TCP connection with a server.

Address   A reference to a particular point within a computer or network environment. A means of identifying a network, subnetwork, or node. A unique location identifier within any finite set. For example: a location of a node within a network.

Address Mask   A way of omitting certain parts of an IP address in order to reach the target destination without broadcasting a message. It is also referred to as a *subnet mask.* The address mask uses the 32-bit IP addressing scheme.

Address Resolution   The mapping of an IP address to a hardware address. In the TCP/IP suite of protocols, Address Resolution Protocol (ARP) performs this function.

Address Resolution Protocol (ARP)   A protocol associated with TCP/IP that maps physical hardware addresses on a network to higher-level protocol addresses (IP).

Address Space   A range of memory addresses available to an application program.

Administrator   A term used to refer to an individual or group that performs the roles of either system administrator or network administrator in a networking environment. *See also System Administrator, Network Administrator.*

American National Standards Institute (ANSI)   The national standards organization for the United States. ANSI is a nonprofit organization that writes the rules for standards bodies to follow and publishes standards produced under its rules of consensus. ANSI accredits standards committees to write standards in areas of their expertise.

American Standard Code for Information Interchange (ASCII)   A 7-bit code for encoding alphanumeric information and control functions that is used to achieve compatibility between data devices.

Anonymous FTP   A service that allows users to transfer files from other hosts on the Internet without having to establish a login and password on the target host. *See File Transfer Protocol (FTP).*

ANSI   *See American National Standards Institute.*

API   *See Application Program Interface.*

Application Layer   In TCP/IP, the uppermost layer of the TCP/IP architecture in which application programs and application protocols and services operate. The application layer provides a means for application programs to access the system interconnection facilities to exchange information. The application layer performs the following functions: establishes the authority to communicate; supports file services, electronic mail, and print services; and transfers information.

In the OSI model, the application layer is layer seven, which is also the uppermost layer. It serves as the window for application processes to access network services. This layer represents the services that support the user applications directly (for example, software for file transfers, database access, and electronic mail).

Application Program Interface (API)   A set of routines that provide specific services used by the system, usually specific to the application's purpose. They define how a program or collection of services can be used by other programs and services.

Application Server   A computing system that implements software that allows other systems to request the services of application programs running on the application server.

Application-Level Gateway   A type of firewall that routes incoming sessions to application programs that perform security filtering and auditing as required.

Archie   An Internet service that searches indexes of anonymous FTP servers for file and directory names.

ARP   *See Address Resolution Protocol.*

ARP Cache   A table maintained by a system containing mappings of Internet addresses to physical hardware addresses for the hosts or routers on the system's own physical network.

ARPANET   Advanced Research Projects Agency Network. An early packet switching network, funded by the Defense Advanced Research Projects Agency (DARPA), that evolved into the Internet.

Array   A group of Proxy Server computers used to provide distributed caching, load balancing, and fault tolerance.

Array Member   A Proxy Server computer that is part of an array.

Array Membership Table   A list of Proxy Server computers within an array. Each Proxy Server computer manages its own table.

ASCII   *See American National Standard Code for Information Interchange.*

Association   In socket programming, the information required in order to exchange data between a process running in the local host and a process running in a remote host. An association is made up of a protocol identifier, local Internet address, local port number, remote Internet address, and remote port number.

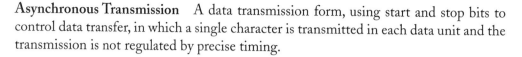

Asynchronous Transmission   A data transmission form, using start and stop bits to control data transfer, in which a single character is transmitted in each data unit and the transmission is not regulated by precise timing.

Audit Trail   Recorded log of specific system activity that can be used to reconstruct an incident for prosecution and recovery. Firewalls should include audit logs.

Authentication   A means by which a reported identity can be validated by either clients or servers to determine permission to access a resource or perform an operation.

Auto Dial   A Microsoft Proxy Server component that enables users to automatically connect to the Internet during predetermined times.

Autonomous System   In TCP/IP, a collection of hosts and routers that are administered by a single authority.

Backbone   A set of nodes and links connected together comprising a network, or the upper layer protocols used in a network. Sometimes used to refer to the physical media that connect components in a network.

Backup Domain Controller (BDC)   A Windows NT server that receives a copy of the security policy and master database for a Windows NT domain. Security data for all domain-assigned users is contained in the centralized master database; updates occur whenever changes in security are made. *See also Primary Domain Controller (PDC), Member Server.*

Bandwidth   A term used to specify the capacity of a communication channel, which refers literally to the difference between the highest and the lowest frequencies that are carried over the channel. The higher the bandwidth, the more information that can be carried.

Baseband   A type of channel in which data transmission is carried across only one communications channel, supporting only one signal transmission at a time. An example of a baseband system is Ethernet.

Basic Authentication   A method of authentication that encodes the user name and password. Often called "clear text" because the encoding (base-64) can be decoded by anyone with a freely available decoding utility. Encoding is not the same as Encryption.

Bastion Host   A multi-homed computer system position on the perimeter of the private network between an outside router and an inside "choke" router. The Bastion Host offers services to users within the intranet, but does not contain resources considered sensitive. The Bastion Host can be directly exposed as a perimeter defense to the Internet. Another type of Bastion Host is single-homed and offers bogus data to a would-be Internet attacker as a diversionary tactic.

Baud   A unit of measure that reflects the number of times a signal changes state in one second. Bauds are equal to bits per second (bps) only at low data rates, when each possible line condition represents a single bit.

BDC   *See Backup Domain Controller (BDC).*

BER   *See Bit Error Rate.*

Berkeley Internet Name Domain (BIND)   A Berkeley implementation of the Domain Name System (DNS).

Berkeley Software Distribution (BSD)   A version of the UNIX operating system that first included TCP/IP support. The UNIX operating systems that included TCP/IP are referred to as 4.2BSD or 4.3BSD.

Best Efforts Service   *See Connectionless Service.*

BGP   *See Border Gateway Protocol.*

Bind Service   *See Domain Name System (DNS).*

Binding   A process that establishes the initial communication channel between the protocol driver and the network adapter card driver.

B-ISDN   Broadband ISDN. *See Broadband ISDN.*

Bit Error Rate (BER)   The number of errors expected in a transmission.

Bit Rate   The rate that bits are transmitted, usually expressed in seconds.

Bits-Per-Second (bps)   The basic rate of data transmission.

BOOTP   A TCP/IP protocol that allows a diskless client computer to determine its own IP address, the IP address of the server, and the name of a file to be loaded into memory and executed. DHCP provides a superset of the functions provided by BOOTP.

Border Gateway Protocol (BGP)   A TCP/IP exterior gateway routing protocol sometimes used as an alternative to the Exterior Gateway Protocol (EGP). BGP allows routers in different autonomous systems to communicate. *See also Exterior Gateway Protocol.*

BPS   *See Bits-Per-Second (bps).*

Bridge   A network device capable of connecting networks using similar protocols. *See also Brouter.*

Broadband   A range of frequencies divided into narrow "bands," each of which can be used for different transmission purposes. Also known as *wideband.*

Broadband ISDN   A high-speed form of integrated services digital network, representing a probable future direction of the telephone industry, that uses fiber-optic transmission. *See also Integrated Services Digital Network (ISDN), SONET.*

Broadband Signaling   The type of signaling used in local area networks that enables multiplexing of more than one transmission at a time.

Broadcast   The simultaneous transmission of the same data to all nodes connected to the network.

Broadcasting   Delivery of data packets to all computers on a network.

Brouter   A network device that is a combination of the functions of a bridge and a router. A brouter routes the data traffic associated with certain protocols and bridges all other data traffic. *See also Bridge, Router.*

Browser   A client application program that allows the navigation of and access to the World Wide Web.

Bulletin Board System (BBS)   BBS is a common acronym for dial-in systems that provide services such as file storage, file retrieval, discussion group support, and online games.

Burst Mode   A transmission mode where data is transmitted in bursts rather than in continuous streams.

Cabling System   A system of cable segments, cable connectors, and attachment units used to physically interconnect the stations to a physical network.

Cache   In Proxy Server 2.0, a means of improving network performance by reducing the number of objects retrieved from the Internet, based on their popularity. A store of frequently retrieved objects and URLs located on the cache drive of Microsoft Proxy Server 2.0.

Cache Drive   The amount of space reserved on a selected server disk drive for use in storing cached files.

Cache Routing   The forwarding of a client HTTP request from one Proxy Server computer to another Proxy Server computer. Also known as *cascading* or *chaining*. *See also Hierarchical Caching.*

Carrier Sense   A signal generated at the physical network layer to inform the data link layer that one or more nodes are transmitting on the underlying medium.

Carrier Sense Multiple Access with Collision Detection (CSMA/CD)   A network media access control protocol wherein a device listens to the medium to monitor traffic.

If there is no signal, the device is allowed to send data. If the sent data collides with data from other nodes, then a random time period is allowed to expire before the data is automatically retransmitted.

CCITT   Consultative Committee on International Telegraphy and Telephony. Now named the ITU-T. *See International Telecommunications Union, Telecommunication (ITU-T).*

CERN-Proxy Protocol   An industry standard for application-aware proxy services over HTTP-based Client/Server communications. The CERN standards are established by the Conseil Européen pour la Recherche Nucléaire (European Laboratory for Particle Physics), located in Switzerland.

CGI   *See Common Gateway Interface (CGI).*

Class A Address   An Internet address in which the first bit is set to 0. A class A address provides 7 bits to identify the physical network and 24 bits to identify hosts. In any Internet there can be up to 126 networks that use class A addresses.

Class B Address   An Internet address in which the first two bits are set to 10. A class B address provides 14 bits to identify the network and 16 bits to identify hosts. A class B address allows for up to 2^{14}-2 different physical networks and up to 2^{16}-2 different hosts on each network.

Class C Address   An Internet address in which the first three bits are set to 110. A class C address provides 21 bits to identify the network and 8 bits to identify hosts. A class C address allows for up to 2^{21}-2 different physical networks but only up to 254 different hosts on each network.

Class D Address   An Internet address in which the first four bits are set to 1110. A class D address is used to implement a form of multicasting in which an address refers to some collection of hosts in an Internet, all of which receive the IP datagrams that have the specified multicast address.

Classification   A means of identifying network types.

Clear Text   *See Basic Authentication.*

Client   In client-server computing, an application component that makes a request for a service of some other application component that operates in the role of a server. Also, a computer that accesses shared network resources provided by a server computer.

Client/Server Architecture   A general phrase used to refer to a distributed application environment where a program exists that can initiate a session and a program exists to answer the requests of a client. The origin of this concept is most strongly rooted in the TCP/IP protocols.

Close System Call   Socket system call used to close a socket descriptor in a manner similar to closing a file descriptor.

CMOT   *See CMIP over TCP/IP.*

Collision   An event that occurs when two or more nodes broadcast packets at the same time, resulting in a collision of packets.

Collision Detection   A device's capability to determine whether a collision has occurred.

Commit Rate   Refers to the speed with which objects or URLs are added to the cache.

Common Gateway Interface (CGI)   A standard interface for HTTP server applications. Used by an application that runs on a server to generate dynamic content based on parameters sent by the requesting Web browser.

Computer Emergency Response Team (CERT)   A government-funded group at Carnegie-Mellon University that provides security clearinghouse and threat information.

Concentrator   Local Area Network (LAN) equipment that allows multiple network devices to be connected to the LAN cabling system through a central point. Sometimes called an Access unit or Hub.

Connect System Call   Socket system call used by the client process in a connection-oriented application protocol that uses TCP to establish a TCP connection with the server process.

Connected Service   Also known as "streamed" service. Refers to a service that provides a managed connection allowing networked computers to communicate reliably. TCP and SPX protocols support this type of service.

Connection   A link between two or more processes, applications, machines, networks, and so on. Connections can be logical, physical, or both.

Connection Oriented   A type of network service wherein the transport layer protocol sends acknowledgments to the sender regarding incoming data. This type of service provides retransmission if problems have been determined as a result of data transfer.

Connectionless   A type of network service that does not send acknowledgments to the sender upon receipt of data. UDP is a connectionless protocol.

Connectionless Service   A data transfer service provided by any layer of a network architecture in which each data unit sent is sent and processed independently of any other data units.

Contention   A condition occurring in some LANs wherein the Media Access Control (MAC) sublayer enables more than one node to transmit at the same time, risking collisions.

Cookie   A customized or personalized file that is assembled and returned by a Web server, usually used to identify users returning to the Web site. Also, in electronic commerce applications, used to hold such information as items added to a shopping cart.

Core Gateway   A router operated by the Internet Network Operations Center to distribute routing information.

Crosstalk   A term referring to signals that interfered with another signal being transmitted.

Cryptography   The technology of encoding and decoding messages. For example, key-managed encryption and decryption of information for confidentiality, authentication, or other services.

Cyclic Redundancy Check (CRC)   A mathematical function performed on the contents of an entity that enables a receiving system to recalculate the value as compared to the original. If the values are different, corruption of the contents has occurred.

Data Circuit Equipment (DCE)   The required equipment to attach Data Terminal Equipment (DTE) to a line or network.

Data Link   A data link protocol also defines the rules that govern how frames are exchanged. A physical circuit in association with a data link protocol forms a data link over which data can be transmitted in an error-free fashion. Each physical network in a TCP/IP Internet takes the form of a data link.

Data Link Layer   Layer two of the OSI model. The Data Link layer is responsible for providing data transmission over a single link from one system to another. Control mechanisms in the Data Link layer handle the transmission of data units, often called frames, over a physical circuit.

Data Link Protocol   A method of handling the establishment, maintenance, and termination of a logical link between nodes. Examples of data link protocols include Token Ring, Ethernet, SDLC, etc.

Data Source Name (DSN)   The logical name that allows a connection to an ODBC data source.

Datagram   The fundamental unit of an Internet Protocol (IP) data transmission. Sometimes also referred to as a *packet*.

Datagram Service   *See Connectionless Service.*

Default Router The router to which a host sends an IP datagram when there is no entry in the host's routing table for the physical network referenced in the destination Internet address field of the IP datagram header.

Destination Unreachable Message An ICMP error message indicating that an IP datagram could not be delivered to the destination host.

DHCP *See Dynamic Host Configuration Protocol (DHCP).*

DHCP Relay Agent The component responsible for relaying DHCP and BOOTP broadcast messages between a DHCP server and a client across an IP router.

Dial-Up Networking (DUN) A component of Windows NT and Windows 95 that enables users to connect to remote networks, such as the Internet or an internal network, over a telephone line.

Digital Referring to a state of on or off; representing a binary 1 or a binary 0.

Distributed Processing The act of processing storage; I/O processing, control functions, and actual processing are dispersed among two or more nodes.

Distributed Caching The forwarding of a client HTTP request from one Proxy Server computer to another Proxy Server computer in an array until the cached item is found. The cache items are distributed among an array or chain of server computers providing load balancing and fault tolerance.

Distributed Processing When a process is spread over two or more devices, it is distributed. It is usually used to spread CPU loads among a network of machines.

DNS *See Domain Name System (DNS).*

DNS Spoofing Assuming the DNS name of another system.

Domain A collection of names that are administered by a single authority. Also, for a Windows NT Server network, a collection of computers that share a common domain database and security policy; also called a *workgroup*. Each domain has a unique name.

Domain Controller For a Windows NT Server domain, the server that authenticates domain logons and maintains the security policy and the master database for a domain.

Domain Filtering Controlling user access to specific Internet sites by denying or granting permission based on the Internet computer's domain name or friendly name.

Domain Name A name that consists of a sequence of simple names separated by periods. Each simple name or set of simple names identifies a domain under the control of some authority.

Domain Name System (DNS)   A service used with the TCP/IP protocol suite to replace the previous method of keeping track with host names, aliases, and Internet addresses. The domain name service is a distributed database used to convert node names into Internet addresses. DNS decentralizes the naming convention by distributing the responsibility for mapping of names and addresses.

Dotted Decimal Notation   A representation of IP addresses. Also called *dotted quad notation* because it uses four sets of numbers separated by periods (such as 255.255.255.255).

Double Byte Character Set   A character set wherein alphanumeric characters are represented by two bytes, instead of one byte, as with ASCII. Double byte characters are often necessary for languages such as Chinese.

Driver   A software component that allows a computer to communicate with a hardware device.

DSN   *See Data Source Name (DSN).*

Dumb Terminal   A terminal that has no significant processing capability of its own, usually with no graphics capabilities beyond the ASCII set.

Dynamic Addressing   The automatic assignment of IP addresses.

Dynamic Filters   Dynamic filters are automatically started by either the WinSock Proxy, Web Proxy, or Socks Proxy services, allowing the Proxy Server services to automatically open and close communication ports on the external interface when transmission of packets is needed.

Dynamic Host Configuration Protocol (DHCP)   A protocol that dynamically assigns IP addresses and related information for temporarily connected network users.

Dynamic Link Library (DLL)   A programming module that contains dynamic link routines that are linked at load or execution time. The files have .dll extensions.

Electronic Mail (Email)   This is a way of sending messages electronically. It is one of the most popular applications that users request from proxy server administrators.

Encapsulation   To include an incoming message within a larger message by adding information at the front, back, or both. Encapsulation is used by layered network protocols. With each layer, new headers and trailers are added.

Encryption   A security mechanism in which enciphering and deciphering functions are used to prevent unauthorized parties from viewing or using transmissions that take place over a network.

End System   In the OSI model, a device in a communication system that serves as the source or final destination of data. In the TCP/IP environment, an end system is typically called a host.

Endpoint Identifier   In socket programming, a data structure that contains an Internet address and a port number that identifies either the local or the remote system.

Enterprise Internetwork   A computer network designed to serve the needs of an entire enterprise. For example, TCP/IP technology can be used to construct all or part of an enterprise internetwork.

Enterprise Network   Generally used as a wide area network, providing services to all corporate sites.

Entity   In the OSI model, an active element within a layer. For example, a particular layer provides services to entities that are running in the layer above.

Ephemeral Port   A port in which the number falls in the range from 1024-4999 that is typically used to send data from the server process back to the client process.

Ethernet   A data link level protocol that implements the IEEE 802.3/ISO 8802-3 CSMA/CED standard. It comprises layers one and two of the OSI reference model. It is a broadcast networking technology. Ethernet can be implemented with different media types, such as thick or thin coaxial cable or copper shielded twisted pair cabling.

Ethernet Address   A 48-bit address, commonly referred to as a *physical or hard address,* which uniquely identifies the Ethernet Network Interface Card (NIC) and, therefore, the device in which the card resides.

Ethernet Version 2   A data link technology, developed by Digital Equipment Corporation, Xerox, and Intel, that served as the basis for the IEEE/ISO CSMA/CD (Ethernet) standard.

Exterior Gateway   A router that communicates with a router in some other autonomous system.

Exterior Gateway Protocol   A routing protocol that allows routers in different autonomous systems to communicate with one another. One of the routing protocols in the TCP/IP suite that is used in the core Internet.

Exterior Neighbor   Two routers that communicate directly with one another and are in different autonomous systems.

Fast Ethernet   Term used to describe the standards developed to define a 100 Mbps version of the CSMA/CD (Ethernet) standard.

FAT   *See File Allocation Table (FAT).*

Fault Tolerance   Fault tolerance allows the recovering of data after a catastrophic event. For example, if one Proxy Server computer is unavailable, other servers in an array or a chain can provide the requested data. Proxy Server's fault tolerance only works if an array or chain of Proxy Server computers is configured.

FDDI   *See Fiber Distributed Data Interface (FDDI).*

Fiber Distributed Data Interface (FDDI)   An ANSI-defined standard for high-speed data transfer over fiber-optic cabling.

Fiber-Optic Cable   A cable that contains one or more thin cylinders of glass, each of which is called a *core*. Each core is surrounded by a concentric cylinder of glass, called the *cladding*, which has a different refractive index than the core. The core of a fiber-optic cable transports signals in the form of a modulated light beam.

File Allocation Table (FAT)   A table or list maintained by various operating systems that keeps track of the status of various segments of disk space used for file storage.

File Server   A process or program that provides access to a file from remote devices.

File Transfer Access Method (FTAM)   A file transfer program and protocol developed by the OSI. It includes some basic management functions.

File Transfer Protocol (FTP)   An Internet standard protocol that provides a means for transferring files across a TCP/IP network. FTP is a user-oriented TCP/IP application layer service.

Filter   An ISAPI feature that allows pre-processing of requests and post-processing of responses, permitting site-specific handling of HyperText Transfer Protocol (HTTP) requests and responses.

Finger   A network program used to obtain information about a particular user or set of users on a host that supports the finger service.

Firewall   An important network protection component, or system, that enforces a boundary between two or more networks, usually public and private. Firewalls are comprised of a packet filter, an application-level gateway, or a combination of the two.

Flags   An Internet header field carrying various control flags.

Fragment   A part of a protocol packet that Internet firewalls must provide a mechanism for handling.

Fragmentation   The breaking of a datagram into several smaller pieces, typically because the original datagram was too large for the network or software.

Frame Check Sequence (FCS)   A mathematical function used to verify the integrity of bits in a frame, similar to the Cyclic Redundancy Check (CRC).

Frame Relay   A form of data link technology that provides services similar to those provided by X.25 packet-switching networks. However, in a Frame Relay network, routing decisions are made in the Data Link layer rather than in the Network layer.

Fresh Data   Cached data that is verified to be current and consistent with its source.

FTAM (File Transfer Access Method)   An OSI file transfer program and protocol. It provides some management functions and permits copying files between systems, performing file management functions, and even deleting files.

FTP   *See File Transfer Protocol.*

Fully Qualifed Domain Name (FQDN)   The full TCP/IP domain name, consisting of simple names separated by periods, that can be used to distinguish a host from all other hosts in an Internet. For example, in the FQDN of *myserver.testbed.com* the host name is *myserver* and *testbed.com* is the domain name.

Gateway   When used with the Internet, this term refers to a device that performs a routing function. Currently, the term refers to a networking device that translates all protocols of one type network into all protocols of another type network.

Gateway-to-Gateway Protocol (GGP)   A protocol used to exchange routing information between core routers.

Gigabyte   One billion bytes, corresponding to the decimal notation 1,073,741,824.

Gopher   A hierarchical system for finding and retrieving information from the Internet or an intranet. An enhanced version available, called Gopher Plus, that returns more information about an item such as file size, last date of modification, and the administrator's name. In the United States alone, there are more than 500 Gopher servers. The collection of all publicly accessible Gopher servers is called Gopherspace. A program called Veronica indexes thousands of resources in Gopherspace, letting you search Gopherspace by keyword.

GOSIP   *See Government Open System Interconnection Profile (GOSIP).*

Government Open System Interconnection Profile (GOSIP)   A government standard using the OSI reference model.

Group   In a Windows NT Server network, an account assigned a unique name within a domain that contains user accounts called members. The permissions and rights granted to a group are also provided to its members. Groups are a convenient way to grant common capabilities to collections of user accounts.

Hardware Layer   The TCP/IP functional layer, generally considered to be outside the scope of the TCP/IP architecture, that is below the Network Interface layer. The Hardware layer is concerned with physical entities, such as the NICS, transceivers, hubs, connectors, and cables that are used to physically interconnect hosts.

Hash   A mathematical algorithm used for routing client requests within an array or a chain. With Proxy Server, the result of the hash determines which specific Proxy Server computer to route the client request to.

Header   Control information at the beginning of a message, segment, datagram, packet, or block of data.

Hierarchical Caching   In Microsoft Proxy Server architecture, the forwarding of a client HTTP request from one Proxy Server computer to another Proxy Server computer upstream. The downstream (source) Proxy Server computer forwards client requests that it cannot service from its own cache. Hierarchical caching uses upstream routing and is a subset of Distributed Caching.

Hit Rate   The percentage of client requests fulfilled through previously cached data, as related to the total of all client requests that have been processed by the caching service.

Hop count   The number of routers or bridges data crosses in a network.

Host   Term used to refer to a computing system that is attached to a TCP/IP network, communicates using the TCP/IP protocols, and runs programs that communicate with programs running on other hosts. A host can be any type of computing system, such as a large mainframe, a minicomputer, a midrange departmental processor, a graphics workstation, or a personal computer.

Host Identifier   The part of an Internet address that identifies an individual host or router within a physical network.

Host Name   A string of alphanumeric characters used to refer to a host in a TCP/IP Internet. Also, the name given to a computer that is part of a Windows NT network domain and that is used for client authentication. Also called the computer name.

HOSTS File   A TCP/IP configuration file that maintains a list of name-to-address mappings for an individual host. *See LMHOSTS file.*

HTML   *See HyperText Markup Language (HTML).*

HTTP   *See HyperText Transfer Protocol (HTTP).*

Hub   *See Concentrator.*

HyperText Markup Language (HTML)   The Internet standard protocol by which WWW clients and servers communicate.

HyperText Transfer Protocol (HTTP)   The most common protocol found on the Web. Used to request documents from HTTP servers.

IAB   *See Internet Activities Board (IAB).*

ICMP   *See Internet Control Message Protocol (ICMP).*

ICMP Echo Request and Reply Messages   ICMP query messages that are used to implement an echo facility. If a host or router receives an ICMP Echo Request message, it replies with an ICMP Echo Reply message.

ICMP Error Message   A message used to implement the Internet Control Message Protocol (ICMP) that is used to report on errors or exceptional conditions that occur during the delivery or attempted delivery of an IP datagram.

ICMP Query Message   A message used to implement the Internet Control Message Protocol (ICMP) that is used to request information and to reply to an ICMP request.

ICMP Subnet Mask Request and Reply Messages   ICMP query messages that are used by a host that needs to obtain its address mask.

ICMP Timestamp Request and Reply Messages   ICMP query messages that are used by a host to request that some other host or router respond with a timestamp indicating the current date and time of day.

IEEE   *See Institute of Electrical and Electronic Engineers.*

IEEE 802.2   An IEEE-approved data link standard used with the 802.3, 802.4, and 802.5 protocol standards.

IEEE 802.3   An IEEE-approved physical layer standard that uses CSMA/CD on a bus network topology.

IEEE 802.4   An IEEE-approved physical layer standard that uses token passing on a bus network topology.

IEEE 802.5   An IEEE-approved physical layer standard that uses token passing on a ring network topology.

IETF   *See Internet Engineering Task Force (IETF).*

IIS   *See Internet Information Server (IIS).*

IMC   *See Internet Mail Connector (IMC).*

Inbound Access   Ability to send information from an external network, such as the Internet, to an internal or private network. *See also Outbound Access.*

Institute of Electrical and Electronic Engineers (IEEE)   A professional organization, comprised of individual engineers, that produced a set of standards for Local Area Network (LAN) technology accepted by ISO as international standards.

Integrated Service Digital Network (ISDN)   A public telecommunications network that supplies end-to-end digital telecommunications services that can be used for both voice and nonvoice purposes.

Interior Gateway   Two routers that communicate directly with one another and are both part of the same autonomous system are said to be *interior neighbors* and are called *interior gateways.* Interior neighbors communicate with one another using an *interior gateway protocol.*

Interior Gateway Protocol   A routing protocol that allows routers in the same autonomous system to communicate with one another.

Interior Neighbor   Two routers that communicate directly with one another and are in the same autonomous system are said to be interior neighbors.

Internet   A collection of TCP/IP networks connected together that spans the entire globe that evolved from ARPANET. It interconnects thousands of networks containing millions of computers in universities, national laboratories, and commercial organizations. Sometimes called the Worldwide Internet.

Internet Activities Board (IAB)   The coordinating committee for the design, engineering, and management of the Internet. The IAB is an independent committee of researchers and professionals with a technical interest in the health and evolution of the Internet system. The IAB focuses on the TCP/IP protocol suite and extensions to the Internet system to support multiple protocol suites.

Internet Address   A four octet (32-bit) source or destination address that consists of a Network field and a Local Address field. Each host and router in a TCP/IP Internet must have at least one unique Internet address.

Internet Control Message Protocol (ICMP)   The Internet standard protocol subset of IP that handles control and error messages. Gateways use ICMP to send problem reports on packets back to the source that sent the packet.

Internet Engineering Task Force (IETF)   A large, open, international group of industry experts working on the technical evolution of the Internet. They specify the protocols and architecture for the Internet.

Internet Information Server (IIS)   The Microsoft Internet server product designed for implementing and managing Web sites. Microsoft Proxy Server requires IIS to be running on the same Windows NT server that Proxy Server runs on.

Internet Layer   TCP/IP functional layer that corresponds to the OSI model network layer. The Internet layer provides routing and relaying functions that are used when data must be passed from a host in one network to a host in some other network in the Internet.

Internet Mail Connector (IMC)   A component of Microsoft Exchange Server that runs as a Windows NT Server service. It is used to exchange information with other systems that use the Simple Mail Transfer Protocol (SMTP).

Internet Protocol   The Internet standard routing protocol that is comprised of an addressing and fragmentation scheme for IP datagrams. The IP datagram is the unit of data transfer. The IP address scheme is a mechanism to route packets from one network location to another. IP fragmentation provides a means for datagrams to fragment during transmission, and then be reassembled upon delivery. IP also includes the ICMP protocol. The Internet protocol suite is often called TCP/IP.

Internet Relay Chat (IRC)   An Internet standard protocol that supports interactive, real-time, text-based communications in established "chat rooms" on the Internet by means of IRC servers.

Internet Research Task Force (IRTF)   A part of the IAB that concentrates on research and development of the TCP/IP protocol suite.

Internet Server Application Programming Interface (ISAPI)   A Microsoft-developed API for establishing procedural calls between Internet-based applications and the underlying operating system.

Internet Service Provider (ISP)   A company or educational institution that enables remote users to access the Internet by providing dial-up connections or installing leased lines to their facilities that connect to the Internet.

Internetwork Packet Exchange (IPX)   A routing protocol developed for Novell Netware networks that, similar to IP, is used to manage data transfer between computers. Windows NT implements IPX through NWLink.

InterNIC   *See Internet Network Information Center (InterNIC).*

Intranet   Any privately operated TCP/IP-based network. Intranets can be connected to the Internet, but are typically protected by an intermediate set of barrier devices, called firewalls, that secure Internet access.

IP *See Internet Protocol (IP).*

IP Address A unique address that identifies a computer on a network by using a 32-bit address that is unique across a TCP/IP network. An IP address is represented in dotted-decimal notation, which depicts an octet (eight bits, or one byte) of an IP address as its decimal value and separates each octet with a period, for example: 102.54.94.97.

IP Datagram The basic unit of information passed through a TCP/IP network. The datagram header contains source and destination IP addresses.

IP Fragmentation A mechanism allowing IP datagrams to fragment during transmission, and then be reassembled upon delivery. Part of the Internet Protocol (IP).

IPX/SPX *See Internetwork Packet Exchange (IPX).*

IRC *See Internet Relay Chat (IRC).*

IRTF *See Internet Research Task Force (IRTF).*

ISAPI *See Internet Server Application Programming Interface (ISAPI).*

ISDN *See Integrated Services Digital Network (ISDN).*

ISO Reference Model The networking model created by the International Standard Organization that defines seven layers of a network, isolating functions within each layer. It is often used as a baseline for comparison and contrast of other network types.

International Telecommunications Union, Telecommunication Standards Sector (ITU-T) The telecommunication branch of the International Telecommunications Union (ITU), within which governments and the private sector coordinate global telecom networks and services, set standards, and make recommendations for international communications, such as telecommunications. Formerly known as CCITT.

IUSR_computername A default account created upon installation of Microsoft's Internet Information Server that allows anonymous logon privileges for accessing Internet-based services, such as FTP, WWW, and Gopher.

Keep-Alives Allow TCP/IP connections to remain intact even after completion of a client request and response. For example, an HTML page might have several inline graphics. Keep-Alives allow the TCP/IP connection to remain open while the graphics download, thus reducing the overhead of establishing TCP/IP connections for the text and for each separate image.

Kerberos A cryptographic authentication scheme developed at MIT; used to prevent unauthorized monitoring of logins and passwords.

LAN   *See Local Area Network (LAN).*

LAT   *See Local Address Table (LAT).*

Leased Line   A dedicated communication line between two points used as a constant vehicle for logical communications to occur at all times.

LMHOSTS file   A text-based file that maps IP addresses to the domain names of Windows NT computers. This file is used as a static routing table in Microsoft Windows NT Server to authenticate and register valid nodes in a local TCP/IP network. A version of a HOSTS file used with Microsoft operating systems.

Load Balancing   Load balancing evenly distributes client requests among server computers in a network. With Proxy Server, if one Proxy Server computer is in use or otherwise unavailable, another server can accept the request, preventing an interruption in service.

Local Address Table (LAT)   A table of all internal IP address pairs set aside for use on the internal network where a Microsoft Proxy Server is installed. This list is used by Proxy Server to control access between clients on the internal network and remote IP addresses on external IP networks. The LAT is registered and stored as a text-based file (Msplat.txt) within the installed directory for Microsoft Proxy Server, which defaults to C:\Msp\Clients. The LAT file is distributed to clients during setup and updated periodically by Microsoft Proxy Server.

Local Area Network (LAN)   A collection of computer-related equipment connected in such a way that communication can occur between all nodes connected to the medium. Usually the term refers to a form of data link technology that is used to implement a high-speed, relatively short-distance form of computer communication.

Log File   The file in which information about events that occurred on a server or a network are stored.

Logical Link Control (LLC)   A sublayer of the Data Link layer, defined by IEEE 802.2 and ISO 8802-2, that is responsible for medium-independent data link functions. It allows the layer entity above to access the services of a LAN data link regardless of what form of physical transmission medium is used.

Mail Exchanger   A system used to relay mail into a network.

MAN   *See Metropolitan Area Network (MAN).*

MBPS   Megabits per second.

Media Access Control (MAC)   A sublayer of the Data Link layer, defined by the IEEE/ISO/ANSI LAN architecture, which is concerned with how access to the physical transmission medium is managed. The MAC sublayer provides services to the Logical Link Control (LLC) sublayer.

Member Server   A server assigned to a Windows NT domain, but not designated as either the Primary Domain controller (PDC) or the Backup Domain Controller (BDC) within the assigned domain.

Message Transfer Agent (MTA)   A process that moves messages between devices.

Metropolitan Area Network (MAN)   A form of networking technology, related to LAN technology, that spans distances up to approximately 20 or 30 miles. Metropolitan area networks are sometimes used to bridge the gap between wide area networks and local area networks. The IEEE 802.6 specifies this standard.

MIME   *See Multipurpose Internet Mail Extension (MIME).*

Modem   A device that enables a computer to transmit information over a standard telephone line using *MODulator-DEModulator* functions to convert between digital data and analog signals.

Mosaic   A popular Internet browser that originated at the National Center for Supercomputing Applications (NCSA) and that helped spawn a revolution in browser-based networking applications.

Multihomed   A computer with network connections to multiple separate physical networks. In TCP/IP, a computer with multiple IP addresses.

Multihomed Firewall   A firewall with network connections to multiple separate physical networks.

Multihomed Host   A host with network connections to multiple separate physical networks.

Multiplex   To simultaneously transmit multiple signals over one channel.

Multipurpose Internet Mail Extension (MIME)   A method of configuring browsers to view files that are in multiple formats. MIME enables the exchanging of objects, different character sets, and multimedia in email on different computer systems.

Name Resolution   The process of mapping aliases to an address. The Domain Name System (DNS) is one system that does this.

Nameserver   Component of the Domain Name System that runs in a limited number of systems in a TCP/IP Internet to provide name resolution services for other hosts.

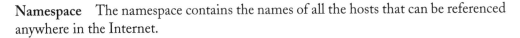

Namespace   The namespace contains the names of all the hosts that can be referenced anywhere in the Internet.

National Institute of Standards and Technology (NIST)   A U.S. standards body, previously called the National Bureau of Standards, that promotes communications-oriented standards.

National Research and Education Network   A network backbone that supports large capacities planned for use with the Internet in the future and might take over the role of the NSFNET as the backbone network of the Internet.

National Science Foundation Network (NSFNET)   The network that acts as part of the Internet backbone.

Negative Caching   A term that refers to the caching of HTTP error conditions associated with accessing a particular URL. If the URL is unavailable, the error response message can be cached and returned to subsequent clients that request the same URL.

NetBEUI   A network protocol typically only used in small, department-size local area networks. It can use Token Ring source routing as its only method of routing.

NetBIOS   *See Network Basic Input/Output System (NetBIOS).*

Network   A number of devices connected to enable a device to communicate with any other device over a physical medium.

Network Adapter Card   A hardware device used to connect a computer to a local area network (LAN). Also called a *network interface card (NIC).*

Network Administrator   An individual or group that assists system administrators by installing networking software on servers, individual workstations, and personal computers, and performs the required networkwide tasks to ensure the proper operation of the network.

Network Architecture   A comprehensive plan that includes a set of rules, or protocols, that govern the design and operation of the hardware, software components, and communication mechanisms used to create computer networks.

Network Basic Input/Output System (NetBIOS)   An API that is available for use by applications on a local area network. NetBIOS provides applications with a uniform set of commands for mapping input/output operations into equivalent network operations.

Network Interface Card (NIC)   A generic term for a networking interface board used to connect a device to the network. The physical connection to the network occurs at the NIC.

Network Interface Layer   TCP/IP functional layer analogous to the Data Link layer of the OSI model. The main purpose of the Network Interface layer is to handle hardware-dependent functions and to present a standardized interface to the TCP/IP Internet layer.

Network Layer   Layer three of the OSI model. The network layer is responsible for making routing decisions and relaying data from one system to another through the network. The facilities provided by the network layer supply a service used by higher layers for moving packets from one end system to another, where the packets can flow through any number of intermediate systems.

Network News Transfer Protocol (NNTP)   A Internet standard protocol that provides a means for news distribution and reading and posting messages on a TCP/IP network.

Network Operating System   A software product, typically used in the personal computer environment, that provides high-level networking functions to users and application programs.

NNTP   *See Network News Transfer Protocol (NNTP).*

Node   A generic term used to refer to any connected network device.

NSFNET   *See National Science Foundation Network (NSFNET).*

NTFS   *See Windows NT File System (NTFS).*

Open Database Connectivity (ODBC)   An API that enables applications to access data from a variety of database systems.

Open Shortest Path First (OSPF)   An Internet routing protocol that can route data traffic via multiple paths using the knowledge of the Internet's topology to make routing decisions.

Open Systems Interconnection (OSI)   A set of ISO-developed standards relating to data communications.

Optical Fiber   A plastic or glass cable that uses light as a communications medium.

Options   The Internet header Options field can contain several options, and each option can be several octets in length.

OSI Model   The seven-layer *Reference Model for Open Systems Interconnection*, developed by members of the ISO and documented in ISO 7498, that provides a common basis for the coordination of standards development for the purpose of systems interconnection.

Outbound Access   The ability to send information from an internal or private network to an external network, such as the Internet.

Packet   In TCP/IP networks, an informal term referring to the IP datagram handled by the Internet Protocol (IP). Also, informal name for the data unit handled at the level of the OSI model network layer.

Packet Filtering   A term used for Proxy Server's or other firewall's ability to intercept packets and either allow or block those packets addressed to specific services on or behind the Proxy Server computer or firewall. *See also Packet-Level Filter.*

Packet-Level Filter   A firewall component or device that filters data based on packet information, such as source and destination address.

Passive Caching   A type of storage service in which data is cached and discarded entirely on the basis of object size, popularity, or time since the requested object was last updated in the cache. Also called *on-demand caching* because all caching updates are user-initiated.

PDC   *See Primary Domain Controller (PDC).*

Peer Web Services   A family of services that enable a computer running Windows NT Workstation to publish a personal Web site from the desktop. Available services include the WWW service, the FTP service, and the Gopher service.

Permission   A rule associated with a networked object (such as a directory or file) to regulate which users have access to the object and in what manner. *See also Rights.*

Physical Hardware Address   An address assigned to a network interface card (NIC) installed in a host or router that uniquely identifies the NIC within an individual physical network. *See also Network Interface Card, Physical Network.*

Physical Layer   The first layer of the OSI model. The Physical layer is responsible for the transmission of communication signals, such as electrical signals, optical signals, or radio signals, between communicating machines. Typically, physical layer mechanisms in each of the communicating machines control the generation and detection of signals that are interpreted as 0 bits and 1 bit.

Physical Network   A collection of two or more hosts, routers, or both, that are interconnected using a particular form of data link technology.

Ping   A TCP/IP utility program that verifies connections to one or more remote computers by sending ICMP packets and listening for reply packets.

Plug-ins   A feature of Proxy Server 2.0. Third-party applications extend and enhance the functionality of Proxy Server to prevent unwanted content, viruses, Java scripts, or

ActiveX controls from being downloaded into your secured network. Plug-ins work with Proxy Server via the Internet Server Application Programming Interface (ISAPI).

Point-to-Point Protocol (PPP)   A TCP/IP protocol that provides host-to-network and router-to-router connections over synchronous and asynchronous dial-up lines.

Point-to-Point Tunneling Protocol (PPTP)   A recent networking protocol that allows remote users to access corporate networks securely across the Internet by dialing into an Internet Service Provider (ISP) or by connecting directly to the Internet. PPTP supports multiprotocol virtual internal networks (VPNs). Because PPTP allows multiprotocol encapsulation, users can send any packet type over an IP network.

Policies   Rules or conditions set by the system administrator. Policies provide the account management required to prevent exhaustive or random password attacks. For example, a policy identifies how quickly account passwords expire and how many unsuccessful logon attempts to allow before a user is locked out.

Popularity   A measurement of the frequency with which client applications, such as Web browsers, request objects or URLs.

Port   In TCP/IP, a number used to identify certain Internet applications with a specific connection. In general, a port is referred to as an entry or exit point. Ports are associated with TCP or UDP transport protocols. *See also Well Known Port Number.*

Port Number   *See Port.*

PPP   *See Point-to-Point Protocol.*

Presentation Layer   Layer six of the OSI model. The presentation layer serves as the data translator for the network. This layer on the sending computer translates data from the format sent by the application layer into a common format. At the receiving computer, the presentation layer translates the common format into a format known to the application layer.

Primary Domain Controller (PDC)   A server assigned to authenticate logons and maintain the security policy for a Windows NT domain. This server stores the master database of all domain-assigned security data for users and must be updated when changes in security are made.

Print Server   A network system that implements software that allows other network systems to share the print server's printers.

Protocol   Rules governing the behavior or method of operation of something. Typically refers to software that allows computers to communicate over a network. For example, the Internet protocol is TCP/IP.

Protocol Conversion   The process of changing one protocol to another.

Protocol Suite   A collection of communication protocols that jointly define the rules governing how messages are exchanged in a computer network. For example, the collection of TCP/IP protocols is a protocol suite. *See also Protocol.*

Proxy   A mechanism where a system functions for another system when responding to protocol requests.

Proxy Client   A client computer that must connect with a proxy server to gain access to network services located outside of the private network.

Proxy ISAPI Application   An ISAPI dynamic link library that provides client authentication, domain filtering, cache searching for requested objects, retrieval of requested objects from the Internet, and updating of cached data.

Proxy ISAPI Filter   An ISAPI dynamic link library that determines if a client-initiated HTTP request is a proxy request. If so, it is handled by the Web Proxy service and forwarded to the Proxy ISAPI application or, in the case of a non-proxy request, forwarded as a standard HTTP request.

Proxy Server   A computer configured as a server that acts as a relay agent between remote servers and clients to intercept requests and process communications on behalf of proxy clients.

Push Service   A service provided by TCP to allow an application to specify when data should be transmitted as soon as possible.

RAS   *See Remote Access Service (RAS).*

RealAudio   A streaming audio protocol that provides continuous sound over the Internet to compatible clients.

Recursive Resolution   A form of name resolution performed by a Domain Name System nameserver in which nameservers contact other nameservers, as required, to completely perform a requested name resolution operation.

Reliable Service   *See Connection-Oriented Service.*

Remote Access Service (RAS)   A Microsoft-developed server service found in Windows NT that allows remote client computers running Microsoft Dial-Up Networking, all Microsoft RAS clients, or any third-party PPP client to dial in to a network server (RAS server). RAS servers can also be configured to allow local client computers to dial out to servers outside a private network.

Remote Administration   Administering a computer from another computer connected across the network.

Remote Procedure Call (RPC)   A specific protocol that permits calling a routine that executes a server; the server returns output and return codes to the caller.

Remote Procedure Call (RPC) Facility   An application layer service for interprocess communication in which an application program issues function and procedure calls by name to program modules that might reside in other network systems. Arguments and results are automatically sent through the network transparently to the application program.

Repeater   A network device that captures and retransmits incoming signals, thereby boosting the strength of the signal in order to extend the length of a network.

Request for Comments (RFC)   Documentation of the operation of one of the protocols that make up the TCP/IP protocol suite. RFCs are available in machine-readable form on the Internet or in hard-copy format from the Internet Network Information Center (InterNIC).

Resolver   A software component of the Domain Name System that makes it possible for clients to access the Domain Name System (DNS) database and acquire an address.

Retrieve Rate   Refers to the speed with which objects or URLs are taken from the cache.

Reverse Address Resolution Protocol (RARP)   A TCP/IP protocol that allows a device to acquire its IP address by performing a broadcast on the network.

Reverse Hosting   Allows any server sitting behind Proxy Server to publish to the Internet. *See also Reverse Proxying.*

Reverse Proxying   Allows a server behind Proxy Server to publish to the World Wide Web without compromising security. *See also Reverse Hosting.*

RFC   *See Request for Comments.*

Rights   Authorize a user to perform certain actions on the network. Rights apply to the network or the system as a whole and are different from permissions, which apply to specific objects.

Router   Hardware or software that manages data traffic between networks or subnetworks that have similar transport protocols. *See also Brouter, Gateway.*

Routing   A process of determining which path is to be used for data transmission.

Routing Algorithm   Algorithm defined by a routing protocol that describes how routers update their routing tables.

Routing Information Protocol (RIP)   A protocol used to exchange information between neighboring routers.

Routing Table   A list of valid paths through which data can be transmitted.

RPC   *See Remote Procedure Call (RPC).*

RS232C   A physical layer specification for connecting devices, it's commonly used for serial lines.

Segment   A protocol data unit that consists of TCP header information and optional data. Segments are transparent to TCP users and are encapsulated in IP datagrams for transmission using the services of the Internet Protocol. Also used to refer to parts of a network that are divided into smaller parts (segments).

Serial   A sequence of events occurring one after another.

Serial Line Interface Protocol (SLIP)   An older industry standard communications protocol that standardizes dial-up networking. *See also Point-to-Point Protocol (PPP).*

Server   An application that answers requests from other devices (clients). Also used as a generic term for any device that provides services to the rest of the network, such as printing, high-capacity storage, and network access. Also referred to as a *host*.

Server Message Block (SMB) Protocol   The underlying protocol by which Microsoft Windows NT-based servers communicate critical service information with one another.

Service   A process that performs a specific system function and often provides an API for other processes to call. The Web Proxy Service and WinSock Proxy Service are examples of two services provided by Microsoft Proxy Server.

Service Pack   An update to the operating system or application software.

Service-Data-Unit (SDU)   In the OSI model, the data unit that a layer or sublayer entity passes down to the adjacent layer or sublayer below it in requesting a data transmission service.

Session Layer   Layer five of the OSI model. The session layer establishes a communications session between processes running on different computers; it can support message-mode data transfer.

Share   An object, such as a directory, file, application, or device, that is made available for users to access over the network.

Simple Mail Transfer Protocol (SMTP)   In TCP/IP, an Application layer protocol used for the transfer of electronic mail messages. An Internet standard protocol, SMTP is used by electronic mail software that provides the user with access to messaging facilities.

Simple Network Management Protocol (SNMP)   The standard Internet network management protocol used to monitor and control network devices.

SMDS   *See Switched Multimegabit Data Service (SMDS).*

SMTP   *See Simple Mail Transfer Protocol (SMTP).*

SNMP   *See Simple Network Management Protocol (SNMP).*

Socket   A data structure that uniquely identifies a process that is communicating with some other process in a TCP/IP application. Sockets are created by using a combination of device IP addresses and reserved TCP/UDP port numbers to indicate connection and delivery service information. *See also Windows Sockets.*

SOCKS   SOCKS provides a secure proxy data channel from a client computer to the Proxy Server computer. After establishing the connection, SOCKS transfers data between the client and the server. SOCKS is a cross-platform, open version of the WinSock Proxy service. Proxy Server can act as a SOCKS client to an upstream SOCKS server, or Proxy Server can be a SOCKS server to a client computer with SOCKS software on it. Proxy Server 2.0 supports SOCKS version 4.

SONET   Physical layer communication facilities, using fiber optics, on which broadband ISDN services are based. OC-1 SONET provides a 51 Mbps data rate, OC-3 SONET provides a 155 Mbps data rate, OC-12 SONET provides a 622 Mbps data rate, and OC-48 SONET provides a 2.4 Gbps data rate.

SPX   *See Sequenced Packet Exchange (SPX).*

SQL   *See Structured Query Language (SQL).*

SQL Server   A server that uses the Structured Query Language (SQL) to query, update, and manage a relational database.

Standard Proxy Protocol   Refers to the accepted industry-standard protocol for application-aware services established by CERN. *See also CERN-Proxy Protocol.*

Structured Query Language (SQL)   A database query and programming language widely used for accessing data in, querying, updating, and managing relational database systems. *See also SQL Server.*

Subnet   In TCP/IP, that part of a TCP/IP network that is identified (isolated) by a part of the Internet address.

Subnet address   In TCP/IP, that part of the IP address that identifies the subnetwork.

Subnet Mask   A way to exclude networks from having a broadcast on certain networks, isolating broadcasts to the desired network or networks.

Switched Connection   A data link connection is similar to a telephone call in that it is established on demand. Also called a *switched line*. See also *Leased Line*.

Switched Multimegabit Data Service (SMDS)   A high-speed wide area network packet-switching service that is built on top of broadband ISDN services to provide services similar to those of an X.25 network.

Synchronous Data Transfer   The transfer of data between two nodes at a timed rate (as opposed to asynchronously).

System Administrator   An individual or group responsible for installing and maintaining software on host computers designated as servers and for helping individual workstation or personal computer users install and maintain software on their own individual computers. *See also Network Administrator.*

Systems Management Server (SMS)   A Windows NT Server network server application that remotely manages the computers on a network. SMS detects computers on the network, inventories software and hardware configurations, and installs client applications from a central location.

T1   A digital transmission line that transfers data at 1.544 Mbps.

T3   A digital transmission line that transfers data at 45 Mbps.

T3 Facility   A digital telecommunication facility, available from telecommunications providers, that supports a bit rate of 45 Mbps.

TCP   *See Transmission Control Protocol (TCP).*

TCP/IP   *See Transmission Control Protocol/Internet Protocol (TCP/IP).*

Telnet   The Internet standard protocol for remote terminal connection service. Telnet allows a user to interact with a remote computer as if the user were on a terminal directly connected to the remote computer.

Throughput   The amount of data that can be successfully moved across a medium or processed within a certain time period.

Time-to-Live (TTL)   A standard field in a TCP/IP header that indicates an age-of-expiration value that is examined by receiving stations. The field indicates the upper boundary on how long this Internet datagram can exist.

Tracert   A TCP/IP diagnostic utility that determines the route taken to a destination by sending ICMP packets that have varying TTL values to that destination.

Traffic   A generic term used to describe the amount of data on a network backbone at a given period in time.

Transmission Control Block (TCB)   A data structure that holds information about TCP and UDP connections.

Transmission Control Protocol (TCP)   A transport layer protocol that is part of the TCP/IP protocol suite and provides a connection-oriented transport layer protocol that provides for the reliable, sequenced delivery of a stream of bytes called segments.

Transmission Control Protocol/Internet Protocol (TCP/IP)   A family of networking protocols that is the standard on which the Internet operates. TCP/IP allows computers that have diverse hardware architectures and various operating systems to communicate across interconnected networks. TCP/IP includes standards for how computers communicate and conventions for connecting networks and routing traffic.

Transport Layer   Layer four of the OSI model. The transport layer confirms that messages are delivered in the order in which they were sent and that there is no loss or duplication. It removes the concern from the higher layer protocols about data transfer between the higher layer and its peers.

TTL   *See Time-to-Live (TTL).*

Tunneling   *See Point-to-Point Tunneling Protocol.*

UDP   *See User Datagram Protocol (UDP).*

Uniform Resource Locator (URL)   A naming convention for an object that uniquely identifies the location of a computer, directory, or file on the Internet. The URL also specifies the appropriate Internet protocol, such as HTTP, FTP, IRC, or Gopher.

Usenet   The most popular newsgroup hierarchy on the Internet.

User   The user of the Internet protocol. This might be a higher level protocol module, an application program, or a gateway program.

User Datagram Protocol (UDP)   In TCP/IP, a transport layer protocol that provides a best-effort, connectionless, unacknowledged, datagram delivery service.

User-Defined Port Port in which the port number falls in the range from 5000-65,535, which is typically used for sending data from a client process to a user-written server process. *See also Port.*

VDOLive A stand-alone application that provides stream-oriented service for continuous video imaging.

Verbose Logging Supplying additional or supplemental information for a network event in a log file. Often used for troubleshooting.

Virtual Appearing to exist, but in reality the appearance is achieved by functions or processes.

Virtual Directory A directory outside the home directory that appears to Web browsers as a subdirectory of the home directory.

Virtual Server A computer that has several IP addresses assigned to the network adapter card. This configuration makes the computer look like several servers to a Web browser.

WAIS Service A distributed text searching system that allows the user to make various types of searches based on the contents of one or more indexed text databases. A number of WAIS-structured databases are available on the Internet.

WAN *See Wide Area Network (WAN).*

Web Browser A software program that retrieves a document from a Web server, interprets the HTML codes, and displays the document to the user with as much graphical content as the software can supply.

Web Page A World Wide Web document. Web pages can contain diverse types of information, for example: hypertext, graphics, photographic images, movies, and sounds.

Web Proxy Service This service provides the foundation for Microsoft Proxy Server to act as a proxy server.

Web Server A computer configured with server software that permits it to respond to Web client requests, such as requests from a Web browser. A Web server uses the Internet HTTP, FTP, and Gopher protocols to communicate with clients on a TCP/IP network.

Well Known Port In TCP/IP, an inbound or outbound port used for an expressed purpose generally agreed upon by TCP/IP users. The Well Known Ports are controlled and assigned by the Internet Assigned Numbers Authority (IANA). On Microsoft Proxy Server, port assignments are enabled separately for inbound ports and outbound ports. Inbound ports are used to listen for client requests from Internet clients, and outbound ports are used to listen for requests from clients on the private network.

Well Known Port Number   *See Well Known Port.*

Wide Area Network (WAN)   Usually used to refer to a network that spans large geographic distances. Often this type of network involves interconnecting multiple Local Area Networks (LANs) that use multiple physical topologies.

Windows Internet Name Service (WINS)   A name resolution service that runs on Windows NT Server. WINS maps friendly names to IP addresses. A WINS Server handles name registrations, queries, and releases. *See also Domain Name System (DNS).*

Windows NT Challenge/Response Authentication   A method of authentication in which a server uses Windows NT security to allow access to its resources.

Windows NT File System (NTFS)   An advanced file system used by Windows NT that supports file system recovery, very large storage media, and object-oriented applications. NTFS also offers enhanced security over the older FAT file system.

Windows NT Server Event Viewer   A program provided with Windows NT that enables users to monitor system, security, and application events by viewing the Event Logs.

Windows NT System Event Log   A Windows NT service that records events in the system, security, and application service logs. *See also Windows NT Server Event Viewer.*

Windows Sockets   Windows Sockets is a Windows implementation of the widely used UC Berkeley Sockets API. Windows Sockets is a networking API used to create TCP/IP-based sockets applications. Windows Sockets provides interfaces between applications and the transport protocol and works as a bidirectional connection for incoming and outgoing data. Also called *WinSock. See also Socket.*

WINS   *See Windows Internet Name Service (WINS).*

WinSock Proxy Service   This is an API service used by Microsoft Proxy Server that provides redirection and remote execution of Windows sockets applications over connections that involve a computer on a internal network (intranet) and remote computers on the Internet.

Workgroup   *See Domain.*

World Wide Web (WWW)   The World Wide Web consists of the software, protocols, conventions, and information that enable hypertext and multimedia publishing on computers connected to the Internet.

A Certification Insider Press
Sample Chapter

In the pages that follow, we've included a sqample chapter from our recently published *MCSE Proxy Server 2 Exam Cram*. We've included this material to give you an overview of what's involved in studying for the Proxy Server 2 MCSE elective exam. Whether or not you planning on getting certified, we hope you find this chapter informative and helpful.

Someday we'll all study this way.

The perfect supplement to all certification study guides

EXAM CRAM

The first and last book you need to read before taking your certification exam

Over 400,000 Exam Cram Guides in Print!

Proxy Server 2

Exam #70-088

Microsoft
Certified
Systems
Engineer

David Johnson, Andy Ruth, and J. Michael Stewart

Certification Insider Press

For this and other Certification Insider Press titles, visit the Coriolis Group's Web site at http://www.coriolis.com.

Certification Insider™ Press

MCSE Proxy Server 2 Exam Cram
Table Of Contents

Proxy Server Protocols

Terms you'll need to understand:

√   IP address

√   Subnet mask

√   CIDR

√   Address class

√   Dotted-decimal format

√   Loopback address

√   InterNIC

√   IANA

√   Port

√   Well-known ports

Techniques you'll need to master:

√   Using subnet masks to determine the network ID and host ID of an address

√   Understanding the structure of the TCP/IP protocol suite

√   Understanding TCP and UDP ports

Because TCP/IP is the protocol of the Internet, you need to understand how TCP/IP operates, how it's addressed, and how it's used to communicate over the Internet. Microsoft has an entire test dedicated to TCP/IP and its implementation. Although it's not necessary to understand all facets of TCP/IP for the Proxy Server exam, TCP/IP and its protocols play a significant role in the Proxy Server environment and should be examined.

The TCP/IP Protocol Suite

As a point of reference, it's important to know how TCP/IP was created and how it's structured. TCP/IP is a suite of protocols developed by the Department of Defense's (DOD) Advanced Research Projects Agency (ARPA). ARPA envisioned a network where researchers at the DOD, corporations, and universities in different parts of the country could share information with one another easily and quickly. Out of the need for interconnectivity and interoperability between the disparate computers running at the different sites, the TCP/IP suite was created. The Internet Protocol (IP) was designed to provide transport across a packet-switched network connecting the sites. The interoperability questions were addressed by the creation of many hardware-independent application protocols that worked together to form a comprehensive group, called a *suite*. Application protocols were created for file transfer and management, email, terminal emulation, printing, and network management.

In September of 1969, four sites were combined to create the Advanced Research Projects Agency Network (ARPANet). This network quickly grew to connect all major colleges and universities, eventually allowing connections from corporations not involved in research. Because the DOD originally funded ARPANet, it was deemed a public domain. This was the beginning of today's Internet.

TCP/IP's vast acceptance has been driven by its use in the Unix environment and its ability to interconnect divergent technologies. TCP/IP is by far the most widely used suite of protocols today and is expected to continue to be number one for the foreseeable future. The TCP/IP suite has grown from just a few protocols in 1969 to over 100 individual protocols today. These protocols do everything from managing files, to providing calendaring and scheduling functions, to transporting for World Wide Web pages, to configuring a computer's IP settings automatically.

TCP/IP Structure

The TCP/IP suite is named for its two primary protocols—the Transmission Control Protocol (TCP) and the Internet Protocol (IP). Its protocols are divided into three categories according to their function:

➤ **Application protocols** Protocols such as FTP (used for file transfer and manipulation), SMTP (provides email transfer), and Telnet (a terminal emulation protocol that provides specific functions and interfaces for the user).

➤ **Network protocols** The most prevalent of these is the IP protocol. They move packets around the network and are responsible for addressing and routing them.

➤ **Transport protocols** TCP and UDP are examples of transport protocols. They ensure delivery between computers. They are responsible for providing a low-layer connection for the applications through mechanisms such as flow control.

You should know how these protocols interrelate and how they're used in a Proxy Server environment. The following list describes some of the most-used TCP/IP protocols:

➤ **Address Resolution Protocol (ARP)** ARP is a Network layer protocol that provides logical (IP) address to physical (MAC) address association. As you know, the network interface card (NIC) in a computer looks for packets with its physical address. IP has no knowledge of this address and, therefore, uses ARP to discover the MAC address for a particular IP address. ARP does this by sending a broadcast that requests the MAC address.

➤ **File Transfer Protocol (FTP)** FTP is an upper-layer protocol that encompasses the Session, Presentation, and Application layers. It's used for file transfer, file manipulation, and directory manipulation.

➤ **Hypertext Transfer Protocol (HTTP)** HTTP is perhaps the most widely used protocol today. This upper-layer protocol is used to deliver World Wide Web (WWW) documents that have been written in HTML and other markup languages.

➤ **Internet Control Message Protocol (ICMP)** ICMP is another Network layer protocol that is used to send control messages. The PING utility uses ICMP to request a response from a remote host. ICMP provides information, such as whether or not the response was received and how long it took to make the trip.

➤ **Internet Protocol (IP)** IP is a Network layer protocol that provides source and destination addressing and routing.

➤ **Routing Information Protocol (RIP)** RIP is used to distribute route information throughout a network. It's a Network layer protocol that uses distance-vector routing algorithms to identify the best path through an internetwork.

➤ **Simple Mail Transport Protocol (SMTP)** Another upper-layer protocol, SMTP is used by messaging programs such as email.

➤ **Simple Network Management Protocol (SNMP)** SNMP is used to manage network devices. It can be used to configure devices, such as bridges, repeaters, and gateways, as well as monitor network events using MIBs and SNMP managers.

➤ **Telnet** Surprisingly not an acronym, Telnet is an upper-layer protocol that is used for remote terminal emulation. It allows users to act as if they were directly connected to the computer. Telnet is most often used as a configuration interface for networking devices, such as routers, and as a terminal program for mainframe and microcomputer systems.

➤ **Transmission Control Protocol (TCP)** TCP is a connection-oriented Transport layer protocol that accepts messages of any length from the upper layers and provides transportation to another computer. TCP is responsible for packet fragmentation and reassembly, and sequencing.

➤ **User Datagram Protocol (UDP)** UDP is the counterpart to TCP. It provides connectionless Transport layer functions for the TCP/IP suite.

IP Addressing And Subnet Masks

As mentioned earlier, IP is responsible for addressing and routing packets through the network. To understand how this works, let's take a look at how all packets are addressed.

Before a packet is placed on a network, it is given a physical source and destination address. These addresses tell the computers on the network where a packet came from and where it's going. The physical address for a computer is its Media Access Control (MAC) address. In most cases, the MAC address is burned into the network interface card's (NIC's) ROM when the card is created.

As the packet traverses the wire, each computer looks at the destination address to determine whether it is the destination. If so, it reads the packet, including the source information, and acts on the data in the packet.

Just knowing the physical address of a computer works fine in a small environment where there are no networking devices, such as routers or gateways. Could you imagine, though, if your computer had to know the physical address of every computer on the Internet to communicate? What if every router that makes up the Internet had this information? In addition, how many people know the MAC address of their computer or even their server? Not many.

IP uses a logical address that is assigned to each computer. Each IP address is 32 bits long and is represented as 4 bytes in decimal format. Hearken back to your binary-to-decimal conversion days. Each bit can be either on (1) or off (0). The decimal value of the number is calculated from right to left with each consecutive bit worth twice the previous bit. The first bit on the right is worth either 0 or 1, the second bit from the right is worth either 0 or 2, the third bit is worth either 0 or 4, and so on through 8, 16, 32, 64, and 128. If there are 8 bits together, the decimal representation can be from 0 (00000000) to 255 (11111111 or 1+2+4+8+16+32+64+128), which gives us 256 combinations of numbers. Table 1 shows a few other decimal representations of a byte.

To delineate between each byte in an IP address, the bytes are written in what is called *dotted-decimal format*. Each byte is separated by a period (or *dot*). Therefore, an IP address looks something like this: 205.199.10.1. Remember, though, that this is just a representation of the 32 bits that make up the address.

Table 1   Decimal representations of a byte.

Bit Pattern	Decimal Equivalent	The Math Involved
10000000	128	0+0+0+0+0+0+0+128
01001100	76	0+0+4+8+0+0+64+0
01011100	92	0+0+4+8+16+0+64+0
11000000	192	0+0+0+0+0+0+64+128
01111111	127	1+2+4+8+16+32+67+0
11111010	250	0+2+0+8+16+32+64+128
00001010	10	0+2+0+8+0+0+0+0
01100011	99	0+2+4+0+0+0+64+128
10101001	169	1+0+4+0+16+0+0+128

> *Note: Although IP addresses can range from 0–255, certain addresses are reserved for special use. Numbers 0 and 255 are reserved for broadcasts and should be used in host IDs only in special situations. In addition, any address beginning with 127 is treated as a loopback address. If a program, such as PING, uses this address, the traffic does not hit the network.*

IP addresses are assigned and maintained by the InterNIC. It is the InterNIC's responsibility to ensure that computers connected to the Internet have unique addresses. However, with the growth of TCP/IP and the Internet, unique addresses are in short supply. InterNIC has taken a number of steps to ease this problem, some of which will be discussed later in this chapter in the section titled "Subnet Masks." One of the biggest steps taken has been to assign particular addresses as private addresses, meaning they cannot be used to connect to the Internet. For companies that have closed and secure environments, these addresses are ideal. Three groups of addresses have been assigned as private addresses according to class, which is discussed in the next section. Here are the private addresses:

➤ Addresses beginning with 10 (one Class A address)

➤ Addresses beginning with 172.16 through 172.31 (16 Class B addresses)

➤ Addresses beginning with 192.168.0 through 192.168.255 (256 Class C addresses)

Private addresses cannot be sent over the Internet. If an Internet router receives a packet with either a source or destination address that is private, it drops the packet.

Address Classes

By definition, an *internetwork* is a group of interconnected networks that operate autonomously. In an internetwork, each network is assigned an address, and it's the responsibility of networking devices, such as routers, to move packets through the internetwork.

In a network using IPX/SPX, the network address is assigned by the administrator and is a hexadecimal representation of the bits in the address field. IPX then uses the MAC address of the NIC to ensure the packet reaches its destination. An IPX packet includes separate fields for the network and host address. In contrast, IP uses a single address for both network and host.

The IP address class system was developed to delineate which bits of the IP address represent the network ID and which bits represent the host ID for a particular computer. The class of an IP address is defined by the value of the first octet of the address. The IP address class system is broken down this way:

➤ **Class A** The first octet is assigned by InterNIC, which leaves the last three octets to be assigned by the administrator. Class A addresses begin with ID numbers between 1 and 126. These addresses were designed with very large corporations in mind. A single Class A address provides for 16,387,064 (254 * 254 * 254) hosts. That's a lot of computers!

➤ **Class B** The first two octets are assigned by InterNIC and begin with IDs between 128 and 191. This leaves the last two octets for host IDs and provides 64,516 hosts per network.

➤ **Class C** The first three octets are assigned by InterNIC and begin with IDs between 192 and 223. A Class C address can have up to 254 hosts.

With internetworks using the class system, the network ID/host ID delineation is along octet lines. Even if a corporation has been assigned a Class B address—if it has no need for more than 254 hosts on a network, or for many networks—it can use a Class C delineation.

Subnet Masks

The delineation between network ID and host ID is made by using a subnet mask. This section of the IP packet specifies which bits of the IP address denote the network ID and which bits denote the host ID. As mentioned earlier, in networks using the class system, this distinction is made along class boundaries. Subnet masks are also written in dotted-decimal format. Let's look at how a computer decides which part of an address is the network ID and which part is the host ID by using a subnet mask. It's important to understand subnet masking because this is where many IP problems start.

Remember that IP addresses are 32 bits long. Subnet masks are also 32 bits long and are used by the computer to determine whether the packet's destination is on the local subnet or a remote subnet by making the delineation between network ID and host ID. Bits in a subnet mask are set to 1 starting at the far left. Each bit that is turned on denotes the network ID of the IP address, either source or destination. For example, an IP address using a Class A subnet mask has the first eight bits set to 1. This means that the first octet denotes the network, whereas the remaining three octets are the host ID. Here are a few examples of how this works:

```
IP address:        100.202.230.99
Subnet Mask:       255.255.255.0 (Class C)
```

```
Binary Address:      01100100   11001010   11100110   01100011
Binary Mask:         11111111   11111111   11111111   00000000
Binary Network ID:   01100100   11001010   11100110
Binary Host ID:                                       01100011
Decimal Network ID: 100.202.230
Decimal Host ID:     99

IP address:          87.104.10.19
Subnet Mask:         255.0.0.0 (Class A)
Binary Address:      01010111   01000100   00001010   00010011
Binary Mask:         11111111   00000000   00000000   00000000
Binary Network ID:   01010111
Binary Host ID:                 01000100   00001010   01100011
Decimal Network ID: 87
Decimal Host ID:     104.10.19

IP address:          87.104.10.19
Subnet Mask:         255.255.0.0 (Class B)
Binary Address:      01010111   01000100   00001010   00010011
Binary Mask:         11111111   11111111   00000000   00000000
Binary Network ID:   01010111   01000100
Binary Host ID:                            00001010   01100011
Decimal Network ID: 87.104
Decimal Host ID:     10.19
```

As you can see, even if a Class A address is used, it can have a different subnet mask to provide more networks with fewer hosts per network. If you think about it from a routing perspective, it makes sense. If, for example, a very large corporation has an internetwork covering the entire U.S. and parts of Europe, it would probably get a Class B address from the InterNIC. If this company used its Class B address with only Class B subnet masks, it would have one very large network. From an IP perspective, every host would be on the same subnet and no routing would take place. All packets would be sent to all sites, thus leading to IP chaos. However, the company could use the Class B address with a Class C mask and have 254 individual subnets with 254 hosts per subnet. This type of configuration is much more manageable and gives the routers something to do. Just imagine what would happen with a Class A address using a Class A mask—16 million hosts across the globe with no routing. For this reason, you'll most often find Class C masks being used.

However, with the growth of the Internet and TCP/IP, even using the class system, there aren't enough IP addresses to go around. How many companies do you know that have less than 100 computers to connect to the Internet? If each of these companies were given a Class C address—in the beginning they were—the addresses would quickly disappear. As mentioned earlier, this is one reason the private IP addresses were reserved for companies not connecting to the Internet. However, something else had to be done to make the most of the available addresses until the next generation of TCP/IP is introduced.

To work around this problem, Classless InterDomain Routing (CIDR) was introduced. CIDR (pronounced *cider*) removes the class boundaries for subnet masks and introduces a new system for determining the network and host ID of an address. Rather than using the dotted-decimal notation, CIDR specifies the exact number of bits representing the network ID. This specification is written as a number following a slash after the IP address: 202.248.130.128 / 26. In this case, the network ID occupies the first 26 bits of the 32-bit address. The following two examples show how CIDR works:

```
IP address:          152.98.212.156
Subnet Mask:         /26 (CIDR)
Binary Address:      10011000   01100010   11010100   10011100
Binary Mask:         11111111   11111111   11111111   11000000
Binary Network ID:   10011000   01100010   11010100   10
Binary Host ID:                                        011100
Decimal Network ID:152.98.212.128
Decimal Host ID:     28


IP address:          129.8.242.156
Subnet Mask:         /21 (CIDR)
Binary Address:      10000001   00001000   11110010   10011100
Binary Mask:         11111111   11111111   11111000   00000000
Binary Network ID:   10000001   00001000   11111
Binary Host ID:                            010        10011100
Decimal Network ID:129.8.240
Decimal Host ID:     2.156
```

By using this method, Internet Service Providers (ISPs) and the InterNIC can provide a company with an address or range of addresses to fit its needs more specifically. This also means that an ISP can get one Class B address from InterNIC and provide addresses for a larger number of companies.

As mentioned earlier, the subnet mask helps the computer determine whether the destination is on the local network or a remote network. When the packet is addressed, the computer looks at the network ID and determines whether it matches its own network ID. If so, it sends the packet down the wire, knowing it will reach its destination. If not, it sends the packet to a gateway.

TCP And UDP Ports

As mentioned earlier, the Transmission Control Protocol (TCP) is the primary transport protocol of the TCP/IP suite. It's a connection-oriented protocol that provides reliable service across a network, including the Internet. TCP also increases its reliability by using acknowledgments, flow control, and checksum information. In contrast, the User Datagram Protocol (UDP), which is not used as often as TCP, is a connectionless protocol that does not provide guaranteed delivery.

Although they approach network communication differently, both protocols utilize the same method to identify which application is sending and receiving data—ports. A *port* is used to name the ends of logical connections that carry on long-term conversations. Most TCP/IP protocols have been assigned their own port between 0 and 1023. These are called *well-known ports* and are assigned by the Internet Assigned Numbers Authority (IANA). Other TCP/IP applications, such as proprietary programs, use ports above 1023. Table 2 is a partial list of the well-known ports used in TCP/IP.

Because every packet that uses TCP includes port information, filters can be setup to permit or deny a particular type of application communication on the network. Microsoft Proxy Server takes full advantage of this option, and it's very important to know the most often used ports to successfully configure a proxy server. A complete list of the well-known ports is available at http://www.isi.edu/in-notes/iana/assignments/port-numbers.

Port Number	Keyword	Description
Table 2 The IANA has assigned well-known port numbers to most TCP/IP protocols and functions.		
20	ftp-data	Port used to transfer data using FTP
21	ftp	Control port used by FTP
23	telnet	Port used by Telnet
25	smtp	Port used by SMTP (email)
80	www	Port used by HTTP (WWW)
137	netbios-ns	Port used by the NetBIOS Name Service
161	snmp	Port used by SNMP
532	netnews	Readnews port

Exam Prep Questions

Question 1

> Which type of protocol provides addressing and routing functions?
>
> ○ a. Transport
>
> ○ b. Network
>
> ○ c. Application
>
> ○ d. Routing

The correct answer to this question is b. Network protocols provide addressing and routing functions. Transport protocols ensure delivery between computers. Therefore, answer a is incorrect. Application protocols provide an interface to the user. Therefore, answer c is incorrect. Routing protocols, such as RIP, are a subset of Network protocols, but do not provide addressing information. Therefore, answer d is incorrect.

Question 2

> Which ports are considered well-known ports?
>
> ○ a. Ports greater than 100
>
> ○ b. Ports less than 1000
>
> ○ c. Ports less than 1023
>
> ○ d. Ports greater than 1023

The correct answer to this question is c. Well-known ports are those ports below 1023. All other answers are incorrect.

Question 3

> Which of the following governing bodies of the Internet is responsible for assigning IP addresses?
>
> ○ a. InterNIC
>
> ○ b. IEEE
>
> ○ c. IANA
>
> ○ d. IETF

The correct answer to this question is a. The InterNIC is responsible for assigning IP addresses. Although the IEEE is a governing body, it develops networking standards, not IP addresses. Therefore, answer b is incorrect. The IANA is responsible for well-known ports, whereas the IETF is responsible for RFCs. Therefore, answers c and d are incorrect.

Question 4

> Which of the following is the correct binary representation of the number 216?
>
> ○ a. 11001000
>
> ○ b. 11011000
>
> ○ c. 10011000
>
> ○ d. 11001100

The correct answer to this question is b. Answer a is the binary representation of 200, answer c is the binary representation of 152, and answer d is the binary representation of 204. Therefore, answers a, c, and d are all incorrect.

Question 5

> Which of the following are examples of Application protocols? [Check all correct answers]
>
> ❑ a. Telnet
>
> ❑ b. RIP
>
> ❑ c. FTP
>
> ❑ d. IP

The correct answers to this question are a and c. Telnet and FTP are Application protocols. RIP and IP are both Network protocols. Therefore, answers b and d are incorrect.

Question 6

> Which of the following is the CIDR representation of a Class B
> subnet mask?
>
> ○ a. /12
>
> ○ b. /26
>
> ○ c. /24
>
> ○ d. /16

The correct answer to this question is d (/16). Answer c (/24) is the CIDR representation for a Class C mask, whereas answers a and b are truly classless masks.

Question 7

> Which of the following is used by a computer to determine the
> network ID portion of an IP address?
>
> ○ a. Subnet mask
>
> ○ b. Gateway
>
> ○ c. DNS server
>
> ○ d. network=

Answer a is correct. A computer uses its subnet mask to determine the network ID portion of its address. A gateway is used to send data to remote networks. Therefore, answer b is incorrect. A DNS server is used to resolve host names to IP addresses. Therefore, answer c is incorrect. Finally, there is no such setting as network=. Therefore, answer d is incorrect.

Question 8

> Which of the following are not valid IP addresses? [Check all cor-
> rect answers]
>
> ❏ a. 199.199.200.200
>
> ❏ b. 156.1.256.2
>
> ❏ c. 1.1.1.1
>
> ❏ d. 299.199.299.1

Answers b and d are correct. IP addresses must be between 0 and 255 because they are a decimal representation of 8 bits. Although they may look odd, 199.199.200.200 and 1.1.1.1 are valid IP addresses. 256 and 299 are not valid IP addresses. Therefore, answers a and c are incorrect.

Question 9

> Which of the following protocols provides connectionless trans-
> port for the TCP/IP protocol suite?
>
> O a. UDP
>
> O b. TCP
>
> O c. FTP
>
> O d. HTTP

The correct answer to this question is a, UDP. TCP is a connection-oriented protocol. Therefore, answer b is incorrect. FTP and HTTP rely on TCP for transport. Therefore, answers c and d are incorrect.

Question 10

> Using the Class system, which of the following network numbers
> would be assigned by the InterNIC?
>
> O a. 12.199.0.0
>
> O b. 192.134.0.0
>
> O c. 135.119.0.0
>
> O d. 255.255.0.0

The correct answer to this question is c. The network number 135.119.0.0 is a Class B address (indicated by 135 in the first octet) and would be assigned by the InterNIC. The network number 12.199.0.0 is a Class A address; InterNIC would only assign the first octet, not the first two. Therefore, answer a is incorrect. The inverse applies to answer b, 192.134.0.0. This is a Class C address and InterNIC would assign the first three octets, not just two. The network number 255.255.0.0 is a Class B subnet mask and would not be assigned by the InterNIC. Therefore, answer d is incorrect.

Need To Know More?

 Stevens, W. Richard. *TCP/IP Illustrated, Volume 1*. Addison-Wesley Publishing Company, Reading, Massachusetts, 1994. ISBN 0-201-63346-9. The entire book provides detailed information on TCP/IP and how it works.

 Tittel, Ed, Kurt Hudson, and J. Michael Stewart. *MCSE TCP/IP Exam Cram*. Certification Insider Press, Scottsdale, Arizona, 1998. ISBN 1-57610-195-9. Chapters 2, 4, and 5 provide information on the architecture of TCP/IP, IP addressing, and subnet masks.

 Microsoft Technet. January, 1998. Searches on "TCP," "UDP," "well-known ports," and "subnet masks" will yield a wealth of information.

 A complete list of the well-known ports is available at http://www.isi.edu/in-notes/iana/assignments/port-numbers.

Index

K

L

M

N

V

VDSL (Very-high-data-rate Digital Subscriber Line), 116
Very-high-data-rate Digital Subscriber Line. *See* VDSL.
Virtual hosting, 10

W

WAN (Wide Area Network), 110
Web access bandwidth guidelines, 96–98
Web browsers, 4
    and challenge/response authentication, 77
    client installation using, 175–176
    configuration parameters, 225–227
    popularity of, 22
Web hosting services, 93–94
Web Proxy client application configuration, 244–248
    creating a custom client LAT file, 247–248
    Web browser configuration, 245–247
Web Proxy Permissions dialog box, 252
Web Proxy permissions tab, 251–253
Web Proxy Port, configuring, 142–143
Web Proxy routing, configuring, 291
    Advanced Array Options dialog box, 294–295
    Advanced Routing Options dialog box, 293–294
    Routing tab, 292–293
    routing within an array, 291–292
    upstream routing, 291, 292–293
    using proxy server with single network adapter, 295
Web Proxy service, 7, 8, 15, 19, 21–22
    directly connected browser, 23
    integration with IIS, 25–26
    proxy server and CERN browser, 23–24
Web Proxy Service Selection dialog box, 253
Wide Area Network. *See* WAN.
Windows Internet Name Service. *See* WINS.
Windows NT
    configuration, 141–150
        domain configuration, 141
        ISX/SPX network configuration, 143–148

routing table configuration, 142
        Service Pack installation, 148–149
        Web Proxy Port configuration, 142–143
    Dial-Up Networking (DUN), 17
    RAS (Remote Access Service), 98
    SAP (Service Advertising Protocol), 144
Windows NT/proxy server engineer, 54
Windows NT security, 71
    domains, 71–72
    user management, 72
Windows NT server installation, 131
    external network adapter configuration, 135–136
    hard disk drive preparation, 132
    internal network adapter configuration, 134–135
    modem and ISDN adapter configuration, 136–139
    network adapter configuration, 133–134
    RAS client installation and configuration, 139–140
Windows sockets, 35, 37
WinSock Proxy permissions tab, 253–256
WinSock Proxy service, 7, 9, 15, 19, 35
    client parameters, 224–225
    clients, 40–42
    IPX private networks, 45
    protocol administration using the WspProto utility, 191–194
    protocols, 257
        WinSock Proxy service Protocols tab, 257–260
    redirecting TCP, 42–43
    redirecting UDP, 43–44
    standards, 39
    TCP/IP private networks, 45
    TCP sockets, 37–38
    UDP sockets, 38
    understanding, 39–40
    versions of, 36
    windows sockets, 35, 37
WinSock Proxy service Protocols tab, 257–260
WINS (Windows Internet Name Service), 118, 122–123
    unbinding clients from external network adapters, 215–216
    using multiple proxy servers, 122–123
WWW (World Wide Web), 21

WE DO WINDOWS!

The Ultimate High-Tech Insider Guides for Deploying Microsoft's Windows 98 Operating System.

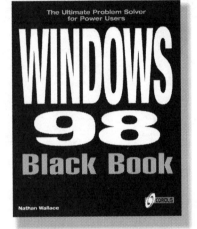

ISBN: 1-57610-295-5 • **Available:** July '98
Price: $29.99 U.S. • $41.99 CANADA

ISBN: 1-57610-265-3 • **Available:** June '98
Price: $39.99 U.S. • $55.99 CANADA

ISBN: 1-57610-294-7 • **Available:** July '98
Price: $29.99 U.S. • $41.99 CANADA

- Delivers the critical core information that power users or system administrators require for a higher level of Windows 98 useability.
- Focuses on boosting system performance and modifying default operations.

- A detailed, hands-on reference for upgrading to, and implementing Windows 98.
- Delivers detailed information on the newest and most powerful features of Microsoft's Windows 98.

- In-depth review of undocumented and little-known Registry functions.
- Demonstrates how to personalize and enhance PC productivity.
- Delivers quick tips and solutions to speed up performance and improve error checking.

CORIOLIS TECHNOLOGY PRESS©
800.410.0192
Int'l Callers: 602.483.0192

Check out www.coriolis.com for detailed information on these books and many more.

COMING SOON!
NT 5: The Next Revolution
Takes readers inside the technology, architecture, and innovation of Microsoft's newest operating system.

ISBN: 1-57610-288-2
Price: $29.99 U.S. • $41.99 CANADA
Available: August '98

Available at Bookstores and Computer Stores Nationwide

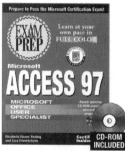
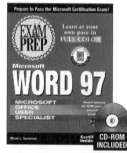

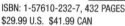

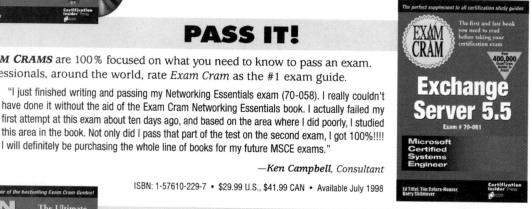